Advances in Empirical Translation Studies

Empirical translation studies is a rapidly evolving research area. This volume, written by world-leading researchers, demonstrates the integration of two new research paradigms: socially oriented and data-driven approaches to empirical translation studies. These two models expand current translation studies and stimulate reader debates around how development of quantitative research methods and integration with advances in translation technologies would significantly increase the research capacities of translation studies. Highly engaging, the volume pioneers the development of socially oriented innovative research methods to enhance the current research capacities of theoretical (descriptive) translation studies in order to tackle real-life research issues, such as environmental protection and multicultural health promotion. Illustrative case studies are used, bringing insight into advanced research methodologies of designing, developing and analysing large-scale digital databases for multilingual and/or translation research.

MENG JI is Professor of Translation Studies and Chinese Studies at the University of Sydney, Australia. She has published extensively on corpus translation studies, contrastive linguistics and quantitative translation methodologies.

MICHAEL OAKES is a reader in Computational Linguistics in the Research Institute in Information and Language Processing at the University of Wolverhampton, UK. His research interests are corpus linguistics, information retrieval and studies of disputed authorship.

Advances in Empirical Translation Studies

Developing Translation Resources and Technologies

Edited by

Meng Ji

University of Sydney

Michael Oakes

University of Wolverhampton

CAMBRIDGE
UNIVERSITY PRESS

CAMBRIDGE
UNIVERSITY PRESS

University Printing House, Cambridge CB2 8BS, United Kingdom

One Liberty Plaza, 20th Floor, New York, NY 10006, USA

477 Williamstown Road, Port Melbourne, VIC 3207, Australia

314-321, 3rd Floor, Plot 3, Splendor Forum, Jasola District Centre, New Delhi - 110025, India

79 Anson Road, #06-04/06, Singapore 079906

Cambridge University Press is part of the University of Cambridge.

It furthers the University's mission by disseminating knowledge in the pursuit of education, learning and research at the highest international levels of excellence.

www.cambridge.org
Information on this title: www.cambridge.org/9781108423274
DOI: 10.1017/9781108525695

First published 2019

A catalogue record for this publication is available from the British Library

Library of Congress Cataloging in Publication data
Names: Ji, Meng, 1982– editor. | Oakes, Michael P., editor.
Title: Advances in empirical translation studies : developing translation resources and technologies / edited by Meng Ji, Michael Oakes.
Description: New York, NY: Cambridge University Press, 2019. | Includes bibliographical references and index.
Identifiers: LCCN 2019008010 | ISBN 9781108423274 (hardback)
Subjects: LCSH: Translating and interpreting – Research – Methodology. | Machine translating – Research – Methodology. | Computational linguistics. | BISAC: LANGUAGE ARTS & DISCIPLINES / Linguistics / General.
Classification: LCC P306.5 .A278 2019 | DDC 418/.02–dc23
LC record available at https://lccn.loc.gov/2019008010

ISBN 978-1-108-42327-4 Hardback
ISBN 978-1-108-43719-6 Paperback

Contents

Figures

Tables

Contributors

ALEX WAIBEL, Professor of Computer Science, Karlsruhe Institute of Technology (KIT), Germany

CARLA PARRA ESCARTÍN, Research Fellow, ADAPT Centre, Dublin City University, Ireland

CONSTANTIN ORĂSAN, Associate Professor, University of Wolverhampton, UK

EDUARD BARBU, Research Fellow, University of Tartu, Estonia

FUKUMOTO FUMIYO, Professor of Computer Science, Yamanashi University, Japan

GLENN HOOK, Professor Emeritus of Japanese Studies, University of Sheffield, UK

JORGE DÍAZ-CINTAS, Professor of Translation Studies, University College London, UK

LAURA LÖFBERG, Research Fellow, University of Lancaster, UK

LIANET SEPÚLVEDA TORRES, Pangeanic, Spain

MARK SELIGMAN, President, Spoken Translation, Inc., Berkeley, USA

MASAAKI NAGATA, Senior Research Fellow, NTT Communication Science Laboratories, NTT Corporation, Japan

MENG JI, Associate Professor of Translation Studies, University of Sydney, Australia

MICHAEL OAKES, Reader in Computational Linguistics, University of Wolverhampton, UK

PAUL RAYSON, Associate Professor of Computer Science, University of Lancaster, UK

SARA MOZE, Lecturer in Corpus Linguistics, University of Wolverhampton, UK

SIMON KREK, Research Fellow, Centre for Language Resources and Technologies, University of Ljubljana; Jozef Stefan Institute, Ljubljana, Slovenia

ZHAOMING GAO, Associate Professor of Translation Studies, National Taiwan University

Preface

This book introduces socially oriented and data-driven approaches to empirical translation studies. Using case studies, it illustrates the interaction and growing interdependency between theoretical and applied translation studies in recent times, in an effort to mitigate the long-standing divide between the two, which has hampered the growth of translation studies in general.

The first four chapters of the book come under the umbrella of understanding empirical translation studies. The book opens with Ji's account in Chapter 1 of the advances which have been made in empirical translation studies, which have occurred in four main waves: pure and applied research; product- and process-oriented translation research; data concerning written translations and interpreting written translations and interpreting data; and now the development of data- and technology-intensive subfields that have important social and practical applications. In Chapter 2, Ji expands on the ideas of data intensiveness and social innovation in the field. In Chapter 3, Oakes then distinguishes between data-based and data-driven approaches, both of which are data-intensive approaches to empirical translation studies, by showing how it is possible to distinguish the original languages of translations from various European languages into English. In Chapter 4, a leading practitioner in the field, Mark Seligman, describes the evolving treatment of semantics in machine translation. The theme of the next four chapters is the development of multilingual resources and data-driven analytical tools. In keeping with the social turn in empirical translation studies, Ji, Hook and Fukumoto look at the translation and dissemination of WHO drinking-water-quality guidelines in Japan in Chapter 5. In Chapter 6, Löfberg and Rayson describe their work on the USAS semantic-tagging system, which assigns a meaning code to each word in the input text. They describe how the tool has been made to work for many languages, and look at its social usefulness. In Chapter 7, Moze and Krek then write about Sketch Engine, which is a powerful suite of corpus tools for cross-linguistic analysis. It can be used with large web-based corpora for computer-aided translation. In Chapter 8, Ji and Gao describe digital analytical instruments that they have developed for assessing the readability of Chinese health translations. The following group of four chapters is concerned with the development of practical and industrial applications for end users. In Chapter 9, Nagata describes his experience of how machine-translation techniques can be enhanced by reordering the words of the text, when the source and target languages have very different word orders. In Chapter 10, Díaz-Cintas gives a comprehensive overview of advances in audiovisual translation and subtitling. Orăsan et al. in Chapter 11 follow the data-driven paradigm by describing the EU-funded EXPERT project, which exploited empirical approaches to translation, including the evaluation of machine-translated outputs. Seligman again draws on his practical experience in Chapter 12 to describe advances in speech-to-speech translation technologies. In Chapter 13, Ji and Oakes conclude by looking at the opportunities and challenges ahead for empirical translation studies.

We hope that this book will bring together theoretical (descriptive) and applied translation studies, so as to expand the horizon of the field of empirical translation studies as a whole, and that we have shown how data-intensive approaches will enable the tackling of new and significant social and research issues.

MENG JI AND MICHAEL OAKES
Sydney and Wolverhampton
March 2018

1 Advances in Empirical Translation Studies

Meng Ji

1.1 Advances in Product and Process-Oriented Translation Studies

This emerging academic discipline was divided into pure and applied research schemes in the Holmes-Toury map of translation studies (Toury, 1995). Within the pure research paradigm, the two large research schemes were descriptive translation studies and theoretical translation research. These two schemes interacted with each other in the study of translation products, processes and functions as the research objects of the discipline. The proposition that descriptive translation was a key component of the field was intrinsically linked with the perception of translation studies as an empirical or scientific research field, as 'no empirical science may make a claim for completeness, hence be regarded a (relatively) autonomous discipline, unless it has developed a descriptive branch' (Toury, 1982). Since its inception, the mission of descriptive translation studies has been to 'study, describe (to which certain philosophers of science add: predict), in a systematic and controlled way, that segment of "the real world" which it takes as its object' (Toury, 1982). Toury's vision succinctly captured the nature and significance of the empirical branch of translation studies. Perhaps more importantly, it emphasised its identity and instrumental role in transforming and advancing translation studies as a young and rapidly growing academic discipline at that time. In the four decades since Toury's visionary statement, descriptive translation studies or its later form, empirical translation studies, has become one of the most dynamic research fields of translation studies, distinguishing itself for its constant pursuit of scientifically rigorous research methodologies to advance our understanding of translation.

In the development of descriptive translation studies since the 1990s, two of its main subfields, product- and process-oriented translation research, have emerged as productive and influential research areas which have largely driven the growth of the field. The study of translation products is chiefly text-based, and involves the contrastive linguistic analysis of source and target text pairs or comparison amongst various versions of translation with reference to the source text. Contrastive analysis between the source and target texts represents one of the most-practised approaches to translation studies, an area of study which was informed by the search for linguistic and textual equivalence (Nida, 1964; Koller, 1995). Since the late 1990s, there has been a gradual, yet decisive shift from source and target text-pair comparison towards the search for features and recurrent patterns in translations (Baker, Francis and Tognini-Bonelli, 1993; Laviosa, 1998; Olohan, 2004). The traditionally perceived authority and influence of the original material over translation outputs has been enthusiastically debated and critically challenged (Toury, 1980; Puurtinen, 1989; Lambert, 1995; Baker, 1996; Laviosa, 2004). The shift towards target-oriented translation research has benefited from the increasing availability of digital language corpora, which facilitate the testing and verification of research hypotheses. As the corpus-based approach to translation-product analysis has become widely accepted, a new wave of research innovation has crystallised in the new research field of corpus-translation studies (Baker, 1993, 1996; Tymoczko, 1998; Laviosa, 2002; Granger, 2003).

Process-oriented translation study has followed a distinct path of development. The process-oriented branch concerns the translators' behaviour and skill development (Wilss, 1996). More recent process-oriented studies have explored the cognitive mechanisms of translators and interpreters (Jakobsen, 2006). Interpreting is the oral practice of cross-cultural and cross-lingual communication, which has gained importance in recent years due to growing demands for high-quality interpreters for special purposes, such as legal, medical and conference interpreting. The process-oriented research paradigm has come to be known as *interpreting studies* in recent years (Salevsky, 1993; Pöchhacker and Shlesinger, 2002). This research paradigm has been strongly associated with and informed by advances in cognitive studies and psychology. Important and fruitful research efforts have been made to explore the cognitive mechanisms that underlie translators' or interpreters' learning patterns and working styles under natural or purposely designed experimental conditions, with a view to improving the translation or more often, the interpreting process and outcomes (Denzin, 2008).

Over the past few decades, product- and process-oriented translation paradigms have evolved into two distinct and interdisciplinary research fields: whilst the product-oriented research scheme has been chiefly applied in the study of written translations, the process-oriented scheme has been explored extensively using natural or simulated interpreting data. The two subfields have developed distinct empirical methodologies informed by different theoretical hypotheses and priorities. Text-based descriptive translation research has been strongly influenced by theoretical assumptions that seek to identify and account for universal patterns in translations across languages. Translation universals are descriptive hypotheses which have been formulated to capture the relationship between the source and target texts, as well as the relations between translations and original texts written in the target languages. Translation universals include, for example, the tendency to simplify, normalise or conventionalise source language and textual patterns when translating into a distinct language and cultural system (Mauranen and Kujamäki, 2004). In terms of the differences between translations and untranslated comparable texts in the target language, the concept of translationese has been created to describe any consistent patterns or salient features of translations as compared with texts written in the original target language (Tirkkonen-Condit, 2002). Unlike translation universals, translationese is more language-dependent and provides a useful and practical framework with which to gauge the impact of the source text on the target language. Translationese can be analysed productively at morphological, lexical, syntactical, phrasal, lexico-grammatical or phraseological and typographical levels.

By contrast, process-oriented research has been informed by theoretical assumptions from cognitive or neuroscience and psycholinguistics (Flores D'Arcais, 1978; Chernov, 1979). Despite their distinct research topics and foci on translation or interpreting materials, these two subfields, as aspects of descriptive translation studies on the Holmes-Toury map, continue to share an explicit and strong emphasis on the analysis and modelling of empirical data in order to test and verify research hypotheses pertinent to translation phenomena (Shlesinger, 1989; Gile, 1994; Lambert and Moser-Mercer, 1994). In more recent times, with the introduction of quantitative research methodologies, both subfields have become increasingly exploratory and experimental, as important and revealing patterns have begun to emerge from the systematic processing and modelling of large amounts of translation or interpreting corpus data (Shlesinger, 1998; Tirkkonen-Condit and Jääskeläinen, 2000). Descriptive translation research is no longer confined to the objective documentation and recording of translation information, but is gradually moving towards the identification of recurrent or predictive patterns in translations, as Toury rightly envisioned four decades ago.

1.2 Increasing Interaction between Descriptive and Applied Translation Studies

Another important direction in the development of descriptive translation studies is that the field has developed a strong association with applied translation research, as the findings from 'pure' translation studies have both informed and benefited from advances in applied translation studies. The applied branch within the Holmes-Toury framework of the discipline covers practical research areas from translation training and translation aids to translation criticism. Translation aids encompass a wide range of translation tools and instruments such as multilingual glossaries, dictionaries and, more recently, digital resources; these include language corpora, terminologies and integrated translation-resource creation and management systems such as local or cloud-based translation memories (Wright and Wright, 1993; Bowker, 2002). Translation aids, tools or information-management systems enable the construction of parallel or comparable corpora of large sizes. The development of language corpora has proven instrumental and cost-effective for both applied translation studies, such as translation training and teaching, and theoretical translation research, such as descriptive translation studies. The exploration of digital language corpora facilitates the identification, retrieval and quantitative analyses of textual and linguistic patterns in translations, which lies at the heart of descriptive translation studies. The creation and utilisation of digital language corpora has offered an important platform of cross-disciplinary collaboration, for example between translation-studies scholars and computer scientists on the development of hybrid translation models that integrate translation memories and machine translation systems (see Chapter 11). With the rise of globalisation, new research fields have emerged that can be incorporated into the applied branch have emerged, and that have significantly changed the landscape and our understanding of translation studies. These highly interdisciplinary and technology-intensive research fields examine aspects such as audiovisual or multimedia translation and localisation, speech-to-text or speech-to-speech translation, and service- or user-oriented multilingual translation applications which are illustrated by the case studies presented in this book.

Within the disciplinary framework devised by early translation studies scholars, the division between the descriptive and the applied research schemes has influenced the interaction and the cross-fertilisation of ideas and methodologies between the two research paradigms. For a long time after the circulation of the disciplinary map, descriptive research was largely driven by intellectual efforts to verify or contest theoretical assumptions such as translation universal patterns, norms and laws, whereas the applied branch continued to evolve, whilst the global translation industry thrives and diversifies amidst intensified intercultural and interlingual communication at a modern industrial scale. New applied research has emerged which provides academic support to new forms of industry-based translation and interpreting practices, such as game and web localisation, terminology standardisation and subtitling and dubbing for the global entertainment industry (O'Hagan and Ashworth, 2002; Remael and Díaz-Cintas, 2004).

The key adjectives used by early translation studies scholars to define and delineate the boundaries or the identity of the field were *theoretical, descriptive* and *applied*. In the early stages of its development, descriptive translation studies was intrinsically related to and influenced by theoretical translation research. In the following decades, this subfield of 'pure' translation research became increasingly scientific, problem-oriented and data-driven, characterised by its clear and strong focus on the robustness of the analysis conducted on translation materials, and the verifiability and reliability of the outcomes obtained through replicable research designs. It is useful to notice that since the 1990s, as the two subfields of descriptive translation research have undergone rapid growth, they have developed distinct research methodologies: *corpus, corpus-based, corpus-driven, frequency analysis* or *pattern recognition* have become common descriptors for product-oriented research, whilst *experimental, empirical, cognitive mechanisms and functions* or *psycholinguistic modelling* emerge as recurrent keywords in process-oriented translation or interpreting projects.

In more recent times, useful and productive efforts have been made to deliberately integrate the two sets of research methodologies to advance descriptive research, especially the empirical study of interpreting data. The benefits of combining and leveraging the two sets of empirical research methodologies are evident. On the one hand, the construction and development of parallel or comparable corpora with data gathered from the monitoring of real-time interpreting assignments can enable the discovery of useful patterns that reveal the association between interpreters' cognitive capacities and features of interpretation outputs. On the other hand, the construction of translational or interpreting corpora, which entails the investment of significant time and resources, can be informed by theoretical hypotheses formulated for process-oriented research to increase the cost-effectiveness of the digital corpus resources being built. In this new wave of methodological exploration, a large and growing number of innovative interpreting research projects have been designed to engage with the corpus-based or the corpus-driven approaches, which were developed initially for product-oriented or text-based translation studies.

Less than four decades after the development of the Holmes-Toury map of translation studies, this young and once 'invisible' academic discipline has successfully developed its own disciplinary identity. It has evolved amidst waves of globalisation to encompass a wide range of highly specialised, data- or technology-intensive subfields that have important social and practical applications. As discussed above, the shared and increasing use and exploration of translational corpora and empirical resources has reduced, and continues to push, the intra-disciplinary boundaries imposed in early times between the fields of descriptive and applied translation research. Process-oriented research has contributed to the emergence and the rapid growth of the new research field of interpreting studies. The aim of this book on advances in empirical translation studies is to reflect and add momentum to this general trend of disciplinary growth and development by encouraging continued exchange, interaction and dialogue between descriptive and applied translation studies. This trend has attracted great attention as the data-based and socially oriented turn in translation studies. In a manner differentiated from early disciplinary mapping, which separates descriptive and applied research, this book integrates these subfields based on their increasingly shared use of empirical language resources and advanced research methodologies to identify, analyse and provide practical solutions to changing social issues and research topics pertinent to translation studies.

1.3 Advances in Empirical Research Methodologies

The development of empirical research methodologies has contributed to the growth of descriptive translation studies. Since the introduction of corpus resources to translation studies in the late 1990s, there has been a constant search for scientifically rigorous and replicable methodologies with which to move the translation debate from emotional and rhetorical arguments to more data- and evidence-based research. Such evidence-based research facilitates the discovery of underlying patterns and features of translation products and processes that can be predicted, controlled and managed for better translation practice, training and education. Research efforts and discussions have revolved around topics closely related to empirical research methodologies. These include the purposes and aims of using language resources of varying sizes in empirical translation studies; the functionality and representativeness of different types of language corpora and their impact on the validity and wider applicability of corpus findings (Teubert, 1996); the role and relevance of theoretical hypotheses in the study of translation corpora; the advantages and limitations of using corpus-based (with theoretical assumptions) versus corpus-driven (without theoretical assumptions) approaches in the exploration of language corpora; the productivity of the combined use of different types of language corpora or the triangulation of corpus information; and the feasibility and reliability of using advanced quantitative methods to process large amounts of corpus data.

Early descriptive or corpus-based language studies focused on the search for meaningful patterns in language corpora (Hunston and Francis, 2000; Bowker, 2001; Baker, 2004). A number of frequency-based indicators and examples of subject-specific terminology have been developed to facilitate the analysis of corpus texts. These include type-token ratios, keywords and key-ness, low- and high-frequency words, hapax legomena, word clusters, word collocates and collocation, colligation, n-grams and so on (Kenny, 2014). Language-specific terminologies and corpus-analysis systems have been developed for character-based writing systems, for example, Chinese, which has been studied extensively at morphological and lexical levels: these developments have been useful in the study of low- and high-stroke characters, lexical density and difficult words. Recently, more sophisticated analytical schemes such as lexical complexity and textual readability or accessibility have been enabled by means of widely used corpus-analysis software that can effectively process multilingual written scripts. These frequency-based indicators for corpus analyses represented the building blocks of early corpus translation studies, which through constant peer discussions of findings uncovered through corpus text analysis have since gradually led to the development of a set of widely tested and largely replicable empirical research methodologies. Cognitive translation studies has also made important use of empirical research methodologies in the collection, such as the testing and evaluation of translation and/or interpreting resources and data (Tirkkonen-Condit and Jääskeläinen, 2000; Shreve and Angelone, 2010; O'Brien, 2011). The empirical branch of translation studies, which is capable of studying, describing and predicting translation phenomena in a systematic and controlled way, as predicted by Toury, has taken shape.

Whilst the study of useful or meaningful patterns in corpus texts through close observation was widely practised at the early stage of corpus translation research, this soon proved less productive or reliable with the large amounts of parallel, comparable or translational corpus data that were made available for empirical translation research. There has been a growing need for more advanced and systematic analytical methods with which to delve into quantitative multilingual corpus data and to unlock the potential of the once controversial corpus-driven approach to descriptive translation studies. Efforts have been made to introduce and adapt statistical methods from cognate fields such as quantitative linguistics and textual statistics to the young research field of corpus-translation studies (Oakes and Ji, 2012). This trend represents the second stage in the methodological advancement of the field, as the introduction of inferential statistics has solved one major bottleneck issue within it, i.e. what is to follow after the identification of 'meaningful' textual patterns that are largely based on individual researchers' observation of limited amounts of corpus data.

With the introduction of inferential statistics, the study of language corpora has moved away from one-dimensional to two- or multidimensional analysis, as researchers are now able to study the complex correlation or causal relationship between different sets of linguistic and textual features retrieved from large-scale language corpora. Different sets of recurrent textual patterns and linguistic features of translations that used to be studied in isolation can now be analysed within a single statistical model to reveal any latent associations amongst them. These analytical techniques are particularly useful when studying and comparing differences and similarities between large-scale translational, parallel and comparable language corpora, as corpus statistics can effectively detect the impact and influence of source textual features on translations, as well as the strength of correlation between translations and the non-translation-related comparable texts in the target language. Exploratory statistics have been introduced to the study of multidimensional translation creativity, as well as to that of the cognitive and contextual factors which may explain translators' working styles.

1.4 Towards a Social Turn in Empirical Translation Studies

The book revisits and challenges the traditional intra-disciplinary division between pure and applied research. Through various interdisciplinary case studies, it demonstrates that with the rapid growth of the field, empirical translation research that combines both product-oriented and applied research schemes has shown important potential in the development of data- or technology-intensive and socially oriented tools and analytical instruments with which to advance both applied and theoretical translation studies. This book envisions the growth of proposed data-based and socially oriented empirical translation studies in three main research areas: the development of the advanced research methodologies applied in translation studies, of large-scale multilingual resources and integrated multilingual analytical infrastructure and tools, and of user-oriented multilingual translation products and services. This requires substantial intra-disciplinary and interdisciplinary collaboration by experts from translation studies, statistics, social sciences, health, computer science and engineering. In this regard, this book makes useful efforts to expand the current horizons of empirical translation studies, especially those of corpus-translation research, by means of interdisciplinary collaboration with international environmental politics and cross-lingual health communication.

The case studies presented in this book represent important efforts to expand the current methodological framework of empirical translation studies, particularly the exploration of language corpora pertinent to socially oriented translation studies. The book proposes and illustrates new models of hypothesis formulation and verification which are being developed through interdisciplinary collaboration with 'remotely' related research fields such as environmental politics and public health. If the first stage of development of corpus-translation studies is pattern recognition, the second stage, the statistical exploration of textual patterns, is well illustrated by the case studies in this book. These case studies demonstrate the productivity of developing more sophisticated analytical instruments. These are based on high-quality multilingual resources that utilise the official multilingual terminologies and ontologies developed for specialist domains, for example, environmental agreements and laws and international environmental health guidelines and recommendations. The third stage of development of corpus-translation research aims to redefine our current understanding of descriptive or corpus translation studies as a subfield of pure translation research.

This book illustrates the development of analytical instruments that can be applied in the study of social phenomena and events at a cross-cultural and cross-lingual level. The first type of analytical instrument covers country-based ranking scales and systems that can be applied in the study of complex social phenomena, for example, multi-sectoral interaction amongst different social agents around the communication of environmental knowledge endorsed by international environmental agreements. The construction of a new ranking scale of multi-sectoral interaction was based on the computation of correlation scores amongst different pairs of social communication agencies such as governments, official reports, legal sources, top industries, major news and business sources, research institutions and digital media which facilitate the transmission and wide dissemination of translated concepts of environmental protection and sustainable development. The strength of this new ranking system, which had been developed using multilingual domain terminologies, was tested in terms of the wide range of countries that the scale can effectively compare and rank: fifteen countries in the Asia Pacific, Latin America, Europe and North America regions, with distinct social, economic and cultural profiles, were compared using the ranking scale. The validity of the multi-sectoral interaction scale was further tested by comparing the scale with authoritative international ranking systems developed for the ranking of country-based environmental performance, and the results of this showed the two ranking scales were largely consistent.

The second type of analytical instrument presented in this book is the structural equation modelling of a diffusion mechanism which imparts the attribution of social accountability across industrial sectors in terms of maintaining drinking-water safety for public health. The construction of the diffusion model utilised high-quality bilingual Japanese and English terminologies which had been developed by authoritative agencies for the translation of World Health Organization drinking-water-quality guidelines. The diffusion model tested the total, direct and indirect effects of first-tier social communication agencies on the attribution of social accountability across industrial sectors in terms of their adaptation to and compliance with international health guidelines and recommendations. The model tested the role of the digital media in enhancing or diminishing the intended effects of the efforts of the first-tier social communicators on the industrial sectors engaged in relevant social activities.

The case studies in this book illustrate recent developments in empirical translation studies, especially its increasing engagement with the study of complex and pressing social issues and problems which have emerged amidst growing multilingualism and multicultural communication in different regions of the world. This book reviews and demonstrates the increasing association between empirical translation studies, which was once categorised as 'pure' translation studies, with more applied and socially oriented translation research.

For example, the use of multilingual translation terminologies and resources can effectively assist with the development of evidence-based analytical instruments for assessing and comparing national performance in the communication of environmental knowledge; and the study of the dissemination of the translation of international health policies and guidelines can offer valuable insights into the social mechanisms that support the adaptation of global health recommendations in distinct national contexts. With the availability and convenience afforded by the increase in digital language resources and advanced corpus research methodologies, empirical translation studies has shown important potential to reveal complex mechanisms of cross-cultural and cross-lingual communication in our contemporary world. The field can thus make original contributions with which to identify and solve complex and pressing practical problems and to drive social innovation, through intra- and interdisciplinary collaboration. As the empirical branch of general translation research has advanced to its fourth stage, that of disciplinary growth, it is beneficial and necessary to review its disciplinary identity, directions of further growth and areas for research innovation that could effectively target and solve social problems such as those associated with the environment, health and social equality.

Further Reading

Hansen, Gyde (2002). Empirical translation studies: Process and product. Copenhagen Studies in Language, vol. 27. Copenhagen: Samfundslitteratur.

Hansen, Gyde (2003). Controlling the process: Theoretical and methodological reflections. In Fabio Alves (ed.), Triangulating Translation: Perspectives in Process Oriented Research, vol. 45. Amsterdam: John Benjamins, 25–42.

Holmes, James (1975/1988). The name and nature of translation studies. In James S. Holmes, Translated! Papers on Literary Translation and Translation Studies. Amsterdam: Rodopi, 66–80.

Pym, Anthony, Miriam Shlesinger and Daniel Simeoni (2008). Beyond Descriptive Translation Studies: Investigations in Homage to Gideon Toury, vol. 75, Amsterdam: John Benjamins.

Schaffner, Christina (1998). The concept of norms in translation studies. Current Issues in Language and Society 5(1–2), 1–9.

Toury, Gideon (2000). The nature and role of norms in translation. In Lawrence Venuti (ed.), The Translation Studies Reader, vol. 2. London: Routledge.

References

Baker, Mona (1993). Corpus linguistics and translation studies: Implications and applications. In M. Baker, G. Francis and E. Tognini-Bonelli (eds.), Text and Technology: In Honour of John Sinclair. Amsterdam: John Benjamins.

Baker, Mona (1996). Corpus-based translation studies: The challenges that lie ahead. In Harold Somers (ed.), Terminology, LSP and Translation: Studies in Language Engineering in Honour of Juan C. Sager. Amsterdam and Philadelphia: John Benjamins.

Baker, Mona (2004). A corpus-based view of similarity and difference in translation. International Journal of Corpus Linguistics 9(2), 167–193.

Baker, Mona, Gill Francis and Elena Tognini-Bonelli (eds.) (1993). Text and Technology: In Honour of John Sinclair. Amsterdam: John Benjamins.

Bowker, Lynne (2001). Towards a methodology for a corpus-based approach to translation evaluation. Meta: Journal des traducteurs/Meta: Translators' Journal 46(2), 345–364.

Bowker, Lynne (2002). Computer-Aided Translation Technology: A Practical Introduction. Ottawa: University of Ottawa Press.

Chernov, Ghelly (1979). Semantic aspects of psycholinguistic research in simultaneous Interpretation. Language and Speech 22(3), 277–295.

Denzin, Norman K. (2008). Collecting and Interpreting Qualitative Materials. London: Sage.

Flores D'Arcais, Giovanni (1978). The contribution of cognitive psychology to the study of interpretation. In David Gerver and H. Wallace Sinaiko (eds.), Language, Interpretation and Communication: NATO Symposium on Language, Interpretation and Communication. New York: Plenum Press, 385–402.

Gile, Daniel (1994). Methodological aspects of interpretation and translation research. In Sylvie Lambert and Barbara Moser-Mercer (eds.), Bridging the Gap: Empirical Research in Simultaneous Interpretation. Amsterdam: John Benjamins, pp. 39–56.

Granger, Silvia (2003). The corpus approach: a common way forward for Contrastive linguistics and Translation Studies. In S. Granger, J. Lerot and S. Petch-Tysin (eds.), Corpus-Based Approaches to Contrastive Linguistics and Translation Studies, vol. 20. Amsterdam: Rodopi, 17–29.

Hunston, Susan and Gill Francis (2000). Pattern Grammar: A Corpus-Driven Approach to the Lexical Grammar of English. Amsterdam: John Benjamins.

Jakobsen, Arnt Lykke (2006). Research methods in translation: Translog. In Studies in Writing. Oxford: Pergamon Press, 95–105.

Kenny, Dorothy (2014). Lexis and Creativity in Translation: A Corpus-Based Approach. London: Routledge.

Koller, Werner (1995). The concept of equivalence and the object of translation studies. Target: International Journal of Translation Studies 7(2), 191–222.

Lambert, José (1995). Translation, systems and research: The contribution of polysystem studies to translation studies. TTR traduction terminologie redaction VIII (1),105–152.

Lambert, Sylvie and Barbara Moser-Mercer (1994). Bridging the Gap: Empirical Research in Simultaneous Interpretation. Amsterdam and Philadelphia: John Benjamins.

Laviosa, Sara (1998). Universals of translation. In M. Baker (ed.), Routledge Encyclopedia of Translation Studies. London: Routledge.

Laviosa, Sara (2002). Corpus-Based Translation Studies: Theory, Findings, Applications. Amsterdam: Rodopi.

Laviosa, Sara (2004). Corpus-based translation studies: Where does it come from? Where is it going? Language Matters 35(1),6–27.

Mauranen, Anna and Pekka Kujamäki (eds.) (2004). Translation Universals: Do They Exist? Amsterdam: John Benjamins.

Nida, Eugene (1964). Principles of correspondence. In Towards a Science of Translating: With Special Reference to Principles and Procedures Involved in Bible Translating. Leiden: Brill, 156–171.

Oakes, Michael P. and Meng Ji (2012). Quantitative Methods in Corpus-Based Translation Studies: A Practical Guide to Descriptive Translation Research. Amsterdam: John Benjamins.

O'Brien, Sharon (2011). Cognitive Explorations of Translation. London: Continuum.

O'Hagan, Minako and David Ashworth (2002). Translation-Mediated Communication in a Digital World: Facing the Challenges of Globalization and Localization. Bristol: Multilingual Matters.

Olohan, Maeve (2004). Introducing Corpora in Translation Studies. London: Routledge.

Pöchhacker, Franz and Miriam Shlesinger (eds.) (2002). The Interpreting Studies Reader. Oxon: Routledge.

Puurtinen, Tiina (1989). Assessing acceptability in translated children's books. Target: International Journal of Translation Studies 1(2), 201–213.

Remael, Aline and Jorge Díaz-Cintas (2004). Audiovisual Translation: Subtitling. Oxon: Routledge.

Salevsky, Heidemarie (1993). The distinctive nature of interpreting studies. Target: International Journal of Translation Studies 5(2), 149–167.

Shlesinger, Miriam (1989). Extending the theory of translation to interpretation: Norms as a case in point. Target: International Journal of Translation Studies 1(1), 111–116.

Shlesinger, Miriam (1998). Corpus-based interpreting studies as an offshoot of corpus-based translation studies. Meta 43(4), 486–493.

Shreve, Gregory M. and Erik Angelone (eds.) (2010). Translation and Cognition. Amsterdam: John Benjamins.

Teubert, Wolfgang (1996). Comparable or parallel corpora? International Journal of Lexicography 9(3), 238–264.

Tirkkonen-Condit, Sonja (2002). Translationese – A myth or an empirical fact? A study into the linguistic identifiability of translated language. Target: International Journal of Translation Studies 14(2), 207–220.

Tirkkonen-Condit, Sonja and Riitta Jääskeläinen (eds.) (2000). Tapping and Mapping the Processes of Translation and Interpreting: Outlooks on Empirical Research. Amsterdam: John Benjamins.

Toury, Gideon (1980). The adequate translation as an intermediating construct: A model for the comparison of a literary text and its translation. In In Search of a Theory of Translation. Tel Aviv: Porter Institute, 112–121.

Toury, Gideon (1982). A rationale for descriptive translation studies. Dispositio 7 19/21, The Art and Science of Translation, 23–39.

Toury, Gideon (1995). Descriptive Translation Studies and Beyond. Amsterdam: John Benjamins.

Tymoczko, Maria (1998). Computerized corpora and the future of translation studies. Meta: journal des traducteurs/Meta: Translators' Journal 43(4), 652–660.

Wilss, Wolfram (1996). Knowledge and Skills in Translator Behaviour. Amsterdam: John Benjamins.

Wright, Sue-Ellen and Leland D. Wright (1993). Scientific and Technical Translation. Amsterdam: John Benjamins.

2 Development of Empirical Multilingual Analytical Instruments

Meng Ji

2.1 Introduction

As outlined in the opening chapter, the focus of this book is to introduce and highlight the rise of the data-intensive turn in empirical translation studies in response to new social and research problems in translation amidst the latest waves of globalisation. Empirical translation studies has been limited to academic research, whilst rarely touching upon its adaptation to practical domains in order to identify and solve pressing social issues. Discussions in this chapter draw upon a case study on environmental translation and communication. This case study, together with other illustrative empirical translation projects presented in this book, provides useful and practical guides for the development of multilingual analytical tools for interdisciplinary empirical translation research. These case studies demonstrate that important efforts have been made beyond disciplinary boundaries, as translation scholars, social scientists, domain specialists such as medical professionals and environmental scientists, and computer scientists work jointly to increase the exchange and cross-fertilisation of research ideas and methods. This collaboration has enabled the development and testing of more integrated and innovative approaches with which to solve complex social problems which require the leveraging of multidisciplinary expertise.

The case studies discussed in this book exemplify and illustrate the feasibility and productivity of the data-intensive and socially orientated approach to translation studies. These translation projects cover important yet understudied issues such as the patterns and social mechanisms that highlight the translation and dissemination of international environmental health policies in national contexts; assessment of the readability of healthcare translations for migrant patients with limited English proficiency and health literacy levels; and development of multilingual environmental terminologies and associated analytical instruments to enable the formulation and evaluation of new environmental performance indicators amongst the countries of the world at different stages of economic and social development. Despite the diverse topics and research aims of these empirical translation projects, they focus on the development of problem-orientated analytical tools and instruments that can be applied in the practical domains, where need of them is especially great, and at large scales.

This chapter will discuss in detail the development of an empirical multilingual analytical instrument that can be used effectively for assessing the multi-sectoral interaction around social sectors in the communication of environmental knowledge. A core component of the analytical instrument is a multilingual environmental terminology framework derived from multilateral environmental agreements and international environmental laws. This new multilingual environmental performance assessment instrument will illustrate how empirical translation research can effectively integrate methodologies and analytical approaches from corpus linguistics, environmental health and media studies; and more importantly, how empirical translation research can be geared towards the new data-intensive and socially orientated research paradigm.

2.2 Multilingual Terminology for Environmental Knowledge Communication and Management

Environmental risks such as pollution of air, water and soil produce substantial health burdens globally and nationally (Lim et al., 2012). Combatting environmental risks provides a focus for collaboration amongst countries to develop strategic partnerships for greater mutual economic, social and environmental benefits. The cross-sectoral nature of the impact and management of environmental health risks requires the development of multi-sectoral interaction for effective policy making. The current intra-sectoral nature of environmental risks management has been a major limiting factor in cross-sectoral collaboration (Bäckstrand, 2006). The extent to which sectors align with or diverge from each other in environmental health management, and national variations in multi-sectoral interaction, remain largely unknown. This has resulted in the lack of an empirical basis for joint action across sectors to tackle environmental risks both domestically and internationally.

Environmental risks are strongly correlated with social development. Environmental risk transition models provide useful analytical tools to explain changes in environmental risks that occur during a country's development from poor to middle-income or rich (Smith and Ezzati, 2005). However, most transition models since the 1940s have focused mainly or exclusively on the demographic and economic influences on environmental risks. This approach has overlooked the mechanism of multi-sectoral interaction – a growing social phenomenon underscored by technological advances in information sharing and knowledge transfer – in managing environmental health risks (Briggs, 2008).

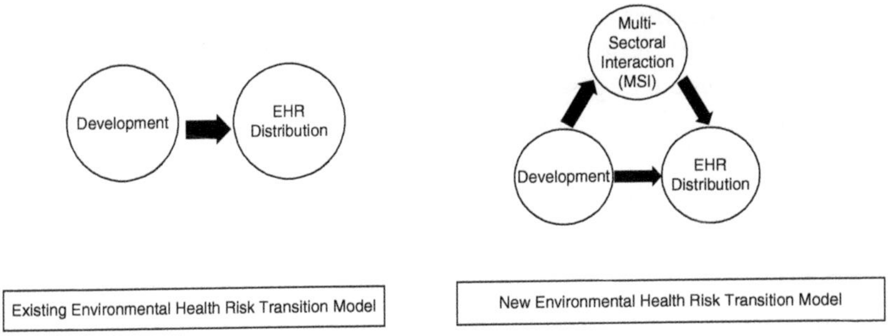

Figure 2.1 Introducing multi-sectoral interaction to advance environmental health risk (EHR) transition

Figure 2.1 illustrates the introduction of multi-sectoral interaction as an important mediating factor in the management of environmental risks. This is particularly relevant for developing countries undergoing environmental risk transition. This study will demonstrate that multi-sectoral interaction can be a powerful intervention mechanism for effective policy making in tackling environmental risk management issues which require important cross-sectoral collaboration. The development of the empirical analytical instrument for multi-sectoral interaction will help close gaps in intra-sectoral understanding and will assist with action planning around environmental health communication and management amongst sectoral stakeholders to build much-needed multi-sectoral and cross-national cooperation.

The core component of multi-sectoral interaction as a cross-national comparison instrument is multilingual terminology for the communication and management of environmental knowledge. The determination of multilingual equivalents and the development of multilingual specialised terminology systems represent an important research area of empirical translation studies (Kockaert and Steurs, 2015; Bowker and Delsey, 2016). In this case, multilingual terminology draws upon the original English terminology compiled by the Multilateral Environmental Agreements Information and Knowledge Management Initiative, which is supported and facilitated by the UN Environment (Chambers, 2008; Adger and Jordan, 2009). Part of the mission of the Initiative is the development of interoperable information systems for the benefit of the participating countries and the environmental community at large. The Initiative has developed an extensive English glossary which contains key terms and concepts common to all or several Multilateral Environmental Agreements. The fifteen countries selected in this study, i.e. Australia, USA, New Zealand, UK, Spain, Taiwan, Portugal, Brazil, China, Mexico, Argentina, Chile, Colombia, Peru and Equatorial Guinea, are participating countries in various multilateral environmental agreements (InforMEA, 2017). The four languages spoken and used as the official language in these countries are English, Chinese, Spanish and Portuguese.

The original English environmental terminology contains a large number of highly specialised expressions that cover a wide range of disciplines from law, international politics and communication to environmental sciences and technologies. In order to expand the English environmental ontology to include the other three languages, extensive search for high-quality equivalents for specialised environmental terms and expressions was conducted with authoritative multilingual translation databases. For Chinese and Spanish equivalents, this study uses the UN Term Portal, which contains hundreds of thousands of terms from four UN conference centres and regional commissions (UNTERM, n.d.). The Term Portal includes a few specialised data sets for legal, political, economic and environmental issues. For Portuguese translation, the translation database used in this study is the Interactive Terminology for Europe (Interactive Terminology for Europe, n.d.), or IATE, which is an inter-institutional terminology database (Johnson and Macphail, 2000). It is used in EU institutions and agencies for the collection, dissemination and management of specialised terminology. Similar to the UN Term Portal, IATE contains specialised terms from a wide range of areas and domains such as law, environment, information technology and many others. The IATE currently has more than 8.5 million terms, including approximately 540,000 abbreviations and 130,000 phrases, and covers all twenty-four official EU languages. In this study, both official multilingual translation databases were consulted to ensure the representativeness and quality of the multilingual environmental terminology compiled.

The total number of lexical entries for each language included in the environmental communication terminology is 450, and the total size of the multilingual terminology is 1,800 words including Chinese character words. Each English lexical entry has its corresponding translation into Spanish, Portuguese and Chinese. In the case of Chinese, the environmental terminology is recorded in the two writing systems of the language, i.e. simplified Chinese (CH) and traditional Chinese (ZH). Translation equivalents are extracted directly from quality and authoritative databases to ensure the consistency of the multilingual corpus search. The original English terminology framework of multilateral environmental agreements and international environmental laws was used. The theory-based classificatory framework will enable the analysis of the communication and management of environmental issues related to human health and national ecosystems. Benner, Reinicke and Witte (2004) propose a pluralist and networked system of accountability for various existing forms of governance which can be examined along three key dimensions, i.e. actors, process and outcomes. In the current study, the proposed multi-sectoral interaction represents essentially a process-orientated form of governance, for which there needs to be strong engagement in terms of 'common goals, and guidelines for cooperation, clear timetables and decision-making procedures' (Benner, Reinicke and Witte, 2004).

Five conceptual categories were developed for the study of the differences and contrastive patterns amongst the fifteen countries in terms of the engagement of and interaction amongst a number of social agencies in the communication and diffusion of environmental knowledge, and the management strategies established and endorsed by multilateral environmental agreements. The first two categories of *Target* and *Action* underscore the development of networked accountability in a society. The other three conceptual or term categories, i.e. *Research, Materials and Technology, and Economics and Management*, refer to the national strategic deployment of sources and funding which were highlighted as another key element in the examination of the process dimension of networked accountability (Benner, Reinicke and Witte, 2004).

The first conceptual category, Target, includes words and expressions that represent pressing environmental issues such as water shortage, acid precipitation, afforestation, air pollution, biodegradation, biodiversity loss, biological contamination, black carbon, deforestation, marine pollution, nuclear energy, ocean acidification, oil pollution, radioactive contamination, vulnerable ecosystems, water pollution, greenhouse gases, habitat loss, extreme weather, climate change, hazardous waste, domestic waste, electronic waste, ocean acidification, sea level rise, and so on. The second conceptual category, Action, includes expressions that denote actions that can be taken or recommended in multilateral environmental agreements to safeguard or improve environmental management: benefit sharing, accession, climate-change adaptation, adoption, allocation, amendment, arbitration, best practice, bioaccumulation, capacity building, certification, mitigation, ratification, recycling, reforestation, registration, public participation, sustainable use and so on.

The third category is defined as Research, which encompasses phrases and expressions indicating concepts, frameworks and key research areas related to environmental protection and management: clean development mechanisms, early warning system, emission standard, integration principle, intra-generational equity, land-degradation neutrality, multilateral systems, polluter-pays principle, precautionary principle, principle of non-regression, sustainable development, environmental impact assessment, and so on. The fourth category is Materials and Technology, which includes expressions related to the use of new resources and technologies to improve environmental management: alternative substances, biofuels, biomass, genetic resources, geothermal energy, hydropower energy, marine genetic resources, plant genetic resources, renewable energy, solar energy, wind energy, biotechnology, genetic engineering, geo-engineering, technology and so on. The last word category is Economics and Management, which encompasses economic, financial and managerial interventions that could improve a country's environmental performance: adaptation fund, carbon stock, development aid, economic instruments, emissions trading, financial mechanism, food aid, green economy, payment for ecosystem services, resource accounting, stakeholder engagement, sustainable tourism, trade in species, coastal management, integrated management, local administration, sound environmental management, waste management, water resources management and so on.

2.3 Patterns of Cross-Cultural Environmental Knowledge Communication and Management

This section uses the multilingual terminology constructed to investigate the underlying patterns of the communication of environmental knowledge and management across a wide range of countries at different stages of economic and social development: Australia, the USA, New Zealand, the UK, Spain, Taiwan, Portugal, Brazil, China, Mexico, Argentina, Chile, Colombia, Peru and Equatorial Guinea. The exploration of differences and similarities amongst the countries in terms of environmental knowledge communication will take advantage of multilingual databases which contain many licensed digital resources published by key sectors in each country. This study uses the FACTIVA open-end database, developed by the Dow Jones company in the 1990s (Johal, 2009). The original database encompasses twenty-one sources of information covering business, industries, governments, trade, newspapers, magazines, journals, official reports, non-governmental organisations, research institutes and sports. In this study, nine main sources of information were selected as the targeted social agencies for the analysis of the hypothesised multi-sectoral interaction mechanism; the sources were limited to this number due to the practical consideration of the limited available relevant data across the fifteen countries. The nine large sources of information cover key social agencies and influential institutions working in the area of the communication of environmental knowledge and management in the countries under comparison: governmental agencies, legal sources, political sources, official sources, top industries, major news and business sources, magazines and journals and newspapers and research institutes.

It is hypothesised in this study that in the communication of environmental management policy based on multilateral agreements and international environmental laws, strong multi-sectoral interaction within a society amongst the nine main sources of information listed above may effectively enhance the environmental performance of the country. Based on this hypothesis, the higher the multi-sectoral interaction amongst the various environmental communication agencies, the better the overall environmental performance of that country may be. This study will test and verify, based on large amounts of environmental publication data, whether the hypothesised multi-sectoral interaction mechanism holds true for these fifteen countries, which represent a wide spectrum of social and economic development and distinct environmental cultures. The multi-sectoral interaction instrument which draws upon the multilingual environmental terminology compiled may serve as an indicator of the effectiveness of cross-sectoral environmental communication, thereby providing a further insight into the environmental performance of the fifteen countries under comparison.

The multi-sectoral interaction index has been developed as an empirical analytical instrument to enable cross-country comparison. The multi-sectoral interaction index provides the breakdown of the correlation scores for each pair of the nine main environmental communication agencies in each country, for example, between governmental sources and top industrial sources, or business sources and newspapers, or legal sources and official sources, magazines and newspapers. The correlation scores for each sectoral pair are indicative of the strength of association between two sectors across the five dimensions developed for measuring and assessing cross-sectoral interaction. These correlation scores by sector pairs reveal the level of multi-sectoral interaction within each of the fifteen countries under comparison.

In order to compare the fifteen target countries, the composite scores for each country were computed by averaging the sum of inter-sectoral correlation scores with the number of environmental communication sectors. The resulting composite scores can be used to compare the average levels of multi-sectoral interaction across the target countries (see Table 2.3). As discussed from the outset of the study, the newly developed ranking of multi-sectoral interaction will be compared with the widely used Environmental Performance Index developed by the Yale Center for Environmental Law and Policy and Yale Data-Driven Environmental Solutions Group at Yale University, and the Center for International Earth Science Information Network at Columbia University, in collaboration with the World Economic Forum (Färw, Grosskopf and Hernandez-Sancho, 2004). The Environmental Performance Index provides the ranking of world countries based on their national performance in achieving two objectives, i.e. protection of human health and maintenance of the country's ecosystems. The availability of the index has enabled evidence-based environmental policy making at national and international levels (Hsu and Zomer, 2016).

The multi-sectoral interaction index developed in this study and the Environmental Performance Index deploy different measurement scales, so to enable cross-index comparison, standardised z-scores are computed for both indexes (Aron, Coups and Aron, 2013). The standardised composite scores of multi-sectoral interaction are then compared with the z-scores of countries' overall environmental performance scores. If the hypothesis proposed in this study holds true, one would expect to detect similar and consistent patterns between the two ranking schemes measuring multi-sectoral interaction amongst environmental communication agencies in each country, and the country's environmental performance, respectively. By contrast, if important differences seem to emerge from comparing the two ranking instruments, one may need to reject or reformulate the original hypothesis in terms of the relevance of the multi-sectoral interaction to national environmental performance.

The development of the multi-sectoral interaction instrument entailed data-intensive corpus analyses using the multilingual environmental communication terminology described in the previous section. The first stage was the search for and extraction of the combined raw frequencies of occurrence of lexical entries in each of the five categories of environmental knowledge communication and management. In order to retrieve the frequencies of each word category in each country, search parameters were first set in the FACTIVA database online interface regarding the range of date, country and language of the digital publications. The source of information for the publications was specified by each of the nine environmental communication agencies: for example, official sources, industries, business sources, or research institutions to the media. Table 2.1 shows the breakdown of the combined frequencies by sector in Australia for the time period under study, i.e. from the mid-1990s to 2017. Similar searches were conducted in the multilingual corpus for the other fourteen countries, where necessary using translations of the English environmental terminology in Chinese, Spanish and Portuguese. The information provided in the cross-tabulation can be used to compute the cross-sectoral correlation scores of each country. A chi-squared test on the data in Table 2.1 (X^2 = 33833, df = 32, p-value $< 2.2 \times 10^{-16}$) showed that the distribution of word categories was not the same for each lexical category.

Table 2.2 shows the cross-sectoral correlation scores amongst the nine large sources of information in Australia. For example, the correlation between business sources and government/politics was found by finding the Pearson's correlation coefficient between the five values in the business sources column and the five values in the government/politics column. The correlation coefficient provides a measure of the strength of association between two variables, or two environmental communication agencies in this study. The coefficient scores range between negative one and positive one. Zero indicates no relation between two variables. Within the positive spectrum of correlation, the larger the correlation coefficient, the stronger the relation between two variables, with positive one indicating two identical variables. For example, the first column shows that in Australia, business sources have strong correlations with government/politics (0.977), top industry sources (0.994), major news and business sources (0.992), magazines and journals (0.949) and newspapers (0.934).

Table 2.1 *Word frequencies of occurrence by category in FACTIVA (Australia)*

Category	Business sources	Government/ politics	Legal sources	Official sources	Research	Top industries	Major news and business	Magazines	Newspapers
Action	209,769	30,986	922	1,215	5,557	84,693	295,210	15,987	575,809
Economics and management	147,285	18,292	597	802	2,894	58,714	180,362	9,473	289,749
Research	74,616	12,227	250	645	2,276	20,695	91,595	4,917	215,546
Target	119,605	18,005	240	895	2,355	38,482	168,220	7,099	358,744
Materials and technology	69,766	8,832	474	475	2,428	22,112	74,361	6,712	117,101

The last row of Table 2.2 displays the sum of the correlation scores by source of information. When there is no relation between any pair of sectors, the sum of correlation coefficients is zero. The sum of correlation scores ranges between positive nine and negative nine. The mean of the cumulative correlation coefficients in Australia is 8.133, and eight of the nine sectors show sums for correlation scores above the mean: business sources (8.498), government and politics (8.483), top industry sources (8.432), major news and business sources (8.503) and magazines and journals (8.402). The four sectors that have limited correlations with other sources of information are legal sources (7.339), official sources (8.112), research (8.165) and newspapers (8.153). The conversion of word frequencies to inter-sectoral correlation scores will enable the development of a new empirical indicator, i.e. the composite inter-sectoral interaction which measures the average cross-sectoral association of each country (see Table 2.2).

Table 2.3 shows the comparison between the scores in the Environmental Performance Index (EPI) and the composite scores of multi-sectoral interaction for the fifteen countries under comparison. The EPI provides an empirical analytical instrument which ranks the countries in the world on nine priority environmental issues including air quality, forests, fisheries, climate and energy, amongst others. The chief objective of the EPI is to facilitate the transition from rhetorical environmental debates to the empirical study of environmental accountability amongst stakeholders and of the outcomes in terms of a country's overall performance. Since its first pilot edition was published in 2002, the EPI has served as an international reference standard for comparing country performance on international policies, including the UN Sustainable Development Goals (Hsu et al., 2010). The current study uses the latest (2016) edition of the national EPI.

The composite scores of multi-sectoral interaction were calculated by dividing the grand total of multi-sectoral interaction scores for each country by the number of environmental communication sectors under study, which is nine. The mean of the composite multi-sectoral interaction scores amongst the fifteen countries is 6.0299 with a standard deviation of 2.184. Eight countries reported strong multi-sectoral interaction around the communication and dissemination of environmental knowledge, a result partly attributable to its purposely constructed multilingual environmental terminology. These are New Zealand (8.34), the UK (8.29), Australia (8.23), the USA (8.15), Spain (7.91), Portugal (7.84), Chile (6.76) and Taiwan (6.45). The other seven countries, including China, five in Latin America (Mexico, Brazil, Colombia, Argentina and Peru) and one in Africa (Equatorial Guinea), are positioned below or well below the average multi-sectoral interaction of approximately 6.

The mean of environmental performance scores amongst the fifteen countries is 61.92, with a standard deviation of 14.535. Similar patterns began to emerge

Table 2.2 *Cross-sectoral correlation scores: Australia*

	Business sources	Government and politics	Legal sources	Official sources	Research report	Top industry sources	Major news and business sources	Magazines	Newspapers
Business sources	1.000	0.977	0.820	0.941	0.891	0.994	0.992	0.949	0.934
Government and politics	0.977	1.000	0.754	0.985	0.908	0.952	0.994	0.927	0.986
Legal sources	0.820	0.754	1.000	0.629	0.912	0.867	0.771	0.938	0.647
Official sources	0.941	0.985	0.629	1.000	0.833	0.899	0.975	0.853	0.997
Research report	0.891	0.908	0.912	0.833	1.000	0.896	0.892	0.973	0.860
Top industry sources	0.994	0.952	0.867	0.899	0.896	1.000	0.972	0.960	0.892
Major news & business sources	0.992	0.994	0.771	0.975	0.892	0.972	1.000	0.936	0.971
Magazines	0.949	0.927	0.938	0.853	0.973	0.960	0.936	1.000	0.866
Newspapers	0.934	0.986	0.647	0.997	0.860	0.892	0.971	0.866	1.000
Grand total	8.498	8.483	7.339	8.112	8.166	8.432	8.503	8.402	8.153

Table 2.3 *Comparison between EPI and Multi-Sectoral Interaction (MSI)*

Country	EPI	Z_EPI	MSI composite	Z_MSI composite (z-score)
Argentina	49.55	−0.8511	4.22	−0.82958
Australia	82.4	1.40898	8.23	1.00821
Brazil	52.97	−0.61581	4.81	−0.55846
Chile	69.93	0.55104	6.76	0.33427
China	43	−1.30174	1.1	−2.25857
Colombia	50.77	−0.76717	5.16	−0.39675
Equatorial Guinea	41.06	−1.43522	3.81	−1.0179
Mexico	55.03	−0.47408	5.43	−0.27311
New Zealand	76.41	0.99687	8.34	1.05938
Peru	45.05	−1.1607	3.95	−0.95299
Portugal	75.8	0.9549	7.84	0.82738
Spain	79.79	1.22941	7.91	0.85983
Taiwan	62.18	0.01784	6.45	0.19402
UK	77.35	1.06154	8.29	1.03298
USA	67.52	0.38523	8.15	0.97128

when comparing the two indexes: countries which have strong and verified multi-sectoral interaction around the communication of environmental knowledge and management endorsed by multilateral environmental agreements also feature high in the overall environmental performance ranking. Countries with the highest overall environmental performance scores are Australia (82.4), Spain (79.79), the UK (77.35), New Zealand (76.41), Portugal (75.8), Chile (69.93), the USA (67.52) and Taiwan (62.18). These are the countries with strong internal cross-sectoral networks for the communication of environmental knowledge and shared management strategies, as their country-specific multi-sectoral interaction scores are either above or well above the mean of the fifteen countries under comparison. Table 2.4 shows the result of Spearman's correlation test of the EPI values and the MSI composite values. The correlation coefficient is 0.932, which is significant at the 0.01 level (two-tailed). This again confirms the strong correlation between the two ranking schemes.

The country scores for the EPI were measured on a different scale from the proposed multi-sectoral interaction index. To enable the comparison between the two indexes, especially each country's position relative to the other countries under comparison, the scores of both indexes were transformed to their respective z-scores (a measure of the standardised deviation from the population mean) to facilitate the comparison of the two lists of country-based environmental communication and overall environmental performance scores. The comparison of the two sets of z-scores again points in a similar

Table 2.4 *Spearman's correlation test*

			MSI composite score	EPI
Spearman's rho	MSI Composite Score	Correlation coefficient	1.000	0.932**
		Sig. (two-tailed)		0.000
		N	15	15
	EPI	Correlation coefficient	0.932**	1.000
		Sig. (two-tailed)	0.000	
		N	15	15

** Correlation is significant at the 0.01 level (two-tailed)

direction with regard to the countries' overall environmental performance, and the strengths amongst the different sectors in the communication of environmental knowledge and management information within each country. With a z-score for environmental performance of 0.01784, and a z-score of within-country multi-sectoral interaction of 0.19402, Taiwan again serves as the division point between two groups of countries: those with high environmental performance and high-level multi-sectoral interaction internally and those with low environmental performance and low-level multi-sectoral interaction at the national level. Whilst the former group of countries (Australia, Spain, the UK, New Zealand, Portugal, Chile, the USA and Taiwan) are indicated by their positive z-scores on the two indexes, the latter group of countries (Mexico, Brazil, Colombia, Argentina, Peru, China and Equatorial Guinea) are marked by their negative z-scores with regard to both empirical measurements. A comparison of the two country-ranking scales suggests strong correlation between a country's environmental performance and the highlighted interaction amongst key social sectors in the communication and diffusion of environmental knowledge and management strategies. It would be interesting to further explore in future research the association between multi-sectoral interaction and a country's overall environmental performance using longitudinal data, for example by generating the composite cross-sectoral correlation scores between two ten-year periods, 1997–20007 and 2007–2017, and comparing the differences between the two periods in terms of the change in inter-sectoral interaction and the countries' overall environmental performance.

2.4 Conclusion

The case study presented in this chapter, along with case studies in other chapters in this book, illustrates the feasibility and productivity of developing evidence-based analytical tools and instruments by taking advantage of the growing multilingual translation resources and materials that have been developed for important practical social applications; this range from the UN or the EU official multilingual databases, to specialised terminology systems based on multilateral environmental agreements and international environmental laws. Whilst the development of multilingual translation resources has provided a focus for important research in translation studies, few have touched upon the development of multilingual analytical tools and instruments that can be used to bring insights into social and research issues of contemporary significance. Based on the development of the cross-sectoral interaction index for assessing the communication of environmental knowledge and shared management strategies to the structural modelling or the path analysis of the translation and diffusion of international environmental politics in national contexts, and the development of empirical assessment tools to label and diagnose the readability or accessibility of national health translations and education resources, the various case studies presented in this book have made useful efforts in expanding and broadening the current research scope of empirical translation studies.

From the perspective of disciplinary growth, empirical or corpus translation studies, which is intrinsically linked with cognate fields such as corpus linguistics, multilingual studies, digital humanities and digital media, has benefited and will continue to benefit from the growing data-intensive and socially orientated turn in the humanities in general. Since its inception in the late 1990s, corpus translation research has placed a strong focus on the development of robust and verifiable research methodologies to enhance the capacity of this relatively young research paradigm in the identification, analysis, processing and interpretation of underlying patterns in large-scale translation and multilingual databases. It is demonstrated and argued in this book that experimentation with and integration of advanced empirical research methodologies from 'remotely-related' disciplines such as public health and environmental politics could provide further stimulus for the disciplinary growth of empirical translation studies, as these fields are facing pressing social and research issues that have been emerging from the growing trends of globalisation and of intensified cross-lingual and cross-cultural communication. In this book, the proposed social turn in translation studies, especially in the specialised branch of multilingual corpus translation research, thus envisions the continued growth of the field as a distinctively problem-driven and interdisciplinary research paradigm which has made original contributions to, and will continue to advance understanding of, translation as an integral and essential part of human communication.

References

Adger, W. Neil and Andrew Jordan (eds.) (2009). Governing Sustainability. Cambridge, UK: Cambridge University Press.

Aron, Arthur, Elliot Coups and Elaine N. Aron (2013). Statistics for the Behavioral and Social Sciences. London and New York: Pearson Higher Education.

Bäckstrand, Karin (2006). Multi-stakeholder partnerships for sustainable development: Rethinking legitimacy, accountability and effectiveness. Environmental Policy and Governance 16(5), 290–306.

Benner, Thorsten, Wolfgang H. Reinicke and Jan Martin Witte (2004). Multisectoral networks in global governance: Towards a pluralistic system of accountability, Government and Opposition 39(2), 191–210.

Bowker, Lynne and Tom Delsey (2016). Information science, terminology and translation studies. In Yves Gambier and Luc van Doorslaer (eds.), Border Crossings: Translation Studies and Other Disciplines. Benjamins Translations Library, vol. 126. Amsterdam: John Benjamins, 73–96.

Briggs, David J. (2008). A framework for integrated environmental health impact assessment of systemic risks. Environmental Health 1(1), 61.

Chambers, Bradnee W. (2008). Interlinkages and the Effectiveness of Multilateral Environmental Agreements. New York: United Nations University Press.

Environmental Performance Index. (n.d.) https://epi.envirocenter.yale.edu.

Färw, R., S. Grosskopf and F. Hernandez-Sancho (2004). Environmental performance: An index number approach. Resource and Energy Economics 26(4), 343–352.

Hsu, A., J. Emerson, M. Levy, A. de Sherbinin, I. Johnson, O. Malik, J. Schwartz and M. Jaitch (2010). Environmental Performance Index. New Haven, CT: Yale Centre for Environmental Law and Policy, vol. 87.

Hsu, Angel and Alisa Zomer (2016). Environmental Performance Index. Wiley StatsRef: Statistics Reference Online.

InforMEA (2017). Multilateral environmental agreements and international environmental law. InforMEA (web). https://informea.org/terms.

Interactive Terminology for Europe (Portuguese) (n.d.). (web) https://iate.europa.eu/home

Johal, Rajiv (2009). Factiva: Gateway to business information. Journal of Business and Finance Librarianship (15)1, 60–64.

Johnson, Ian and Alastair Macphail (2000). IATE-Inter-Agency Terminology Exchange: Development of a single central terminology database for the institutions and agencies of the European Union. In Workshop on Terminology Resources and Computation.

Kockaert, Hendrik J., and Frieda Steurs (2015). Handbook of Terminology. Amsterdam: John Benjamins.

Lim, S., T. Vos and A. D. Flaxman et al. (2012). A comparative risk assessment of burden of disease and injury attributable to 67 risk factors and risk factor clusters in 21 regions, 1990–2010: A systematic analysis for the Global Burden of Disease Study 2010, Lancet 380(9859), 2224–2260.

Smith, Kirk R. and Majid Ezzati (2005). How environmental health risks change with development: The epidemiologic and environmental risk transitions revisited. Annual Review of Environment and Resources 30, 291–333.

UNTERM: The UN Terminology Database (n.d.) Welcome. The UN Terminology Database (web). https://cms.unov.org/UNTERM/portal/welcome.

3 Statistics for Corpus-Based and Corpus-Driven Approaches to Empirical Translation Studies

Michael Oakes

3.1 Introduction

In this chapter we follow the distinction between the two main approaches to corpus studies: 'corpus-based' and 'corpus-driven'. Corpus-based studies are used to describe and explain patterns of variation and use of known linguistic constructs, rather than to discover new ones. Corpus-based studies have shown the importance of register in linguistic variation. In this chapter, we will look at corpus-based studies which examine such hypotheses as 'Type-token ratio (TTR) depends on language of origin for translated texts in the ENNTT corpus', the t-test, linear regression, ANOVA and mixed modelling. In contrast, corpus-driven approaches make very few initial assumptions regarding the linguistic features that should be chosen for the corpus analysis. In their most extreme form, we assume only the existence of words, 'words' here being simply defined as strings of alphabetic characters surrounded by other characters such as punctuation and white space. We consider only the surface forms of words, and even inflected variants of the same lemma are regarded as separate entities. Through the corpus-driven analysis, we discover co-occurrence patterns among words (or between words and texts) and use these as the basis for making linguistic descriptions afterwards. In this way we can use the corpus to identify linguistic categories for the first time (Tognini-Bonelli, 2001, 81). Biber's (2009) MDA (Multi-Dimensional Analysis) is a hybrid approach, since it assumes pre-defined categories (such as nominalisations and past-tense verbs) and syntactic features (such as WH-relative clauses and conditional adverbial clauses). However, the hitherto undiscovered groupings of such features which represent dimensions of linguistic variation (as they commonly co-occur in texts of a given type such as genre) did reveal new linguistic constructs, not previously recognised by linguistic theory.

In Section 3.4 we describe studies in which we use Principal Components Analysis (PCA), a technique related to Factor Analysis, to examine the variation in texts translated into English according to which language family the originals were written in. We start with no linguistic assumptions, and use only the surface forms of the 100 most frequent words in the total vocabulary in the text collection. Once the first two principal components (each representing groups of words which tend to occur together in similar texts) have been extracted, we examine which sets of words are most typical of those components, to form hitherto undiscovered linguistic constructs consisting of those sets of words.

3.2 The ENNTT Corpus

Philipp Koehn's (2005) 'Europarl' corpus is a parallel corpus consisting of transcripts of the European parliament since 1996 in twenty-one languages, each aligned sentence by sentence with their English translations. The speech turns are each annotated with the language of the text, the speaker's identification number, and in many cases what language the original speaker was using.

Nisioi et al. (2016) describe one version of the Europarl Corpus of Native, Non-Native and Translated Texts (ENNTT) corpus, which is a subset derived from Europarl.[1] The corpus built by Nisioi et al. (2016) is monolingual, consisting only of texts in English, as follows:

- a Texts produced directly by native speakers in English;
- b Texts in English produced directly by native speakers of other languages (who are highly competent in English);
- c Texts originally in another language translated into English by native speakers of English.

According to Nisioi et al. (2016, 4197), '[c]orpora of original and translated language are essential for empirical investigation of theoretically-motivated hypotheses from the field of translation studies'. In this chapter, we explore for example the theory that TTR (in 2000-word samples) in native, non-native and translated texts is different: supporting the hypothesis that the lexical diversity of non-native speakers is poorer than that of native speakers.

The files accessible from this link are not annotated with speakers' data, including knowledge about the speaker's native language. However, the file names are given meaningful prefixes, where 'ensc' denotes texts by native speakers, 'eu' denotes texts written directly into English by non-native speakers and 'translated' refers to those texts not originally written in English, but translated by professional translators. There are 354 individual files for each of the 3 language varieties.

Rabinovich et al. (2016) clustered these text samples by k-means clustering. Their choice of features to characterise the texts were the 400 function words

[1] The corpus is freely available from: http://nlp.unibuc.ro/resources/ENNTT.tar.gz.

from a list by Koppel and Ordan (2011). The advantages of using function words for text classification are (a) they are less biased by topic; (b) they are very high frequency, so their selection is outside the author's conscious control; and (c) they are assumed to contain grammatical information, and thus provide a proxy for full grammatical analysis. They also looked at positional token frequency, meaning the frequency of each word when it occurs in first position or second position in the sentence, and so on. In other experiments they used the 3000 most frequent POS (part of speech) trigrams and cohesive markers. Each time, when they selected three-way clustering they obtained separate clusters for native, non-native and translated texts, and when they selected two-way clustering, obtained one cluster for native speaker texts, and another combined cluster for non-native and translated texts.

The same team (Rabinovich et al., 2016) describe a second version of ENNTT, which consists of two subcorpora: languages and families. Both consist of raw text not divided into individual speeches, and have no annotation.[2] The 'Families' sub-corpus is itself divided into four subcorpora: texts written by non-native speakers from Germanic and Romance languages; and translated texts from both the Germanic and Romance languages. The 'Languages' sub-corpus has English texts written by native speakers of eight different languages: Spanish, French, German, Italian, Dutch, Portuguese, Romanian and Swedish.

Rabinovich et al. (2017) examined the hypothesis that due to L1 interference, translations into English from a pair of closely related languages will resemble each other more than two translations into English from a pair of more distantly related languages. Thus by using clustering techniques on a set of translations into English from a variety of source languages, they felt they should be able to build a phylogenetic tree in which nearby branches correspond to closely related languages. In their experiments they used agglomerative (hierarchical) clustering with Ward's linkage method and Euclidean distance (of the most frequent word vectors) as the dissimilarity metric. The best trees were found using POS trigrams, which, working on a seventeen-language set, achieved clustering similar to the gold standard set of Serva and Petroni (2008).

All the experiments performed in this chapter made use of the ENNTT corpus.

3.3 Corpus-Based Experiments

In Section 3.3.1 we make use of the t-test to compare two groups of texts according to how often they contain the word 'that'. ANOVA, described in Section 3.3.3, is an extension of the t-test to compare three or more groups, so we can use it to find out whether the word 'that' is used in English texts at

[2] The data set is available at: http://nlp.unibuc.ro/resources.html.

different rates by native speakers of all eight languages represented in the ENNTT corpus. ANOVA is an example of a linear model, as is linear regression, described in Section 3.3.2. An excellent tutorial on linear models (and the linear mixed-effects models we will encounter in Section 3.3.4), from which the R commands used in this chapter have been derived, has been prepared by Bodo Winter at the University of California (Winter, 2013). The R commands for ANOVA were derived from Baayen (2008, 104–108).

3.3.1 *The T-Test*

We are interested in knowing whether the word 'that', in English texts written by non-native speakers, is relatively more frequent in texts written by Spanish speakers or in texts written by French speakers. We may express this in a negative way, in the so-called 'null hypothesis': There is no difference in the frequency of 'that' in English texts written by non-native speakers of Spanish and French. One way to measure this is to examine suitable texts in the 'Languages' section of the ENNTT corpus. Since we have formed the hypothesis before examining the corpus, this is an example of a 'corpus-based' study. By selecting the relevant texts in the corpus, we find that the number of times 'that' occurs per hundred words in the twenty-four texts by Spanish speakers is:

> 2.40, 2.25, 2.00, 1.50, 1.80, 2.00, 1.85, 1.35, 1.55, 1.55, 1.00, 0.90, 0.70, 0.85, 1.10, 1.10, 0.90, 1.20, 0.55, 0.80, 1.15, 0.45, 0.75 and 0.95.

The corresponding data for the twelve texts by French speakers is:

> 2.10, 2.15, 1.10, 2.25, 2.20, 1.50, 0.95, 1.25, 1.95, 1.70, 2.15 and 1.75.

To compare this data using the R statistical programming language, we place the 'Spanish' data into a file called 'that_e' and the 'French' data into a file called 'that_f'. The t-test is run using the command:

```
> t.test(that_e,that_f)
```

and the computer responds as follows:

```
Welch Two Sample t-test
data: that_e and that_f
t = −2.7582, df = 25.883, p-value = 0.01052
alternative hypothesis: true difference in means is not equal to 0
95 per cent confidence interval:
−0.8327004 −0.1214663
```

Sample estimates:

```
mean of x mean of y
1.277083 1.754167
```

The two mean values on the last line show that on average, the French speakers in our sample used ‘that’ more often than the Spanish speakers (about 1.75 per cent of the total word count as opposed to about 1.27 per cent). However, it may be that in general the two groups of native speakers use the word ‘that’ equally frequently, and we just happened to choose some texts by French speakers with unusually high counts of the word ‘that’. We need to know how likely this is to have been the case, and the answer to this question is returned by the t-test (and all ‘frequentist’ statistical tests) in the form of a p-value. Here the p-value is 0.01052, so the chance that we simply chose an unlucky sample is just over 1 per cent. This means that we are almost 99 per cent confident that native speakers of French use the word ‘that’ more than native speakers of Spanish. This is more than an arbitrary (though widely accepted) threshold of 95 per cent, so we say that the difference is statistically significant. We also see a 95 per cent confidence interval, showing that we are 95 per cent confident that the true difference in the occurrence of ‘that’ in the texts written by the two sets of speakers is between about 0.12 per cent and 0.83 per cent.

3.3.2 Linear Regression

The first type of linear model we will look at is linear regression. We start with the null hypothesis that there is no relation between the number of times the word ‘that’ is found in a 2000-word text written by a non-native speaker and the number of times the word ‘of’ is used. Linear regression is suitable for experiments such as this, where we study how one numeric variable varies with another one. The frequencies of the two words in each of the 137 texts of the ENNTT ‘non-native’ sub-corpus are stored in files called ‘that_freq’ and ‘of_freq’. The data in these files are shown below, where the numbers in the square brackets simply indicate the ordinal number of the data item which appears first in the row. Thus the first data item in the second row is the sixteenth item in the whole data set.

a) Frequencies of ‘that’, expressed as percentages of the whole text.

```
[1]   2.40 2.25 2.00 1.50 1.80 2.00 1.85 1.35 1.55 1.55 1.00 0.90 0.70 0.85 1.10
[16]  1.10 0.90 1.20 0.55 0.80 1.15 0.45 0.75 0.95 2.10 2.15 1.10 2.25 2.20 1.50
[31]  0.95 1.25 1.95 1.70 2.15 1.75 1.55 2.05 2.10 1.85 1.50 1.65 1.00 2.10 2.40
[46]  1.70 1.50 1.50 1.45 1.45 1.80 1.70 1.85 1.85 1.75 1.65 1.85 2.30 3.45 2.20
[61]  3.00 2.10 2.35 1.45 2.55 2.00 2.30 2.50 2.10 1.55 1.60 2.10 2.55 2.25 3.00
[76]  3.10 3.50 2.65 2.00 1.65 1.70 2.35 1.40 2.10 1.25 1.40 1.65 1.85 1.50 2.00
[91]  1.80 1.50 1.55 1.45 1.75 2.05 1.70 2.25 2.55 2.60 2.10 1.70 1.80 0.70 1.35
[106] 1.80 1.40 1.00 1.20 1.10 1.20 0.80 1.15 0.95 2.10 1.65 2.15 2.15 2.40 1.25
[121] 1.75 1.70 1.40 2.20 1.90 2.60 1.50 1.45 1.10 2.15 1.20 1.60 2.25 1.70 1.80
[136] 1.65 1.80
```

b) Frequencies of 'of', expressed as frequencies of the whole text.

```
[1]   3.60 3.65 4.90 4.95 4.00 3.25 2.60 3.55 3.20 3.35 4.90 4.55 4.95 4.15 4.70
[16]  4.20 5.05 4.15 4.10 4.55 4.45 7.00 3.60 4.05 3.60 2.90 3.90 3.90 3.90 4.15
[31]  4.60 5.05 4.35 4.90 4.70 4.00 4.20 3.00 3.05 2.35 4.05 4.05 4.35 2.65 3.10
[46]  2.65 4.40 3.60 4.75 3.65 3.70 3.20 3.35 2.90 3.40 3.00 2.15 3.25 3.30 3.15
[61]  2.80 3.05 3.05 3.30 2.35 2.70 3.00 2.85 3.15 2.45 2.85 3.75 2.80 2.75 2.60
[76]  2.75 3.75 4.75 5.00 3.55 4.50 4.20 3.55 4.45 4.05 3.50 4.65 4.25 3.85 5.70
[91]  4.80 4.20 3.60 4.70 3.55 2.90 4.45 2.55 2.25 3.00 4.00 3.55 3.15 3.85 3.75
[106] 3.00 3.50 3.75 4.05 3.75 3.60 3.80 3.85 3.60 2.90 2.65 2.80 3.10 2.95 4.15
[121] 2.90 2.65 4.55 3.00 3.25 2.90 3.30 3.95 3.25 3.50 3.35 3.45 3.00 3.15 2.70
[136] 3.00 3.40
```

To create a linear model (lm) where the frequency of the word 'that' is a function of the frequency of the word 'of' in R, we can use the command

```
> that_of.lm = lm(that_freq ~ of_freq)
```

and then view the output with

```
> that_of.lm
```

The output is shown below. The coefficients show that the percentage frequency of the word 'that' is about 2.9715 minus 0.3378 times the percentage frequency of the word 'of'. Thus in general, the higher the frequency of 'that' in the text, the lower the frequency of 'of'. The 'plot' and 'abline' commands cause this relationship to be depicted in Figure 3.1, where the straight line shows the general trend and the small circles represent individual texts. The 'cor.test' command shows that the correlation between the frequencies of 'that' and 'of' is −470747 (where a correlation coefficient of 0 would show no relation between the frequencies of the two words, and a coefficient of −1 would show a perfect inverse relation between the two. The p-value shows that this relation is highly statistically significant.

Call:

lm(formula = that_freq ~ of_freq)

Coefficients:

(Intercept) of_freq
2.9715 −0.3378

```
> plot(of_freq, that_freq, xlab = 'of', ylab='that')
> abline(that_of.lm)
> cor.test(of_freq, that_freq)
```

Pearson's product-moment correlation

data: of_freq and that_freq
t = −6.1995, df = 135, p-value = 6.438e-09
alternative hypothesis: true correlation is not equal to 0
95 per cent confidence interval:
−0.5917434 −0.3290072

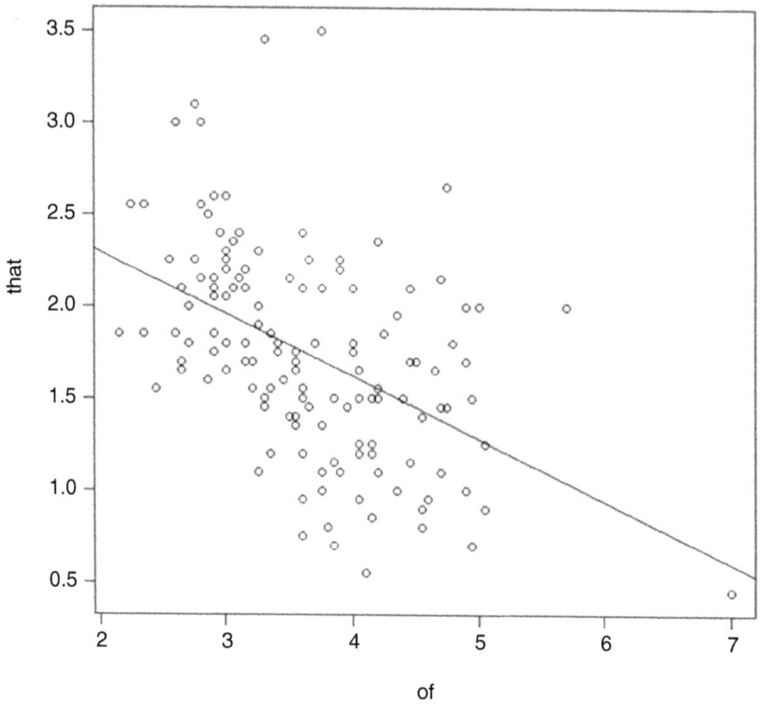

Figure 3.1 Regression line showing the relation between the percentage frequencies of the words 'that' and 'of' in English texts written by non-native speakers

```
sample estimates:
cor
−0.470747
```

3.3.3 *ANOVA*

In Section 3.3.1, by using the t-test, we saw that the frequency of 'that' was significantly greater in English texts by native speakers of French than in those by native speakers of Spanish. In this section we use the ANOVA test to make a similar comparison, between not just two but all eight groups of native speakers in the ENNTT corpus. As was the case for the regression example in Section 3.3.2, we again create a linear model. Here we have a data file called 'that' containing for each text the percentage frequency of the word 'that' it contains, and the native language of the author of that text. The linear model is that the frequency of the word 'that' depends on the native language of its writer, and the relevant R command is as follows:

```
> summary(lm(that ~ lang, data=that))
```

The output of the computer is as follows:

Call:
lm(formula = that ~ lang, data = that)

Residuals:
Min 1Q Median 3Q Max
−0.8271 −0.3589−0.0750 0.3411 1.2911

Coefficients:

<table>
<tr><th></th><th>Estimate</th><th>Std. Error</th><th>t value</th><th>Pr(>|t|)</th></tr>
<tr><td>(Intercept)</td><td>1.27708</td><td>0.09586</td><td>13.322</td><td>< 2e-16***</td></tr>
<tr><td>langF</td><td>0.47708</td><td>0.16604</td><td>2.873</td><td>0.004751**</td></tr>
<tr><td>langG</td><td>0.39435</td><td>0.20173</td><td>1.955</td><td>0.052770.</td></tr>
<tr><td>langI</td><td>0.49792</td><td>0.21435</td><td>2.323</td><td>0.021751*</td></tr>
<tr><td>langN</td><td>0.93185</td><td>0.13064</td><td>7.133</td><td>6.29e-11***</td></tr>
<tr><td>langP</td><td>0.58958</td><td>0.13557</td><td>4.349</td><td>2.75e-05***</td></tr>
<tr><td>langR</td><td>−0.03478</td><td>0.16172</td><td>−0.215</td><td>0.830082</td></tr>
<tr><td>langS</td><td>0.52509</td><td>0.13703</td><td>3.832</td><td>0.000198***</td></tr>
</table>

—
Signif.codes:0 ‘***’ 0.001 ‘**’ 0.01 ‘*’ 0.05 ‘.’ 0.1 ‘ ’ 1

Residual standard error: 0.4696 on 129 degrees of freedom
Multiple R-squared: 0.3458, Adjusted R-squared: 0.3103
F-statistic: 9.74 on 7 and 129 DF, p-value: 1.058e-09

The coefficients show that for Spanish native speakers (the intercept), the mean percentage frequency was 1.27708 (as was found by the t-test in Section 3.3.1). For native speakers of French, shown in the langF row, it was 0.47708 higher, giving a value of about 1.65416. In the final column we have Pr(>|t|) values, which are like p-values, which relate to statistical significance. The very small value at the end of the intercept column shows that the value of 1.27708 in the estimate column was significantly different to 0. The slightly larger value of 0.004751 has two asterisks next to it, showing that the p-value was less than 0.01, so we can be 99 per cent confident that the native speakers of French really do use ‘that’ more often than native speakers of Spanish. Looking down the estimates column, we see that the native speakers of all the other languages use ‘that’ more often than the native speakers of Spanish, except for native speakers of Romanian, who use it fractionally less, although this is not statistically significant. An overall p-value is given at the end of the very bottom line for the F-statistic. This means that the differences between the groups of native speakers were significantly greater than the differences between the individual texts within groups. To find out if native speakers of specific pairs of languages use the word ‘that’ significantly more or less than each other, we can use the 'aov' version of ANOVA in R, followed by a test called the Tukey test, using the following R commands (Baayen, 2008, 106–107):

```
> that.aov = aov(that ~ lang, data=that)
> TukeyHSD(that.aov)
```

The resulting output is as follows:
Tukey multiple comparisons of means

```
95% family-wise confidence level
Fit: aov(formula = that ~ lang, data = that)
```

$lang

	diff	lwr	upr	p adj
F–E	0.47708333	−0.03452648	0.9886931440	0.0866946
G–E	0.39434524	−0.22725341	1.0159438894	0.5163245
I–E	0.49791667	−0.16256876	1.1584020922	0.2894444
N–E	0.93184524	0.52931279	1.3343776845	0.0000000
P–E	0.58958333	0.17185567	1.0073109945	0.0007085
R–E	−0.03477564	−0.53309461	0.4635433316	0.9999989
S–E	0.52509058	0.10284681	0.9473343469	0.0047569
G–F	−0.08273810	−0.77094815	0.6054719619	0.9999526
I–F	0.02083333	−0.70269220	0.7443588662	1.0000000
N–F	0.45476190	−0.04451815	0.9540419563	0.1023829
P–F	0.11250000	−0.39910981	0.6241098107	0.9974488
R–F	−0.51185897	−1.09114301	0.0674250647	0.1252267
S–F	0.04800725	−0.46729655	0.5633110387	0.9999917
I–G	0.10357143	−0.70149346	0.9086363214	0.9999249
N–G	0.53750000	−0.07399068	1.1489906825	0.1294582
P–G	0.19523810	−0.42636056	0.8168367466	0.9781203
R–G	−0.42912088	−1.10750888	0.2492671241	0.5201661
S–G	0.13074534	−0.49389718	0.7553878660	0.9981349
N–I	0.43392857	−0.21705297	1.0849101140	0.4503137
P–I	0.09166667	−0.56881876	0.7521520922	0.9998748
R–I	−0.53269231	−1.24688164	0.1814970207	0.3026762
S–I	0.02717391	−0.63617697	0.6905247985	1.0000000
P–N	−0.34226190	−0.74479435	0.0602705417	0.1583787
R–N	−0.96662088	−1.45227278	−0.4809689771	0.0000003
S–N	−0.40675466	−0.81397176	0.0004624464	0.0504852
R–P	−0.62435897	−1.12267795	−0.1260400017	0.0043017
S–P	−0.06449275	−0.48673652	0.3577510135	0.9997623
S–R	0.55986622	0.05775548	1.0619769639	0.0176027

For each pair of native languages, we see: the initials of the language pair; the mean difference in the use of 'that' between speakers of the native languages; the lower and upper bounds of the confidence limits; and the p-value for that language pair. Once again, if this p-value is less than 0.05, there is a significant

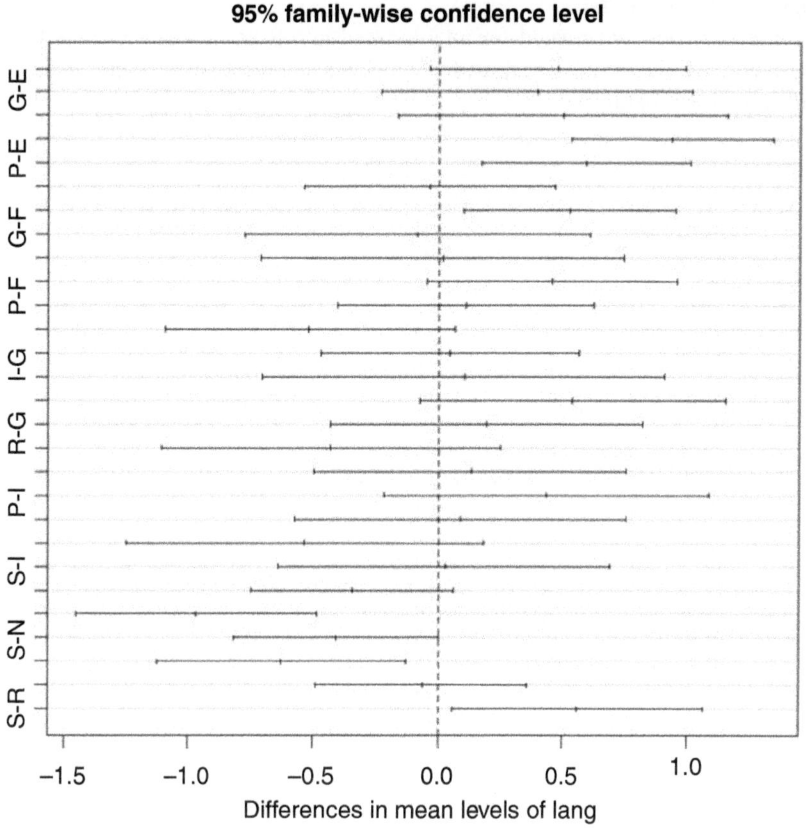

Figure 3.2 Confidence limits for the use of 'that' in English texts by native speakers of various language pairs

difference in the use of 'that' by native speakers of that language pair. The data above can be summarised graphically using the R command

```
>plot(TukeyHSD(that.aov))
```

to produce the plot in Figure 3.2. In this plot, just some of the language pairs are written down the side. There is one language pair for each notch, starting with F-E (French and Spanish), then G-E, I-E, N-E and P-E and so on (in the same order as in the data table above). If both the upper and lower confidence limits have the same sign (positive or negative), then the difference between the native speakers of the two languages (such as Dutch and English) in their use of 'that' is significant.

3.3.4 Mixed Models

A mixed model was created for a table (read into R and given the name ‘l’), derived from the ENNTT corpus, for which a section for some of the Spanish texts is shown below:

types	chars	lang	mode	topic
462	5082	E	N	languages
413	4802	E	N	spanish
450	4816	E	N	basque
462	4920	E	N	evans
457	4982	E	N	basque
425	4848	E	N	spanish
474	4868	E	N	spanish
492	5119	E	N	basque
450	4962	E	N	torture
440	4835	E	N	basque
425	4874	E	N	judging
391	4830	E	N	mother
397	4844	E	N	languages
409	4816	E	N	iranian
440	5054	E	N	company
445	5074	E	N	languages
445	4907	E	N	defence
459	5034	E	N	motion
450	4865	E	N	longstay
395	4959	E	N	writing
390	4909	E	N	writing
418	4927	E	N	egf

Column 1 is the number of word types in a 1,000-word sample, which is a measure of vocabulary richness; ‘chars’ is the number of characters per 1,000 words, and thus an indication of word length; ‘lang’ is the language of the text – either the mother tongue of a non-native speaker writing directly in English, or the original language of a text translated into English; and ‘mode’ denotes whether the text is a translation (T) or written directly by non-native speakers (N). For each text a one-word topic descriptor was automatically generated, by making use of the tf.idf measure widely used in search engines. Each word in each text of a collection has a tf.idf value, which depends both on the frequency of the term in that text, and the total number of texts the term appears in altogether. N is the total number of documents in the collection, which is 400 for the translations, and 271 for the non-native-speaker productions. Various variants of the tf.idf measure exist, but the one we have used for this experiment is

$$tf.idf = tf \times \log\left(\frac{N}{df}\right)$$

The idea of the formula is to find out to what extent a word is characteristic of the text in which it appears. A very common word tends not to be characteristic

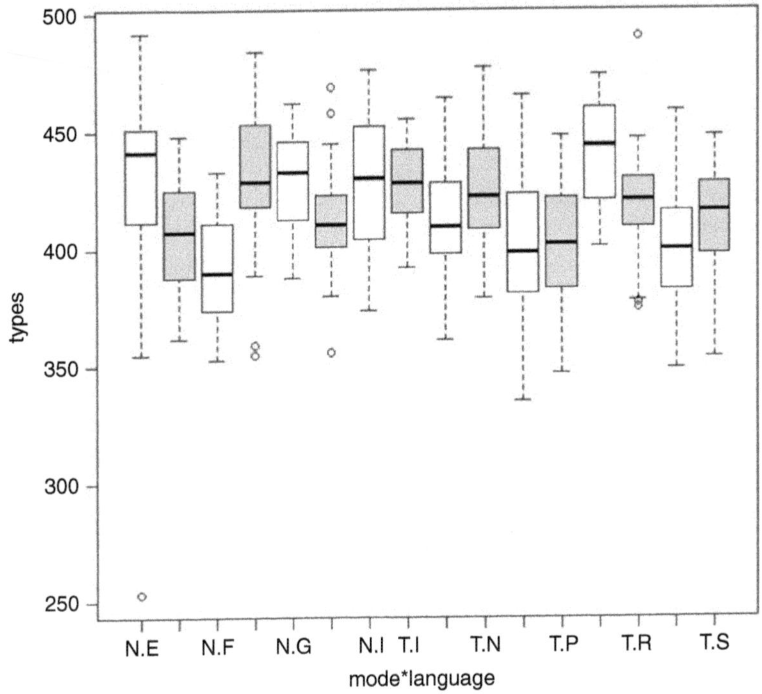

Figure 3.3 Boxplot showing how the number of types per 1,000 words depends on the interaction between mode and language

of an individual text, because it is found in nearly all of the texts in the collection. A very rare word tends not to be characteristic of any text, because its frequency is very low even in the texts in which it occurs. However, a word which is characteristic of a text tends to be fairly common in that text, but not to occur very often in the other texts of the collection. The word with the highest tf.idf value in each text was chosen to represent the topic of that text. Using the R command below, the boxplot in Figure 3.3 was produced to illustrate the interaction between mode and language.

```
> boxplot(types ~ mode*lang, data = l, col = (c('white', 'gray')), xlab = 'mode*
language', ylab = 'types')
```

The thick horizontal bars through each box show the median value of types per 1,000 words, where half the texts have more types and the other half have fewer types. The number of types per 1,000 words is exactly 1,000 times the more commonly cited TTR. The limits of the boxes themselves is the inter-quartile range. Twenty-five per cent of the texts have more types than the top of the box (the upper quartile), while twenty-five per cent of the texts have fewer types than the bottom of the box (the lower quartile). The limits of the 'whiskers' are the greatest and least numbers of types, excluding outliers, and the small circles are outlying values for individual texts. Although not all of the boxes are labelled on the horizontal axis, from left to right they are N.E. (mode = N, language = E), T.E., N.F, T.F, N.G, T.G and so on.

The light boxes show mode N while the grey boxes show mode T. On average, texts from Romanian sources have slightly more types than the rest, and those from Spanish sources have the second most. Again on average, translated texts have fewer types than those written by non-native speakers of English. The number of types in the texts is also affected by the interaction between language and mode. For example, even though number of types in translated texts is generally less than that of non-native-speaker productions (seen especially strongly in the case of Spanish), for French the number of types of the translated texts is actually much higher. This is an example of interaction between language and mode.

However, knowing the language, the mode and the degree of interaction between language and mode does not tell us everything we need to know to calculate the number of types in each text. There is also individual variability between the texts due to differences in topic, individual author and other factors we do not know of. Genre is often a factor leading to differences between texts, but this is relatively homogeneous in the Europarl corpus, where all the texts are political speeches. In the mixed model described below, we take into account language, mode, the interaction between language and mode, and topic in an attempt to fully explain the differences in the number of types between the texts.

The topics of the texts are random effects of the model. Within a linear model we have a number of 'fixed effects', which are relatively well understood or systematic, and can be controlled for (Winter, 2013). In our case these are language and mode, since we know we have a finite set of eight languages and two modes of text production. However, we also have a number of 'random effects' which are less well understood. In our case we have at least topic and individual variation, and there will be yet other factors that we cannot account for. We do not know how many topics there are altogether in the Europarl corpus, nor the identity of every speaker. If we were to repeat the experiment, we could sample the texts again to find representatives of each language and both modes, but it would be difficult to sample the same range of topics or individual speakers. In the model below we include topic as a random effect. The following R command:

```
> l.model = lmer(types ~ lang*mode + (1|topic), data = l)
```

means that we build a linear model in which the number of types per 1,000 words is a function of the fixed effects language, mode and their interaction, and the random effect of topic, read in from a data file called l which is in the format of the file given at the start of this section. The output from this model can be viewed using the command

> summary(l.model)

The 'random effects' section shows how much variation ('variance') in TTR is due to the topic of the text (81.76). However, a much greater amount of variation is 'Residual' (529.32), i.e. attributable to other factors. One such factor may have been individual speaker, but we were unable to explicitly encode this in the model as the corpus did not carry this information. 'The fixed effects' section shows that the mean types per 1,000 words for the texts written by native speakers of Spanish was 430.356, since the relevant value for the first language in the alphabet (E) and the earlier mode in the alphabet (N) is shown by '(Intercept)'. The mean number of types per 1,000 words for the other languages are given relative to the value for Spanish. Thus the mean types per 1,000 words for the French (langF) texts in mode N is 430.356 – 38.299 = 392.057. The effect of mode can be seen in the line starting 'modeT'. This shows that the translated texts (mode T) had on average a number of types 25.508 lower than those written in mode N. From this, we can calculate that a text translated from French would have an average TTR of 430.356 – 38.299 – 25.508 = 366.549. Finally we take into account the interaction between language and mode, where 'langF:modeT' shows the effect of the interaction between French language and translation mode, which is to increase the average number of types by 64.914. The overall value for mean types per 1,000 words for texts translated from French is 430.356 – 38.299 – 25.508 + 64.914 = 431.463, but there is also an unspecified effect of topic and other random effects that we have not included in the model.

Linear mixed model fit by REML ['lmerMod']
Formula: types ~ lang * mode + (1 | topic)
Data: l
REML criterion at convergence: 6113.6

Scaled residuals:
Min 1Q Median 3Q Max
−6.6774 −0.5928 0.0142 0.6304 2.8060

Random effects:
Groups Name Variance Std.Dev.
topic (Intercept) 81.76 9.042
Residual 529.32 23.007
Number of obs: 671, groups: topic, 489

Fixed effects:

	Estimate	Std. Error	t value
(Intercept)	430.356	3.749	114.80
langF	−38.299	6.210	−6.17
langG	−1.202	7.383	−0.16
langI	−3.821	7.799	−0.49
langN	−17.782	5.135	−3.46
langP	−28.308	5.215	−5.43
langR	9.429	6.117	1.54
langS	−30.180	5.229	−5.77
modeT	−25.508	5.122	−4.98
langF:modeT	64.914	7.933	8.18
langG:modeT	10.478	8.860	1.18
langI:modeT	28.274	9.214	3.07
langN:modeT	37.552	7.114	5.28
langP:modeT	25.082	7.170	3.50
langR:modeT	4.418	7.859	0.56
langS:modeT	39.151	7.193	5.44

In a second experiment derived from table l, a model was built to estimate the lengths of the texts in characters (hence average word length) as a function of language, mode (fixed effects), the interaction between language and mode, and topic (a random effect). The intercept value for English texts written by native speakers of Spanish was 5097.51 characters. The texts originating from all the other languages were on average shorter than those from Spanish, and for Spanish, translated texts were on average 206.64 characters shorter than those written directly into English by non-native speakers. However, due to the interaction between language and mode, for all the other languages there was less effect of mode, and for Italian and Romanian the effect was even slightly reversed: translated texts were on average slightly longer than those written directly by non-native speakers. The results were as follows:

```
> l2.model = lmer(chars ~ lang*mode + (1|topic), data = l)
> summary(l2.model)
Linear mixed model fit by REML ['lmerMod']
Formula: chars ~ lang * mode + (1 | topic)
Data: l
REML criterion at convergence: 8613.6
```

Scaled residuals:

Min 1Q Median 3Q Max
−2.97578 −0.58297 0.02119 0.59239 3.09195

Random effects:

Groups Name Variance Std.Dev.
topic (Intercept) 7147 84.54
Residual 21158 145.46
Number of obs: 671, groups: topic, 489

Fixed effects:

	Estimate	Std. Error	t value
(Intercept)	5097.51	25.97	196.30
langF	−217.46	42.28	−5.14
langG	−123.25	50.20	−2.46
langI	−335.02	53.05	−6.32
langN	−330.78	35.18	−9.40
langP	−114.54	35.89	−3.19
langR	−51.50	41.58	−1.24
langS	−216.92	35.88	−6.05
modeT	−206.64	34.95	−5.91
langF:modeT	270.55	53.75	5.03
langG:modeT	32.53	59.89	0.54
langI:modeT	363.99	62.37	5.84
langN:modeT	246.36	48.26	5.10
langP:modeT	196.09	48.71	4.03
langR:modeT	322.88	53.16	6.07
langS:modeT	218.46	48.88	4.47

3.4 Corpus-Driven Experiments: Principal Components Analysis

The PCA used in this study is like the Factor Analysis (FA) used by Biber (2009) in that it starts with a matrix of frequencies of linguistic features, where each feature has its own column and each text has its own row. The techniques then automatically identify groups of features which tend to vary together across the set of analysed texts. First the set of features which together explain most of the differences (or variation) between the texts are extracted, and these constitute the first principal component (PC1). Then the group of features which together explain the second greatest amount of variation in the data are defined, and these constitute the second principal component. Altogether there are as many principal components as linguistic features, but usually just the first few are taken into consideration. In this chapter, we plot just PC1 and PC2 on two-dimensional plots. On these plots, both the texts and the features can be shown. The features closest to a particular text occur frequently in that text. The co-ordinates of the words are called the 'loadings' of the words on each principal component. We can begin to interpret each principal component by which words have the most positive and most negative loadings on that component.

3.4.1 Comparison between Texts by Native Speakers, Non-native Speakers and Translated Texts

The first experiment with PCA was an attempt to replicate the results of Rabinovich et al. (2016), using the same corpus, which was a comparison between English texts written by native speakers (n), those written directly in English by non-native speakers (u) and those translated from various European languages into

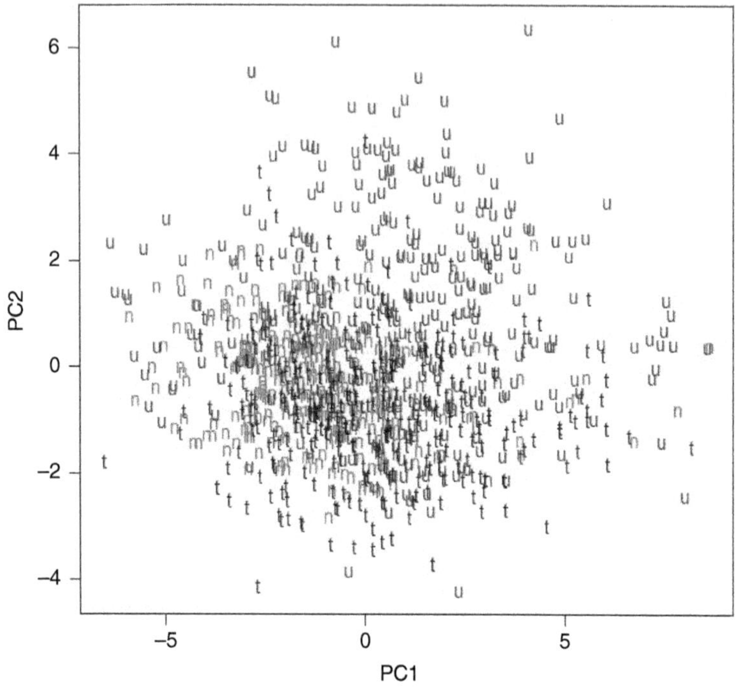

Figure 3.4 PCA for native-speaker-authored (n), non-native-speaker-authored (u) translated (t) texts in the ENNTT corpus

English by professional translators. In this experiment, clearest separation between the three types of texts was obtained when the texts were characterised by the frequencies of the fifty most common words. Unlike Rabinovich et al. we were unable to get clear separation between the three text types, but as shown in Figure 3.4, we did see some separation between u and n, where the n samples form a much tighter cluster, at more negative co-ordinates on both PC1 and PC2. This is seen more clearly in Figure 3.5, where the translated texts (t) have been removed. The t samples in general are at more negative co-ordinates on PC2 than the n samples, which may reveal some overcompensation in translation, as the t samples are on the opposite side of the n samples to the u samples. Rabinovich et al. also found the u and t samples hardest to separate.

3.4.2 *Experiment with the 'Families' Sub-Corpus of ENNTT*

Here, using PCA, it was possible to completely separate the texts according to whether they had been translated from Germanic or Romance

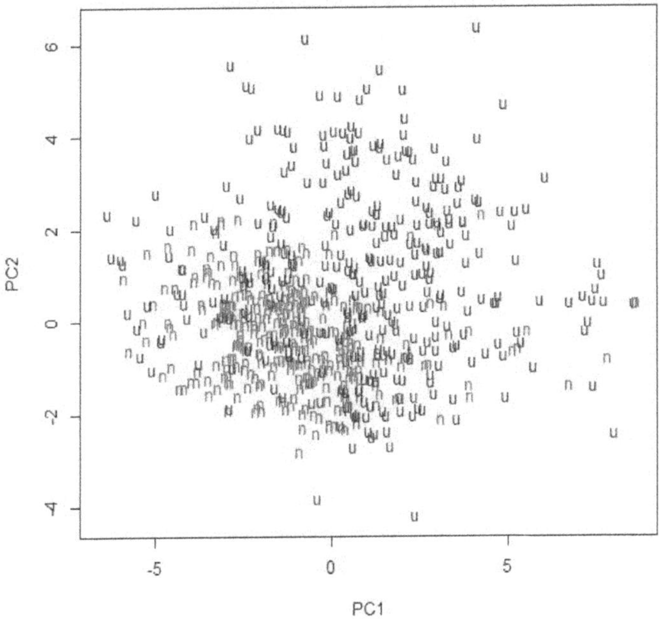

Figure 3.5 PCA for native-speaker-authored (n) and non-native-speaker-authored (u) texts in the ENNTT corpus

languages. In Figure 3.6, the texts were characterised by the top 100 most frequent single words (MFW), and 100 random samples each of 1,000 words of texts from each family were taken using the 'random' sampling function on stylo. The separation between clusters was equally clear when the texts were characterised by the top 100 adjacent word pairs (2-grams) and consecutive word triples (3-grams). Since the separation occurred on PC1, the main source of variation between the texts was language family.

In order to find out which words or word groups most characterised the two language families, we first note that the Germanic-family originals are plotted at negative values of PC1. We can find the loadings of the individual words (or word sequences) used as features to characterise the texts, and those which are most negative will be most associated with the Germanic-family originals. First the PCA is run on stylo, and the output data is stored in a variable (here called a):

```
>a = stylo()
```

We can then store every word in the feature set and its loading on every single factor into a variable called c:

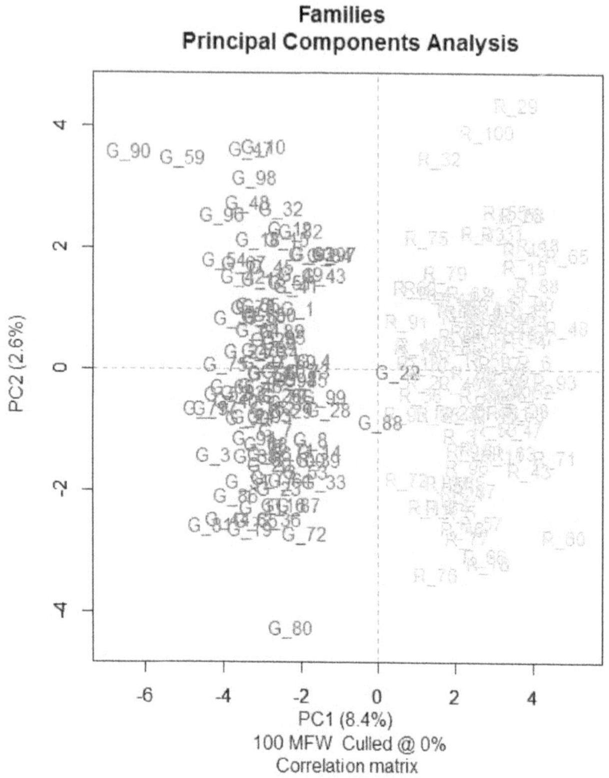

Figure 3.6 PCA for texts translated into English from Germanic- and Romance-language-family originals

> c = a$pca.rotation

We then concentrate on the loadings for PC1, and sort them from most negative to most positive:

> sort(c[,1])

The twenty words most associated with Germanic-family-original texts (with negative loadings on PC1) and the twenty words most associated with Romance-family-original texts (with positive loadings on PC1):

we	should	that	about	also	is
−0.215515173	−0.190013726	−0.183946759	−0.168547759	−0.168285019	−0.160277028
what	can	now	if	important	there
−0.158474631	−0.156793389	−0.150369140	−0.148258716	−0.137641339	−0.136656285

very	not	eu	a	so	do
−0.131915185	−0.128146360	−0.119023648	−0.118512752	−0.113580692	−0.112905812
it	you				
−0.108797581	−0.106736617				

new	to	rights	member	parliament	therefore
0.045007406	0.046581951	0.051998080	0.053015917	0.055086579	0.057090176
their	countries	europe	believe	between	union
0.059386695	0.071658311	0.083346803	0.098582038	0.127683941	0.140467256
economic	its	european	by	and	which
0.148239474	0.150202535	0.172255783	0.172429102	0.192044919	0.202669162
the	of				
0.235393277	0.253896614				

The twenty word pairs most associated with Germanic-family originals (with negative loadings on PC1) and the twenty word pairs most associated with Romance-family originals (with positive loadings on PC1):

that we	i should	the eu	of course
−0.2095920245	−0.2061562790	−0.1992775465	−0.1861006447
we should	that is	about the	as a
−0.1850826634	−0.1841361118	−0.1528375727	−0.1347555957
fact that	we have	in the	and that
−0.1313584069	−0.1291055375	−0.1252562512	−0.1250526714
want to	to make	the council	like to
−0.1246743574	−0.1164799090	−0.1150050690	−0.1149390926
have to	if we	i am	the same
−0.1113500156	−0.1100467602	−0.1018389227	−0.0985515237

i believe	between the	favour of	of our
0.0722911687	0.0832418592	0.0837414404	0.0838891835
of this	to the	european parliament	order to
0.0885816096	0.0960031664	0.0979565564	0.1063544132
for the	need to	the union	which is
0.1183902012	0.1235039229	0.1388230961	0.1391779174
european union	of a	the European	all the
0.1446086344	0.1576658451	0.1587445561	0.1621665616
by the	and the	in order	of the
0.1876790574	0.1923063276	0.2036609595	0.2323911416

The ten word triples most associated with Germanic-family originals (with negative loadings on PC1) and the ten word triples most associated with Romance-family originals (with positive loadings on PC1):

should like to	and that is
−1.098395e-01	−9.507554e-02
do not want	is to be
−8.311819e-02	−7.286355e-02
make it clear	in the netherlands
−7.240401e-02	−7.052803e-02

the group of	i hope that
−7.049404e-02	−7.016229e-02
to do so	to do with
−6.966617e-02	−6.882851e-02

the united nations	enable us to
6.710723e-02	6.853438e-02
the work of	treaty of lisbon
6.946765e-02	7.003026e-02
the european union	the adoption of
7.107581e-02	7.201061e-02
the countries of	take into account
7.228378e-02	7.228511e-02
the development of	the reform of
7.285345e-02	7.529046e-02

Figure 3.7 shows the results of a PCA where the texts have been automatically grouped according to the original languages of the translated texts. For each original language, twenty random samples of 2,000 words were taken from the corpus. The original languages are E (Spanish), F (French), G (German), I (Italian), N (Dutch), P (Portuguese), R (Romanian) and S (Swedish).

Nearly all the translations from the Germanic family are in the top right quadrant, with all positive co-ordinates on PC1, and mainly positive or only slightly negative co-ordinates on PC2. The translations from Swedish form a distinct cluster, with higher scores on PC2 than the cluster for German and Dutch originals, which overlap with each other. A large cluster of Romance-language originals appears below the German/Dutch cluster, with mainly positive scores on PC1 and all negative scores on PC2. The three original languages within this cluster are Italian and Spanish, which are distinct from each other, and French, which overlaps with them both. Both Portuguese and Romanian originals form distinct clusters. The members of the Romanian cluster all have highly negative scores on PC1, and the Portuguese originals are placed intermediately between the Romanian cluster and the rest of the Romance languages. Using the following R commands it was possible to see which words had the most positive and negative loadings on PC1 and PC2:

```
> a = stylo()
> summary(a)
> b = a$pca.rotation
> sort(b[,1])
> sort(b[,2])
```

The twenty words with the most negative and the twenty words with the most positive loadings on PC1 were as follows:

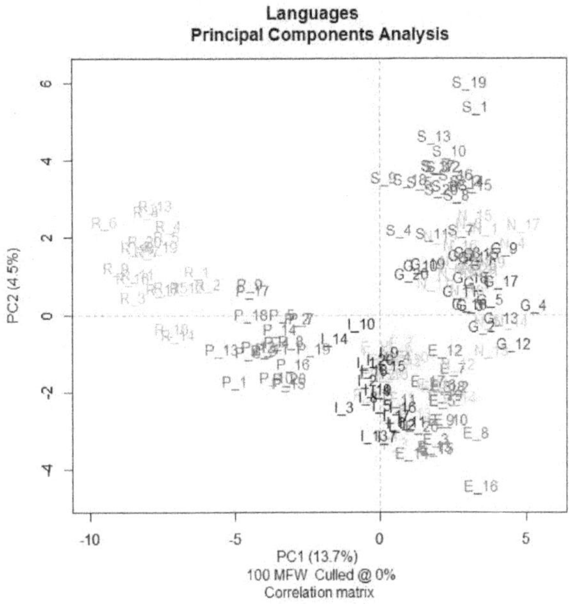

Figure 3.7 PCA where translated texts are grouped according to their original languages

the	of	to	and	in
−0.1708411789	−0.1034129285	0.0271294598	−0.1149752561	−0.0321335945
that	a	is	for	this
0.1722000435	0.0576394347	0.1624539363	−0.0994259614	0.0340593573
i	we	on	be	it
0.0051827094	0.2141132464	−0.0410362174	0.1166383817	0.1608093089
as	are	not	which	with
−0.1221571669	0.1203830366	0.1408497005	−0.1140155360	0.0008197426

now	our	was	there	would
0.1236102534	0.1248334271	0.1268969701	0.1270476899	0.1289581829
should	not	very	but	if
0.1384728200	0.1408497005	0.1410890115	0.1443053182	0.1516858289
have	what	it	is	you
0.1536110847	0.1581390033	0.1608093089	0.1624539363	0.1658859368
that	do	president	mr	we
0.1722000435	0.1757236891	0.1814879520	0.1836713579	0.2141132464

The 20 words with most negative and positive loadings on PC1 were as follows:

of	our	union	because	and
−2.667993e-01	−1.837969e-01	−1.777946e-01	−1.640012e-01	−1.587302e-01
mr	president	by	its	us
−1.539630e-01	−1.426549e-01	−1.296030e-01	−1.266008e-01	−1.234013e-01
europe	commission	you	which	am
−1.123702e-01	−1.103663e-01	−9.910877e-02	−8.708184e-02	−8.554713e-02
the	political	would	with	therefore
−8.454747e-02	−8.391750e-02	−8.239707e-02	−7.592811e-02	−7.540009e-02

be	countries	any	for	support
9.957081e-02	1.017769e-01	1.032297e-01	1.049295e-01	1.075306e-01
a	such	people	being	however
1.119552e-01	1.146718e-01	1.231736e-01	1.255459e-01	1.296685e-01
policy	member	now	in	is
1.339520e-01	1.356525e-01	1.361127e-01	1.519039e-01	1.556487e-01
about	also	important	s	eu
1.790939e-01	2.077698e-01	2.261871e-01	2.328161e-01	3.573825e-01

3.5 Conclusion

In this chapter we have compared the corpus-based and corpus-driven approaches. With corpus-based approaches we start with an initial hypothesis, and use tests of statistical significance to see whether this hypothesis holds. In Section 3.3.1 we used the t-test to examine the hypothesis that the word ‘that’ is used more commonly in English texts written by native speakers of Spanish than in those written by native speakers of French. Related to the t-test is the idea of a linear model, where we create an a priori model and fit the parameters to that model. For example, in our experiment on linear regression described in Section 3.3.2, we first imagine a model where the frequency of the word ‘that’ in texts written by non-native speakers of English is related to the frequency of the word ‘of’. The regression process finds the closest mathematical relation between the two which can be plotted as a straight line is (frequency of ‘that’) = 2.9715 – (0.3378 x frequency of ‘of’), and thus texts which use the word ‘that’ to a greater extent have fewer occurrences of ‘of’. The values 2.9715 and -0.3378 are the intercept and slope of the straight line, and are the parameters of the model. ANOVA, another linear model described in Section 3.3.3, is an extension of the t-test in that we could use it to compare the frequency of ‘that’ in English texts among native speakers of all eight languages represented in the ENNTT corpus.

In Section 3.3.4 we described mixed models, which have rarely been used in corpus-based studies. They are a direct extension of ANOVA, designed to deal with both fixed (selectable again if the study were to be repeated) and random (varying according to individual subject, or in this case, text) effects. Our mixed model (or multi-level model) showed that TTR depends on language, mode (whether translations or written directly into English by non-native speakers), the interaction between language and mode, and the random effect topic of the text.

Corpus-driven approaches are a form of exploratory data analysis. They do not require the creation of a priori hypotheses, but through the patterns produced in the data, possible relations between texts about which we could form hypotheses will often become apparent. Corpus-driven approaches are illustrated in Section 3.4. We have only used one technique, that of PCA, but there are a family of matrix analysis techniques which fall under the umbrella term 'factor analysis'. The differences between them are described by Baayen (2008). Although we were only partially successful in finding systematic differences between English texts by native speakers of English, texts written by non-native speakers and translations, this chapter has shown for the first time that English texts translated from different language families (and even, to a lesser extent, different languages) form separate clusters. Once PCA has been carried out, we can perform a second analysis, to find which linguistics features (in our case, words), load most on each principal component. This enables us to discover linguistic constructs in the form, 'text type A is associated with linguistic features B, C, and so on'. Although this is not a common method, it is possible to quantify the patterns found in correspondence analysis by performing a corpus-based statistical test afterwards. This can be done, since we are often able to form hypotheses as a *result* of the corpus-driven analysis. Using the example from Section 3.4.2, we could perform a t-test to show whether the co-ordinates of the texts on PC1 are significantly different for the two language family groups (they probably are), and also whether there is any significant difference for PC2 (there probably is not). An ANOVA test could be used to show whether there are significant differences in Figure 3.7 between the co-ordinates of the translations from the various source languages.

References

Baayen, R. Harald (2008). Analysing Linguistic Data: A Practical Introduction to Statistics Using R. Cambridge, UK: Cambridge.

Biber, Douglas (2009). Corpus-based and corpus-driven analyses of language variation and use. In Bernd Heine and Heiko Narrog (eds.), The Oxford Handbook of Linguistics (1st edition). Oxford, UK: Oxford University Press.

Koehn, Philipp (2005). Europarl: A parallel corpus for statistical machine translation. In Proceeding of the Tenth Machine Translation Summit (MT Summit X), Phuket, Thailand. Tokyo: Asia-Pacific Association for Machine Translation.

Koppel, M. and N. Ordan (2011). Translationese and its dialects. In Proceedings of ACL, Portland OR, June 2011. Stroudsberg, PA: Association for Computing Machinery, pp. 1318–1326.

Nisioi, Sergiu, Ella Rabinovich, Liviu P. Dinu and Shuly Wintner (2016). A corpus of native, non-native and translated texts. In Nicoletta Calzolari et al. (eds.), Proceedings of the Tenth International Conference on Language Resources and Evaluation (LREC), Portoroz, Slovenia May 23–28, 2016. European Languages Resources Association, pp. 4197–4200.

Rabinovich, Ella Sergiu Nisioi, Noam Ordan and Shuly Wintner (2016). On the similarities between native, non-native and translated texts. In Antal van den Bosch (General Chair) (ed.), Proceedings of the 54th Annual Meeting of the Association for Computational Linguistics, Berlin, Germany, 7–12 August. Stroudsburg, PA: Association for Computing Machinery, pp. 1870–1881.

Rabinovich Ella, Noam Ordan and Shuly Wintner (2017). Found in translation: Reconstructing phylogenetic language trees from translations. Proceedings of the 55th Annual Meeting of the Association for Computational Linguistics, Vancouver, Canada, 30 July–4 August. Stroudsburg, PA: Association for Computational Linguistics, pp. 530–540.

Serva, Maurizio and Filippo Petroni (2008). Indo-European languages tree by Levenshtein distance. Europhysics Letters 81(6), 68005.

Tognini-Bonelli, Elena (2001). Corpus Linguistics at Work. Amsterdam: John Benjamins.

Winter, Bodo (2013). Linear models and linear mixed effects models in R with linguistic applications. Tutorials 1 and 2. arXiv:1308.5499. http://arxiv.org/pdf/1308.5499.pdf.

4 The Evolving Treatment of Semantics in Machine Translation

Mark Seligman

4.1 Introduction

Language is primarily a way of conveying meaning, and translation is primarily a way of assuring that, so far as possible, a surface-structure segment conveys the same meaning in language B as in language A. In the face of this painfully obvious observation, it is striking how far present-day machine translation (MT) systems have come without any consensus among translation researchers on the meaning of meaning.

In fact, influential theorists have argued that MT programs have always operated, and can only ever operate, without understanding what they are talking about. Philosopher John Searle has notoriously contended that current translation programs, and more generally current computer programs of all sorts, necessarily function without semantics, as he understands the term (Searle, 1980).[1] In his notorious Chinese Room thought experiment, a locked-in homunculus slavishly follows rules to successfully translate into another language Chinese text passed to him through a slot. He understands neither the design of the rules nor the text which he processes: To him, they are literally meaningless – ergo, *sans* semantics. Computer programs arguably follow rules just as blindly.

It is true that MT and many other natural language processing (NLP) systems have made steady and impressive progress, while use of explicit semantic processing has undergone a rise and fall. With the ascent of the statistical era of MT and the decline of the rule-based era and its symbolic representation, Google research leader Peter Norvig and colleagues have observed "the unreasonable effectiveness of data": given enough data and effective programs for extracting patterns from it, many useful computational tasks – NLP among them – can be accomplished with no explicit representation of the task, and, in particular, no explicit representation of meaning. Machine translation has become perhaps the quintessential example.

[1] Throughout this chapter, we will be treating John Searle as representative of skepticism regarding the possibility of true semantics in computer programs. We intend no slight to other skeptics.

It is also true that, even when explicit semantic representations have been most used, consensus has remained elusive concerning their philosophical and psychological foundations: Controversy has persisted concerning their ability to provide contact with the external world of things and the internal world of thinking.

In this chapter, however, we observe renewed interest in semantic representation and processing for MT and other NLP. Vector-based semantic representation is alive and well, and neural-network-based semantics is receiving increased attention. Even symbolic semantic representation is enjoying something of a rebirth, though currently in other areas of NLP more than in MT. We will speculate that this comeback might soon extend to MT as well.

In addition, we foresee a gradual movement toward semantic approaches grounded upon artificial perception – that is, incorporating audio, visual, or other sensor-based input. We will distinguish these *perceptually grounded* semantic approaches from most current methods, which until now have tended to remain *perception-free*. And from a philosophical and cognitive viewpoint we will risk the suggestion that perceptually grounded approaches to automatic NLP have the potential to display *intentionality*, and thus after all to foster a truly meaningful semantics that, in the view of Searle and other skeptics, is intrinsically beyond computers' capacity.

To lay the groundwork for these predictions and speculations, we will survey the role of semantics in MT to date. Conveniently enough, progress in MT can be divided into three eras or paradigms: those of rule-based, statistical, and neural MT. We will devote a section to each paradigm, with discussion of their respective treatments of semantics: Rule-based methods have generally emphasized symbolic semantics; statistical methods have generally avoided semantic treatment or employed vector-based semantics; and neural methods have until now handled meaning as implicit within networks. We reserve speculations on the road ahead for a final section.

We are not undertaking a full history of MT research and development. For that purpose, see instead, for example, Hutchins (2010). Readers interested in the history of speech-to-speech translation specifically can turn to Seligman and Waibel (Chapter 12 in this volume).

4.1.1 Rule-Based Machine Translation

We begin our survey of MT semantics with a review of rule-based approaches. These employ handwritten grammatical and morphological rules side by side with handwritten programs, so that the style might instead have been termed handmade MT. Three sub-approaches can be distinguished within the rule-based paradigm: direct, transfer-based, and interlingua-based.

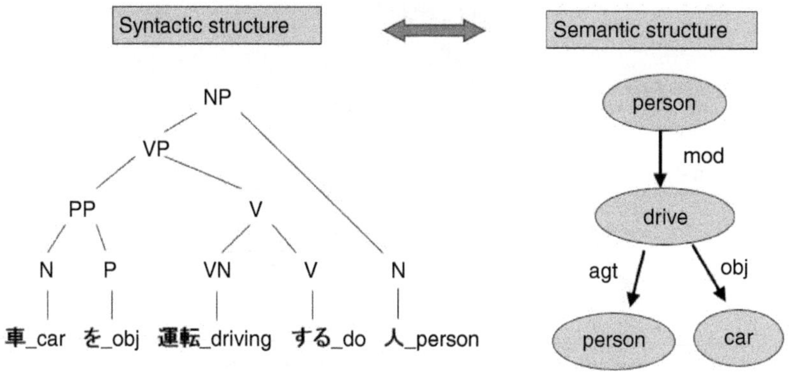

Figure 4.1 Contrasting syntactic and semantic intermediate structures

4.1.2 *Intermediate Structures: Syntactic versus Semantic*

In comparing the three rule-based approaches, we will refer to the presence or absence of syntactic or semantic *intermediate structures* which may be derived through analysis of the source language or may be intended to facilitate generation of the target language. Figure 4.1 displays a pair of simplified examples.

Consider first the syntactic or structural analysis of the Japanese phrase on the left. In their original order, the English glosses of the relevant Japanese words would be "car, (object marker), driving, do, person" – that is, "car-driving person," "person who drives/is driving a car." The syntactic analysis shows that we are dealing with a noun phrase; that it is composed of a verb phrase on the left and a noun on the right; that the verb phrase in turn contains a post-positional phrase; and so on. This part-to-whole analysis makes no explicit claim about the meaning of the phrase, though this might be computed via programs not shown.

By contrast, on the right, we do see an attempt to capture the meaning of this phrase. PERSON is this time shown as a semantic object, presumably one which could be related within an *ontology* – typically, a graph relating classes, subclasses, and instances – to other semantic objects such as ANIMALS AND LIVING-THINGS. The PERSON in question is *modified* – a semantic rather than syntactic relationship – by the *action* DRIVE, and that modifying action has an *agent* (the same PERSON, though the identity is not shown) and an *object*, CAR. In practice, intermediate structures often mix syntactic and semantic features, as we will see.

4.1.3 *Vauquois Triangle*

We are ready now to contrast the three principal approaches within the rule-based MT paradigm. For orientation, we refer to a familiar diagram of the

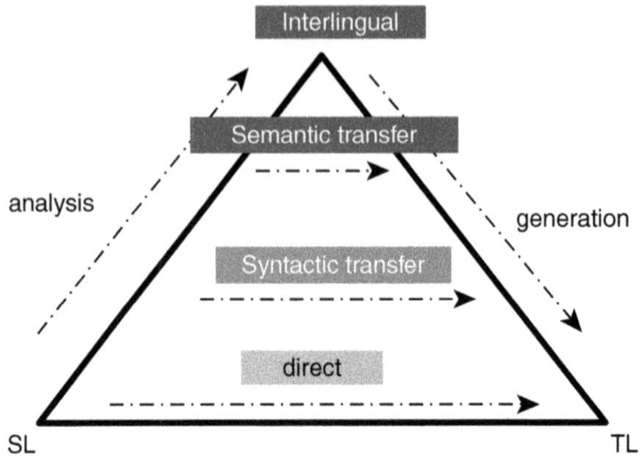

Figure 4.2 The Vauquois Triangle

relationships between direct, transfer-based, and interlingua-based methods (Figure 4.2), the Vauquois Triangle (Boitet, 2000).

The diagram depicts various paths for departing from the source language (SL, at lower left) and arriving at the target language (TL, at lower right).

4.1.4 Direct Translation

If a *direct* translation method is adopted, no attempts will be made to derive intermediate structures as go-betweens or stepping-stones between SL and TL. As a first step, *surface* elements of the SL – that is, the words and expressions in the input – will undergo lookup to discover TL elements that can serve as their respective translations. (Several candidates might be found per element.) Programs will then be invoked to "massage" the target elements to compose a complete translation based upon them: to choose among translation candidates; to order the selected target elements properly; and to make necessary adjustments for TL morphology and syntax, e.g., by handling agreement and adding function words or morphemes.

For such direct translation regimes, the diagram depicts a horizontal line between SL and TL which remains low in the triangle – low because, as mentioned, translation methods higher in the diagram use intermediate structures to mediate in the translation process, whereas direct methods do without them. These intermediate structures are considered more *abstract* than the surface elements; and height in the diagram is interpreted as degree of abstraction, concerning which more in a moment. The intermediate structures include those derived through programs which perform *analysis* of the SL input (shown by the ascending line on the left): The structures produced by analysis should indicate the construction and/or meaning of the original SL input in ways not obvious from the surface language.

4.1.5 *Transfer-Based Translation*

Above the horizontal line labeled "direct" is a line labeled "syntactic transfer." *Transfer-based* translation methods use two main intermediate structures. The first is the output of SL analysis, as just described. The second intermediate structure should represent the construction and/or meaning of the input structure's translation into the TL. As such, it is intended to serve as the starting point for *generation* of the TL surface structure (shown by the descending line on the right), and is derived from the analysis output through the *transfer process* for which transfer-based methods are named. Transfer processes are somewhat analogous to the processes of direct translation in that they, too, begin by selecting TL elements which will translate source elements, and then go on to "massage" by reordering, adding and subtracting, etc. However, instead of massaging surface language elements, they massage the associated analysis output structure, for example by replacing one substructure with another to account for structural differences between source and target.

As mentioned, intermediate structures are intended to be increasingly *abstract* in the following special sense: The more abstract an intermediate structure, the greater the number of SL utterances which may have given rise to it during analysis or the greater the number of target utterances which might result during generation.[2] At the level of *syntactic transfer*, the structure produced by analysis should represent a range of SL surface input utterances: Any utterances analyzed as having equivalent meaning *and* equivalent syntactic structure should be assigned the same analysis result. At the higher level of *semantic transfer*, however, the syntactic constraint is partly relaxed, so that many more utterances having equivalent meaning should receive the same analysis result, though in practice some syntactic and/or morphological commonalities will also be captured. See e.g., Seligman, Suzuki, and Morimoto (1993) for some examples from a semantic-transfer-based system for Japanese-German, with discussion of persisting syntactic elements. In any case, if there is a transfer process at any level of abstraction, whether syntactic or semantic, its objective is to produce a TL structure at the same level, from which generation of surface language can proceed.

[2] In many linguistic discussions, "abstraction" is discussed in terms of "depth," as in "deep structure." This terminology can be confusing, and not only because elements *higher* in the Vauquois Triangle would be described as "deeper." Several metaphors are in competition: "deeper" may mean "dominant in a phrase structure"; "superordinate in an ontology"; "earlier in a derivation sequence"; and so on.

4.1.6 Interlingua-Based Translation

If the tendency toward abstraction is taken to its extreme, analysis aims to produce a maximally semantic result – one which could in principle result from any source utterance having an equivalent meaning, regardless of syntax or morphology.[3] The result should then be an *interlingua representation*, one intended to represent the semantics for *both* SL and TL, and ideally for many, or even all, additional languages. At this extreme, a transfer process will no longer be needed to mediate between intermediate structures on the source and target side. Hence *interlingua-based* translation methods are shown at the apex of the Vauquois Triangle, where horizontal transfer lines will no longer fit.

Having outlined rule-based or handmade translation methods – direct, transfer-based, or interlingua-based – we can comment on their treatment of semantics.

4.1.7 Semantics in Rule-Based Machine Translation

Direct MT methods might be assumed to dispense with explicit semantic processing, since their approach concentrates upon the surface elements of SL and TL.

Of course, no translation could take place without at least implicit consideration of meaning. In purely direct rule-based MT, the meaning of an expression is shown only by its translations: One could say that the translations *are* the meanings. There are typically several possible translations, and examination can reveal semantic relations like SL polysemy (when one or more SL expressions map to several groupings of synonymous TL expressions) and SL synonymy (when several SL expressions map to one grouping of synonymous TL expressions).

Even in direct rule-based translation, however, explicit information concerning the meanings of words and phrases can still be useful, for example to aid in the selection of the correct word meaning, and thus the correct translation, for ambiguous expressions – that is, for *lexical disambiguation*. An example appeared in the direct MT system of Word Magic for English↔Spanish, in which translation lexicons listed not only surface expressions but *word senses*, e.g., *bank1* ("financial institution"), *bank2* ("shore"), and *bank3* ("row, e.g. of switches"), where each listed word sense pointed to a set of synonymous Spanish translations, in which one member was the default translation. During analysis, the appropriate word sense – that is, meaning – for the current

[3] Some qualification is necessary: Some syntactic or morphological information may be included, even at this "purely semantic" level, to help create a translation structurally similar to the input. The structural information would itself be represented quite abstractly to maximize cross-linguistic universality.

translation segment was chosen according to handwritten rules taking account of the context. For maximum generality, the disambiguation rules referred to *semantic classes* (e.g., VEHICLES) rather than individual semantic instances (e.g., CAR.1); and those classes were collected and arranged in an ontology. Among direct rule-based approaches, this treatment is typical (Hutchins, 2010).

Example-based translation systems (Nagao, 1984; Hutchins, 2005) make up a class of rule-based translation systems, often of the direct variety, which depend heavily upon semantic categorization. For instance, to render Japanese *kyouto no kaigi* or *toukyou no kaigi* fluently as "conference in Kyoto/Tokyo" or "Kyoto/Tokyo conference" rather than generically and clumsily as e.g., "conference of Kyoto/Tokyo," example-based systems have exploited semantic symbols drawn from an ontology, indicating that *kyouto* and *toukyou* are examples of the CITIES class and that *kaigi* is an example (or subclass) of MEETINGS. Phrases in the relevant example base (including "conference in Kyoto") were enriched with such symbols to enable matching against the current input. In thus using symbolic semantic symbols to constrain the matching of input segments against example base segments linked to translations, example-based translation is a *semantic grammar*. Bundy and Wallen (1984) discuss other semantic grammars: In many, syntactic rules can match during syntactic analysis (parsing) only if input elements being scanned meet certain semantic as well as syntactic requirements. For instance, a noun-phrase rule can match only if its head noun belongs to the HUMANS class.

So direct systems have certainly used symbolic semantic representations to good advantage. However, within the rule-based MT paradigm, such representations are most associated with transfer-based and interlingua-based methodologies.

The ASURA system for English, German, and Japanese, an early speech-translation system,[4] included a transfer-based MT component intended to operate at the semantic level, in order to better bridge the gap between the disparate languages involved. However, ASURA's intermediate structures actually contained an admixture of semantic and syntactic constraints: See for example Figure 4.3, a structure produced by the transfer process during translation of "Could you make the hotel arrangements?" into German (Seligman, 1993). The structure contains both semantic symbols like REQUEST and POLITE and syntactic symbols like MACHEN-V ("to make," a verb) and HOTELBUCHUNG-N ("hotel booking," a noun). In this case, no explicit ontology was used for generalization: Transfer rules referred to specific semantic tokens, ignoring their interrelation.

Separate ontologies were nevertheless exploited outside the scope of ASURA's MT per se, as has been typical in rule-based translation systems.

[4] Concerning ASURA, see further Seligman and Waibel, Chapter 12 in this volume.

```
;;;=========== Transfer Result ============
 [[SEM [[RELN REQUEST]
        [AGEN !X3[[LABEL *SPEAKER*]]]
        [RECP !X1[[LABEL *HEARER*]]]
        [OBJE [[RELN MACHEN-V]
               [TENSE PRES]
               [AGEN !X1]
               [OBJE [[PARM !X2[]]
                      [RESTR [[RELN HOTELBUCHUNG-N]
                              [ENTITY !X2]]]
                      [INDEX [[DETERM DEFART]
                              [NUMBER SING]
                              [OWNER [[LABEL *UNKNOWN*]]]]]]]]]
        [ATTD INTERROGATIVE]]]
  [PRAG [[RESTR [[IN [[FIRST [[RELN POLITE]]]
                      [REST [[FIRST [[RELN EMPATHY-DEGREE]
                                     [LESS !X1]
                                     [MORE !X3]]]
                             [REST [[FIRST [[RELN POLITE]]]
                                    [REST !X4[]]]]]]]]
                 [OUT !X4]]]
         [HEARER !X1]
         [INTIMACY LOW]
         [POLITENESS [[DEGREE 3]]]
         [SPEAKER !X3]]]]
```

Figure 4.3 A hybrid intermediate structure from the ASURA system

For example, see Seligman (1994) for description of an experimental topic-tracking auxiliary program in which the ontology of a Japanese thesaurus was used to smooth lexical co-occurrence data. Also described is an example-based speech-translation system featuring exploitation of similarity hierarchies (in effect, ontologies), not only of semantic elements but of sounds and syntactic structures as well, to aid both speech recognition and translation.

As might be expected, the most extensive use of explicit symbolic semantic tokens has been in interlingua-based MT. Here a mature example is the ATLAS system for English and Japanese, developed at Fujitsu under the direction of Hiroshi Uchida (1986). Uchida is also the founder of the most extensive multilingual and multi-partner interlingua-based research effort, the Universal Networking Language (UNL) project.[5] Its foundation is a rich set of word senses,

[5] See www.unl.ru/introduction.html.

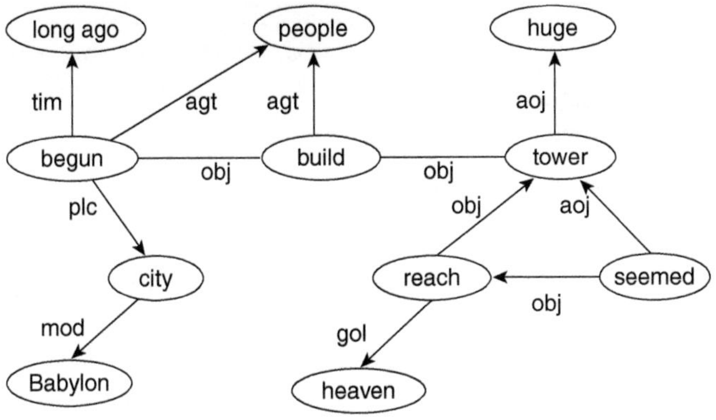

Figure 4.4 A sentence representation in the UNL interlingua

originally based upon that of a complete English dictionary. Combinatory relations then enable construction of UNL representations for phrases, sentences, etc. Figure 4.4, for instance, shows the combination representing this sentence and its many paraphrases and translations: "Long ago, in Babylon, the people began to build an enormous tower, which seemed to reach the sky."

The task of each UNL partner group is to map each sense into native words or expressions and each relation into native syntax, in order to develop encoder (i.e., analysis or surface-to-UNL) and decoder (i.e., generation or UNL-to-surface) programs for their respective languages. Translation of web pages and other documents can then follow. Some fifteen institutions have taken part, with prominent roles played by the Russian team, headed by Igor Boguslavsky (Boguslavsky et al., 2005), and the French team, under Christian Boitet (Boitet, 2002).

The collection of UNL word senses can be treated as a flat listing, but some project members have exploited graphically arranged ontologies, e.g., to assist in lexical disambiguation (Boguslavsky, 2009). Interlingua-based structures have also been useful in speech-translation research. See (Seligman and Waibel, Chapter 12 in this volume) and (Levin et al., 1998) regarding the Interchange Format (IF) structures used by the C-STAR consortium (Figure 4.5 shows three examples) and concerning a separate interlingua used in IBM's MASTOR project (Gao et al., 2006).

4.2 Statistical Machine Translation

In the 1990s, Eduard Hovy was heard to say, "A plague of statistics has descended upon our houses." He was accurately describing the dramatic rise of *statistical machine translation* (SMT) (Koehn, 2009).

We have single, and twins and also Japanese rooms available on the eleventh.
a:give-information+availability+room (room-type=(single&twin&Japanese_style), time=md11)

I'd like a twin room, please.
c:accept+features+room(room-type=twin)

A twin room is fourteen thousand yen.
a:give-information+price+room(room-type=twin, price=(currency=yen, quantity=14000))

Figure 4.5 Sentence representations in the IF interlingua

In initial implementations, statistical information was treated as a supplement or add-on to the existing mechanisms – the rules and programs – of rule-based MT (Brown et al., 1990, 1993). However, the new paradigm soon gravitated toward methods that in some respects recalled those of direct rule-based MT. Rather than manipulate abstract structures like those of transfer-based methods – structures representing some mixture of compositional and semantic commonalities among surface structures – statistical methods returned to operations upon the surface structures themselves. As in direct rule-based methods, the first step is to determine which TL surface segments might serve as translations for SL surface segments; and later steps relate to the ordering of target elements, possible additions or subtractions from them, possible grammatical adjustments, etc. But while in rule-based methods these steps depend on rules and programs created by hand, in SMT they depend upon probabilities discovered in parallel corpora of human translations. The goal in SMT is to produce the most *probable* translation of a source segment given that corpus, so actual production of a translation (*decoding*) becomes an *optimization* process often visualized as hill climbing: The probabilities of alternative translations are iteratively compared in the attempt to arrive at the highest probability peak (and avoid getting stuck on a lower one).

In most SMT, the translations of words and phrases *are* their meanings (just as they are in "pure" or unadorned direct rule-based MT). SMT's translations are indicated in a system's *phrase table*, a listing of SL-to-TL correspondences (e.g., English *cool* to French *frais*), each with a probability determined during training (Figure 4.6). The rows in a table can be examined to discover semantic relations like polysemy and synonymy.

While symbolic semantic representation received a boost in the rule-based paradigm as direct methods gave way to transfer-based and interlingua-based styles, this representational style was heading for a fall as the field shifted dramatically toward SMT. Throughout its decade-long reign, mainstream SMT exploited symbolic semantic representation only rarely. In compensation, *vector-based* semantic treatments have gradually become influential.

Source language expression	Target language expression	Probability
cool	frais	.34
cool	chouette	.21
nippy	frais	.88
man	homme	.68

Figure 4.6 Part of a phrase table for statistical machine translation

Vector-based semantic research aims to leverage the statistical relationships among text segments (words, phrases, etc.) to place the segments in an abstract space, within which closeness represents similarity of meaning (Turney and Pantel, 2010). Intuitively, words that occur in similar contexts and participate in similar relations with other words should turn out to be semantically similar. The intuition goes back to Firth's declaration (1957, p. 11) that "You shall know a word by the company it keeps," and has been formalized as the *distributional hypothesis*. The clustering in this similar-neighbors space yields a hierarchy of similarity relations, comparable to that of a handwritten ontology. Figure 4.7 (Mikolov, Le, and Sutskever, 2013) shows two examples from English with corresponding examples from Spanish.

Representation of a given segment's meaning as a location in such a vector space can be viewed as an alternative to representation as a location in an ontology. The vector-based approach is much more scalable in that there is no need to build ontologies manually; but relations can be harder for humans to comprehend in the absence of appropriate visualization software tools.

Historically, the vector-based approach grew out of document-classification techniques, whereby a document can be categorized according to the words in it and their frequency. The converse was then proposed: A word or other linguistic unit can be categorized according to the documents it appears in, or more generally, according to surrounding or nearby text segments of any size – minimally, just the few words surrounding it. (Turney and Pantel [2010] survey the various sorts of contexts explored to date.) Note also an interesting relation to semantic categorization in the style of WordNet (Fellbaum, 1998): In this popular semantic ontology, synonyms are defined as words that can be substituted in identical contexts. That is, words of (practically) *identical* meaning are those which can be employed in *identical* contexts. (See Seligman [1994]; Knott and Dale [1992] for earlier suggestions along these lines.) In vector-based semantic approaches, this criterion is generalized: Words of *similar* meaning are those found in *similar* contexts.

Vector-based semantic approaches have indeed been used experimentally to improve statistical MT systems. Alkhouli, Guta, and Ney (2014) provide a clear

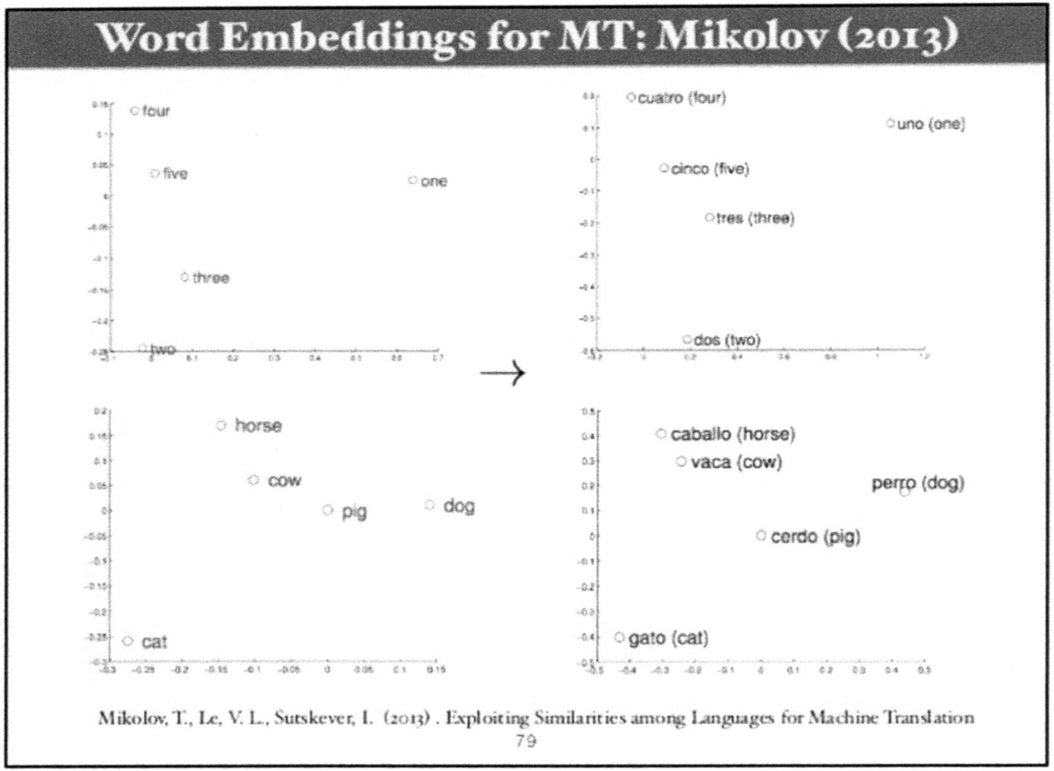

Figure 4.7 Two vector spaces for English, with corresponding Spanish spaces

example. Their study employs *phrase-based SMT*, in which the rows in the phrase table show groups of source words (as opposed to only individual words) corresponding to groups of target words.[6] Hence the elements that are located in vector space according to their respective contexts are likewise phrases (word groups) rather than only words. It then becomes possible to measure distances between phrases, interpretable as semantic similarity; and this interpretation in turn enables enhancement of the translation process via enlargement of the relevant phrase tables. The trick is to add new rows to the current table, rows not found in the training corpus, as follows. For the current corpus:

- Find phrases monolingually on both source and target sides.
- Establish a translation phrase table. Some source phrases and target phrases will be aligned with sufficiently probable translations, and some will not.
- Select a row in the current table; extract its source and target elements; and for each, find nonaligned phrases that are sufficiently similar to it semantically. Call them *paraphrases* of the current source and target elements.
- Compose new rows, each containing a paraphrase of the current source and/or a paraphrase of the current target.
- Handle the probabilities of the new and old rows appropriately, as described in the paper.

This artificial enlargement of the phrase table imitates an enlargement of the training corpus, which rarely contains all the examples one would wish. That is, the technique potentially reduces the endemic problem of OOV (out of vocabulary) items.

4.3 Neural Machine Translation

Neural machine translation (NMT) has proved to be a late bloomer. While early neural experiments (Waibel et al., 1989; Waibel et al., 1991) garnered interest, especially in view of potential insights into human language processing, the computational infrastructure that would eventually make neural approaches practical did not yet exist. Now that they do, the approach has experienced an explosive renaissance: Google announced its first neural translation systems as recently as 2016 (Johnson et al., 2016); SYSTRAN has since then gone fully neural;[7] and most other major MT vendors are converting at full speed.

[6] Confusingly, the term "phrase table" is used in *word*-based as well as phrase-based SMT. Also potentially confusing: In phrase-based SMT, word groups may simply be contiguous words rather than linguistically motivated phrases.

[7] See tutorial by Jean Senellart, "Training Romance multi-way model," at Open NMT forum (October 9, 2018): http://forum.opennmt.net/t/training-romance-multi-way-model/86.

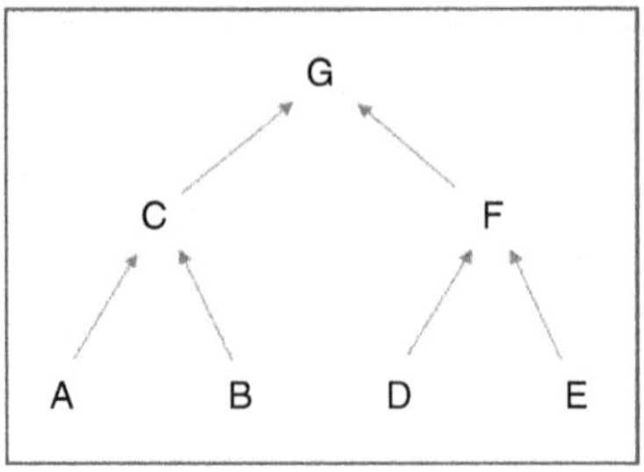

Figure 4.8 Connections among rules forming a network

A conceptual introduction to neural network operation may help to explain the methodology's application to translation. Think first of logical rules, for instance those of the predicate calculus:

If A and B, then C
If D and E, then F
If C and F, then G

If the premise-to-conclusion relations are depicted as lines, we obtain a tree-like diagram (Figure 4.8).

Imagine that the lines are electric wires, and that there is a bulb at each premise or conclusion which lights up if manually switched on, or if all incoming wires are active; and that, when a light is illuminated, the outgoing wire is activated. Switch on A, B, D, and E. Then C and F will be activated and will propagate activity to G. *Et voilà*: a neural network! However, several refinements are needed to complete the picture.

- First, rather than being simply on or off, each line should have a *degree* of activation; and illumination of a conclusion bulb should require not full activation of all wires, but only summed activation passing a specified threshold.
- Second, some wires may inhibit rather than promote the conclusion – that is, their activation may subtract from the sum.
- Third, rather than only three "rules," there should be many thousands.
- And fourth, and perhaps most important, all of the network's parameters – the wires' activation levels, thresholds, etc. – should be learned from experience rather than set by hand. They may be learned through a *supervised* process, whereby a trainer provides the expected conclusions given the switches thrown at the input, and appropriate programs work backward to adjust the parameters; or through an *unsupervised* process, whereby adjustment depends on frequency of activation during training, perhaps assisted by hints and/or rewards or punishments.

Such networks can indeed be applied to translation, since they provide general-purpose computational mechanisms: With sufficient available wires, "rule" layers, etc., they can in principle learn to compute any *function* – any mapping of input patterns to output patterns. Thus they can learn to map input bulbs coding for SL segments into patterns analogous to the analysis results of an interlingua-based MT system – that is, to perform operations analogous to the analysis phase of such a system. (In NMT, the analysis phase is called *encoding*.) Likewise, the networks can also learn to map those result patterns into the surface structures of the TL – that is, to perform operations (called *decoding*) analogous to a system's generation phase. And they can learn the alignment between surface elements of the source segment with those of the target segment, alignment information helpful during generation – and in this context termed *attention*, since the generator employs it to determine which source element to attend to when selecting the next target output as it moves through the input, normally left to right (Figure 4.9).

Neural networks were born to learn abstractions. The "hidden" layers in a neural network, those which mediate between the input and output layers, are designed to gradually form abstractions at multiple levels by determining which combinations of input elements, and which combinations of combinations, are most significant in determining the appropriate output. (In our conceptual introduction above, each abstraction level was viewed as a stage in a chain of implied "rules." Rules close to the input, at the bottom of the network, use surface elements specific to particular inputs as their "premises," while those at higher layers use "premise" combinations taken from many

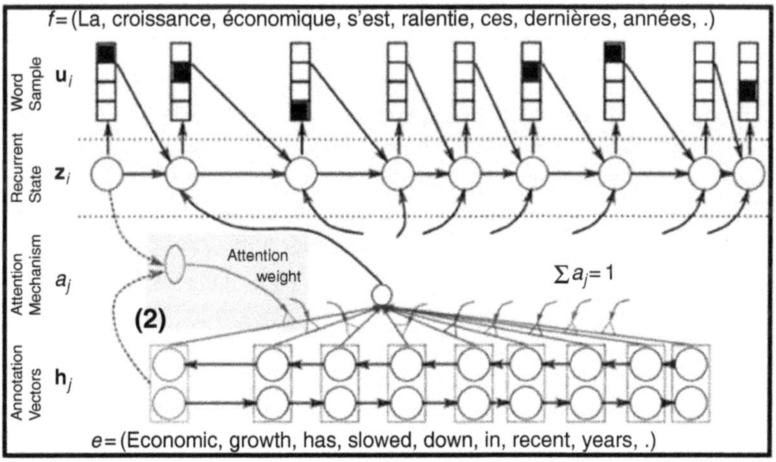

Figure 4.9 A neural network showing encoding, decoding, and attention

inputs.) The more hidden layers, the more levels of abstraction become possible; and this is why *deep* neural networks are better at abstracting than shallow ones. This advantage has been evident in theory for some time; but deep networks only became practical when computational processing achieved sufficient capacity to handle multiple hidden layers.

Where MT is concerned, this hidden learning raises the possibility of training neural translators to develop internal semantic representations automatically and implicitly (Woszczyna et al., 1998). A new neural-network-based approach to semantics then suggests itself: *Within a network, nodes or pathways shared by input elements having the same translation or translations can be seen as representing the shared meanings*. Input elements sharing a translation can originate in a single SL (when in that language the source elements are synonyms in the current context) or in several SLs (when across the input languages in question the source elements are synonymous in their respective contexts). And in fact, the shared translations, too, can be unilingual or multilingual.

Thus, if translation is trained over several languages, semantic representations may emerge that are abstracted away from – that become relatively independent of – the languages used in training. Taken together, they would compose a *neurally* learned interlingua, a language-neutral semantic representation comparable to the *handmade* symbolic interlingua discussed above in relation to rule-based systems. A successful neural interlingua could facilitate handling of under-resourced or long-tail languages, thus opening a path to truly universal translation at manageable development costs. Several teams have begun work in this direction (Le, Niehues, and Waibel, 2016; Firat et al., 2016)[8] and early results are already emerging: Google, for instance, has published on "zero-shot" NMT, so named because the approach allows translation between languages for which zero bilingual data was included in training corpora (Johnson et al., 2016); and SYSTRAN, in a similar spirit, has already announced combined translation systems for Romance languages.[9] Zero-shot NMT works because the encoding (analysis) phase of translation has been generalized across all currently trained SLs, while the decoding (generation) phrase has similarly been generalized across all currently trained TLs. Thus any current source can be paired with any current target. Expectations would be low, however, if completely untrained SLs or TLs were tried.

[8] See e.g., "Google's new multilingual neural machine translation system can translate between language pairs even though it has never been taught to do so," *Kurzweil AI Digest* (November 25, 2016): www.kurzweilai.net/googles-new-multilingual-neural-machine-translation-system-can-translate-between-language-pairs-even-though-it-has-never-been-taught-to-do-so.

[9] See Senellart, "Training Romance multi-way model." http://forum.opennmt.net/t/training-romance-multi-way-model/86.

4.4 Future Directions for Semantics in Machine Translation

Having surveyed past and present approaches to semantics for MT, we are ready to look ahead. We first consider possibilities for a renaissance of symbolic semantics in MT. Second and finally, we address the development we consider most significant: The advent of perceptually grounded semantics for NLP in general and for MT in particular.

4.4.1 Resurgence of Explicit Symbolic Semantics?

We have observed a marked decline in explicit symbolic representation in MT since the rule-based era. The difficulties and frustrations for this representational style are well known (Hutchins, 2010). Why then do we suggest that a comeback is possible, at least for some purposes?

In the first place, better results may sometimes be obtained: As we saw above, translation of Japanese *kyouto no kaigi* or *toukyou no kaigi* could be enhanced through exploitation of symbols drawn from ontologies, indicating that *kyouto* and *toukyou* are examples of the CITIES class and that *kaigi* is an example (or subclass) of MEETINGS.[10] Such processing advantages remain, though issues also persist concerning the costs and difficulties of obtaining semantically labeled corpora. It is also arguable that sufficiently big data can eventually yield such high accuracy via statistical or neural techniques that the advantages of explicit symbolic processing for translation accuracy will not be worth the trouble.

However, other significant advantages of explicit semantics relate to universality and interoperability. Regarding universality, the original argument for interlingua-based MT in the rule-based era was after all that the number of translation paths could be drastically – in fact, exponentially – reduced if a common pivot could be used for many languages. In that case, the meaning representation for English would be the same as that for Japanese or Swahili, and all analysis or generation programs could be designed to arrive at, or depart from, that same pivot point. And concerning interoperability, the same representation could be shared not only by many languages but by many MT systems. Thus the ambition to overcome the Tower of Babel among human languages would be mirrored by the effort to overcome the current Babel of translation systems.

A common meaning representation, beyond bridging languages and MT systems, could also bridge NLP tasks. And in fact, we do see explicit semantic representation taking hold now in tasks other than translation. Google, for example, has already begun to make extensive use of its Knowledge Graph

[10] See the Wikipedia entry for example-based MT: https://en.wikipedia.org/wiki/Example-based_machine_translation.

ontology in the service of *search*. "Thomas Jefferson" is now treated not only as a character string, but as a node in a taxonomy representing an instance of the PERSONS class, and of its LEADERS subclass, and of its PRESIDENTS sub-subclass, and so on (Figure 4.10). This knowledge guides the search and enables more informative responses.

Similarly, IBM's Watson system uses its own Knowledge Graph, this time in the service of *question answering* – initially focused especially upon the healthcare domain.[11] Unsurprisingly, Google and IBM presently use their own ontologies. However, eventual movement toward a common standard seems likely: one semantic representation that could bridge languages, tasks, and competing or cooperating organizations. Meanwhile, efforts to inter-map or mediate among competing taxonomies also seem likely.

4.4.2 Perceptually Grounded Semantics

The semantic representations discussed above – explicit symbolic, vector-based, and early neural-network-based – have in common that they have been based on text alone. In contrast, we now turn to the possibility of *perceptually grounded semantics*.

As a starting point, we return to John Searle's claim that computer programs in general, and translation programs specifically, currently – and even necessarily – lack semantics. If shown a translation program making extensive use of perception-free semantic representation as discussed so far – that is, of symbols drawn from ontologies, or of vectors drawn from vector spaces, or even of common nodes and paths in today's neural networks – Searle would be unlikely to change his mind. He would probably argue that these symbols, vectors, or net elements, like the text strings that they accompany, could be manipulated blindly by a computer, or by a homunculus aping a computer, with no relation at all to their real-world content. Such a translation system, he might say, could compute from the string "elephant" that an instance of the class ELEPHANTS was represented, and thus, according to the relevant steps, an instance of the classes PACHYDERMS, MAMMALS, ANIMALS, etc. (or a participant in the corresponding vector clusters or convergent neural paths). However, no matter how much further ontological, taxonomical, or relational information might be manipulated via rules, vectors, or networks, the system would still utterly fail to recognize an elephant if confronted with one. There would be no relation between the rules, vectors, or networks and the world of sights, sounds, tastes, smells, and textures.

These arguments would be correct. The ontologically equipped system, despite its taxonomic sophistication, would remain devoid of any worldly

[11] See https://sites.google.com/site/anshunjain/knowledge-graphs.

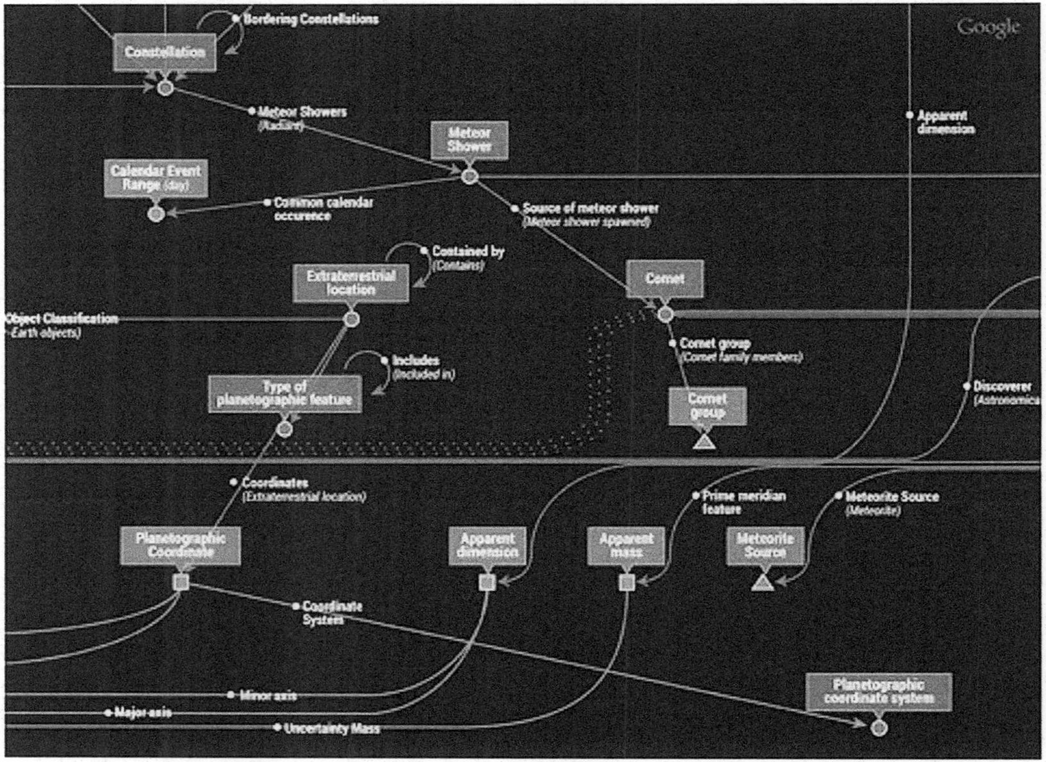

Figure 4.10 A fragment of Google's Knowledge Graph

experience. But we can recognize now that this innocence is not an irremediable condition. It has now become possible for computational systems to learn categories based upon (artificial) perception. If, based on perceptual input, categories representing things like elephants are learned alongside categories representing linguistic symbols, and if associations between these categories are learned as well, then arguably the systems will come to have semantic knowledge worthy of the name – that is, perceptually grounded semantic knowledge which can eventually inform translation and other NLP programs.

We can, for example, imagine a computational system that learns from visual, audio, or other sensor-based examples to recognize members of the category CATS, thereby internalizing this category;[12] learns from examples to recognize members of the graphic category NEKO-KANJIS (the Japanese character 猫, symbolizing the meaning "cat"), thereby internalizing this second category; and learns from examples to associate the two categories in both directions, so that activation of CATS triggers activation of NEKO-KANJIS and vice versa. We can also imagine a second computational system with similar learning mechanisms that learns likewise, but based on completely different examples. And finally, assuming that at least one of the systems can learn to generate and transmit *new* instances of NEKO-KANJIS, we can imagine communication between the two systems mediated by transmission of such instances and confirmed through some objective functional test, such as reliable selection from a barnyard lineup. The argument then is that, to both systems, instances of 猫 have a kind of meaning absent from handmade, vector-based, or even neural-network-based "semantic" constructs divorced from (even artificial) perception.

This linguistic communication scenario could in fact be implemented using current technology. The DeepMind neural net technology acquired by Google can indeed form the category CATS (minus the label) based upon perceptual instances in videos (much as the perceptual systems of self-driving cars are daily internalizing and refining categories like PERSONS, VEHICLES, etc.). And as for the learning of communicative symbols like NEKO-KANJIS, in fact every speech recognition or handwriting recognition program already forms implicit categories such that a new instance is recognized as belonging to the relevant category. What remains is to learn the association between categories like CATS and NEKO-KANJIS, and then to demonstrate communication via the symbol categories between computers whose respective learning has depended upon unrelated instances.

We can extend this story of perceptually grounded semantics to translation by assuming that, while one computational system learns an association with NEKO-KANJIS, the other learns a different linguistic symbol category instead,

12 Pun intended.

say that of the written word "cat" in English, call it CAT-GRAPHEMES. Then for communication to take place, an instance of NEKO-KANJIS must be replaced during transmission by an instance of that graphic class (or vice versa). *If the replacement involved activation in a third system – the translator system – of a perceptually learned* CATS *class associated with both the learned SL and TL symbols, then the translation process as well the transmission and reception would be perceptually grounded.*

Such demonstrations may emerge within a few years, but practical use of perceptually grounded semantic categories for automatic translation purposes will likely take longer. (Perceptually grounded experiments in other areas of NLP are ongoing, however, for instance in *automatic tagging of photos* by Kyunghyun Cho of NYU and others (Cho, 2015). There have also been suggestions that self-driving vehicles should learn to communicate about their percepts to human drivers. Such communication would demonstrate perceptually grounded semantics on the vehicle's part, though a human rather than a computer would be on the receiving end.) Meanwhile, integration of ontology-based, vector-based, or perception-free neural semantic representation might well move faster. The two strands of semantic research might thus proceed in parallel, with a perception-free strand advancing alongside a perceptually grounded strand. We can hope that the two strands would in time meet and enrich each other.

From a philosophical viewpoint, with respect to arguments like Searle's that NLP and other computer programs necessarily lack true semantics, we are suggesting here that a crucial missing factor can now be supplied. Since the absentee is most often called intentionality, we cautiously use that term here, with due recognition of the considerable but inconclusive associated literature.[13] Searle provides a serviceable definition:

> The primary evolutionary role of the mind is to relate us in certain ways to the environment, and especially to other people. My subjective states relate me to the rest of the world, and the general name of that relationship is "intentionality." These subjective states include beliefs and desires, intentions and perceptions, as well as loves and hates, fears and hopes. "Intentionality," to repeat, is the general term for all the various forms by which the mind can be directed at, or be about, or of, objects and states of affairs in the world. (Searle, 1999, 85)

Intentionality thus defined, then, is a relation or link between processes internal to a cognitive system and "the rest of the world." Searle and others have correctly identified a gap between that perceptible world and computational systems to date; but we suggest that this gap can after all be crossed, and that artificial perception can be the bridge. When the classes or categories involved in translation and other NLP processes are learned through artificial perception

[13] See the Wikipedia entry for intentionality: https://en.wikipedia.org/wiki/Intentionality.

of that world, the linkup will be achieved. Intentionality will indeed be engendered, and semantics worthy of the name – truly meaningful semantics – will enter the computational universe. Communication based upon semantics evincing intentionality, whether among computers or between computers and humans, will then be amenable to operational definition and confirmation. Perceptually grounded NLP programs will have broken out of Searle's Chinese room . . . through the doors of perception.[14]

A necessary coda: Does perceptual grounding of concepts imply consciousness? No. While the capacity to learn conceptual classes via perception may well be a necessary condition for consciousness, we are by no means suggesting that it is a sufficient condition. Consciousness seems likely to require a range of additional elements, probably including a self-concept based upon memory of past experiences and perhaps anticipation of the future; the ability to direct attention, and perhaps actions, in response to internal and external stimuli; and much more. Nevertheless, progress toward consensus on the meaning of meaning will certainly be a significant – all right, a meaningful – step on the way toward understanding of cognition.

References

Alkhouli, Tamer, Andreas Guta, and Hermann Ney (2014). Vector space models for phrase-based machine translation. In *Proceedings of SSST-8, Eighth Workshop on Syntax, Semantics and Structure in Statistical Translation*. Doha, Qatar, October 25, pp. 1–10.

Boguslavsky, Igor, Jesus Cardeñosa, Carolina Gallardo, and Luis Iraola (2005). The UNL initiative: An overview. In Alexander Gelbukh (ed.), Computational Linguistics and Intelligent Text Processing. CICLing 2005. *Lecture Notes in Computer Science*, vol. 3406. Berlin, Heidelberg: Springer.

Boitet, Christian (2000). Bernard Vauquois' contribution to the theory and practice of building MT systems: A historical perspective. In William John Hutchins (ed.), *Early Years in Machine Translation: Memoirs and Biographies of Pioneers*, *Studies in the History of the Language Sciences* 97, pp. 331–349.

Boitet, Christian (2002). A rationale for using UNL as an interlingua and more in various domains. In *Proceedings of LREC-02: First International Workshop on UNL, Other Interlinguas, and Their Applications*. Las Palmas, Canary Islands, pp. 26–31.

Brown, Peter F., John Cocke, Stephen A. Della Pietra, Vincent J. Della Pietra, Frederick Jelinek, John D. Lafferty, Robert L. Mercer, and P. Roossin (1990).

[14] As goes without saying, numerous knotty philosophical and practical issues will persist. Since all perception occurs within a cognitive system, how is "the rest of the world" to be defined? For example, would a cognitive system's perceptions of its own artificial hunger or fear qualify? Would artificial perception of a fully simulated external world? Would Searle's Chinese Room homunculus handle perceptual computations just as blindly as all others, leaving him just as shut in as when lacking perception? We hope to address such questions elsewhere.

A statistical approach to machine translation, *Computational Linguistics* 16(2) (June), 79–85.

Brown, Peter F., Stephen A. Della Pietra, Vincent J. Della Pietra, and Robert L. Mercer (1993). The mathematics of statistical machine translation: Parameter estimation, *Computational Linguistics* 19(2) (June), 263–311.

Bundy, Alan, and Lincoln Wallen (1984). Semantic grammar. In Alan Bundy and Lincoln Wallen (eds.), *Catalogue of Artificial Intelligence Tools: Symbolic Computation (Artificial Intelligence)*. Berlin, Heidelberg: Springer.

Cho, Kyunghyun (2015). Introduction to neural machine translation with GPUs (Part 1). NVIDIA Developer Blog (May 27, 2015), at: https://devblogs.nvidia.com/parallelforall/introduction-neural-machine-translation-with-gpus/.

Dikonov, Vyacheslav, and Igor Boguslavsky (2009). Semantic network of the UNL dictionary of concepts. In *Proceedings of the SENSE Workshop on Conceptual Structures for Extracting Natural Language Semantics*. Moscow, Russia, July.

Fellbaum, Christiane (ed.) (1998). *WordNet: An Electronic Lexical Database*. Cambridge, MA: MIT Press.

Firat, Orhan, Kyunghyun Cho, and Yoshua Bengio (2016). Multi-way, multilingual neural machine translation with a shared attention mechanism. In Proceedings of NAACL-HLT 2016 (June 12–17), San Diego, California. Association for Computational Linguistics, pp. 866–875: www.aclweb.org/anthology/N16-1101.

Firth, John Rupert (1957). A synopsis of linguistic theory 1930–1955. In *Studies in Linguistic Analysis*. Oxford: Special Volume of the Philological Society 1(32).

Gao, Yuqing, Bowen Zhou, Liang Gu, Ruhi Sarikaya, Hong-kwang Kuo, Antti-Veiko I. Rosti, Mohamed Afify, and Wei-zhong Zhu (2006). IBM MASTOR: Multilingual automatic speech-to-speech translator. In *Proceedings of ICASSP 2006*. Toulouse, France, May 14–19, pp. 1205–1208.

Hutchins, William John (2005). Towards a definition of example-based machine translation. In *MT Summit X: Proceedings of Workshop on Example-based Machine Translation*. Phuket, Thailand, September 16, pp. 63–70.

Hutchins, William John (2010). Machine translation: A concise history. *Journal of Translation Studies* 13(1–2): *Special Issue: The Teaching of Computer-Aided Translation*, Chan Sin Wai (ed.), 29–70.

Johnson, Melvin, Mike Schuster, Quoc V. Le, Maxim Krikun, Yonghui Wu, Zhifeng Chen, Nikhil Thorat, Fernanda Viégas, Martin Wattenberg, Greg Corrado, Macduff Hughes, and Jeffrey Dean (2016). Google's multilingual neural machine translation system: Enabling zero-shot translation. Transactions of the Association for Computational Linguistics, [S.l.] 5 (October 2017), 339–351. ISSN 2307-387X. Available at: https://transacl.org/ojs/index.php/tacl/article/view/1081.

Knott, Alistair, and Robert Dale (1992). Using linguistic phenomena to motivate a set of rhetorical relations: Human Communication Research Centre Technical Report Rp-34. Edinburgh: University of Edinburgh.

Koehn, Philipp (2009). *Statistical Machine Translation*. Cambridge: Cambridge University Press.

Le, Than-He, Jan Niehues, and Alex Waibel (2016). Toward multilingual neural machine translation with universal encoder and decoder. In *Proceedings of the International Workshop on Spoken Language Translation (IWSLT) 2016*. Seattle, WA, December 8–9.

Levin, Lori, Donna Gates, Alon Lavie, and Alex Waibel (1998). An interlingua based on domain actions for machine translation of task-oriented dialogues. In *Proceedings of the Fifth International Conference on Spoken Language Processing, ICSLP-98*. Sydney, Australia, November 30–December 4.

Mikolov, Tomas, Quoc V. Le, and Ilya Sutskever (2013). Exploiting similarities among languages for machine translation. At arXiv:1309.4168.

Nagao, Makoto (1984). A framework of a mechanical translation between Japanese and English by analogy principle. In Alick Elithorn and Ranan Banerji (eds.), *Artificial and Human Intelligence*. Amsterdam: Elsevier Science Publishers.

Searle, John. R. (1980). Minds, brains, and programs, *Behavioral and Brain Sciences* 3 (3), 417–457.

Searle, John R. (1999). *Mind, Language and Society: Philosophy in the Real World*. London: Phoenix.

Seligman, Mark (1993). *A Japanese-German Transfer Component for ASURA*. Kyoto, Japan: ATR (Advanced Telecommunications Research Institute International) Technical Report TR-I-0368.

Seligman, Mark (1994). *CO-OC: Semi-Automatic Production of Resources for Tracking Morphological and Semantic Co-Occurrences in Spontaneous Dialogues*. Kyoto, Japan: ATR (Advanced Telecommunications Research Institute International) Technical Report TR-I-0084.

Seligman, Mark, Masami Suzuki, and Tsuyoshi Morimoto (1993). Semantic-level transfer in Japanese–German speech translation: Some experiences. Technical Report NLC93-13 of the Institute of Electronics, Information, and Communication Engineers (IEICE), May 21. Tokyo, Japan: IEICE.

Turney, Peter D., and Patrick Pantel (2010). From frequency to meaning: Vector space models of semantics, *Journal of Artificial Intelligence Research* 37(2010), 141–188.

Uchida, Hiroshi (1986). Fujitsu machine translation system: ATLAS. *Future Generation Computer Systems* 2(2) (June), 95–100.

Waibel, Alex, Toshiyuki Hanazawa, Geoffrey E. Hinton, and Kiyohiro Shikano (1989). Phoneme recognition using time-delay neural networks. *IEEE Transactions on Acoustics Speech and Signal Processing* 37(3) (April), 328–339.

Waibel, Alex, Ajay N. Jain, Arthur E. McNair, Hiroaki Saito, Alexander G. Hauptmann, and Joe Tebelskis (1991). JANUS: A speech-to-speech translation system using connectionist and symbolic processing strategies. In *Proceedings of the International Conference on Acoustics, Speech and Signal Processing (ICASSP) 1991*. Toronto, Canada, May 14–17, pp. 793–796.

Woszczyna, Monika, Matthew Broadhead, Donna Gates, Marsal Gavaldà, Alon Lavie, Lori Levin, and Alex Waibel (1998). A modular approach to spoken language translation for large domains. In *Proceedings of the Third Conference of the Association for Machine Translation in the Americas (AMTA) 98*. Langhorne, PA, October 28–31, pp. 31–40.

5 Translating and Disseminating World Health Organization Drinking-Water-Quality Guidelines in Japan

Meng Ji, Glenn Hook and Fukumoto Fumiyo

5.1 Introduction

The policies adopted by multilateral organisations at the global and regional levels are regularly translated from one language into another, usually from English into the national language of a member state. The social network at the heart of the translation and dissemination of these policies is a critical yet largely under-explored research area, given the dominance of the English language in policy documents worldwide. As evidenced in the case of the World Health Organization (WHO), many of these policies impact directly on the lives and well-being of the citizens of the member states, none more so than the compound essential for all living organisms: H_2O. Whilst the consumption of water is regulated at international, regional and national levels, central to the establishment of a regulatory framework for water standards is the WHO, which drafts authoritative guidelines on the quality of water that is healthy for healthy human consumption. In this chapter we take up the impact of WHO policy on Japan, interrogating how the standardisation of drinking-water quality is translated and disseminated in a range of industrial sectors. The analysis offers an illuminating example of how regulatory procedures in the development of national health policies coherent with guidelines from international health agencies are transferred from the international to the national level through different social networks. To this end, policy documents such as the WHO Guidelines for Drinking-Water Quality form the basis for the setting of national standards aimed at regulating water safety in support of national public health policies.

Looking back historically (Kosuge, 1981), we find Japan's Waterworks Ordinance (the 'old Waterworks Act') of 1890 did not include any provisions for drinking-water-quality standards (DWQS). By 1908, however, the Council on Waterworks had laid down the 'Agreed Method for Water Examination' as the national standard for regulating water quality. In 1958, the DWQS were established based on the Waterworks Act, enacted the previous year. After minor amendments in 1960, 1966 and 1978, the standards went through substantial revision in 1992. In 1958, after the establishment of the Waterworks Act, twenty-nine items were set as the first DWQS. Since then, the Ministry of Health, Labour and Welfare (MHLW) has carried out a series of amendments of the standards to comply with the latest scientific findings. The amendments of 1992 were especially significant as the number of standard items covered was increased from twenty-six to forty-six in order to substantially enhance the regulation of drinking-water quality. In 2004, in response to the WHO's third Guidelines for Drinking-Water Quality, the MHLW consulted with the Health Science Council of Japan on the revision of the DWQS and special task forces were set up to examine the revision of the water-quality management systems. As a result, new standards were established and new water-quality management systems went into effect in the same year as the WHO published its third edition of the Guidelines.

The first and second editions of the WHO Drinking-Water-Quality Guidelines were used by both developed and developing countries as the basis for the standardisation and regulation of water quality, with the aim of establishing regulatory standards for the safe human consumption of drinking water. The third edition of the Guidelines was comprehensively updated to take account of developments in risk assessment and risk management that had taken place since the second edition was published. It puts forward a regulatory framework for drinking-water safety and outlines the roles and responsibilities of different stakeholders, including the complementary roles of national regulators, suppliers, communities and independent surveillance agencies. The expanded third edition contains two key improvements on the earlier versions of the Guidelines. The first improvement relates to embedding a norm on drinking-water-quality regulation and management, in particular through the introduction of comprehensive, system-specific water-safety plans. Second, recognising the need for different tools and approaches in supporting large community supplies of drinking water, the third edition describes the norms in the approaches to each, and the surveillance of small community supplies.

These two improvements at the international level were fully represented in the revision of DWQS carried out by the Japanese government in 2004. This illustrates how improvements in international policy changed the way water-quality standards were implemented at the national level, as before this amendment the DWQS were set only in regard to issues seen as common throughout the nation. That is, instead of the government relying on administrative guidance to deal with issues arising in specific localities (on administrative guidance, see Johnson 1982), or in regard to specific water-purification methods, as heretofore, the norm of dealing with water safety as a national-level system of regulation can be seen to have cascaded down from the international level of the WHO, changing Japan's regulatory framework for human consumption of drinking water (on 'norm cascade', see Finnemore and Sikkinh 1998). In the amendment, new standards were established based on these two fundamental principles, closely in line with the third WHO Guidelines. The implementation of these new standards now means that all aspects of drinking-water safety are taken into account, regardless of the particular nature of the locality, types of water source or purification method used, even if the detection level of a particular risk is low on a national basis. We see here how standards have as a result come to be viewed through a *national* lens in terms of the level of risk posed to human health, well-being or living conditions. What is more, the water regulators are now obliged to carry out the testing of drinking water in order to ensure it is fit for human consumption, prepare an 'Annual Water Quality Testing Plan' outlining the boundaries for analysis and publish their plans for water consumers beforehand, thereby ensuring the new system is transparent.

5.2 Development of the Bilingual Japanese-English Terminology for Translating WHO Guidelines for Drinking-Water Quality

As the above transition only became possible as a result of international-level regulatory norms cascading down to the national level through the translation and dissemination of the English of the WHO into the Japanese of the MHLW, we now turn to examine this topic using an approach based on an empirical analysis of the translation of the WHO Guidelines (third edition, 2004) into the target language. We start with an examination of the bilingual terminologies developed in the Japanese translation in 2004, the same year that the original English policy documents were published. It goes without saying that, in two languages as different as Japanese and English (Miyagawa, 2008), the translation of international health-policy documentation into Japanese required significant effort in order to devise specialised terminology able to convey both international scientific and policy principles in linguistic expressions that were both understandable and acceptable to the national audience. To extract, review and assess the bilingual Japanese and English nomenclature used in the translation, an English–Japanese parallel corpus was constructed. This corpus contains the original English source text and the Japanese translation aligned at the sentence level. The extraction of bilingual terms is focused on the statistical extraction of term pairs of content words, especially named entities in the aligned parallel corpus. The empirical results reveal the combination of script required to convey in Japanese the meaning of the original, given the range of new scientific knowledge, especially health and safety standards and newly introduced water management instruments like the Water Safety Plan (WSP) in the third WHO Guidelines. More specifically, to ensure the new terminology was both understandable and acceptable, the translation of named entities from English to Japanese utilised a variety of translation techniques combining the mixed use of the three parallel writing systems in Japanese, i.e. *hiragana*, *katakana* and *kanji* characters (Tsujimura, 2013).

The WSP acts as an instrument through which the WHO introduced a regulatory framework encompassing the norms of comprehensive risk assessment and management at all stages of water supply. Prior to the third edition of the WHO Guidelines, an earlier Japanese version of the second edition of those Guidelines was produced in 1993. A comparison of the two versions shows high terminological consistency. Following the 2004 translation (Guidelines for Drinking Water Quality, 2004), the MHLW compiled the Japanese version of the Guidelines and disseminated them to the regulatory bodies dealing with the management of drinking water across Japan in 2008. To facilitate the analysis of the social dissemination of the translated material, bilingual terminology (see Appendix 5A.1) was developed and classified into four conceptual categories, i.e. *Targets*, *Standards and Principles*, *Approaches and Methods* and *Action*. The temporal range of the analysis is between 2000 and 2017, four years prior to the third edition's publication.

The first semantic category of *Targets* contains Japanese translations of original English terms which are mostly content words and proper nouns: water-resource management (水源資管理); community drinking-water supplies (コミュニティー飲料水供給); healthcare facilities (ヘルスケア施設); health-outcome targets (健康成果目標); Millennium Development Goals (ミレニアム開発目標); performance targets (処理性能目標); water-quality targets (水質目標); health-based targets (健康に基づく目標); performance target setting (性能目標の設定); and so on. These terminological equivalents are closely related to agenda setting in the development of national guidelines for drinking-water quality based on the original WHO document.

The second semantic category of *Standards and Principles* contains Japanese equivalents of English terms such as: acceptability (受容性); adequacy of supply (水供給の充足度); affordability (経済的負担能力); equitability (公平性); fitness for purpose (目的への適合性); fit for purpose (目的に適合した); independent surveillance (独立機関によるサーベイランス); local adaptation (地域での適用); national priorities (国としての優先度); international standards (国際基準); access to water (水へのアクセス); treatment achievability (処理による達成度); practical considerations (現実的配慮); priority setting (優先順位付け); regional adaptive use (地域での活用); prioritisation of hazards (危害因子の優先順位付け); or risk-based development policy formulation (リスクに基づくの策定).

The third semantic category, *Approaches and Methods,* encompasses Japanese translations of terms such as: benchmark (ベンチマーク); quantitative risk assessment (リスクの定量評価); response plans (対応計画);

preventive integrated management approach (総合予防管理アプローチ); audit-based surveillance (監査によるサーベイランス); framework for safe drinking water (安全な飲料水の枠組み); grading schemes for the safety of drinking water (飲料水の安全性に関する格付け); holistic approach (総合的アプローチ), problem formulation (問題の明確化); risk characterisation (リスク特性評価); risk–benefit approach (リスク一便益アプローチ); water-safety plans (水安全計画); and so on.

The last semantic category, *Actions*, includes Japanese equivalents regarding specific actions and procedures taken to maintain the drinking-water safety and quality standards set out in the third WHO Guidelines: approval (承認); audit (監査); control measures (制御手段); maintaining control (制御の維持); operational monitoring (運転監視); risk assessment (リスク評価); risk management (リスク管理); system assessment (システム評価); surveillance (サーベイランス); system design (システム設計); verification (検証); quality assurance (品質保証); quality control (品質管理); process control (プロセス制御); ranking of complexity (複雑さのランク付け); and ranking of costs (コストのランク付け).

These four categories of term equivalents offered the foundation for developing a number of integrated search strings in order to retrieve large amounts of licensed digital materials from diverse sources of information. The extracted digital materials in original Japanese were then subjected to the formalised analysis of the complex paths for the dissemination of translated drinking-water-quality guidelines in the Japanese social system, which will be discussed in Section 5.3 of this chapter.

5.3 Exploring the Translation and Dissemination Network of the Third Edition of the WHO Guidelines for Drinking-Water Quality

Structural equation modelling, or path analysis, is a powerful statistical technique used widely in the social sciences. It provides a formalised approach for testing theoretical hypotheses regarding the combined effects of two sets of external factors or variables: i.e. the independent variables, on the one hand, and the mediating or the observed dependent variable(s), on the other. The underlying hypothesis explored in this study is that, in the dissemination of translated international health guidelines, here the WHO's third set of Guidelines for Drinking-Water Quality, the target Japanese social and cultural system is susceptible to the combined effects of different sources of information. This includes the direct sources of information such as government and politics and top industrial organisations and businesses, on the one hand, and indirect, mediating social agencies such as newspapers, journals and magazines on the other. The corpus analysis demonstrates that, in the social diffusion of the WHO Drinking-Water-Quality guidelines, different sources of information played distinct roles in fostering the accountability borne by certain industrial sectors in giving life to specific aspects of the guidelines. In the structural equation modelling of the social dissemination of translated health knowledge and guidelines, the hypothesised independent variables are the direct sources of information, e.g. governmental, top industrial or business sources; the mediating variable is the Japanese mass media, including newspapers, journals and magazines; and the dependent variables are a range of Japanese industrial sectors as the end users of the institutionally translated and socially disseminated key information in the third edition of the WHO Guidelines.

The latent links, associations and interconnections identified between the international recommendations found in the WHO Guidelines for improved water management, on the one hand, and certain industrial sectors in the target social system, on the other, are depicted as the pathways of international policy translation and adaptation in the national context, in this case that of Japan. The corpus analysis offers evidence that, whilst the main sources of information play a central role in this process, whether governmental, industrial or business, the mediating effect of the media can significantly enhance or attenuate the direct impact of the main sources on the intended industrial sectors, which adds to the complexity of the social-diffusion model proposed. Nevertheless, we argue that our study provides a formalised and largely replicable approach to the formulation and analysis of the hypothesised pathways that underline the national adaptation and utilisation of international health recommendations made by organisations such as the WHO. Policy makers at the national level will benefit from an in-depth understanding of the complex pathways involved, and the interaction and dynamics between the sources of information and the mediating agents, as well as of these factors' combined impact on the industrial sectors engaged in relevant social activities, such as agriculture, consumer goods, business and consumer services, retail and wholesale and transport and logistics.

Figure 5.1 illustrates the hypothesised pathway of the dissemination of translated health guidelines in the target social and cultural system of Japan. The simplest model of the transmission of translated information is from an authoritative main source of information directly to the intended end user, i.e. the industrial sector engaged in the related social or economic activities. For example, government agencies and industrial bodies may develop, refine and publish national regulatory guidelines in the Japanese language based on the key principles and suggestions found in the drinking-water-quality documents issued by the WHO. Related industrial sectors such as consumer goods, business and consumer services, agriculture, retail and wholesale and transport and

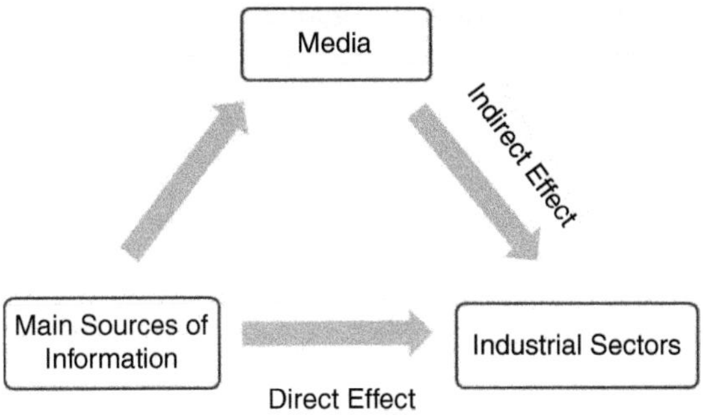

Figure 5.1 Path analysis of the translation and dissemination of WHO Guidelines in Japan

logistics may then be addressed in these guidelines. As a result, these industrial sectors take on their share of social accountability for certain aspects of the Guidelines as they have been translated and adapted for the target social context.

As shown in Figure 5.1, another layer has been added to this simplified transmission model by including the media as a mediating variable. This means that the effects of the sources of information on the intended end user are the combination of the direct and indirect effects mediated by media agents. The corpus analysis in the Section 5.3.1 not only offers compelling evidence of how the hypothesised mediating process has significantly improved the predictive regression model, but also reveals the shifting and dynamic role played by the media in either enhancing or moderating the information provided to the intended users from different sources, e.g. government, business and industries. By focusing on how the transmission and social assimilation of the WHO's drinking-water guidelines have been translated at the national level, our case study provides germane, needed and timely insights into the complex pathways as well as potential social interventions available to stakeholders to enhance the social dissemination and uptake of both translated guidelines and best-practice suggestions from international health organisations in the national context.

5.3.1 Direct Effects from Main Sources of Information

This section examines the strengths identified between the dependent variables and the hypothesised exogenous variables in the structural equation modelling which include both the independent variables and the mediating variables. Four independent variables and two mediating variables are examined: the four independent variables are Business Sources, Government and Political

Table 5.1 *Regression weights (targets and goals)*

Field	Dependent variable	Independent variable	Estimate	S. E.	C. R.*
Target	Business & Consumer Services	Government and Politics	12.739	4.059	3.139
Target	Consumer Goods	Government and Politics	5.959	2.564	2.324
Target	Retail & Wholesale	Government and Politics	2.527	0.926	2.729
Target	Transport & Logistics	Business Sources	0.374	0.114	3.289
Target	Business & Consumer Services	Business Sources	0.976	0.378	2.583
Target	Business & Consumer Services	Major News and Business Sources	0.495	0.167	2.958

S. E. (Standard Errors); C. R. (Critical Ratios) * larger than 1.96 is significant at 0.05 level

Sources, Major News and Business Sources and Top Industry Sources,[1] and the two mediating variables are (1) Newspapers and (2) Magazines and Journals. Five industrial sectors have been selected as the dependent variables: (1) Agriculture, (2) Business and Consumer Services, (3) Consumer Goods, (4) Retail and Wholesale and (5) Transport and Logistics. This classification aligns with the structure of the large-scale database used in this study, i.e. the open-end FACTIVA database that has been developed by the Dow Jones company from the mid-1990s onwards. FACTIVA includes a large range of licensed digital materials published by government, industrial and business sources in different countries in their original languages over the last twenty years. The following section examines the social and cross-sectoral dissemination of four semantic categories of terminologies derived from the Japanese translation of the third WHO Guidelines between 2000 and 2017.

Table 5.1 shows the breakdown of the statistically significant regression weights identified in the path analysis of the disseminated target-related Japanese translations of the third WHO Guidelines. In the formalised analysis of the disseminated information translated into Japanese, the predictive relationship between the independent variable, i.e. a specific source of information, and the dependent variable, is measured by the statistical indicator of regression weight or repression coefficient. In structural equation modelling, unstandardised regression weight or coefficient represents the amount of change in the dependent variable per single unit change in the predicator variable.

In Table 5.1, for example, the unstandardised regression weight of government and political sources of information when used as the independent

[1] In the FACTIVA database: Major News and Business Sources refer to key sources covering general and business news; Business Sources refer to key sources from various regions covering business news; Government and Politics sources of information refer to sources in which government and political news comprise a significant portion of the content.

Table 5.2 *Regression weights (standards and principles)*

Field	Dependent variable	Independent variable	Estimate	S. E.	C. R.
Standards	Consumer Goods	Government and Politics	2.188	0.939	2.329
Standards	Transport & Logistics	Government and Politics	1.491	0.435	3.429
Standards	Transport & Logistics	Business Sources	0.097	0.043	2.267

variable to explain the change in the business and consumer services sector is 12.739. This means that, with each article published in the Government and Politics category of the FACTIVA database, which contains expressions in the 'targets and goals' word category, there is an increase of more than twelve articles in the Business and Consumer Services Sector category of the database. In contrast, the unstandardised regression coefficient of government and political sources of information when used as the independent variable to explain changes in the retail and wholesale sector is 2.527. Table 5.1 includes only regression weights which indicate statistically significant relationships between the direct sources of information and the industrial sectors as the end users of the translated information.

Table 5.2 shows the regression models constructed for different pairs of independent and dependent variables. These models were built using Japanese translations of original English expressions related to the standards and principles outlined in the third WHO Guidelines such as acceptability, adequacy of supply, affordability, equitability, fitness for purpose, local adaptation, national priorities, international standards, treatment achievability, accessibility of quality water supplies and so on. As can be seen in Table 5.2, government and political sources of information have assumed the role of the largest source of information for two industrial sectors, Consumer Goods and Transport and Logistics. Comparing the information in Tables 5.1 and 5.2, we can see that, whilst in the dissemination of target- and goal-related translation terminology, a variety of sources of information have actively engaged with industrial sectors, Government and Politics remain as the key sources of information in the social diffusion of the principles and standards regarding drinking-water quality control and management given by international health organisations.

Table 5.3 shows the relationships between the various sources of information as the observed explanatory variables and the different industrial sectors as the dependent variables. Similar to the findings revealed in Table 5.2, Japanese government and political sources of information continue to play the key role in disseminating and promoting the methods and approaches to drinking-water management recommended by the third WHO Guidelines in the target Japanese social and cultural system. Across the five industrial sectors examined in our study, i.e. Agriculture, Business and Consumer Services, Consumer

Table 5.3 *Regression weights (approaches and methods)*

Field	Dependent variable	Independent variable	Estimate	S. E.	C. R.
Approach	Agriculture	Government and Politics	1.083	0.445	2.436
Approach	Business & Consumer Services	Government and Politics	8.006	1.146	6.988
Approach	Consumer Goods	Government and Politics	4.735	0.833	5.686
Approach	Retail & Wholesale	Government and Politics	0.936	0.217	4.316
Approach	Transport & Logistics	Government and Politics	1.287	0.201	6.413
Approach	Business & Consumer Services	Major News and Business Sources	0.052	0.026	1.996

Table 5.4 *Regression weights (actions)*

Field	Dependent variable	Independent variable	Estimate	S. E.	C. R.
Action	Transport & Logistics	Business Sources	0.103	0.042	2.467
Action	Business & Consumer Services	Government and Politics	6.937	1.122	6.181
Action	Consumer Goods	Government and Politics	3.157	0.591	5.341
Action	Retail & Wholesale	Government and Politics	1.022	0.237	4.316
Action	Transport & Logistics	Government and Politics	1.113	0.324	3.436

Goods, Retail and Wholesale and Transport and Logistics, the regression weights for Government and Politics, which explain important changes in the frequency of occurrence of these sectors in the FACTIVA database, are 1.083 (2.436), 8.006 (6.988), 4.735 (5.686), 0.936 (4.316) and 1.287 (6.413). The critical ratios (C. R.) (in brackets) of these regression weights all point to a significant relationship between the category of Government and Politics and these industrial sectors.

Table 5.4 displays the dependent relationships between the direct sources of information and the four industrial sectors as the end users of the translated and socially disseminated WHO Guidelines. The relationship revealed in Table 5.4 is based on the frequency analysis of sectoral publications containing translated expressions derived from the Action word category. Similar to the patterns uncovered in Table 5.3, Government and Politics continues to serve as the largest source of information for the four industrial sectors; i.e. Business and Consumer Services 6.937 (6.181), Consumer Goods 3.157 (5.341), Retail & Wholesale 1.022 (4.316) and Transport & Logistics 1.113 (3.346). The large, critical ratios indicate a strong relationship between the government and political sources of information and four distinct industrial sectors in Japan, thereby illuminating the important role of the government in ascribing social accountability amongst industrial sectors, and in creating and establishing pathways for the social dissemination of international health guidelines and policy materials in the target social system.

The formalised analysis of the distribution of translated water-quality guidelines has revealed important patterns regarding the effects of direct sources of information on different industrial sectors, and the latent social accountability created by these main sources of information between aspects of the WHO water-quality guidelines – summarised in four lexical categories of the WHO's translation terminology – and Japanese industrial sectors. Across the four areas – i.e. *Targets, Standards and Principles, Approaches and Methods* and *Actions* – Government and Politics proved to be the largest and most important source of information. Materials published by government and political sources covered a variety of industrial sectors ranging from Consumer Goods and Retail and Wholesale to Transport and Logistics. The high frequencies of occurrence of these industrial sectors in materials produced by direct sources of information point to the salient intention to establish and reinforce the social accountability of these sectors in implementing the recommendations given in the WHO's Guidelines. Specifically, in terms of achieving the targets and goals set out in the third set of WHO Guidelines, the four industrial sectors which were frequently mentioned in the direct sources of information were Consumer Goods, Business and Consumer Services, Retail and Wholesale and Transport and Logistics. Regarding the adoption and adherence to the general standards and principles stipulated in the Guidelines, the two Japanese industrial sectors which were highlighted by government and business sources of information were Transport and Logistics and Consumer Goods. In the adoption of specific methodologies to improve drinking-water quality, government and political sources of information have actively engaged a range of industrial sectors covering Agriculture, Consumer Goods, Consumer Services, Retail and Wholesale and Transport and Logistics. Lastly, in discussions around taking actions to highlight the recommendations from the third set of WHO Guidelines, the patterns are similar to those uncovered with the term category of *Approaches and Methods*, i.e., government and political sources of information have widely engaged Japanese industrial sectors.

5.3.2 The Social Communication and Mediation Role of the Mass Media

This section explores the intervening role of the mass media in the social diffusion of the third WHO Guidelines in Japan. It examines the contrastive approaches taken by the mass media to the reporting and communication of key information from the Guidelines. The corpus analysis shows that important, revealing differences exist between direct sources of information and the mass

Table 5.5 *Regression weights between the media and industrial sectors*

Field	Dependent variable	Independent variable	Estimate	S. E.	C. R.*
Target	Agriculture	Magazines and Journals	2.049	0.772	2.655
Target	Agriculture	Newspapers	0.161	0.072	2.21
Target	Transport & Logistics	Magazines and Journals	0.915	0.347	2.639
Standards	Agriculture	Newspapers	0.043	0.01	4.232
Approach	Transport & Logistics	Magazines and Journals	0.939	0.256	3.663
Approach	Agriculture	Newspapers	0.037	0.01	3.737
Approach	Transport & Logistics	Newspapers	0.01	0.004	2.163
Action	Agriculture	Magazines and Journals	1.233	0.598	2.062
Action	Agriculture	Newspapers	0.046	0.014	3.257

* larger than 1.96 is significant at 0.05 level

media when fostering the accountability borne by certain industrial sectors in giving life to specific aspects of the Guidelines.

Table 5.5 shows the corpus findings regarding the role of the mass media in the development of social accountability amongst industrial sectors in implementing aspects of WHO drinking-water guidelines and recommendations. For example, in the dissemination of targets and goals related to translation terminology, the unstandardised regression coefficients of Magazines and Journals, when used as the predictor variable for the Agriculture and Transport and Logistics sectors, were 2.049 and 0.915, respectively. Their associated critical ratios were 2.655 and 2.639, which were much larger than the threshold value of 1.96 required for the regression coefficients to be significant at the 0.05 level. This corpus finding suggests that Japanese mass media have highlighted and foregrounded Agriculture and Transport and Logistics sectors when discussing specific issues related to terms and expressions in the *Targets* term category of the third edition of the WHO Guidelines. This corpus finding stands in contrast with the social visibility and accountability ascribed to the Agriculture sector by direct sources of information, for example, government, business and industrial sources in Japan when discussing similar topics and issues. Table 5.1 shows that this sector has not been given much importance in materials published by direct sources of information, as no statistically significant relationship has been detected between the agriculture sector and direct sources of information. This contrastive corpus finding suggests that, in the social dissemination process, the mass media can exert important effects on or alter to a large extent the knowledge diffusion pathways from direct sources of information to the intended end users and consumers of the translated international policy materials.

In discussions around the standards and principles in the WHO Guidelines, the agriculture sector remains susceptible to influence from the mass media.

The unstandardised regression coefficient for newspapers as the independent variable for the Agriculture sector was 0.043, with a large critical ratio of 4.232. In discussing specific methods and approaches to drinking-water-quality management and surveillance, two of the five industrial sectors exhibit statistically significant relationships with the media, i.e. Transport and Logistics and Agriculture. The regression coefficients for magazines and journals and for newspapers as the independent variables for Transport and Logistics were 0.939 (3.663) and 0.01 (2.163). Similarly, the regression coefficient for newspapers as the explanatory variable for the Agriculture sector was 0.037 (3.737). These regression weights and their associated critical ratios point to statistically significant relationships between the mass media and relevant industrial sectors. In discussions around taking actions to adopt relevant WHO health recommendations, both newspapers, and magazines and journals have foregrounded the Agriculture sector. The regression weights and associated critical ratios for the two explanatory media sources of information were 1.233 (Magazines and Journals) and 0.046 (Newspapers). This result points to a statistically significant relationship between the media and the Agriculture sector.

5.3.3 Comparison of Effects from Direct Sources of Information and the Media on Industrial Sectors

The corpus analyses presented in the previous sections show that, in the communication and dissemination of the translated WHO Guidelines, Japanese mass media have taken a contrasting approach to that of more direct sources of information, i.e. government and political, top industrial and major business sources. Specifically, government and political sources have proven to be the most important sources of information. These sources of information have engaged with a range of industrial sectors in the discussion of specific aspects of the third WHO Guidelines. By contrast, the mass media (newspapers, and magazines and journals) have mainly focused on the agriculture sector, and to a lesser extent, the transport and logistics sector when discussing specific aspects of the translated WHO Guidelines. This section examines the impact of different sources of information and the media on the attribution of social accountability amongst industrial sectors. This is based on the Spearman's correlation test of the standardised effects from direct sources of information and the mass media on the five industrial sectors.

Table 5.6 shows the result of the Spearman's correlation test. The correlation coefficient provides a measure of the strength of association between direct sources of information and the two varieties of the mass media under study, i.e. newspapers, and magazines and journals. Coefficient scores range between negative one and positive one. Zero indicates no relationship between two

Table 5.6 *Spearman's correlation test of effects from direct sources of information and the mass media*

	Magazines and Journals		Newspapers	
	Correlation coefficient	Sig. (2-tailed)	Correlation coefficient	Sig. (2-tailed)
Government & Politics	−0.472*	0.035	−0.611**	0.004
Top Industrial Sources	−0.015	0.950	−0.668**	0.001
Major Business Sources	−0.241	0.307	−0.773**	0.000
Business Sources	−0.149	0.531	−0.238	0.313

* Correlation is significant at the 0.05 level (2-tailed).

variables. Within the positive spectrum of correlation scores, the larger the correlation coefficient, the stronger the relationship between two variables. A positive one indicates two identical variables. By contrast, if the correlation coefficient is negative, the larger the absolute value, the more different the two variables. In Table 5.6, an asterisk indicates that the correlation coefficient is significant at the 0.05 level. If the significance level is equal to or larger than 0.05, the correlation coefficient is not significant statistically. Table 5.6 shows that whilst Japanese magazines and journals were significantly different from government and political source of information (−0.472), they were largely similar to the other three direct sources of information. By contrast, Japanese newspapers were significantly different from three of the four direct sources of information: Government and Politics (−0.611); Top Industries (−0.668) and Major Business Sources (−0.773). Such results confirm the distinct approaches to the attribution of social visibility and accountability amongst industrial sectors on the part of direct sources of information and the media within the Japanese social and cultural system.

5.4 Conclusion

This chapter offered an original, quantitative analysis of how the rules, regulations and norms associated with the WHO drinking-water-quality guidelines have been translated and disseminated in the Japanese social and cultural system. It illustrated the important social role that direct sources of information such as government and politics and business have played in attributing social accountability amongst Japanese industrial sectors as the end users of the translated information. The corpus study analysed and reconfigured the complex process and pathways of the transmission of global health-policy materials, from international organisations to industrial sectors as the end users of translated materials in national contexts. We can see here evidence of how the bureaucracy in Japan acts as an agent of change (Pempel, 1992), disseminating information to promote the health of the citizenry as norms on water quality cascade down from the international to the national level. Along with the analysis of direct sources of information, we have also seen how newspapers, as a source of indirect information, play a distinctive role compared with three other direct sources of information: Government and Politics, Top Industrial Sources and Major Business Sources. This is especially salient in regard to the accountability of the agricultural sector. The evidence here shines a light on the continuing importance of newspapers as a source of information in Japan, with the household distribution of newspapers in 2016 standing at over 43 million (Nihon Shimbun Kyōkai, 2017). Whilst a decline in the number of newspapers distributed is taking place in the context of digital media, the agricultural sector continues to treat newspapers as an essential source of information in the area of water quality. Our study has developed formalised, analytical methods for the study of the role of institutional translations in facilitating and aiding important social and cultural changes. It has been able to deepen current understanding of the way information from international agencies becomes part of the national social and cultural systems by both direct and indirect means. In the case of the dissemination of the WHO Drinking-Water-Quality Guidelines in Japan, the government has provided the most important direct path and newspapers have served as the most important indirect path for the social diffusion of these guidelines. In this way, our study has highlighted the role of direct and indirect agents in the translation and dissemination of international water-quality standards in Japan.

References

Finnemore, Martha and Kathryn Sikkink (1998). International norm dynamics and political change, *International Organization* 52(4), 887–917.

Guidelines for Drinking Water Quality [Japanese version] (2004). Tokyo: Japan Water Works Association.

Johnson, Chalmers (1982). *Miti and the Japanese Miracle: The Growth of Industrial Policy: 1925–1975*. Stanford, CA: Stanford University Press.

Kosuge, Nobuhiko (1981). Development of waterworks in Japan, *Developing Economies* 19(1), 69–94

Miyagawa, Shigeru (2008). *The Oxford Handbook of Japanese Linguistics*. Oxford: Oxford University Press.

Nihon Shimbun Kyōkai [The Japanese Newspaper Publishers and Editors Association] (2017). Facts and figures. Pressnet (web). Available at: www.pressnet.or.jp/english/data/index.html.

Pempel, T. J. (1992). Bureaucracy in Japan, *Political Science and Politics* 25(1), 19–24

Tsujimura, Natsuko (2013). *An Introduction to Japanese Linguistics*. John Wiley and Sons.

World Health Organization (WHO) (2004). *Guidelines for Drinking-Water Quality* (3rd edition), Geneva: WHO.

Appendix 5A.1 *Bilingual Japanese-English terminology for translating WHO drinking-water-quality guidelines*

水源資管理	water-resource management
優良作業規程	code of good practice
コミュニティー飲料水供給	community drinking-water supplies
コミュニティー水源	community sources
コミュニティー給水システム	community water-supply system
コミュニティー管理水供給	community-managed supplies
障害調整生存年数	disability-adjusted life years
ヘルスケア施設	healthcare facilities
健康上の懸念	health concerns
健康危害因子	health hazards
健康上の成果	health outcome
健康成果目標	health-outcome targets
健康増進	health improvement
健康リスク	health risks
自家給水システム	household water-supply systems
ミレニアム開発目標	Millennium Development Goals
国の飲料水供給政策	national drinking water
処理性能目標	performance targets
潜在的健康便益	potential health benefits
公衆衛生の観点	public-health aspects
サービスレベル	service level
水質目標	water-quality targets
水資源保護	water-resource protection
健康に基づく目標	health-based targets
性能目標の設定	performance target setting
処理による達成度	treatment achievability
受容性	acceptability
許容レベル	acceptable level
水へのアクセス	access to water
水供給の充足度	adequacy of supply
経済的負担能力	affordability
公平性	equitability
目的に適合した	fit for purpose
目的への適合性	fitness for purpose
サーベイランスの独立性	independence of surveillance
独立機関によるサーベイランス	independent surveillance
国際基準	international standards
地域での適用	local adaptation
国としての優先度	national priorities
国の基準	national standards
国での適用	national adaptation
現実的配慮	practical considerations
危害因子の優先順位付け	prioritisation of hazards
飲料水中における重大さ	significance in drinking water
優先順位付け	priority setting
リスクに基づく策定	risk-based development

Appendix 5A.1 (*cont.*)

地域での活用	regional adaptive use
基準設定への住民参加	involvement in setting standards
耐容リスクの判定	judgement of tolerable risk
ベンチマーク	benchmarking
危害因子同定	hazard identification
リスクの定量評価	quantitative risk assessment
放射能分析	radioactivity analysis
対応計画	response plans
改善計画の立案と実施	planning and implementing improvement
代替アプローチ	alternative approaches
総合的予防の管理アプローチ	preventive integrated management approach
監査によるサーベイランス	audit-based surveillance
制御方策	control strategies
文書化	documentation
安全な飲料水の枠組み	framework for safe drinking water
飲料水の安全性に関する格付け	grading schemes for the safety of drinking water
総合的アプローチ	holistic approach
国の規制	national regulations
届け出レベル	notifiable level
問題の形式化	problem formulation
リスク特性	risk characterisation
リスク対有益性のアプローチ	risk–benefit approach
低減方策	strategies for reducing . . .
水安全計画	water-safety plans
管理手順	management procedures
承認	approval
監査	audit
制御手段	control measures
制御の維持	maintaining control
管理	management
運転監視	operational monitoring
再吟味	review
リスク評価	risk assessment
リスク管理	risk management
サーベイランス	surveillance
システム評価	system assessment
システム設計	system design
検証	verification
検証試験	verification testing
維持管理体制の確保	ensuring maintenance
運転の確保	ensuring operation
品質保証	quality assurance
品質管理	quality control
優先度設定のためのデータ活用	use of data for priority setting
プロセス制御	process control
複雑さのランク付け	ranking of complexity
コストのランク付け	ranking of costs

6 Developing Multilingual Automatic Semantic Annotation Systems

Laura Löfberg and Paul Rayson

6.1 Introduction

Early developments in the fields of natural language processing and corpus-based language studies were driven by the needs of descriptive language analysis, in particular for grammatical analysis and for lexicography. In addition, much early groundbreaking research was carried out on collecting, annotating and analysing English language corpora. In recent years, the focus has moved to higher levels of language analysis such as semantics, pragmatics and discourse, some of which are more amenable to automated methods than others. Similarly, the focus has widened to major European and world languages with larger national corpora being created, and the collection of web-derived and online social media corpora of many languages. This has supported and driven advancements in methods and resources in a wide range of human language technologies and linguistic description, not least for empirical translation studies of both manual and automatic translation.

In parallel with these developments, over the last couple of decades, a wide variety of semantic lexical resources have been created to support psycholinguistic, computational and corpus linguistics research projects. These include WordNet (Miller, 1995) and the UCREL Semantic Analysis System (USAS) semantic lexicon (Rayson et al., 2004). Large international collaborations have been organised to extend these semantic frameworks to cover more languages, for example EuroWordNet and Global WordNet. In this chapter, we report on the development and extension of USAS, originally developed for English only, to many more languages. This entails research on extending the semantic lexicons which provide the knowledge base for USAS, and also extending the USAS tagger itself to become a multilingual semantic analysis system.

The original English Semantic Tagger (EST) was developed in two research projects (1990–1996), motivated by the need to build a bridge between qualitative and quantitative analysis for market research interview transcripts. The original aim was to enable triangulation between the multiple-choice answers, that could be analysed quantitatively, and open-ended free text responses, where only small-scale manual qualitative studies could be employed. Previous content-analysis systems for text carried out their analyses on a subset of content-bearing words in interviews, in a restricted number of categories derived from prior psycholinguistic research. Such systems employed simple word lists and did not consider contextual disambiguation, so could not distinguish, for example, the modal verb ‘may’ from the temporal noun ‘May’, or determine whether ‘bank’ was related to finance, geographical features or aircraft manoeuvres. Another significant limitation of existing content-analysis systems was the lack of awareness of multi-word expressions (MWEs). A vast amount of research from a number of different perspectives has revealed the importance of MWEs. They impact on a number of areas including phraseology, theoretical and descriptive linguistics, foreign-language learning and teaching and lexicography, and take a number of potential forms: fixed expressions and idioms, collocations, lexical bundles, clusters and formulaic sequences. The key definitional criterion in the application of a semantic tagger was therefore to mark a phrase, which may be discontinuous (i.e. with intervening words as in the case of phrasal verbs), as an MWE if it needs to be assigned one coarse-grained meaning as a whole rather than to be tagged as separate words. In English, this can take the form of phrasal verbs (‘stubbed out’), noun phrases (‘riding boots’), proper names (‘United States of America’) or true non-compositional idioms (‘living the life of Riley’).

Such requirements led to the manual development of a large-scale single-word lexicon alongside an MWE lexicon, where entries in both were manually categorised into a set of possible coarse-grained semantic fields. Although as part of the original system design it would have been useful to apply full word sense disambiguation to words in a text, there needed to be a compromise in terms of what could be achieved automatically. A key decision was also required in terms of what categories or tags would be applied by the new semantic tagger. Unlike part-of-speech tagging, where there was little controversy about which word-class categories would be applied, in semantic analysis many different approaches could have been taken to encode semantic categories or what type of semantic relations were being modelled. The linguistic theory of semantic fields was adopted, and the initial category set from Tom McArthur’s Longman Lexicon of Contemporary English (McArthur, 1981) was applied and expanded based on experience with application and practice in a number of projects. The resulting USAS taxonomy centres on 21 major domains (as shown in Table 6.1) with a further 232 semantic tags arranged in a hierarchy, extending with positive and negative markers on some categories to indicate relationships within categories such as antonyms. Such a system allows for a general semantic analysis to be undertaken with a high degree of accuracy, resulting in applications such as an

Table 6.1 *USAS semantic taxonomy*

A general and abstract terms	B the body and the individual	C arts and crafts	E emotion
F food and farming	G government and public	H architecture, housing and the home	I money and commerce in industry
K entertainment, sports and games	L life and living things	M movement, location, travel and transport	N numbers and measurement
O substances, materials, objects and equipment	P education	Q language and communication	S social actions, states and processes
T time	W world and environment	X psychological actions, states and processes	Y science and technology
Z names and grammar			

intelligent dictionary and providing assistance for translators, which will be described later in this chapter.

The two semantic lexicons provide an invaluable knowledge base for the semantic tagger, where each word or MWE is assigned one or more potential semantic tags. The task of the automatic tagger itself is then to apply these to the text and make decisions about which tag is correct in each context, a process of semantic disambiguation. Multiple pieces of information come into play when deciding on the most appropriate tag for a word or MWE. The immediate sentence context, part of speech, and topic of the whole text can be used to inform this decision. A key element of the USAS semantic tagger framework is therefore a part-of-speech (POS) tagger, and for English the CLAWS tagger Garside and Smith (1997) also developed at Lancaster University, is employed. In general, the major word class rather than fine-grained POS tag is sufficient to help eliminate some contextually inappropriate semantic tags. Further, a lemmatiser which maps the input word to a dictionary headword with grammatical category, is vital to help in improving the coverage of the dictionary to inflectional variants. Thus, the USAS semantic tagger framework for English was created. In the early evaluations, it was deemed to be around 91 per cent accurate in determining the correct semantic tag in context (Rayson et al., 2004).

In the remainder of this chapter, in Section 6.2 we provide a brief summary of the development history of the semantic taggers from English into new languages and employing new methods. Section 6.3 provides a recipe or potentially a set of recipes for the computational extension of the general language system into new languages. Then, in Section 6.4, we turn to recent developments and domain-specific adaptations that may be needed in order to apply the system to particular challenges and topics. Finally, in Section 6.5, we look forward to more potential applications that the multilingual semantic framework will enable.

6.2 Development History beyond the English Tagger

The Finnish Semantic Tagger (henceforth FST) was the first non-English semantic tagger in the USAS framework. It was developed within an EU-funded language-technology project called Benedict – The New Intelligent Dictionary (2002–2005). This project produced various novel electronic-dictionary solutions, but the most innovative aim was to develop a context-sensitive dictionary search tool. This tool was based on semantic taggers for English and Finnish which provided semantic field information for the words under consideration. During the project, the existing semantic tagger for English was further refined and an equivalent semantic tagger for Finnish was developed (Löfberg et al., 2005). The second non-English semantic tagger in the framework was the Russian Semantic Tagger (henceforth RST). The RST was developed in the ASSIST (Automatic Semantic Assistance for Translators) project (2005–2007) to provide contextual examples of translation equivalents for words from the general lexicon between the language pair English and Russian (Mudraya et al., 2006).

The development processes of the EST, FST and RST were relatively similar, involving manual construction of the semantic lexicons by expert linguists who were native speakers of their respective languages. They created the initial versions of the lexicons by exploiting frequency lists, various other types of word lists of different domains and dictionaries. After a 'seed lexicon' for each language had been constructed, it was saved into the software component of the respective semantic tagger, and thus the working prototype of the semantic tagger was ready. Thereafter, candidates for new lexicon entries were collected by feeding texts and corpora from various sources into the semantic tagger and classifying words that remained unrecognised. No doubt there are still many single words and MWEs which would be worthwhile additions to the semantic lexicons; these should be detected and added to the lexicons. In addition, since language changes and evolves constantly, this necessitates updating the lexicons on a regular basis in the future as well to ensure that all the relevant and current vocabulary is included. In addition to including missing words, it would also be important to add missing senses for the existing lexicon entries. Expanding the single-word lexicons by adding new entries is a well-defined task. It would be practical to start by feeding newly produced text, e.g. newspapers or blogs, into the semantic taggers and again adding the unrecognised words which would be considered worthwhile additions to the lexicons. It would also be useful to substantially expand the coverage of the Z category for each language. This top-level category includes personal names (Z1), geographical names (Z2) and other proper names (Z3), such as trademarks and names of companies and institutions. By way of illustration, the geographical database GeoNames[1] could be a beneficial source. In addition, Wikipedia[2] offers various lists which could be utilised for this purpose. Senses which are discovered to be missing must also be included in the existing single-word lexicon entries. However, detecting missing senses is more challenging than detecting missing words, since missing senses cannot be searched for automatically, but this task requires manual checking.

The further development of the MWE lexicons is a much more complex and time-consuming task than the further development of the single-word lexicons. The first step involves expanding the size of each MWE lexicon in terms of entries. For this purpose as well, GeoNames and Wikipedia would be useful, along with information contained in freely available idiom dictionaries. Secondly, the MWE lexicon entries need to be written into templates (Rayson et al., 2004). The requirements for these templates vary depending on the structure and grammar of the language in terms of what types of MWEs exist.[3] The main aim in the development of such general language resources is to try to incorporate the core vocabulary of these languages into them. In other words, the purpose is not to include all the vocabulary in the language exhaustively, such as jargon, technical terms, colloquialisms or very rarely occurring proper nouns or other words; this would only result in an unmanageable lexicon size. In regard to adding missing senses to existing lexicon entries, it would be sensible to include all the commonly used senses and, additionally, develop better disambiguation mechanisms in order to be able to choose the correct sense in a given context.

It was evident that such manual construction of semantic lexicons is a very laborious and time-consuming task, and for this reason the UCREL team began to seek alternative methods for lexicon construction to further expand the USAS framework. During recent years, new semantic taggers have been developed, and new methods have been used to carry out lexicon development much more easily and rapidly. These methods involve bootstrapping new semantic lexical resources via automatically translating the semantic lexicons of the EST into other languages, followed by manual checking and

[1] www.geonames.org/. [2] www.wikipedia.org/.

[3] By way of illustration, some ideas for expanding the Finnish MWE lexicon and creating MWE templates which can recognise and tag Finnish MWEs are presented in Löfberg (2017).

improvement. As described in more detail in Section 6.3, this has proved a very successful approach for languages for which there are appropriate high-quality bilingual lexicons available (Piao et al., 2015). Another very promising approach for the lexicon construction for new languages is crowd-sourcing. El-Haj et al. (2017) carried out experiments using Mechanical Turk workers who were native speakers of their respective languages and compared the results obtained with the results from similar tasks performed by expert linguists. The authors came to the conclusion that the results were comparable and that it is indeed possible for non-expert native speakers to apply the hierarchical semantic taxonomy without prior training by utilising an easy-to-use graphical interface to assist the semantic tag selection and the annotation process.

Consequently, in addition to the English, Finnish and Russian Semantic Taggers, there are equivalent semantic taggers and semantic lexicons now for Czech, Chinese (Piao, Hu and Rayson 2015), Dutch, French, Italian, Malay, Portuguese, Spanish (Jiménez et al., 2017), Urdu and Welsh (Piao et al., 2017b). Furthermore, there are plans to extend the USAS framework next for Arabic (Mohamed, Potts and Hardie, 2013), Norwegian and Swedish. The lexical coverage potential of twelve languages was evaluated in Piao et al. (2016). Many of these semantic taggers and lexicons are available via the USAS web interface.[4]

When developing the semantic lexicons for the FST and the RST, it was discovered that the semantic categories developed originally for the EST did not require any modification, but they were found entirely suitable for the semantic categorisation of objects and phenomena in Finnish and Russian as well. The shared semantic categories thus function as a type of a 'meta-dictionary' or 'lingua franca' between the languages (Löfberg et al., 2005; Mudraya et al., 2006, 293–294). Partly, this may be due to the fact that the cultures of these three countries share many similarities. Another reason may be the fact that the USAS semantic categories are relatively general and can thus be successfully applied across many cultures. However, the semantic categories may well require adjustment if they are to be applied to the analysis of languages in significantly different cultures. Qian and Piao (2009, 189–191) reported interesting findings which emerged when they were modifying the USAS tag set to develop a semantic annotation scheme for Chinese kinship terms. They noticed that the Chinese kinship system is not only much finer-grained but is also quite different from the English kinship system. Thus, even if the USAS scheme was made finer-grained by subdividing the existing categories further, the scheme would not be able to cover the type of distinctions which are made in the Chinese language.

[4] For more information, see http://ucrel.lancs.ac.uk/usas/.

The purpose of the USAS category system has been to provide a conception of the world that is as general and wide a coverage as possible, and, therefore, it does not include detailed fine-grained distinctions. This is illustrated with the example of birds. The USAS category system does not have a specific category for birds, but birds as well as other animals are all grouped together in the category L2 ('Living Creatures Generally') which belongs in the top-level category L ('Life and Living Things'). If necessary for a particular task, the category system can be flexibly expanded further by adding more subcategories, such as 'Creatures of the Land', 'Creatures of the Sea' and 'Creatures of the Air'. The subcategory 'Creatures of the Air' could be further expanded into subcategories, such as 'Wild Birds' and 'Domestic Birds'. However, the classification of words into such finer-grained categories might be problematic, since, for instance, birds which are considered to be wild by one culture may be considered pets by another (Archer et al., 2004, 823–824).

The EST has not only been ported to many new languages but it has also been redesigned to create a historical semantic tagger for English, the Historical Thesaurus Semantic Tagger (HTST; Piao et al., 2017a). The HTST complements the semantic tags used in the EST; it offers finer-grained meaning distinctions for use in word sense disambiguation (WSD) by incorporating a large-scale historical English thesaurus linked to the *Oxford English Dictionary*. Its historically valid semantic annotation scheme contains in all approximately 225,000 semantic concepts and 4,033 thematic semantic categories. The development of the HTST has been closely connected to the development of the *Historical Thesaurus of English* at the University of Glasgow (Kay et al., 2009).

6.3 A Computational Recipe for Extending USAS to New Languages

As already outlined in the previous two sections, manual creation of the semantic lexicons for EST, FST and RST was a painstaking long-term process. Supervised methods tend to produce better results than unsupervised ones, so the intention was to follow a similar knowledge-based framework for further new languages. In the case of FST and RST, the new semantic lexicons took around 1–2 person years to create and evaluate in each case. Thus, to allow further expansion in a shorter amount of time, it was necessary to carry out a feasibility study for automatically porting semantic lexical resources to new languages. The first approach taken was to employ existing bilingual lexicon resources and POS taggers to bootstrap prototype USAS lexicons and taggers for Chinese, Italian and Portuguese. Good quality bilingual dictionaries are important for such a process, and FreeLang word lists[5] were used for

[5] www.freelang.net/dictionary.

English–Italian and English–Portuguese, alongside Routledge frequency dictionaries for Chinese (Xiao, Rayson and McEnery, 2009) and Portuguese (Davies and Preto-Bay, 2007).[6] Combined with this were the Stanford Chinese word segmenter and POS tagger (Toutanova et al., 2003), and the TreeTagger for Italian and Portuguese (Schmid, 1994). Full details are described in Piao et al. (2015), but these initial experiments resulted in reasonable lexical coverage figures for Chinese (81 per cent), Portuguese (73 per cent) and Italian (65 per cent) and tagging precisions for Chinese (76 per cent), Italian (56 per cent) and Portuguese (83 per cent). Further manual checking and improvement of the prototype lexicons will clearly be required. However, the experiments reported in Piao et al. (2015) show that it is feasible to automatically transfer existing semantic lexicons to new languages to develop prototype taggers. Further approaches to generate a new semantic lexicon in a different language are to use machine translation or translation memory approaches. For the Czech language, a parallel corpus aligned at the word level using GIZA++, can be tagged by the EST and then semantic tags are transferred to Czech using the word alignments, and finally a Czech semantic lexicon can be derived (Piao et al., 2016). As described above, a crowdsourcing approach has also been adopted to evaluate the potential for non-experts (those who are not trained on the USAS taxonomy in advance) to assign semantic categories to words.

Further work is ongoing, for example in Welsh and Urdu, to use distributional vector-based approaches to derive and group words in a second language by porting the English system. Named entity recognition and gazetteers will also be employed to extend the coverage of proper nouns and MWEs representing organisational entities and place names in new languages. A key challenge remains in the automatic assignment of semantic categories to previously unclassified words and MWEs. Although it is straightforward to list the unmatched words in a text, it is more difficult to select appropriate semantic fields. Thesauri and similar distributional groupings are potential solutions here. The automatic assignment of semantic categories to new MWEs is doubly difficult, especially for non-compositional idiomatic expressions, where the individual word components of an MWE offer no clue as to its meaning as a whole expression.

6.4 Domain-Specific Applications

In Section 6.3, we discussed different approaches for the development of the USAS semantic lexicons as general language resources. Manual development involves a large investment of time and effort, but the process can nevertheless

[6] However, for many languages, such as Finnish, this approach would not be feasible because of the lack of freely available high-quality bilingual lexicons.

be made more efficient and facilitated by utilising computational methods, as became evident above. However, much less work would be required if the semantic lexical resources were tailored for a specific purpose to deal with only one particular domain or task. In such a case, only the relevant single words and MWEs would need to be recognised and thus recorded in the semantic lexical resources, rather than any single word or MWE which could be considered as belonging to general standard modern language, as would be the case when developing a general language resource.

In the following subsections, we will briefly suggest how to tailor and extend the existing general language resources for specific tasks, using Internet content monitoring and psychological profiling.[7] These suggestions do not only apply to tailoring existing semantic lexicons for domain-specific tasks, but, naturally, it is also possible to create domain- and task-specific semantic lexicons to new languages from scratch in similar manner, without developing a general language lexicon first.

6.4.1 Semi-Automatic Internet Content Monitoring

The semantic lexicons could be reoriented for developing a semi-automatic Internet content-monitoring program which could be used for browsing quickly and efficiently through Internet text in order to detect certain predefined characteristics of speech. To achieve this, it would first be necessary to identify and record the type of speech which is to be detected, and, subsequently, incorporate a search engine component within the semantic tagger to locate such speech. The monitoring program would not be fully automatic, but it would rather be a semi-automatic preprocessing tool. If the monitoring program discovered questionable content, it would alert a human supervisor, such as a moderator of a discussion forum, and guide him to the relevant spot on the website. This person could check to see if there is reason for concern and then intervene, if considered necessary. This type of arrangement could be seen as a sensible division of work between the human being and the computer. The human being would write the rules according to which the computer would do all the hard and monotonous work, while the human being would still be in charge of the end result by manually checking the possible findings of the computer.

Detecting hate speech targeted at immigrants, which is a common problem among user-created content in social media websites, provides a good example case. The first step in the creation of the proposed application would be to study

[7] In addition, the EST has already been tested for the task of sentiment analysis (Simm et al., 2010) and the FST has been tested for the task of named entity recognition (Kettunen and Löfberg, 2017). For further details of the domain-specific applications, see Löfberg (2017).

the relevant linguistic features which need to be recognised. Various sources could be utilised for gathering the necessary background information. A particularly valuable source would be the logging of messages which have been deemed unacceptable earlier by the moderators and which, therefore, have been deleted from the website. Many websites also provide a possibility for their users to report inappropriate messages; these would undoubtedly contain very useful material as well. Furthermore, consulting specialists, literature and studies in the given field would be beneficial.

The lexicon construction should not occur only at the initial stages of the development process, but the lexicons should continuously be updated and improved. The most practical method for this could be to examine the material which the monitoring program has identified as possibly alarming and has sent over to the moderators to check manually. In case this material indeed contains unacceptable content, it is likely that in the vicinity there are also other relevant single words and MWEs which would be important to recognise but which are not recorded in the application yet. Constant lexicon development is also necessary because, to evade an automatic moderation system, writers may try to obscure the words in their questionable text with, for example, intentional misspellings and expanded spelling, that is, they may separate the characters by spaces or punctuation marks (Warner and Hirschberg, 2012, 21). Such attempts must be detected, and, subsequently, the monitoring program must be trained to recognise questionable words and MWEs nevertheless.

The first procedure in the development of the proposed application would be to find hits for certain relevant single words and MWEs irrespective of the semantic category they fall into. Derogatory words used for referring to immigrants[8] and other words which often occur in such text type would be important to recognise, for example, 'race', 'racial', 'scum', 'terrorist', 'rape', 'rapist', 'patriot', 'home country', 'multiculturality' and 'ethnic cleansing'. Perhaps also some proper names which tend to appear in connection with this type of writing would provide useful clues for detecting questionable content, for example, Hitler or Breivik (Anders Behring Breivik, the Norwegian who committed the Norway 2011 attacks).

Even though the single words and MWEs listed above could be of interest here irrespective of the semantic category they fall into, they should somehow be labelled together as alarming and thus relevant patterns for the program to recognise. It would be practical to group all of them under the same semantic tag for the suggested application. Such a semantic tag could be, for example, A15-/E3,[9] in which the semantic tag A15- signifies risk and danger, while the

[8] See, for example, the list of ethnic slurs in English at https://en.wikipedia.org/wiki/List_of_ethnic_slurs_by_ethnicity.

[9] The full tag set can be viewed at http://ucrel.lancs.ac.uk/usas/.

semantic tag E3- signifies violence and anger. An alternative solution would be to establish an entirely new semantic category for these single words and MWEs or subdivide further an existing category.

Secondly, in addition to looking for certain predefined single words and MWEs within text, it would also be possible to make use of semantic field information to find relevant results. Such semantic tags which could provide useful clues for revealing the sentiments behind the text in the proposed application include, for example:

E3- (e.g. 'angry', 'attack', 'torture', 'beat half to death', 'drive mad')
L1- (e.g. 'assassinate', 'kill', 'drop dead', 'wipe out')
G3 (e.g. 'ambush', 'shoot', 'machine gun')
S9 (e.g. 'Islam', 'Christian', 'mosque', 'Day of Judgement',)
Z2/S2 (e.g. 'immigrant', 'foreigner', 'Kurd', 'Somali', 'asylum seeker')
X7+ (e.g. 'intend', 'plan', 'want')

The Internet content-monitoring program could monitor the incoming messages in real time. Such messages in which the program does not detect any questionable content could be passed on directly to the website. In turn, such messages in which the program does discover questionable content could be directed to the moderators for manual checking. Statistical methods could be utilised for weighting the findings of the program to be able to arrange them in the order of urgency and to detect the most questionable spots in text. Successful implementation of weighting mechanisms would significantly further improve the performance of the program and eliminate the possibility of false alarms. In addition, machine learning techniques could be utilised to combine the potential features and learn which were most productive for that specific task.

Yet another issue to consider in the development of such applications is the often quite informal nature of 'Internet language' which includes various colloquialisms in terms of vocabulary, spelling and grammar. It would be possible to train the program to cope with these features, for example by incorporating an additional semantic lexicon containing colloquial vocabulary and emoticons into the semantic tagger as well a tool to help deal with spelling variation. One example of such a tool is Variant Detector (VARD) which was originally developed at Lancaster University for the analysis of Early Modern English texts. Utilising techniques which are employed in modern spellchecking software, VARD processes spelling variants in texts into an output with modernised forms. This enables the study of historical texts with the same linguistic tools and methods which are used for modern language (Baron and Rayson, 2009). VARD has lately been enabled to process any form of possible spelling variation, and it can also be applied to languages other than English by incorporating a new language dictionary and spelling rules into the VARD software.[10] Spelling errors, which often appear in online discussions and blog postings, could also be addressed by using VARD or similar mechanisms to preprocess the text and to match the erroneous forms with correct forms. VARD has already been applied for the detection of spelling errors in written learner corpora (Rayson and Baron, 2011).

Following the procedures suggested above, it would also be possible to tailor the semantic taggers and their lexical resources for detecting, for example:

- hate speech characteristic of violent offenders, such as school shooters,
- hate speech targeted at sexual or other minorities,
- rape threats,
- paedophiles,
- suicidal ideation, and
- cyber-bullying, cyber-harassment and cyber-stalking.

6.4.2 Psychological Profiling

The semantic taggers and their lexicons could be tailored for the purposes of psychological profiling as well. In fact, the EST has already been tested for this task. It was used together with the *Dictionary of Affect in Language* (Whissell and Dewson, 1986) in a study by Hancock, Woodworth and Porter (2013) which examined the features of crime narratives provided by psychopathic homicide offenders. The results revealed that the offenders of the test group described their crimes, powerful emotional events, in an idiosyncratic manner. Their narratives contained an increased number of cause-and-effect statements, with a relatively high number of subordinating conjunctions, and a great number of references to basic physiological and self-preservation needs, such as eating, drinking and money. They were less emotional and less positive, and their increased use of past tense indicated that they wanted to distance themselves from the murders (Hancock, Woodworth and Porter, 2013, 110–111).

If the semantic taggers of the USAS framework and their lexicons were used for psychological profiling in the future, it might be useful to expand their affective vocabulary. This would potentially obviate the need to use a complementary dictionary of affect in language. For instance, the following semantic categories contain affective vocabulary:

E2 Liking
E3 Calm/Violent/Angry
E4.1 Happy/Sad: Happy
E4.2 Happy/Sad: Contentment

[10] For more information, see http://ucrel.lancs.ac.uk/vard/about. Unfortunately, VARD is not yet applicable to highly inflectional languages, such as Finnish, which would require lemmatisation as preprocessing.

E5 Fear/Bravery/Shock
E6 Worry, Concern/Confident
S7.2 Respect
X5.2 Interest/Boredom/Excited/Energetic

Thus, to create different types of psychological profiles, the relevant combinations of semantic categories need to be recognised and, if necessary, expanded with new entries which are relevant for the task at hand. As was the case with the Internet content-monitoring application suggested above, this application would also benefit from the incorporation of an additional semantic lexicon containing colloquial vocabulary and VARD or similar mechanisms to help to deal with the spelling variation and possible spelling errors.

6.5 Multilingual Applications

The USAS framework now includes equivalent semantic taggers based on equivalent semantic lexicons for Czech, Chinese, Dutch, English, Finnish, French, Italian, Malay, Portuguese, Russian, Spanish, Urdu and Welsh. In addition to developing monolingual applications, the equivalent structure enables the development of multilingual applications. Two bilingual applications already exist. The first bilingual application was the context-sensitive dictionary search tool for English and Finnish which was developed in the Benedict project. The second bilingual application was the automatic semantic assistance tool for translators developed in the ASSIST project which utilised the semantic taggers for English and Russian. It would now be possible to try the semantic taggers in such applications between many more language pairs. It would also be possible to utilise the semantic taggers, for example, for the purposes of machine translation and cross-lingual plagiarism detection.

Moreover, it would be intriguing to apply the semantic taggers for cross-lingual information extraction. In fact, in March 2016, the BBC organised a multilingual NewsHACK event themed ‘Multilingual Journalism: Tools for Future News’ in which they offered an opportunity for teams of language-technology researchers to work with their own tools with multilingual data from the BBC’s connected studio. ‘Team 1’ from Lancaster University used the semantic taggers for English, Chinese and Spanish and built a prototype tool named ‘Multilingual Reality Check’ to bridge related news stories across these languages. As a result, journalists can simply click on news stories in the system, and the system will show them related articles in the other languages, ranked in order of relevance (ESRC Centre for Corpus Approaches to Social Science, 2016). A similar application might be found very useful worldwide across many more languages.

6.6 Conclusion

In this chapter, we have summarised the development of the USAS software framework and semantic lexicons over a period of twenty-seven years. With the original application of the English system to market research interview analysis, it has significantly expanded to cover many other languages and to be employed in a wide range of applications including manual and automatic translation assistance. We have described manual and automatic processes and recipes for expanding the coverage of the lexicons and semantic taggers, along with proposals for domain-specific applications and extensions, not just of individual language systems, but together these will be powerful tools to support research in cross-lingual and multilingual scenarios.

Acknowledgements

Paul Rayson's involvement in this research work is partially funded by the UK Economic and Social Research Council (ESRC) and Arts and Humanities Research Council (AHRC) as part of the CorCenCC (Corpws Cenedlaethol Cymraeg Cyfoes; The National Corpus of Contemporary Welsh) Project (Grant Number ES/M011348/1).

References

Archer, D., P. Rayson, S. Piao and T. McEnery (2004). Comparing the UCREL semantic annotation scheme with lexicographical taxonomies. In G. Williams and S. Vessier (eds.), *Proceedings of the 11th EURALEX Congress* (pp. 817–827). Morbihan: Université de Bretagne Sud.

Baron, A., and P. Rayson (2009). Automatic standardization of texts containing spelling variation: How much training data do you need? In M. Mahlberg, V. González-Díaz and C. Smith (eds.), *Proceedings of Corpus Linguistics 2009*. Liverpool: University of Liverpool.

Davies, M. and A. Preto-Bay (2007). A Frequency Dictionary of Portuguese. London: Routledge.

El-Haj, M., P. Rayson, S. Piao and S. Wattam (2017). Creating and validating multilingual semantic representations for six languages: Expert versus non-expert crowds. In *EACL 2017 Workshop on Sense, Concept and Entity Representations and Their Applications*. Valencia. Association for Computational Linguistics.

ESRC Centre for Corpus Approaches to Social Science (2016). NewsHack 2016 retrospective. ESRC Centre for Corpus Approaches to Social Science (website). Retrieved from http://cass.lancs.ac.uk/?p=1978.

Garside, R., and N. Smith (1997). A hybrid grammatical tagger: CLAWS4. In R. Garside, G. Leech and A. McEnery (eds.), *Corpus Annotation: Linguistic Information from Computer Text Corpora* (pp. 102–121). London: Longman.

Hancock, J. T.,M. T. Woodworth and S. Porter (2013). Hungry like the wolf: A word-pattern analysis of the language of psychopaths. *Legal and Criminological Psychology* 18(1), 102–114.

Jiménez, R. M., H. Sanjurjo-González, P. E. Rayson and S. S. Piao (2017). Building a Spanish lexicon for corpus analysis. In The 35th International Conference of AESLA. 2017.AESLA.

Kay, C., J. Roberts, M. Samuels and I. Wotherspoon (2009). Unlocking the *OED*: The story of the Historical Thesaurus of the OED. In C. Kay, J. Roberts, M. Samuels and I. Wotherspoon (eds.), *Historical Thesaurus of the Oxford English Dictionary* Oxford: Oxford University Press, pp. xiii–xx.

Kettunen, K. and L. Löfberg (2017). Tagging named entities in 19th century and modern Finnish newspaper material with a Finnish semantic tagger. Paper presented at NoDaLiDa 2017, Gothenburg.

Löfberg, L. (2017). Creating large semantic lexical resources for the Finnish language. Doctoral thesis. Lancaster University.

Löfberg, L., S. Piao, P. Rayson, J-P. Juntunen, A. Nykänen and K. Varantola (2005). A semantic tagger for the Finnish language. In *Proceedings of the Corpus Linguistics 2005 Conference*. Proceedings from the Corpus Linguistics Conference Series online e-journal: www.birmingham.ac.uk/Documents/college-artslaw/corpus/conference-archives/2005-journal/LanguageProcessingandCorpustool/Asemantictagger.doc.

McArthur, T. (1981). Longman Lexicon of Contemporary English. London: Longman.

Miller, G. A. (1995). WordNet: A lexical database for English, Communications of the ACM, 38(11), 39–41.

Mohamed, G., A. Potts and A. Hardie (2013). AraSAS: A semantic tagger for Arabic. Paper presented at Second Workshop on Arabic Corpus Linguistics, Lancaster University, United Kingdom.

Mudraya, O.,B. Babych, S. Piao, P. Rayson and A. Wilson (2006). Developing a Russian semantic tagger for automatic semantic annotation. In *Proceedings of Corpus Linguistics 2006* St. Petersburg, pp. 290–297.

Piao, S., F. Bianchi, C. Dayrell, A. D'Egidio and P. Rayson (2015). Development of the multilingual semantic annotation system. In The 2015 Conference of the North American Chapter of the Association for Computational Linguistics – Human Language Technologies (NAACL HLT 2015). Association for Computational Linguistics, pp. 1268–1274.

Piao, S. S., X. Hu and P. Rayson (2015). Towards a semantic tagger for analysing contents of Chinese corporate reports. Paper presented at the 4th International Conference on Information Science and Cloud Computing (ISCC 2015).

Piao, S., P. Rayson, D. Archer, F. Bianchi, C. Dayrell, M. El-Haj, R. Jiménez, D. Knight, M. Kren, L. Löfberg, R. A. Nawab, J. Shafi, P. L. Teh and O. Mudraya (2016). Lexical coverage evaluation of large-scale multilingual semantic lexicons for twelve languages. In Proceedings of the *10th Edition of the Language Resources and Evaluation Conference (LREC2016)* European Language Resources Association (ELRA), pp. 2614–2619.

Piao, S. S., F. Dallachy, A. Baron, J. E. Demmen, S. Wattam, P. Durkin, J. McCracken, P. Rayson and M. Alexander (2017a). A time-sensitive historical thesaurus-based semantic tagger for deep semantic annotation, *Computer Speech and Language* 46, 113–135.

Piao, S. S., P. E. Rayson, D. Knight, G. Watkins, and K. Donnelly (2017b). Towards a Welsh semantic tagger: Creating lexicons for a resource poor language. Paper presented at the Corpus Linguistics Conference 2017, University of Birmingham, United Kingdom.

Qian, Y., and S. Piao (2009). The development of a semantic annotation scheme for Chinese kinship, *Corpora* 4(2), 189–208.

Rayson, P., D. Archer, S. Piao and T. McEnery (2004). The UCREL semantic analysis system. In Proceedings of LREC-04 Workshop: Beyond Named Entity Recognition Semantic Labeling for NLP Tasks. Lisbon, Portugal: European Language Resources Association (ELRA), pp. 7–12.

Rayson, P., and A. Baron (2011). Automatic error tagging of spelling mistakes in learner corpora. In F. Meunier, S. De Cock, G. Gilquin and M. Paquot (eds.), *A Taste for Corpora: In Honour of Sylviane Granger.* Amsterdam: John Benjamins, pp. 109–126.

Schmid, H. (1994). Probabilistic part-of-speech tagging using decision trees. Proceedings of International Conference on New Methods in Language Processing. Manchester, UK: University of Manchester.

Simm, W., M. A. Ferrario, S. Piao, J. Whittle and P. Rayson (2010). Classification of short text comments by sentiment and actionability for VoiceYourView. In *2010 IEEE Second International Conference on Social Computing (SocialCom)* IEEE, pp. 552–557.

Toutanova, K., D. Klein, C. Manning and Y. Singer (2003). Feature-rich part-of-speech tagging with a cyclic dependency network. In Proceedings of HLT-NAACL 2003. Stroudsburg, PA: Association for Computational Linguistics, pp. 252–259.

Warner, W., and J. Hirschberg (2012). Detecting hate speech on the World Wide Web. In *Proceedings of the Second Workshop on Language in Social Media.* Stroudsburg, PA: Association for Computational Linguistics, pp. 19–26.

Whissell, C. M. and M. R. Dewson (1986). A dictionary of affect in language: III. Analysis of two biblical and two secular passages. Perceptual and Motor Skills 62(1), 127–132.

Xiao, R., P. Rayson and T. McEnery (2009). A Frequency Dictionary of Mandarin Chinese: Core Vocabulary for Learners. London: Routledge.

7 Leveraging Large Corpora for Translation Using Sketch Engine

Sara Moze and Simon Krek

7.1 Introduction

Recent advances in computer science and information technology have completely revolutionised the way linguists and language professionals carry out their jobs. In the Digital Age, data availability is no longer an issue, with a wide selection of open-source databases, dictionaries, glossaries, data sets and software being freely accessible online to users all across the globe. Computers have become increasingly sophisticated over the past couple of decades, and this fact has had important implications for users and developers of language technologies alike – not only do these powerful machines enable us to build very large, linguistically annotated text corpora, but they can also be used to develop and run robust and user-friendly software suites that allow users to process and analyse large collections of data, completing simple search queries in a mere fraction of a second. To create a corpus, linguists and language professionals are no longer required to perform time-consuming, tedious tasks involving slow machines – instead, they can either access pre-existing online corpora or create their own from the comfort of their homes. Both the accessibility of computer technology and the amount of linguistic data provided by corpora have opened up endless possibilities for academics, teachers and language professionals, who are now integrating corpus data and tools in their daily workflows. For instance, whilst academics are increasingly using corpora as the main source of linguistic evidence for their research (cf. Sinclair 1991, 2004; McEnery and Wilson, 2001; Hanks, 2013), language teachers can analyse learner corpora to detect common student errors and search monolingual reference corpora to create handouts and to extract good illustrative examples for in-class exercises (cf. O'Keefe, McCarthy and Carter, 2007; Timmis, 2015; Thomas, 2016), and lexicographers use corpus samples to identify word senses and extract good dictionary examples for their entries (cf. Atkins and Rundell, 2008). Translators are not an exception – not only can they search parallel and comparable corpora to identify translation equivalents and collocations, but they can also use monolingual reference corpora to explore the way a word is used in different contexts and to extract domain-specific terminology in support of their projects.

As the past three decades saw the rise of corpora in mainstream linguistics, the need for robust and user-friendly corpus query systems (CQSs) has become increasingly pronounced. Originally, CQSs were imagined as downloadable tools to be installed and run on one's personal computer, with popular CQSs such as the old-school Wordsmith Tools (Scott, 2018) and, more recently, AntConc (Anthony, 2018) dominating the landscape. Whilst these tools are robust and user-friendly, offering users attractive basic features (e.g. concordance, keywords, collocations), they typically do not come with pre-loaded data, which means that is entirely up to the user to gain access to existing corpora or to build their own. One can see how this poses a serious issue for translators, who need access to a wide variety of general and domain-specific textual collections in several languages and language pairs. Building a new corpus entails more than just gaining access to a large text file, as a corpus has to be lemmatised and tagged with linguistic information (e.g. part-of-speech tags) to allow the user to extract relevant information from it (e.g. collocations, terminology). Whilst CQSs integrate functionalities that enable users to pre-process corpora, advanced procedures such as part-of-speech tagging require the use of stand-alone statistical computational tools (i.e. taggers and parsers) and large collections of complementary, language-specific data such as word form lexicons, which might not be easily accessible for the selected language. These procedures also require a certain level of technical expertise to execute, which is partly why translators are still relatively reluctant to integrate corpora into their daily workflow. Sketch Engine provides a solution to this problem by offering users access to both high-quality, linguistically annotated data and a powerful suite of user-friendly corpus tools to process it, therefore enabling users to successfully sidestep the issue altogether.

Sketch Engine (Kilgarriff et al., 2014a) is a web-based, multifunctional corpus query and management system that is widely used by linguists, lexicographers, language teachers and translators all across the globe. Offering state-of-the-art modules, very large monolingual and parallel corpora for more than ninety languages, and advanced lexicographic tools such as Tickbox Lexicography (cf. Kilgarriff, Kovář and Rychlý, 2010), the tool has been used for important large-scale lexicographic projects at all major dictionary houses, including Oxford University Press, Collins, Macmillan, Cambridge University Press, Le Robert, Cornelsen Verlag and Shogakukan. Despite its general popularity and enormous potential for translators, the tool remains majorly under-utilised in commercial translation environments. By means of a case study, this chapter will demonstrate how translators can harness the immense power of corpora and the plethora of tools available through the Sketch Engine, i.e. the multifunctional concordancer, the 'Word Sketches' tool, the statistical thesaurus, the term-extraction feature and the corpus-building tool, to inform their professional practice.

The case study is centred around a real-life translation scenario: a Slovene freelance translator is commissioned to produce translations of several Slovene governmental webpages providing basic information on EU-related topics. As part of the project, they are asked to translate a short informative text titled 'Kaj je Lizbonska pogodba' ('What is the Lisbon Treaty'?)[1] into English. The translator has good computer literacy skills and is accustomed to using computer-assisted translation (CAT) and corpus tools in their everyday professional life. As a result, they regularly use MemoQ for all their translation projects, and have a full subscription to Sketch Engine. Being a freelancer, they do not have access to the same variety of computational and translation resources as translators working for an agency, e.g. very large translation memories (TMs), sophisticated machine translation (MT) systems and post-editing modules. In this chapter, we shall explore how such a translator can make best use of the tools at their disposal, i.e. mainly the Sketch Engine, to enhance the translation process and ensure that quality and consistency are maintained throughout the translation.

7.2 Context and Collocation

7.2.1 Using Parallel Corpora to Find Translation Equivalents

In its most basic function, Sketch Engine serves as a sophisticated concordancer, allowing users to search for any word or phrase in a monolingual, parallel or comparable corpus in order to explore the way it is used in context by real users of the language. Despite being relatively simple and easy to use, the concordancer offers several advanced search options; users are not only able to search for specific word forms, lemmas and phrases, but they can also further refine their search by limiting their query to a specific subcorpus or text type (e.g. medical or legal texts), and to define which words or parts of speech typically co-occur with the searched item in its immediate left and right context. Advanced users can benefit from the integrated Corpus Query Language (CQL) builder, which enables them to search for specific word combinations and syntactic constructions within the selected corpus, as shown in Figure 7.1.

Through Sketch Engine, users are given access to more than 400 corpora covering over 90 languages, which is particularly valuable for translators working with under-resourced languages and language pairs. Whilst parallel

[1] The full text is available online from: https://e-uprava.gov.si/drzava-in-druzba/e-demokracija/o-demokraticnih-procesih/demokracija-v-eu/kaj-je-lizbonska-pogodba.html.

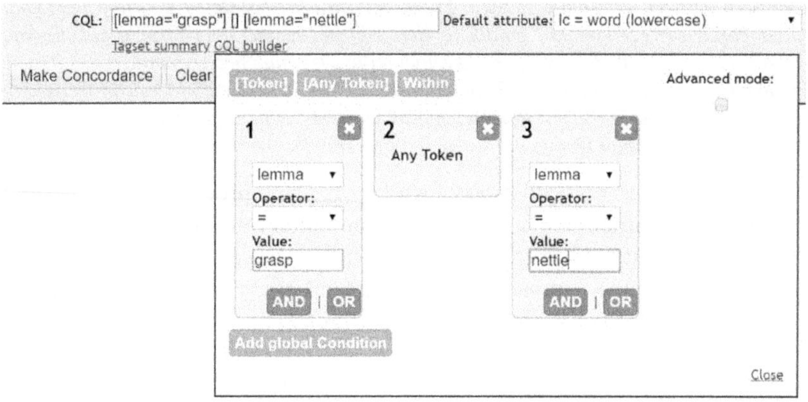

Figure 7.1 Building a query for the idiom *grasp the nettle* with the CQL builder

corpora are by far the most relevant source of data offered by Sketch Engine, translators can also use monolingual corpora to compare how frequently different near-synonyms or translation equivalents appear in the corpus in order to assess which is the most natural to use in a specific context. In addition, monolingual corpora are also typically used as the primary source of data to extract collocations and to generate the thesaurus.

By contrast, parallel corpora are mainly used by translators to identify possible translations of a word or phrase and select the most appropriate option based on the context in which the translation equivalent typically appears. As segments within a parallel corpus are sentence-aligned, these corpora function as large and fully searchable TMs. Although popular CAT tools (e.g. MemoQ and SDL Trados) integrate corpus query and management tools, this often comes at the price of user-friendliness, as the ensuing multi-functional interfaces are often perceived as too complex and difficult to operate by the translators (cf. Zaretskaya, Corpas Pastor and Seghiri, 2016). The Sketch Engine, on the other hand, offers a clean and straightforward interface incorporating several additional modules and functionalities (e.g. 'Word Sketches', the sketch-difference tool and the thesaurus), allowing translators to search through the corpora and extract information more efficiently than they would using a simple CAT tool. Take, for instance, our fellow Slovene translator, who has just started translating the Lisbon Treaty text in MemoQ. As they make their way through the text, they identify a number of terms and multi-word expressions they are not quite sure how to translate. One of the sentences contains the expression 'postopek soodločanja' ('co-decision procedure'):

Original (source language – SL): *Predvsem zaradi pogostejše uporabe* ***postopka soodločanja*** *pri oblikovanju politik je Evropski parlament na področju zakonodaje EU postal enakopraven z Evropskim svetom, ki je zastopnik držav članic.*
Translation (target language – TL): *As the ____________ is being increasingly used to shape policies, the European Parliament has, in terms of EU legislation, gained equal status to the European Community, which represents the member states.*

The translator automatically jots down 'co-decision procedure/process' and 'the procedure/process of co-decision' as potential translations of 'postopek soodločanja', but wishes to seek confirmation from a corpus or dictionary before finalising the sentence. Luckily, Sketch Engine offers several parallel corpora covering the EU domain, most of which are available for the twenty-plus languages of the EU, e.g. Eur-Lex, Eur-Lex judgements (a subset of Eur-Lex), DGT and Europarl. The translator selects the Slovene Eur-Lex judgements subcorpus as the starting point and generates a parallel concordance by entering the Slovene expression into the 'simple query' box and selecting the English Eur-Lex judgement subcorpus in the 'Parallel query' field, as shown in Figure 7.2.

The Eur-Lex judgement corpus contains thirty-nine instances of 'postopek soodločanja', which are displayed, alongside their English translations, in the parallel concordance (cf. Figure 7.3). By inspecting the concordance, the translator can unequivocally determine that the most likely translation of the Slovene phrase is 'co-decision procedure', with 'co-decision' being typically spelled with a hyphen. This is a very simple and straightforward example of how a parallel concordance can help translators instantly identify translation

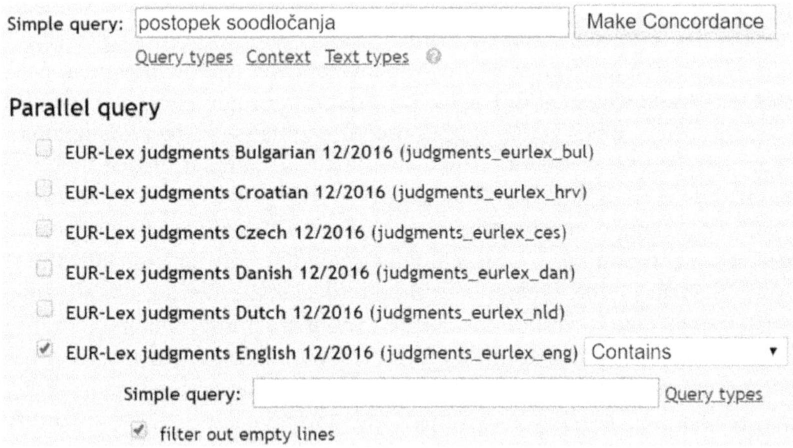

Figure 7.2 Parallel query using the Slovene and English Eur-Lex judgements subcorpora

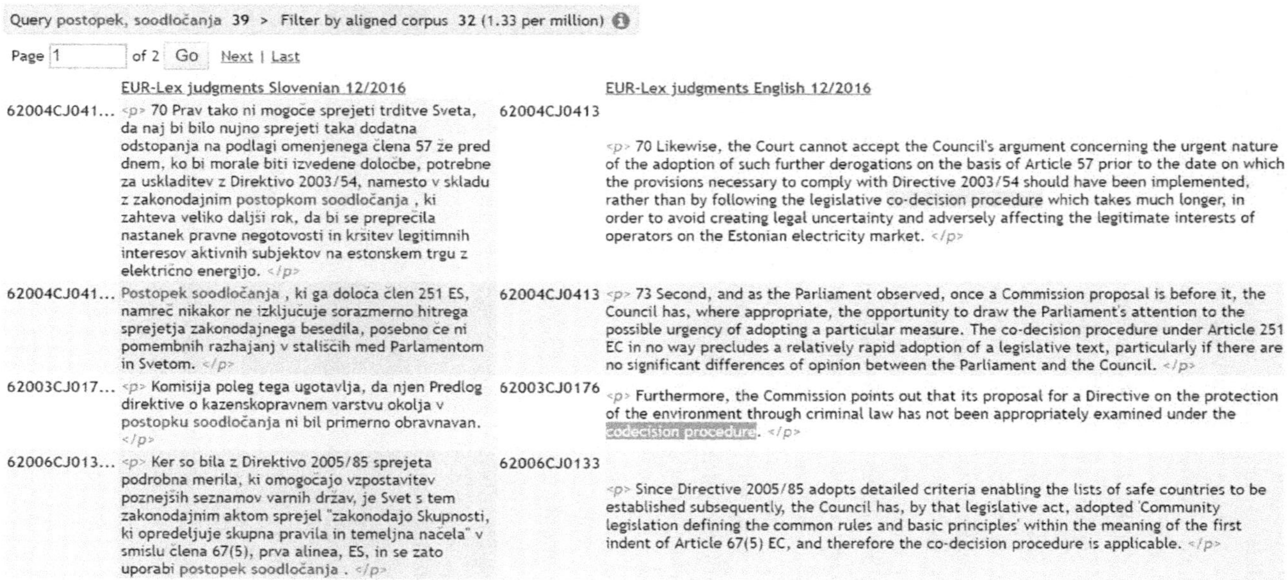

Query postopek, soodločanja 39 > Filter by aligned corpus 32 (1.33 per million)

Page 1 of 2 Go Next | Last

	EUR-Lex judgments Slovenian 12/2016		EUR-Lex judgments English 12/2016
62004CJ041...	<p> 70 Prav tako ni mogoče sprejeti trditve Sveta, da naj bi bilo nujno sprejeti taka dodatna odstopanja na podlagi omenjenega člena 57 že pred dnem, ko bi morale biti izvedene določbe, potrebne za uskladitev z Direktivo 2003/54, namesto v skladu z zakonodajnim postopkom soodločanja , ki zahteva veliko daljši rok, da bi se preprečila nastanek pravne negotovosti in kršitev legitimnih interesov aktivnih subjektov na estonskem trgu z električno energijo. </p>	62004CJ0413	<p> 70 Likewise, the Court cannot accept the Council's argument concerning the urgent nature of the adoption of such further derogations on the basis of Article 57 prior to the date on which the provisions necessary to comply with Directive 2003/54 should have been implemented, rather than by following the legislative co-decision procedure which takes much longer, in order to avoid creating legal uncertainty and adversely affecting the legitimate interests of operators on the Estonian electricity market. </p>
62004CJ041...	Postopek soodločanja , ki ga določa člen 251 ES, namreč nikakor ne izključuje sorazmerno hitrega sprejetja zakonodajnega besedila, posebno če ni pomembnih razhajanj v staliscih med Parlamentom in Svetom. </p>	62004CJ0413	<p> 73 Second, and as the Parliament observed, once a Commission proposal is before it, the Council has, where appropriate, the opportunity to draw the Parliament's attention to the possible urgency of adopting a particular measure. The co-decision procedure under Article 251 EC in no way precludes a relatively rapid adoption of a legislative text, particularly if there are no significant differences of opinion between the Parliament and the Council. </p>
62003CJ017...	<p> Komisija poleg tega ugotavlja, da njen Predlog direktive o kazenskopravnem varstvu okolja v postopku soodločanja ni bil primerno obravnavan. </p>	62003CJ0176	<p> Furthermore, the Commission points out that its proposal for a Directive on the protection of the environment through criminal law has not been appropriately examined under the codecision procedure. </p>
62006CJ013...	<p> Ker so bila z Direktivo 2005/85 sprejeta podrobna merila, ki omogočajo vzpostavitev poznejših seznamov varnih držav, je Svet s tem zakonodajnim aktom sprejel "zakonodajo Skupnosti, ki opredeljuje skupna pravila in temeljna načela" v smislu člena 67(5), prva alinea, ES, in se zato uporabi postopek soodločanja . </p>	62006CJ0133	<p> Since Directive 2005/85 adopts detailed criteria enabling the lists of safe countries to be established subsequently, the Council has, by that legislative act, adopted 'Community legislation defining the common rules and basic principles' within the meaning of the first indent of Article 67(5) EC, and therefore the co-decision procedure is applicable. </p>

Figure 7.3 Slovene–English parallel concordance for 'postopek soodločanja' in the 'Sentence view'

equivalents. For several major languages, Sketch Engine also offers an integrated statistical machine dictionary feature that automatically highlights translation candidates in parallel concordances (cf. Kovář, Baisa and Jakubíček, 2016), which is particularly useful when large concordance samples are being examined.[2] Although in some cases, the translator can achieve the same result by simply turning to a multilingual glossary or term bank, parallel corpora have a wider use, as they enable translators to identify collocations and other multi-word expressions that do not necessarily feature in terminological resources.

Sketch Engine's multifunctional concordancer offers several view and sort options in the left-hand side menu, allowing users to tailor the experience to their needs and requirements. In addition to being able to sort concordances by the node word (i.e. the searched item), left and right context, and set the amount of context displayed for each concordance line (number of characters), users are also able to filter the results in order to either exclude lines containing any unwanted or irrelevant hits, or to only target lines appearing in specific text types or containing a specific word or lemma (positive or negative filter). Furthermore, the concordancer enables users to generate useful frequency lists for the node word and the items appearing in its immediate left and right context using different attributes (e.g. word form, lemma and part-of-speech tag). The 'Frequency' tool supports multi-level queries combining up to four attributes for which frequencies are to be calculated.

Frequency lists are particularly useful when a parallel concordance features several translation equivalents, as they can help translators determine which translation is commonly used in everyday communication or in a specific text type. Our case study provides a good example of how this tool can be utilised by a translator to identify the most natural translation equivalent. Below is a sentence containing the Slovene term 'pravni okvir' ('legal framework'), which can be translated into English in several different ways depending on the context.

Original (SL): *Evropska unija je z Lizbonsko pogodbo dobila potrebni* ***pravni okvir*** *in orodja za spopadanje s prihodnjimi izzivi in za uresničevanje zahtev državljanov.*

Draft translation (TL): *The Lisbon Treaty enabled the European Union to create the necessary _______ and tools to face future challenges and meet the requirements of its citizens.*

To identify potential translation equivalents, the Slovene translator in our case study decided to generate a parallel concordance for 'pravni okvir' from the Eur-Lex judgements corpus using the 'Context' functionality: the nominal lemma 'okvir' was the search and the adjectival lemma 'praven' was set to

[2] This option is unfortunately not yet available for Slovene. The highlighted translations in Figure 7.3 have been manually marked by the authors for presentation purposes.

appear immediately before the search item (i.e. one token right of the 'node'). The query generated 4,422 results, enabling the translator to quickly skim through the first few dozens of corpus examples to identify the following candidate translations for the Slovene term: 'legal context', 'legal framework', 'legislative framework' and 'legal background'. By examining their use in context, the translator was then able to narrow their choice down to two translations, i.e. 'legal framework' and 'legislative framework', with the former being identified as the more likely translation in this context ('pravni okvir' is used in a more general sense in the sentence above, which is why 'legal' seemed the more appropriate near-synonym than the narrower and more specific adjective 'legislative'). To confirm (or dismiss) their linguistic intuition, the translator decided to use quantitative data to see which of the two options is used more frequently in EU texts, thinking that frequency is likely to indicate the more common, generic use. As a result, they repeated the query with one minor difference: when selecting the English corpus in the 'Parallel query' section, they decided to filter the search to only those corpus examples where 'background' appeared as the translation of 'okvir' in order to identify the most appropriate adjectival premodifier.[3] The translator was then able to generate a frequency list based on the amended concordance using the 'Frequency' tool in the left-hand side menu, specifying which attributes they were interested in and how many levels of sorting were to be implemented in the list, as shown in Figure 7.4.

As shown in Figure 7.5, the ensuing frequency list and graph clearly point out to 'legal framework' being by far the most frequently used translation equivalent with 'framework' as its base, appearing in 517 out of the 609 concordance lines in the sample (84.9 per cent). Although frequencies are not necessarily good indicators of technical accuracy (see the above commentary of 'legal' and 'legislative'), they can complement the translator's analysis and help confirm some of their assumptions.

7.2.2 *Exploring a Word's Collocational Behaviour: 'Word Sketches'*

The most distinctive feature of Sketch Engine is 'Word Sketches', i.e. one-page, automatically generated summaries of a word's statistically significant collocates, which are sorted according to the grammatical patterns in which they occur (cf. Kilgarriff et al., 2014a). As languages differ significantly in their grammars, these patterns have to be defined for each language separately. The full set of rules defining these grammatical relations for a specific language are called 'sketch grammar', and different 'sketch grammar' configurations

[3] This was achieved by simply typing 'background' into the 'Simple query' field appearing below the selected corpus in the parallel query section (see Figure 7.3).

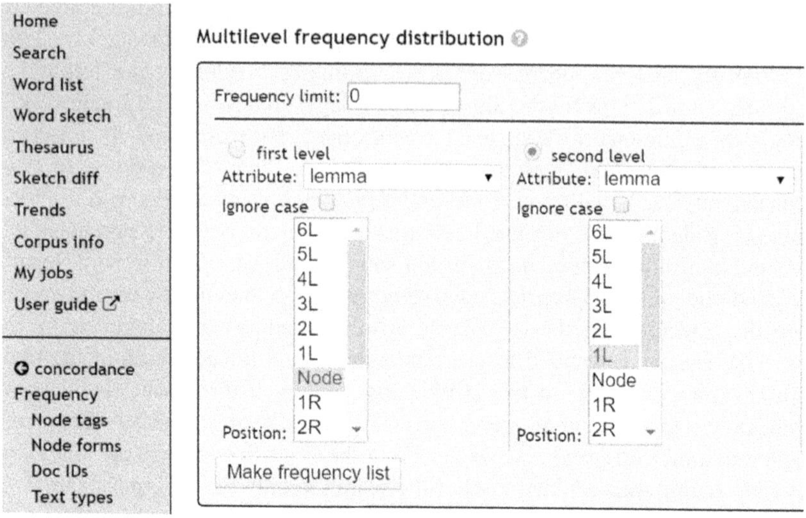

Figure 7.4 Generating a multi-level frequency list in Sketch Engine

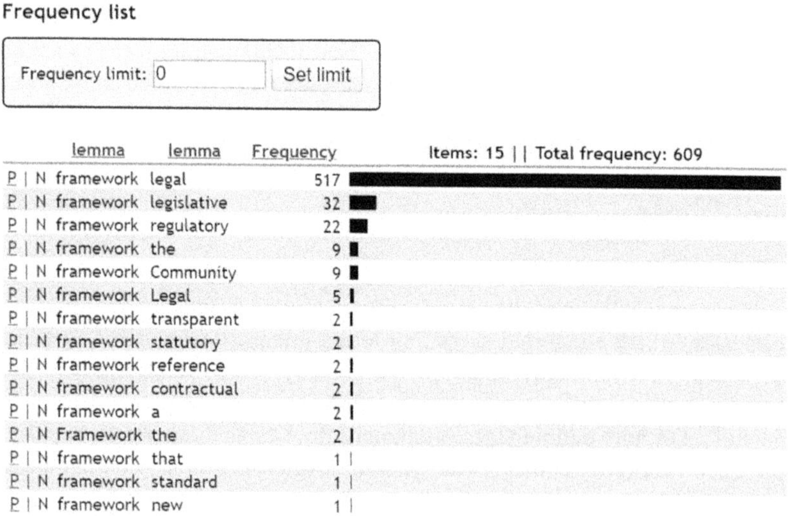

Figure 7.5 Frequency list featuring candidate translations with ‘framework’

may exist for the same language depending on the user's needs and selected corpus. The type of grammatical relations offered by the Sketch Engine also depend on the selected word's part of speech; for instance, when examining a verb's sketch, we mainly wish to know which nouns it typically takes as its subject and object, and which prepositions, particles and adverbs it typically co-occurs with. By contrast, when we analyse noun sketches, we are primarily interested in the adjectival premodifiers and verbs the noun combines with as their subject or direct object. The Sketch Engine provides several other grammatical relations for the selected word, and these serve to complement the analysis and provide the user with additional information on the word's collocational behaviour, semantic preference and prosody. Overall, word sketches serve as an invaluable source of information for both linguists and language professionals alike, as they help users identify not only lexical and grammatical collocations, but also idioms, phrasal verbs and specific syntactic constructions associated with the selected word (cf. Kilgarriff et al., 2014a).

In our case study, the Slovene translator noticed a recurrent word in the source text, i.e. the adjective 'učinkovit'. As the word co-occurs with different nouns within the text, the translator decided to examine the collocational behaviour of its two direct translation equivalents, i.e. 'effective' or 'efficient', in order to gain a better understanding of the type of contexts they typically appear in and therefore establish which of the two equivalents is better suited for each individual use of 'učinkovit' in the text. The translator considered skimming through a monolingual concordance to get a better 'feel' of the two words; however, they realised that this option would be way too time-consuming and would fail to account for the plethora of combinatory possibilities exhibited by high-frequency lexemes such as 'efficient' or 'effective'. A word sketch generated from a balanced reference corpus such as the British National Corpus (BNC) seemed to be a much better solution, as it would enable the translator to get a more comprehensive, well-rounded and systematic account of the two examined words. Word sketches are very easy to generate: after selecting a corpus from the home page, the user clicks on 'Word Sketches' from the left-hand side menu and enters the selected word's base form into the 'Lemma' field (see Figure 7.6). At present, word sketches can only be created for lexical words (nouns, verbs, adjectives, adverbs) and pronouns. Several advanced options are available during this first step, including a bilingual word-sketch option.

The ensuing word sketch is composed of grammatically motivated lists of collocates which are sorted into columns according to their statistical significance. Two figures are provided for each collocate – the first one is raw frequency of co-occurrence in the corpus, whilst the second is a statistical score computed using the logDice formula (cf. Rychlý, 2008). Clicking on the frequency opens a concordance displaying all corpus lines containing the

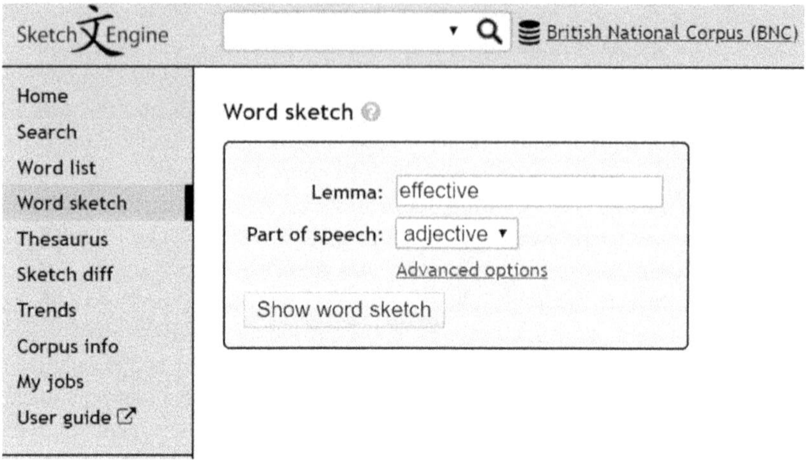

Figure 7.6 The word-sketch functionality

selected collocation. The Sketch Engine offers a few additional options in the left-hand side menu; by clicking on 'More Data', users are able to expand the lists with additional collocates, whilst the 'Cluster' option sorts the collocates into groups based on their semantic similarity. Figure 7.7 shows a word sketch for the first translation equivalent examined by our Slovene translation, i.e. 'effective'.

The BNC-derived sketch for 'effective' provides information on its top adverbial modifiers (e.g. 'highly'), the type of nouns it typically describes (both as a premodifier and when used predicatively in the construction 'X be effective'), prepositional phrases it co-occurs with and co-ordinated adjectives linked with the conjunction 'and' (e.g. 'safe and effective'). The same grammatical relations are displayed in the BNC-derived word sketch for 'efficient', as shown in Figure 7.8.

Based on the two word sketches, our Slovene translator was able to identify several groups of nominal collocates that are typically associated with only one of the two candidate translation equivalents. For instance, only 'efficient' tends to be used when describing people (e.g. 'producer', 'administrator', 'farmer'), whilst 'effective' often co-occurs with nouns describing medical treatments or substances (e.g. 'drug', 'medication', 'vaccine', 'therapy, 'treatment', 'remedy'), and this use is not found for 'efficient'. Similarly, 'efficient' typically collocates with nouns from the domain of Energy (e.g. 'fuel', 'engine', 'energy') and this domain-specific use is not associated with 'effective'. Although both 'effective' and 'efficient' were found to co-occur with nouns denoting abstract concepts and eventuality, 'effective' had a slight edge over

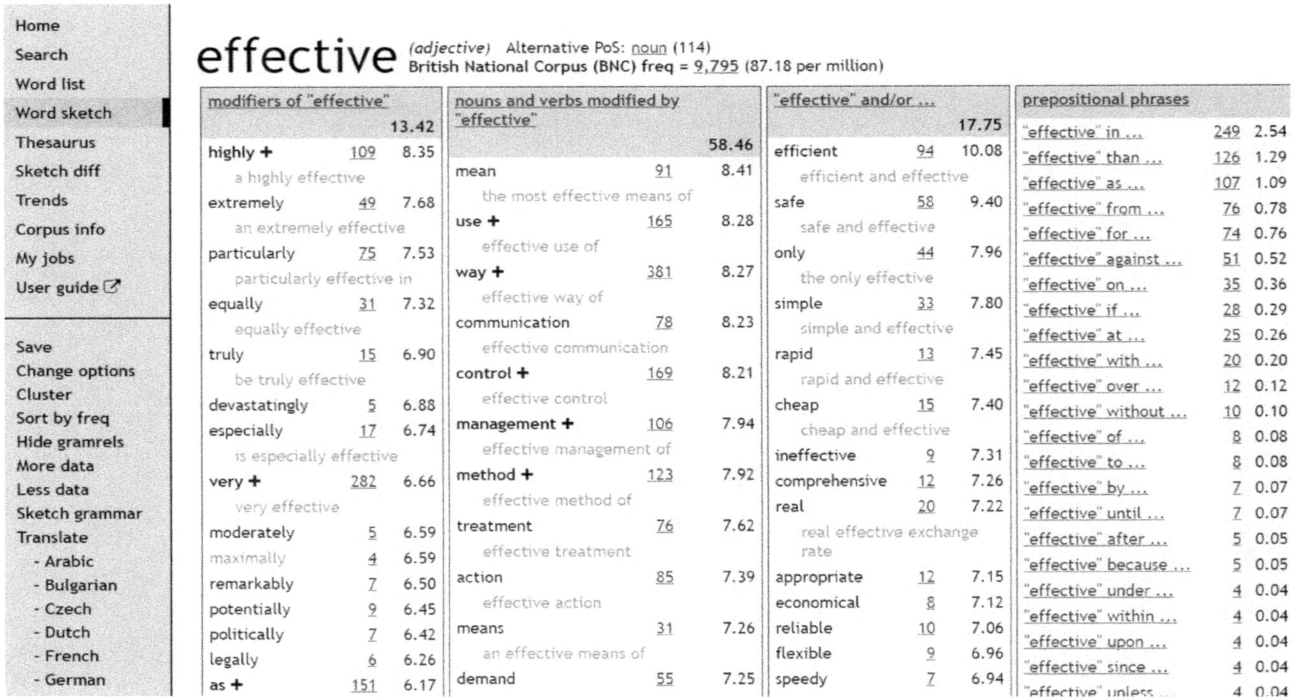

Figure 7.7 Word sketch for ‘effective’

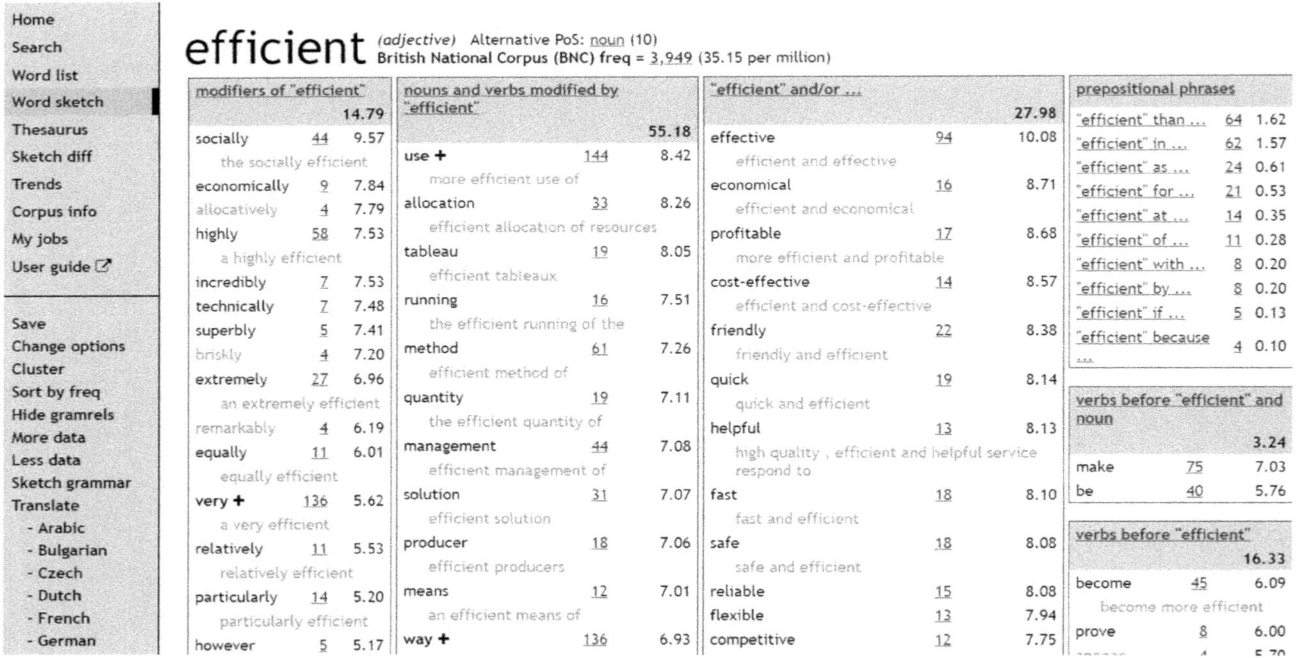

Figure 7.8 Word sketch for 'efficient'

'efficient' as far as nouns describing proactive, dynamic actions were concerned. Going back to the source text, the translator was able to tentatively conclude that 'efficient' should be used when the noun in question describes a human being or, by extension, institutions and legal persons such as Europe (e.g. 'učinkovitejša Evropa' – 'a more efficient Europe'), whereas 'effective' was more likely to be the better translation equivalent when 'učinkovit' was used to describe actions and processes, e.g. 'učinkovitejša zaščita' ('a more effective protection'), and 'učinkovitejše odločanje' ('more effective decision-making'), although the picture provided by the word sketches was not entirely clear. As a result, the translator decided to seek further clarification from a domain-specific corpus by generating word sketches for both 'protection' and 'decision-making' from the English subset of the Eur-Lex corpus. The word sketches helped clarify any remaining doubts – 'effective' was indeed the stronger candidate collocate amongst the two adjectives, although both were found to co-occur with the nouns. More specifically, the Eur-Lex-derived sketch for 'decision-making' showed that 'effective decision-making' (frequency: 51) was used twice as frequently as 'efficient decision-making' (frequency: 28), whilst the gap was significantly wider as far as 'protection' was concerned, with 'effective protection' (frequency: 5,632) being by far the more statistically significant collocation when compared with 'efficient protection' (frequency: 198). Furthermore, a sketch generated for 'Europe' from the same corpus highlighted 'efficient' as a statistically significant collocate of the noun 'Europe' (frequency: 208), thus further confirming the translator's initial analysis of the BNC-generated sketches.

Another option available to users who wish to compare the collocational behaviour of semantically related words (or, in our translator's case, translation equivalents) is 'Sketch Difference', i.e. a concise, one-page contrastive summary of the two selected words' word sketches. The procedure for creating a sketch difference is very similar to that devised for word sketches and similarly takes only seconds to complete: after selecting a corpus, the user simply clicks on the 'Sketch Diff' option in the left-hand side menu and enters the two words they wish to compare. The greatest advantage of using sketch difference has to do with data visualisation, as the tool combines the two words' collocates into the same column and uses colour coding to show which word they typically co-occur with. The ensuing columns are to be interpreted as a cline: collocates appearing at the top and bottom of the list represent the two extremes (i.e. they co-occur exclusively with one of the two words) and are highlighted in a vibrant hue of green or red, whilst collocates that are shared between the two analysed words are displayed in the white field in the middle. Collocates appearing between the white field and the two extremes are highlighted in a lighter shade of green or red to indicate a preference for one of the words despite sporadically co-occurring with the other. Frequencies and logDice scores are displayed alongside the collocates, mimicking the structure of a word sketch, and users can access corpus sentences containing the selected collocation by clicking on their frequency in the corpus.

Figure 7.9 shows a BNC-derived sketch difference contrasting the collocational behaviour of 'effective' (green) and 'efficient' (red). A quick look at some of the top and bottom collocates confirms the results of our previous analysis of the word sketches, with 'drug', 'treatment', 'vaccine' and 'therapy' being listed as 'effective'-only collocates, and 'organisation', 'fuel', 'energy' and 'engine' as co-occurring exclusively with 'efficient'. Using the sketch difference to highlight these uses is much more time-efficient than examining the two word sketches individually; however, there is a downside – as these summaries are relatively short and concise, they do not feature the same level of detail as word sketches. The choice between the two options depends on what we are trying to achieve; whilst word sketches provide a more comprehensive account of the word's collocational behaviour, sketch differences help users identify the main differences and similarities in a systematic and visually appealing way.

Our case study provides us with another good example of how sketch differences can help users decide between candidate translation equivalents. One of the subheadings in the Slovene source text contains the noun 'varnost', which corresponds to the English nouns 'safety' and 'security':

Original (SL): *Evropa pravic in vrednot, svobode, solidarnosti in varnosti*
Draft translation (TL): *A Europe characterised by rights and values, liberty, solidarity and* _______

There are a number of fine-grained semantic distinctions between these two near-synonyms, and these are mainly contextually defined, which is why the sketch differences can serve as a good starting point in determining which of the two translation equivalents is better suited. Therefore, the Slovene translator decided to generate a sketch difference using the domain-specific Eur-Lex corpus to resolve this dilemma (cf. Figure 7.10).

The first thing we notice about the subheading is that 'varnost' is used alongside a number of nouns from the same semantic field – 'right', 'value', 'liberty' and 'solidarity' all denote abstract concepts that are generally accepted as positive societal and personal values. Figure 7.10 shows part of the Eur-Lex-derived sketch difference for the two selected words, which focuses on one grammatical relation only, i.e. co-ordination. According to the list, 'security' is often listed alongside nouns that fall into the same semantic field as nouns co-occurring with 'varnost' (e.g. 'justice', 'freedom' and 'peace') and these nouns only sporadically co-occur with 'safety', indicating that 'security' might be the more appropriate translation equivalent for 'varnost' in this context. This is a good example of how translators can harness the power of collocation to

effective/efficient *(adjective)* Alternative PoS: noun (freq: 114)
British National Corpus (BNC) freqs = 9,795 | 3,949

effective 6.0 4.0 2.0 0 -2.0 -4.0 -6.0 efficient

subjects of "be effective/efficient"	889	402	0.09	0.10
drug	16	0	8.9	--
treatment	16	0	8.7	--
diet	11	0	8.4	--
intervention	9	0	8.2	--
vaccine	7	0	8.0	--
therapy	7	0	7.9	--
technique	8	0	7.6	--
refusal	4	0	7.2	--
latter	5	0	7.1	--
approach	6	0	7.1	--
cost	63	4	10.4	7.0
method	9	5	7.7	7.4
process	6	4	7.0	6.9
system	14	15	7.6	8.0
operation	5	5	7.1	7.8
cent	5	15	6.6	8.7
business	0	4	--	7.1
organisation	0	4	--	7.3
industry	0	6	--	7.7
engine	0	4	--	7.9
filter	0	4	--	8.2
market	0	12	--	8.5

modifiers of "effective/efficient"	1,314	584	0.13	0.15
truly	15	0	6.9	--
devastatingly	5	0	6.9	--
especially	17	0	6.7	--
maximally	4	0	6.6	--
moderately	5	0	6.6	--
potentially	9	0	6.5	--
politically	7	0	6.4	--
legally	6	0	6.3	--
particularly	75	14	7.5	5.2
as	151	56	6.2	4.8
equally	31	11	7.3	6.0
very	282	136	6.7	5.6
highly	109	58	8.3	7.5
extremely	49	27	7.7	7.0
remarkably	7	4	6.5	6.2
however	7	5	5.4	5.2
quietly	0	4	--	5.2
relatively	0	11	--	5.5
briskly	0	4	--	7.2
superbly	0	5	--	7.4
technically	0	7	--	7.5
incredibly	0	7	--	7.5

nouns and verbs modified by "effective/efficient"	5,726	2,179	0.58	0.55
treatment	76	0	7.6	--
action	85	0	7.4	--
demand	55	0	7.2	--
protection	39	0	7.2	--
learning	30	0	7.1	--
strategy	44	0	6.9	--
implementation	24	0	6.8	--
control	169	8	8.2	4.1
communication	78	7	8.2	5.5
mean	91	15	8.4	6.6
way	381	136	8.3	6.9
management	106	44	7.9	7.1
method	123	61	7.9	7.3
means	31	12	7.3	7.0
use	165	144	8.3	8.4
manner	27	21	6.6	6.9
solution	35	31	6.7	7.1
functioning	9	9	5.6	6.9
working	8	11	5.2	6.6
allocation	4	33	4.2	8.3
q	0	8	--	6.5
producer	0	18	--	7.1

Figure 7.9 Sketch difference comparing the adjectives ‘effective’ and ‘efficient’

security/safety *(noun)* EUR-Lex English 2/2016 freqs = 336,144 | 231,437

security 6.0 4.0 2.0 0 -2.0 -4.0 -6.0 safety

"security/safety" and/or ...	77,859	57,905	0.23	0.25
bond	998	0	8.6	--
instrument	1,362	0	8.4	--
share	1,069	0	8.4	--
justice	5,659	22	10.8	3.1
freedom	7,354	59	11.1	4.5
peace	2,448	26	9.9	3.7
network	1,032	18	8.2	2.7
defence	1,119	40	8.7	4.3
policy	4,936	216	9.8	5.5
stability	1,671	72	9.1	4.9
safety	3,317	500	9.6	7.1
order	1,020	337	8.5	7.2
environment	811	1,233	7.6	8.5
protection	1,275	2,935	8.2	9.6
security	1,308	3,317	8.1	9.6
prevention	248	863	6.3	8.4
efficiency	172	637	5.7	7.9
welfare	90	414	5.1	7.7
requirement	226	1,564	5.6	8.6
health	1,942	19,135	8.4	11.9
quality	296	3,307	6.2	10.0
performance	34	957	3.5	8.7
operator	8	708	1.2	7.9
hygiene	12	1,208	2.2	9.3
efficacy	0	1,414	--	9.6

Figure 7.10 Extract from the Eur-Lex-generated sketch difference comparing 'security' and 'safety'

explore semantic preference in order to resolve difficult cases of divergent polysemy.

In addition to the 'Sketch Difference' functionality, there is another extension of 'Word Sketches' that is relevant for translators, i.e. multi-word sketches. This recently implemented functionality allows users to generate a lexical profile for a multi-word expression, which is particularly useful when analysing idioms, phrasal verbs and domain-specific terms. Creating a multi-word sketch is easy: after generating a simple word sketch for one of the words in the expression (i.e. usually the base), the user has to find the relevant collocate, click on the little plus symbol appearing next to it, and they will be redirected to a multi-word sketch for the selected collocation. The lack of a plus sign next to the collocate indicates that there is not sufficient data for the Sketch Engine to create a multi-word sketch. Figure 7.11 shows a multi-word sketch for the term 'legal framework', which was discussed earlier; the sketch was generated from the English subset of the Eur-Lex judgements English corpus.

The multi-word sketch can be used to either find translation equivalents or double-check collocations used in their translations before finalising them. For instance, our Slovene translator can use the sketch to check whether the verb they used in the draft translation (i.e. 'The Lisbon Treaty enabled the European Union to create the necessary legal framework and tools to face future challenges and meet the requirements of its citizens') is a statistically significant collocate of 'legal framework' and identify alternative near-synonyms (e.g. 'establish') in order to avoid repetition and stylistically improve the translation. As the selected verb features at the very top of the list, the translator can be assured that the draft sentence is well-formed. In addition, several collocates in the multi-word sketch are marked with a plus sign, indicating that the user can potentially narrow their search by generating a new sketch for a three-word expression (e.g. 'horizontal legal framework'), which is particularly useful when examining highly specialised terminology.

7.2.3 Searching for Alternative Translation Equivalents

Stylistic appropriateness is not limited to making sure that the target text is in line with genre and domain conventions; every translation should ideally reflect the more general writing style that is typically associated with native speakers of the target language. This is what people usually refer to when they say that a text 'flows' or 'sounds natural'. To put it bluntly, a translator's ultimate objective is to fool the target audience into thinking that they are reading an original text written by a native speaker in the target language, and that entails knowing which constructions and near-synonyms are best suited to specific linguistic contexts and communicative situations. In terms of translation technology, there are a plethora of tools and resources a translator can utilise to render their texts semantically and stylistically appropriate. For instance, translators can use comparable corpora before they start translating to closely examine similar texts in the target language and identify multi-word expressions (e.g. collocations, idioms and phrasal verbs), terms, syntactic constructions and stylistic devices that are typically used by native speakers of the target language. They might also want to use a thesaurus to identify contextually appropriate near-synonyms in order to phrase the sentence in a more natural way.

The Sketch Engine's automatic distributional thesaurus can provide translators with near-synonyms, antonyms and semantically related words for

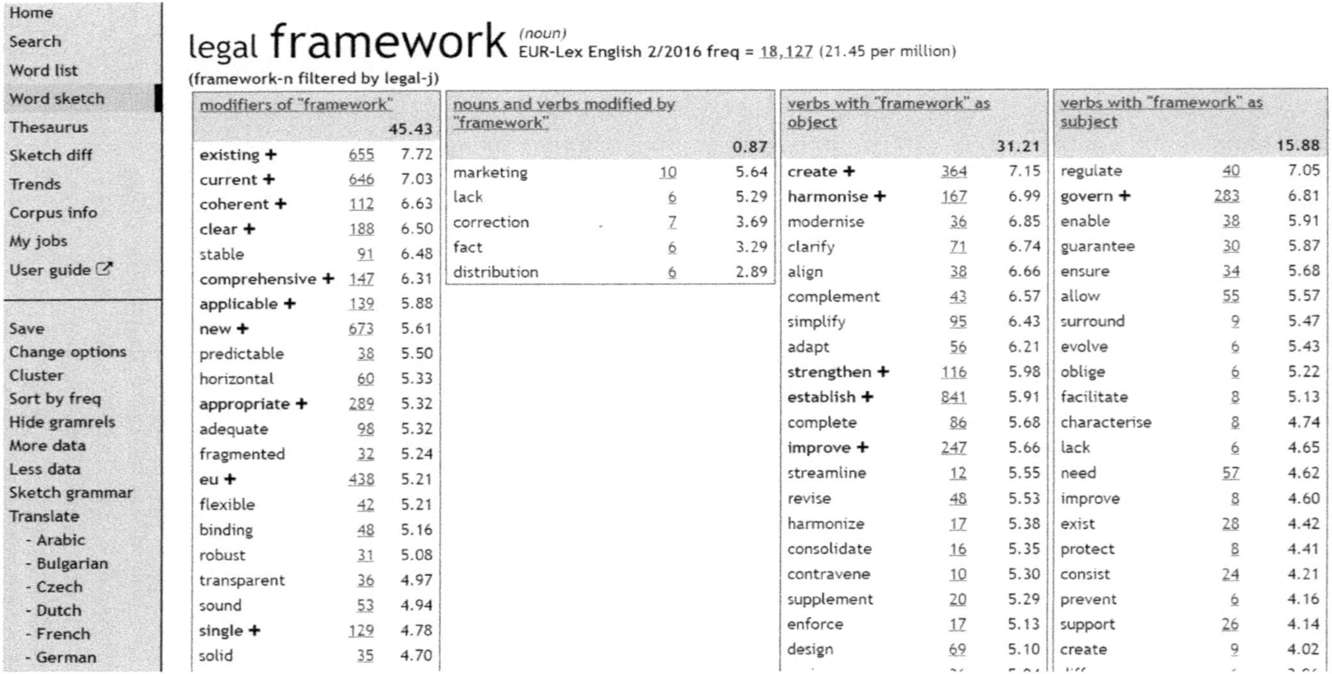

legal framework (noun) EUR-Lex English 2/2016 freq = 18,127 (21.45 per million)

(framework-n filtered by legal-j)

modifiers of "framework"		45.43
existing +	655	7.72
current +	646	7.03
coherent +	112	6.63
clear +	188	6.50
stable	91	6.48
comprehensive +	147	6.31
applicable +	139	5.88
new +	673	5.61
predictable	38	5.50
horizontal	60	5.33
appropriate +	289	5.32
adequate	98	5.32
fragmented	32	5.24
eu +	438	5.21
flexible	42	5.21
binding	48	5.16
robust	31	5.08
transparent	36	4.97
sound	53	4.94
single +	129	4.78
solid	35	4.70

nouns and verbs modified by "framework"		0.87
marketing	10	5.64
lack	6	5.29
correction	7	3.69
fact	6	3.29
distribution	6	2.89

verbs with "framework" as object		31.21
create +	364	7.15
harmonise +	167	6.99
modernise	36	6.85
clarify	71	6.74
align	38	6.66
complement	43	6.57
simplify	95	6.43
adapt	56	6.21
strengthen +	116	5.98
establish +	841	5.91
complete	86	5.68
improve +	247	5.66
streamline	12	5.55
revise	48	5.53
harmonize	17	5.38
consolidate	16	5.35
contravene	10	5.30
supplement	20	5.29
enforce	17	5.13
design	69	5.10

verbs with "framework" as subject		15.88
regulate	40	7.05
govern +	283	6.81
enable	38	5.91
guarantee	30	5.87
ensure	34	5.68
allow	55	5.57
surround	9	5.47
evolve	6	5.43
oblige	6	5.22
facilitate	8	5.13
characterise	8	4.74
lack	6	4.65
need	57	4.62
improve	8	4.60
exist	28	4.42
protect	8	4.41
consist	24	4.21
prevent	6	4.16
support	26	4.14
create	9	4.02

Figure 7.11 Multi-word sketch for 'legal framework'

a selected lexical word, enabling them to quickly identify alternative translation equivalents. One of the advantages of using this feature is that it allows users to generate a list of semantically related words from a corpus of their choice; whilst selecting a balanced, representative target-language corpus will ensure that the extracted words that are generally suited to most text types, a domain-specific corpus such as Eur-Lex (EU), EcoLexicon (Environmental studies) or the Medical Web Corpus (Medicine) will yield even more relevant candidate synonyms, as the results will be tailored to fit the selected domain and genre. Consider, for instance, the following sentence identified by our Slovene translator:

Original (SL): *Evropska unija je pravna oseba, kar je okrepilo njeno pogajalsko moč in* ***učinkovitost*** *na svetovnem prizorišču.*
Draft translation (TL): *The European Union's status as a legal person helped consolidate its negotiating position and _______ on the global stage.*

The most obvious translation equivalents for the Slovene noun 'učinkovitost' are 'effectiveness', 'efficiency' and 'efficacy', none of which seem to be suitable in this context. What is required to make the sentence semantically and stylistically appropriate is a near-synonym. Therefore, the Slovene translator decided to generate a statistical thesaurus using the Eur-Lex judgements corpus. The searched item was 'effectiveness' (see Figure 7.12). Based on the words suggested by the thesaurus, the Slovene translator was able to identify 'competitiveness', 'performance' and 'importance' as contextually appropriate translation equivalents for the word 'učinkovitost' in the sentence above.

The automatically generated thesaurus provides the user with a list of semantically related words, alongside their frequencies in the corpus and their semantic similarity scores, which are calculated by comparing the two words' word sketches. As a result, related words are selected on the basis of their shared collocational behaviour rather than being listed in terms of traditional sense relations such as synonymy, antonymy and hyper-/hyponymy. The list also integrates several useful hyperlinks: by clicking on a related word's frequency, users are redirected to its concordance, whilst clicking on the word itself generates a sketch difference comparing the related word with the searched item. Another advantage of using the thesaurus is data visualisation; in addition to having the list be sorted by similarity score, which results in the most semantically similar words being displayed at the top of the list, a word cloud is automatically generated and displayed alongside the results. The thesaurus can theoretically provide the user with an unlimited number of semantically related words, as there are no space constraints; however, corpus size plays a key role here – if the selected corpus is not large enough, the Sketch Engine will not have enough data to generate useful results.

effectiveness (noun) EUR-Lex English 2/2016 freq = 54,827 (64.88 per million)

Lemma	Score	Freq
efficiency	0.448	78,642
transparency	0.391	52,548
functioning	0.384	76,795
sustainability	0.367	24,498
quality	0.353	236,254
competitiveness	0.330	48,716
availability	0.328	30,803
aspect	0.327	83,052
reliability	0.323	13,925
performance	0.321	117,614
importance	0.321	76,284
achievement	0.321	25,760
existence	0.313	64,481
consistency	0.312	23,896
coherence	0.310	16,453
outcome	0.309	41,250
relevance	0.309	62,022
independence	0.308	23,123
stability	0.304	53,645
scope	0.304	176,834
impact	0.303	244,402
safety	0.301	231,437
integration	0.300	62,589

Figure 7.12 The Sketch Engine thesaurus in action

7.2.4 Comparing the Collocational Behaviour of Source-Language Words and Their Translation Equivalents

Over the past five years, the Sketch Engine has made great strides towards developing useful bilingual options for translators, the main feature being bilingual word sketches, i.e. an extension of the 'Word Sketch' functionality that allows users to create side-by-side comparisons of collocational profiles for a selected lexical word and its translation equivalent. The primary target users the developers of the Sketch Engine had in mind when they started developing bilingual word sketches were lexicographers compiling bilingual dictionaries. Before the feature was developed and implemented, lexicographers would use separate windows to generate and compare word sketches for the source-language word and its corresponding word in the target language, comparing the observed grammatical relations and collocates manually (Kovář, Baisa and Jakubíček, 2016). As the bilingual word-sketch feature was introduced, users were finally able to view both profiles on the same page, therefore saving precious time due to the improved visualisation.

If we turn our attention back to our case study, we can identify several ways our Slovene translator working on the Lisbon Treaty text can utilise this feature. Take, for instance, the previously discussed examples containing the Slovene adjective 'učinkovit'; in addition to analysing BNC-derived word sketches for the two translation equivalents ('effective' and 'efficient'), the translator can also generate a bilingual sketch for each translation pair in order to examine the degree of lexical and syntactic overlap between the two words. Figure 7.13 shows a bilingual word sketch for the pair 'učinkovit'/'effective', which was derived from the domain-specific Eur-Lex parallel corpus. The procedure for generating bilingual word sketches is fairly similar to the one used for monolingual sketches, except that the user needs to select a second language and parallel or comparable monolingual corpus from the drop-down menus offered under 'Advanced options'.

The first thing we noticed when examining the bilingual word sketch is data visualisation: the two sketches are displayed separately on opposite sides of the page, with the target-language collocate lists being highlighted in light green. Several grammatical relations are provided in the partial screenshot featured in Figure 7.13; the four columns displayed for the Slovene adjectives include top nominal collocates the adjective premodifies ('kdo-kaj?' – 'who-what?'), verbs appearing immediately before the adjective ('gl-pred'), prepositions following the adjective ('predlog'), and other adjectives typically co-occurring with 'učinkovit' ('priredje' – 'co-ordination'). As the grammatical relation featured in the first column is comparable to that of the last green column ('nouns and verbs modified by

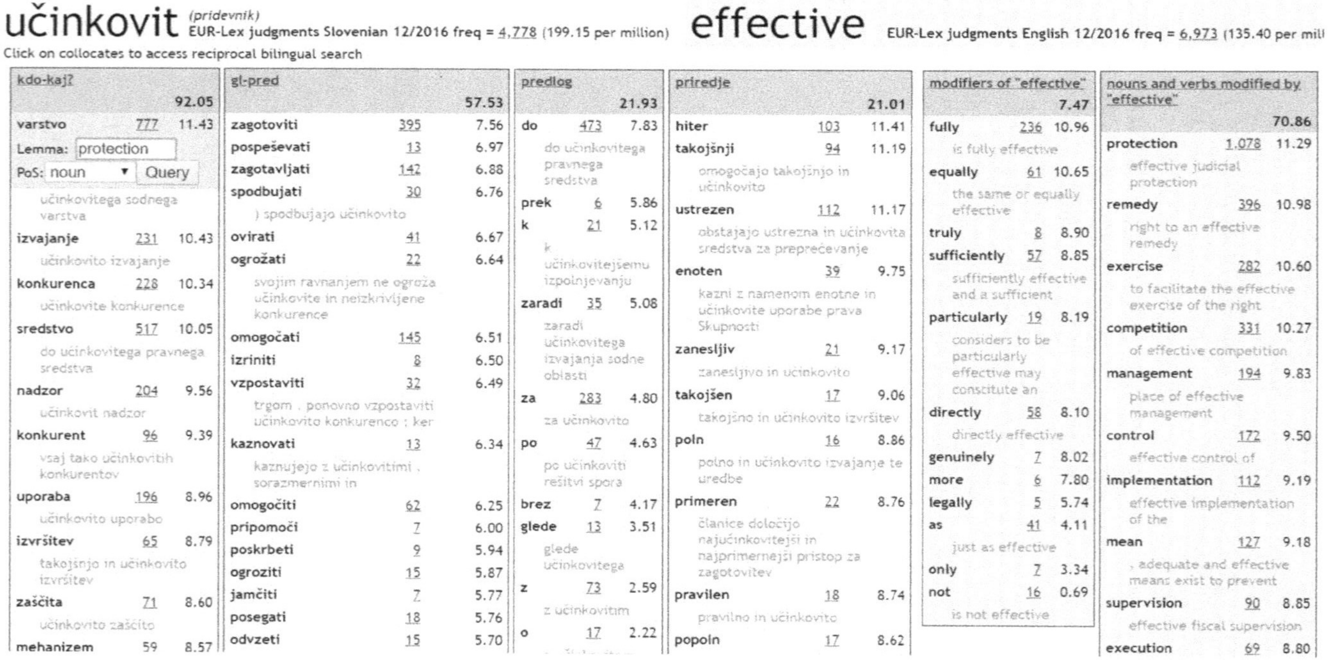

Figure 7.13 Slovene–English bilingual word sketch for ‘učinkovit’ and ‘effective’

"effective"'), the translator can use the collocates appearing in the two lists to identify candidate translation equivalents for multi-word expressions and terms. For instance, the top English collocate 'protection' is the perfect match for the top Slovene collocate 'varstvo'; in addition, the two illustrative examples in dark grey font just below the corresponding collocates ('učinkovitega sodnega varstva' – 'effective judicial protection') also happen to be full translation equivalents. The degree of translation equivalence between the two collocates can be further explored from here – when the user clicks on the collocate, a search form appears, offering that user the option of generating a bilingual word sketch for the selected collocate and a candidate translation equivalent (cf. the grey area in Figure 7.13). The user can then either specify which translation equivalent they wish to contrast with the selected word (e.g. 'protection') or simply leave the 'Lemma' field empty, in which case the Sketch Engine will automatically select the most likely translation based on their statistical translation dictionary.

Currently, the Sketch Engine offers different types of bilingual word sketches, with the one displayed above for the Slovene–English pair of adjectives being the simplest one. If we switch language pairs, the ensuing bilingual word sketch may look significantly different. Consider the Italian–English word sketch for the nouns 'regolamento' and 'regulation', which were generated from the Eur-Lex judgements corpus (cf. Figure 7.14).

There are two main differences between the two bilingual sketches featured in Figures 7.13 and 7.14: firstly, collocate lists for comparable grammatical relations are showcased side by side in the Italian–English sketch, which makes them time-efficient and easier for the user to process in terms of cognitive load. The red lines in Figure 7.14 were added to show how easy it is to identify candidate translation equivalents using the aligned collocate lists (e.g. 'modificare' – 'amend', 'revise'; 'applicare' – 'enforce', 'implement'). Secondly, the Italian–English bilingual word sketch offers another option in the left-hand side menu, i.e. the recently developed 'Translate' button (Baisa et al., 2014), which offers the user translation suggestions for a small selection of well-supported languages, including Italian and English. These translation equivalents are extracted from the Sketch Engine's in-house statistical dictionary, which was derived from parallel corpora. Unfortunately, these statistical dictionaries have only been generated for a small subset of language pairs; as the Sketch Engine has yet to develop a Slovene–English statistical dictionary, the 'Translate' button does not appear in the menu when a Slovene monolingual or parallel corpus is selected. Similarly, the Slovene–English sketch does not feature fully aligned bilingual collocate lists; for this option to be implemented, the two sketch grammars have to be mapped onto each other in order to identify comparable

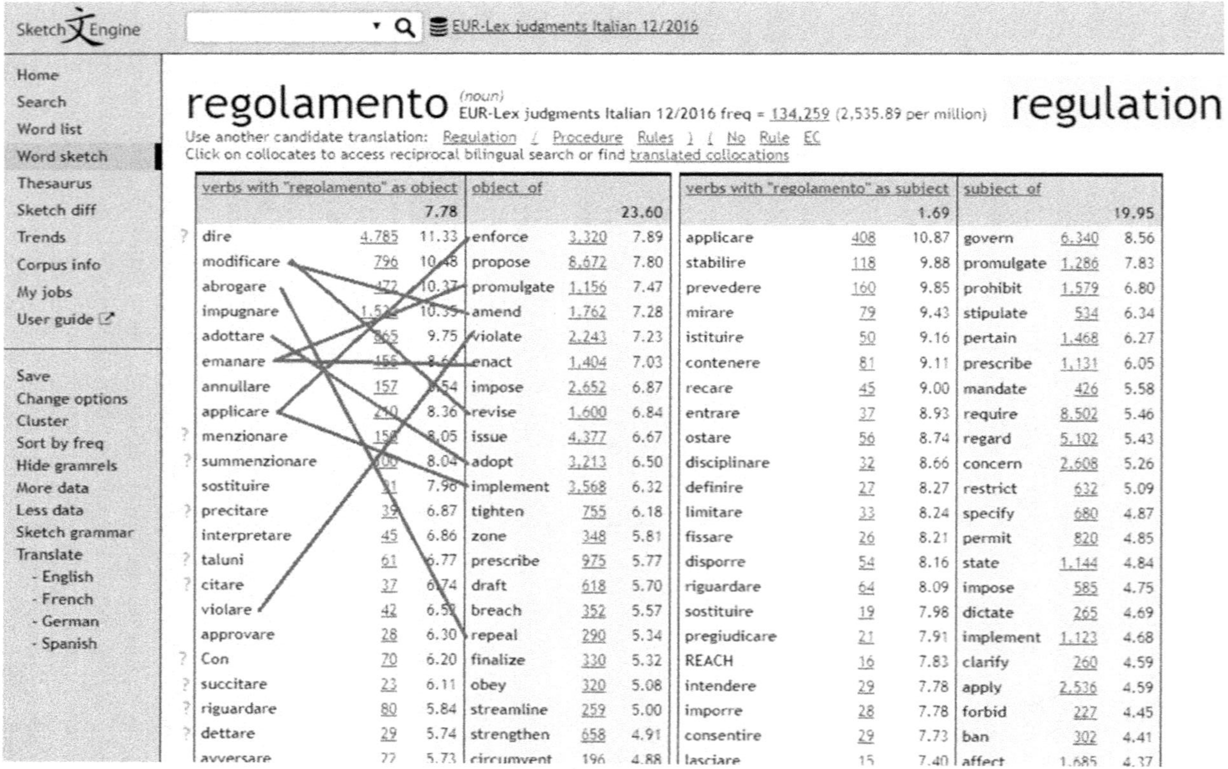

Figure 7.14 Short excerpt from the Italian–English bilingual word sketch for ‘regolamento’ and ‘regulation’

grammatical relations, which does not appear to be the case for any of the sketch grammar developed for the two languages thus far. That is not to say that there are no issues when dealing with major languages, as the availability of resources is not necessarily equal to quality. The Italian word sketch, for instance, included a lot of noisy data, which was most likely the result of part-of-speech tagging errors in the preprocessing stage. Consider, for instance, the Italian collocates marked with an orange question mark – whilst some of these are completely nonsensical (e.g. 'Con'), others have been erroneously parsed as verbs taking 'regolamento' as its object instead of being interpreted as past participles functioning as adjectival premodifiers (e.g. 'menzionare' ('mention') in phrases such as 'summenzionato regolamento' ('the above-mentioned regulation')). The same applies to the translation equivalents offered by the Sketch Engine; whilst 'regulation', 'procedure' and 'rule' are all plausible, the random appearance of 'No', 'EC', '/' and round brackets is unfortunately nothing more than noise, which only serves to confound the user. As these automatically generated translation equivalents have clearly not been manually validated, their accuracy inevitably depends on the quality of the annotated data and third-party tools used to preprocess it.

7.3 Terminology

Sketch Engine's term-extraction feature (Kilgarriff et al., 2014b; Baisa, Cukr and Ulipová, 2015; Kovář, Baisa and Jakubíček, 2016) uses state-of-the-art natural language processing technologies to identify terminology in specialised corpora. The results include both single- and multi-word units and can be exported into the customised CAT tool in the widely supported TBX format. By doing so, translators can easily fill their CAT-tool termbase with terminology for maintaining consistency and quality across all translation jobs from the same area or the same client.

Translators can extract terminology either from one of the many specialised corpora available through the Sketch Engine or by building a new parallel corpus from their TM using Corpus Architect, the corpus-building component of Sketch Engine, which enables users to process and analyse their own translations using Sketch Engine's rich collection of tools and features. As pointed out by a recent user survey (Zaretskaya, Corpas Pastor and Seghiri, 2015, 247), translators are still reluctant to compile their own corpora, mainly due to their unfamiliarity with corpus-building tools and lack of technical expertise in this area. The Sketch Engine provides a solution to this problem by offering a highly simplified, user-friendly tool that enables users to create a new corpus within minutes. As part of our case study, we shall demonstrate how this can be achieved by uploading an open-access

English–Slovene corpus from the same domain (i.e. European legislation) onto the Sketch Engine.[4] The English part of the parallel corpus contains 2,685,188 words in 103,796 sentences. In order to facilitate term extraction, users need to select a general reference corpus against which the specialised parallel corpus will be compared. For our case study, we selected the English web corpus (enTenTen13), which contains well over 19.6 billion words and is available through the Sketch Engine. These parameters are defined in the 'extraction options' box, which is shown in Figure 7.15.

By choosing the 'Keywords/terms' option in the left-hand side menu, the system generates a list of single- and multi-word terms based on a statistical comparison of their frequencies in the general and specialised corpora. Both lists can be downloaded as TBX and CSV files, alongside term-frequency data extracted from the two corpora. In addition, the extracted terms can be used as 'seeds' to create a new web corpus using the integrated WebBootCaT tool (Baroni et al., 2006), which compiles corpora by crawling the Internet for freely available texts containing the specified terms (cf. the grey 'Use WebBootCaT with selected words' button located above the term lists in Figures 7.16 and 7.17).

A short example with the first multi-word term in the downloaded TBX file is shown below:

```
<body>
 <termEntry id="1">
  <langSet xml:lang="">
   <ntig>
    <termGrp>
     <term id="t1">european patent</term>
      <termNote type="score">192.220</termNote>
      <termNote type="frequency">611</termNote>
     <termNote type="ref_frequency">5</termNote>
    </termGrp>
   </ntig>
  </langSet>
 </termEntry>
```

The same procedure can be implemented on the Slovene side, with similar results, as shown in Figure 7.17.

Using this extremely simplified corpus-building procedure, translators can compile new corpora from TMs, texts stored on their personal computers, or web pages, which means that our Slovene translator can also produce a list of Slovene terms used in their source text. After clicking on the 'Create corpus'

[4] The corpus is available for download in the ELRC-SHARE Repository: https://elrc-share.eu/repository/browse/secretariat-general-parallel-corpus-sl-en-and-en-sl-part-1/b0b331a3f42711e6bfe700155d02050215d7a2b820f74b6fa9980b2f06390c17/.

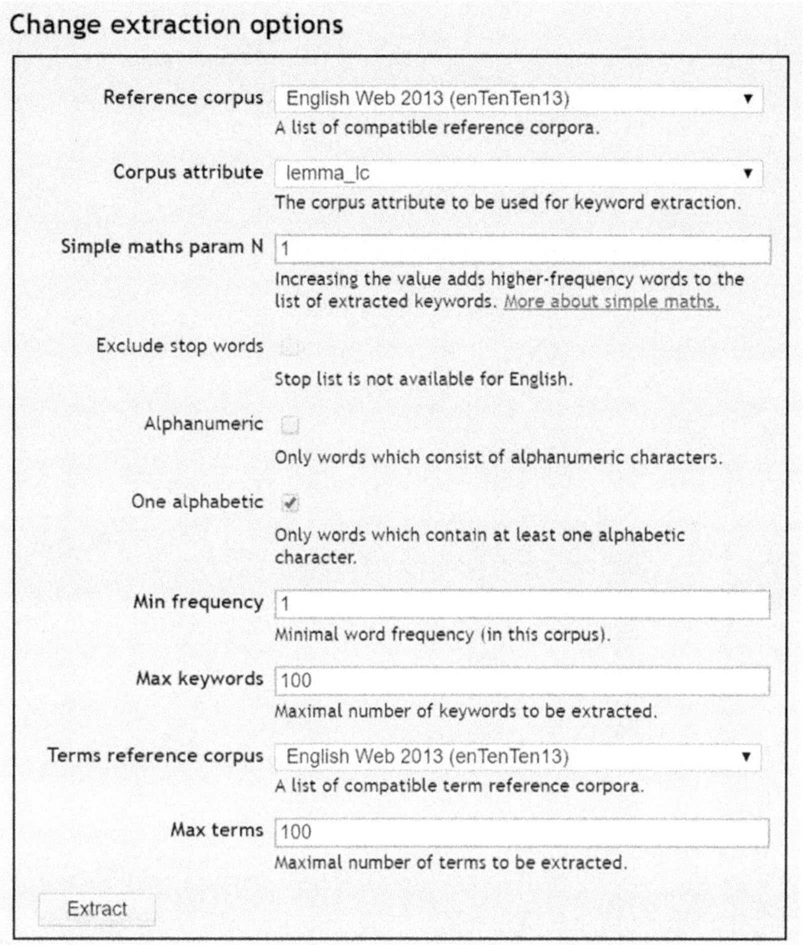

Figure 7.15 The ‘Change extraction options’ box in Sketch Engine

option in the left-hand side menu, the translator will first have to name the new corpus (‘Lisbon Treaty’) and select the language (Slovene) from the drop-down menu, as seen in Figure 7.18.

As the source text is available online, the translator can simply add the webpage’s link to the ‘Download from location’ field to load the text, which simplifies the procedure even further, as shown in Figure 7.19.

After finalising this step, the texts will be made available in the Sketch Engine; however, the corpus itself will still have to be compiled. This can be achieved by clicking on ‘Compile corpus’, as shown in Figure 7.20 below.

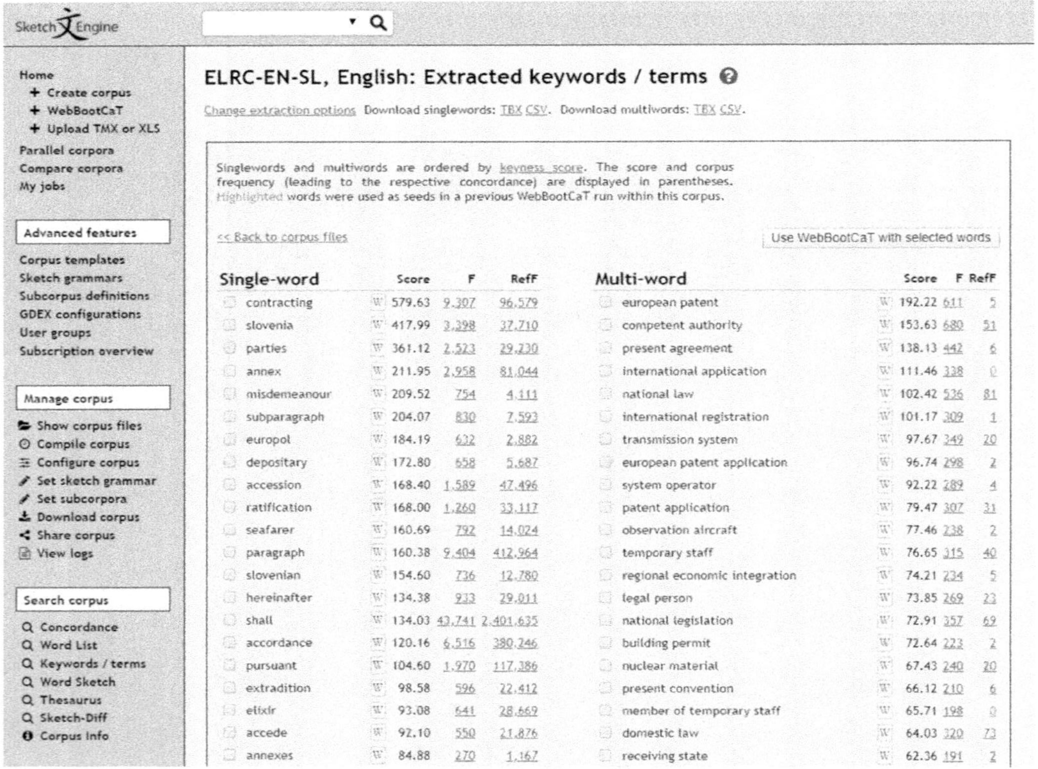

Figure 7.16 English term candidates extracted from the specialised parallel corpus

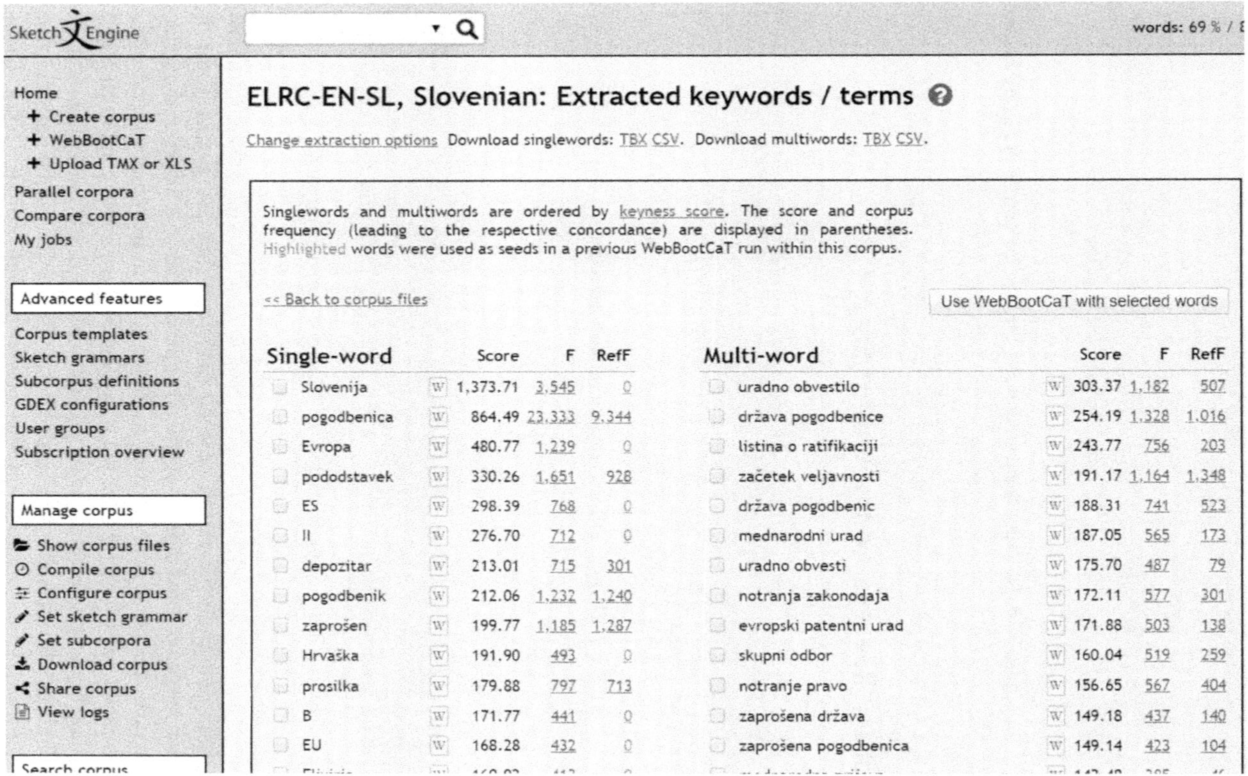

Figure 7.17 Slovene term candidates extracted from the specialised parallel corpus

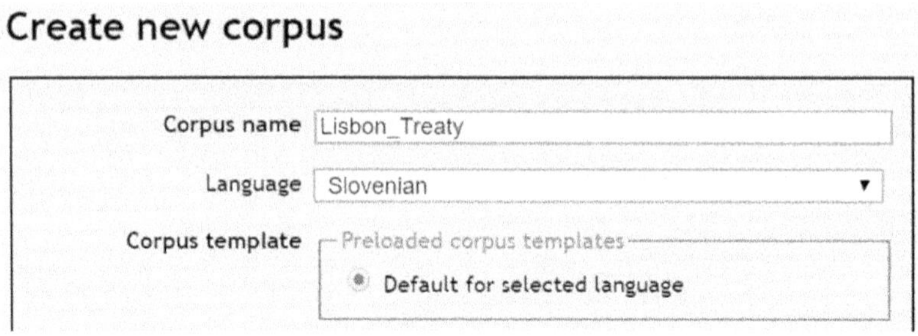

Figure 7.18 Defining basic parameters for the new corpus in Sketch Engine

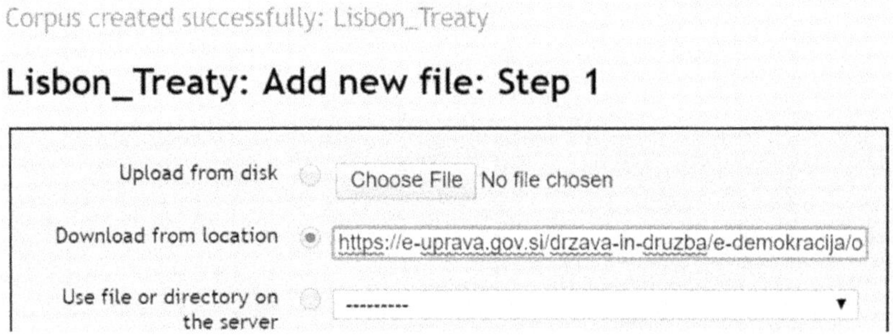

Figure 7.19 Step 1 of the corpus-building procedure

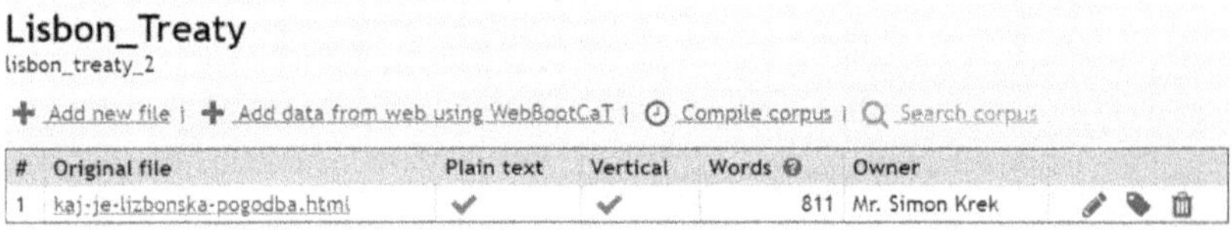

Figure 7.20 Corpus files and the 'Compile corpus' command

When compiling the corpus, the user needs to specify which sketch grammar and term definition file are to be used (provided they are available for the selected language), and define several other parameters, e.g. whether duplicates (i.e. repeated sentences or parts of sentences) are to be removed, and which structural elements are to be used (e.g. sentences, paragraphs), amongst others. Defining these parameters at the preprocessing stage is extremely important, as it will allow our translator to use all Sketch Engine functionalities, including the term-extraction feature, on the newly created corpus. After having compiled the corpus, our Slovene translator will be able to produce a comprehensive list of single- and multi-word terms from the Lisbon Treaty text within a few minutes (cf. Figure 7.21).

A bilingual term-extraction option has also been developed and implemented (cf. Kovář, Baisa and Jakubíček, 2016); however, only a handful of language pairs are currently supported. As part of our case study, we tested the feature on several parallel corpora available through Sketch Engine and were able to generate results only for one corpus (DGT) and a very small subset of languages (English, French, German, Czech, Spanish, Portuguese), which indicates that this feature is under development.

7.4 Conclusion

Sketch Engine is a user-friendly, robust and multifunctional CQS incorporating a wide array of state-of-the-art features with dozens of monolingual and parallel corpora for both major and under-resourced languages. As such, it provides a solid basis for computer-aided translation. Through the lens of a real-life translation scenario, the chapter discussed how translators can take full advantage of the concordancer, the 'Word Sketch' and 'Sketch Diff' tools, the distributional thesaurus and the term-extraction feature to harness the power of corpus data in support of their work. Overall, Sketch Engine performed well in all the designed tasks; however, the case study also highlighted a major weakness, i.e. limited coverage. Although Sketch Engine currently integrates corpora for more than ninety languages, which is impressive, some of the more advanced bilingual features, i.e. fully aligned bilingual word sketches, the 'Translate' button and bilingual term extraction, are available only for a small subset of the supported languages. Nonetheless, as the Sketch Engine is constantly improving in terms of language support and new features, we can safely predict that these issues will be addressed in the near future. In the meantime, the Sketch Engine has just recently committed to providing academic users with free access for the next four years (2018–2022) as part of the ELEXIS infrastructure project.[5] Funded by the Horizon 2020 research programme, ELEXIS will set up a European lexicographic infrastructure to foster research and cooperation in lexicography and natural language processing. Free academic access to Sketch Engine includes all functionalities available to subscribers as of 2018, as well as those to be developed during the project. For instance, one of the new functionalities will be Lexonomy (Měchura, 2017), i.e. a cloud-based, open-source platform for writing and publishing dictionaries, which will be integrated into Sketch Engine. Although freelancers and translators employed by translation companies are not eligible, university students and academics specialising in translation

[5] Further information on the project is available on ELEXIS' website: www.elex.is/.

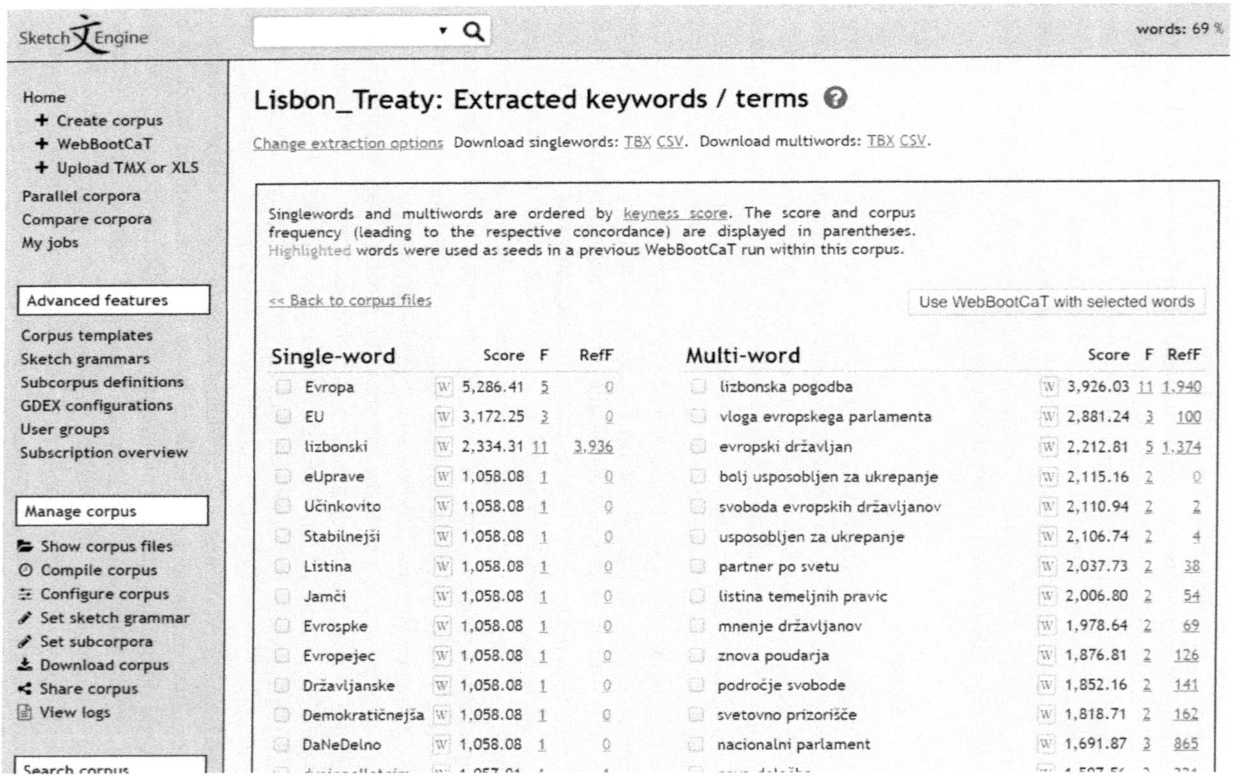

Figure 7.21 Single- and multi-word Slovene terms extracted from the Lisbon Treaty text

studies and translation technology will be able to greatly benefit from having unlimited access to Sketch Engine, which will hopefully lead to an increased awareness of the enormous potential of corpora and corpus query systems for computer-aided translation.

References

Anthony, Lawrence (2018). *AntConc* (Version 3.5.6) [Computer Software]. Tokyo, Japan: Waseda University. Available at: www.laurenceanthony.net/software.

Atkins, B. T. Sue and Michael Rundell (2008). *The Oxford Guide to Practical Lexicography.* Oxford: Oxford University Press.

Baisa, Vít, Miloš Jakubíček, Adam Kilgarriff, Vojtěch Kovář and Pavel Rychlý (2014). Bilingual word sketches: The *translate* button. In *Proceedings of the XVI EURALEX International Congress*. Bolzano: EURAC Research, pp. 505–513.

Baisa, Vít, Michal Cukr and Barbora Ulipová (2015). Bilingual terminology extraction in Sketch Engine. In *9th Workshop on Recent Advances in Slavonic Natural Language Processing (RASLAN 2015)*. Brno: Tribun EU, pp. 65–70.

Baroni, Marco, Adam Kilgarriff, Jan Pomikálek and Pavel Rychlý (2006). WebBootCaT: instant domain-specific corpora to support human translators. In *Proceedings of EAMT, the 11th Annual Conference of the European Association for Machine Translation*. Oslo, Norway, pp. 247–252.

Hanks, Patrick (2013). *Lexical Analysis: Norms and Exploitations*. Cambridge, MA: MIT Press.

Kilgarriff, Adam, Vojtěch Kovář and Pavel Rychlý (2010). Tickbox lexicography. In *eLexicography in the 21st Century: New Challenges, New Applications.* Brussels: Presses universitaires de Louvain, pp. 411–418.

Kilgarriff, Adam, Vít Baisa, Jan Bušta, Miloš Jakubíček, Vojtěch Kovář, Jan Michelfeit, Pavel Rychlý and Vít Suchomel (2014a). The Sketch Engine: Ten years on. *Lexicography* 1, 7–36.

Kilgarriff, Adam, Miloš Jakubíček, Vojtěch Kovář, Pavel Rychlý and Vít Suchomel (2014b). Finding terms in corpora for many languages with the Sketch Engine. In *Proceedings of the Demonstrations at the 14th Conference of the European Chapter of the Association for Computational Linguistics*. Gothenburg, Sweden: The Association for Computational Linguistics, pp. 53–56.

Kovář, Vojtěch, Vít Baisa and Miloš Jakubíček (2016). Sketch Engine for bilingual lexicography. *International Journal of Lexicography* 29(4), 339–352.

McEnery, Tony and Andrew Wilson (2001). *Corpus Linguistics: An Introduction* (2nd edition). Edinburgh: Edinburgh University Press.

Měchura, Michal (2017). Introducing Lexonomy: An open-source dictionary writing and publishing system. In *Electronic Lexicography in the 21st Century: Proceedings of eLex 2017 Conference*. Leiden: Lexical Computing, pp. 662–679.

O'Keefe, Anne, Michael McCarthy and Ronald Carter (2007). *From Corpus to Classroom: Language Use and Language Teaching*. Cambridge, UK: Cambridge University Press.

Rychlý, Pavel (2008). A lexicographer-friendly association score. In *Proceedings of Recent Advances in Slavonic Natural Language Processing, RASLAN*. Brno: Masaryk University, pp. 6–9.

Scott, Mike (2018). *WordSmith Tools Version 7*. Stroud: Lexical Analysis Software. Available at: www.lexically.net/wordsmith/downloads.

Sinclair, John (1991). *Corpus, Concordance, Collocation*. Oxford: Oxford University Press.

Sinclair, John (2004). *Trust the Text: Language, Corpus and Discourse*. London/New York: Routledge.

Thomas, James (2016). *Discovering English with Sketch Engine: A Corpus-Based Approach to Language Exploration* (2nd edition). Brno: Versatile.

Timmis, Ivor (2015). *Corpus for ELT: Research and Practice*. London: Routledge.

Zaretskaya, Anna, Gloria Corpas Pastor and Miriam Seghiri (2015). Translators' requirements for translation technologies: A user survey. In Gloria Corpas-Pastor, Miriam Seghiri-Domınguez, Rut Gutierrez-Florido and Miriam Urbano-Medaña (eds.), *New Horizons in Translation and Interpreting Studies* (Full papers). Malaga, Spain: Tradulex, pp. 247–254.

Zaretskaya, Anna, Gloria Corpas Pastor and Miriam Seghiri (2016). Corpora in computer-assisted translation: A users' view. In Gloria Corpas-Pastor and Miriam Seghiri (eds.), *Corpus-Based Approaches to Translation and Interpreting: From Theory to Applications*. Frankfurt: Peter Lang, pp. 253–276.

8 Developing Computerised Health Translation Readability Evaluation Tools

Meng Ji and Zhaoming Gao

8.1 Introduction

Research in readability has a long history. In 1921, educational psychologist Thorndike published the *Teachers' Word Book*, which contained frequency information for the most frequent 10,000 words in English (Thorndike, 1921). This was the first systematic study on the difficulty of words based on frequency information taken from language corpora. Two years later, Lively and Pressey proposed the first readability formula in which words outside Thorndike's frequent word list were considered difficult (Lively and Pressey, 1923). By the early 1920s, researchers already noticed that sentence length, word length and word frequency were important indicators related to the reading difficulty of written texts. The development of readability formulas represented a landmark in empirical educational research. This trend converted previously subjective evaluations to objective procedures that could be observed and calculated. The importance of readability was not only appreciated by education researchers, but also by health authorities and professionals. Health research was among the earliest applications for readability testing. The relationship between readability and health literacy was very close from the early days when readability formulas were developed. For instance, texts on health topics were analysed by Dale and Tyler (1934) using one of the earliest readability formulas. The Simple Measure of Gobbledygook (SMOG) grading scheme was also recommended for use in health literacy research (Doak, Doak and Root, 1985). In more recent times, readability formulas were used to assess the accessibility of web-based versus printed health education materials among populations with limited education and health literacy levels (Friedman and Hoffman-Goetz, 2006).

While English readability formulas have been employed by health professionals for a long time, readability in non-European languages remains largely under-explored, especially in the context of health literacy and health education. With the increasing number of multicultural immigrants to English-speaking countries, there is a pressing need to explore the readability of health resources translated into the first languages of immigrants to reduce increasing the health and economic burdens caused by populations with limited education and health literacy levels (Kreps and Sparks, 2008). In multicultural societies, effective health communication among a culturally and linguistically diverse population lies at the heart of the prevention and self-management of chronic, lifestyle-related diseases such as diabetes and cardiovascular diseases which represent leading burdens of disease in developed countries. In Australia, for example, despite the large investment in diabetes research, there is a costly long-existing gap in the communication of health risk factors such as physical activities and food choices among culturally and linguistically diverse populations (Thow and Waters, 2005; Caperchione et al., 2011). If not managed effectively, the resulting elevation in blood glucose, blood pressure, cholesterol and depression puts people at high risk of developing complications as well as increasing an individual's risk of developing a range of other chronic conditions, such as cancer and Alzheimer's (Jowsey, Gillespie and Aspin, 2011). This morbidity is accompanied by an increased risk of early death. The development of health translation resources which are of high readability and wide accessibility among the target populations holds the key to the success and sustainability of health promotion and education in multicultural societies. This chapter introduces a computerised system for assessing the readability of Chinese health translations. The development of the health readability system was informed by research in corpus linguistics (Crossley, Greenfield and McNamara, 2008). The system was used to evaluate and label the reading difficulty of a large number of Chinese health-related translations produced by national health authorities in Australia. The resulting readability scores were compared with those computed for non-translated health educational resources published by national health organisations in China. The differences thus identified between the two sets of health education resources in terms of language and communication styles point to areas to further improve the linguistic comprehensibility and accessibility of the health translations resources currently used in Australia for health promotion among Chinese-speaking populations.

8.2 Development of the Chinese Text Readability Analyser

Recent advances in readability research have been made possible by breakthroughs in natural language processing (NLP) and machine learning over the past three decades. The wide availability of NLP resources and tools, such as corpora, lexicons, part-of-speech taggers and parsers, has made recent readability formulas more sophisticated and powerful than those proposed decades ago. For example, Coh-metrix is a state-of-the-art tool for measuring the readability of English texts using various NLP resources and tools (Graesser et al.,

2004; Crossley, Allen and McNamara, 2011). It has over sixty computational indexes for vocabulary, syntax and discourse in English texts. It also includes programs which can compute the coherence and cohesion of a text. In our study, the health translation readability testing instrument has been adapted from readability tools which have been developed for Chinese education materials assessment and general literacy studies.

For example, along the lines of Coh-metrix, Sung et al. (2013) proposed a model for Chinese readability based on twenty-four computational indexes. A total of 386 articles from textbooks ranging from primary to high schools were employed for constructing the model and 96 new articles used for validation, with the grade level as the independent variable. Stepwise regression and the Support Vector Machine (SVM) machine-learning algorithm were chosen as the statistical and machine-learning tools, respectively. The results showed that the number of difficult words, the percentage of simple sentences, average logarithm of content word frequency and the number of pronouns were the most important predictors in the stepwise regression model. For the SVM model, the number of difficult words, the number of two-character words, the number of characters and the number of intermediate-stroke characters were the most significant features. According to Sung et al. (2013), the accuracy rates of stepwise regression and SVM were 55.21 and 72.92 per cent.

It should be noted that Sung et al. (2013) explored the readability of non-translated Chinese texts rather than translations. In addition, the computational indexes proposed by Sung et al. (2013) were limited to individual lexical features. Compound and complex lexical features such as the number of Chinese nominal phrases, n-grams and frequency-based bands of words were not discussed in their study. However, the distribution of compound lexical features serves as a key indicator of textual coherence; and the collocation patterns and frequency statistics of Chinese nominal phrases and n-grams provide important clues regarding the information load and linguistic technicality of the texts, which are particularly relevant for the study of the readability and accessibility of health education resources among populations with limited education and health literacy levels. The new computerised system developed in our research has built on the individual lexical features studied in Sung et al. (2013). For example, we have included dependent variables such as the length of Chinese words in terms of characters and the frequency of character words as an indicator of reading difficulty, the total number of running character words (i.e. tokens), the number of distinct character words (types) and the type–token ratio. In addition, we have included textual features such as the percentage of punctuation, and frequency bands ranging from the most frequent and least-frequent character word bands in Chinese. Each band contains around 6,000 Chinese character words, the average frequency-band ranking, and the average number and length of noun phrases. In total, thirty-nine indexes were incorporated into the computerised Chinese readability testing system which has significantly enhanced its capacity to assess the readability of Chinese texts based on the analysis of the statistical profiles of the lexical complexity, textual coherence and information load of the written materials (Appendix 8.1).

8.3 Research Methodologies and Chinese Health Translation Corpora

The development of the Chinese readability system was an important preparation for the study of linguistic and textual features of Chinese health education resources. The rest of the chapter focuses on the development of a data-driven statistical model that can be used to predict the linguistic readability of Chinese health materials. Despite being an important health communication and social intervention tool, multicultural health translation has been explored to a limited extent. Given the increasing health risks among non-English-speaking populations in multicultural societies, there is a pressing need to conduct systematic research on the approaches and strategies to develop effective health translation and communication materials for populations with distinct language, cultural, ethnic and educational backgrounds.

The rest of the chapter develops an empirical health translation assessment instrument based on the collection, analysis and statistical modelling of a large number of health translations produced in Australia for its diverse and growing Chinese-speaking populations. The statistical translation assessment tool will identify, first of all, specific linguistic, textual and stylistic features which tend to be associated with health translations of low and high reading difficulty; secondly, the patterns of linguistic and textual features that characterise expert ratings of high- versus low-readability translations across the various predictors; and thirdly, linguistic and textual features that are predictive of health translations of high readability and accessibility for Chinese-speaking populations.

The statistical modelling of the Chinese health translations starts with the identification of key dimensions of linguistic and textual features that characterise Chinese health translations. For the purposes of this study, which is to assess the readability of health education resources in Australia among its Chinese-speaking populations, a large corpus of health translations was constructed which contains around 100 Chinese health-related translations produced and widely circulated by national health organisations and governmental health-service providers in Australia. These include Alzheimer's Australia, Cancer Australia, Heart Foundation Australia, Kidney Foundation, National Asthma Council, New South Wales Multicultural Health Communication and Osteoporosis Australia. Each organisation was given a label to facilitate the identification of the source of the translation included in the Chinese health translation corpus. The total size of the corpus is 382,692 Chinese character words.

The health translation corpus features a variety of health education resources commissioned and circulated by different health organisations in Australia. The topics covered by the translation corpus include health guidelines for the prevention and self-management of chronic diseases like type-2 diabetes, cardiovascular diseases, kidney diseases, cancers, asthma and osteoporosis, and advice on healthy diet and physical activities, medication, aged care, women and children's health and wellbeing, etc. Some of the topics are highly specialised and the narrative styles of the translations are more abstract and technical such as the description of diseases and medical syndromes and the explanation of their physiological mechanisms. Some of the translations included in the corpus are more general and practical such as health guidelines, health advice, an introduction to the Australian healthcare system and usage of health facilitates and services.

There is a range of factors that may affect the readability and comprehensibility of the health-related translations and education resources. Apart from the influence of the language style and content of the source English texts, the diverse language, cultural and educational backgrounds and the different translation styles and strategies used by medical translators may also have an impact on the outcomes of translation. Chinese-speaking translators in Australia often have different demographic profiles in terms of the country of origin, gender, age, education, etc. However, the translation market in Australia is well regulated, as health organisations, business entities and governmental agencies are required to contract qualified translators based on formal assessments by the National Accreditation Authority of Translators and Interpreters (NAATI). In the evaluation and qualification of professional translators, NAATI applies a set of national standards and criteria in terms of the clarity, accuracy and linguistic naturalness of the translation outcome, which has an important regulatory effect on the overall translation market.

In this study, a wide range of Chinese health-related translations produced by local translators were purposely included in the Australian Chinese Health Translation Corpus. This not only increases the representativeness of the corpus, but also enhances the robustness and wide applicability of the health translation assessment instrument to be developed for analysing and predicting the readability of Chinese health translation materials.

8.4 Findings of Exploratory Statistical Modelling

This section uses exploratory statistics to identify linguistic and textual features which tend to be associated with health translation materials of low and high readability. Translations included in the Australian Chinese Health Translation Corpus were input into the online Chinese Readability Analyser which returned the frequency data of the thirty-nine lexical indexes which provide important information on the readability of the translations in terms of the linguistic

Table 8.1 *Exploratory factor analysis model*

	Initial eigenvalues			Extraction sums of squared loadings			Rotation sums of squared loadings		
Component	Total	per cent of variance	Cumulative per cent	Total	per cent of variance	Cumulative per cent	Total	per cent of variance	Cumulative per cent
1	6.452	6.4520	6.4520	6.452	6.4520	6.4520	6.428	6.4285	6.4285
2	1.907	19.072	83.593	1.907	19.072	83.593	1.931	19.308	**83.593**

complexity, textual coherence and information load. Exploratory factor analysis is a useful exploratory technique that can be used to identify the latent factors or variables in the original data set. The latent factors extracted often contain a number of the independent variables which underline the theoretical structure of the original data set. This technique is particularly useful when the original data set has a large number of independent variables which makes it difficult to detect the internal structure of the original data set.

In this study, the computerised Chinese readability testing system has as many as thirty-nine lexical indexes which requires the use of dimension deduction techniques to streamline the corpus analysis. Following the calculation of the lexical profiles of the translations included in the Australian Chinese Health Translation Corpus, exploratory factor analysis constructed a statistical model which was based on the computation of the correlation matrix of the independent variables or the lexical indexes of the Chinese Readability Analyser. The factor analysis model has a Kaiser-Meyer-Olkin (KMO) score of 0.875, and the significance level of the Bartlett Test (0.00) is well below the threshold value of 0.05. Both these statistics which measure the sampling adequacy and sphericity of the data point to a statistically significant model.

Table 8.1 shows the internal structure of the two-dimensional model which classifies the original thirty-nine lexical indexes into two large latent factors. The first latent factors accounts for almost two-thirds (64.285 per cent) of the total variance in the original data set. The second latent factor accounts for another 20 per cent (19.308 per cent) of the total variance in the original data set. In exploratory factor analysis, the variance explained by different factors is accumulative, which means that the total amount of variance explained by the two-dimensional model in this study is 83.593 per cent. This indicates a model which has largely explained the complex internal structure of the thirty-nine lexical indexes included in the Chinese readability testing system.

Table 8.2 shows the two-dimensional model and the loadings of the lexical indexes on each of the two dimensions. The two dimensions of independent variables are extracted from the original linguistic and textual features of

Table 8.2 *Rotated component matrix of the two-dimensional factor analysis model*

	Quantifiable textual features	Component 1	Component 2
1	Total words	**0.974**	0.09
2	Total characters	**0.966**	0.146
3	Punctuations	**0.965**	0.09
4	Types of words	**0.963**	0.06
5	Consecutive noun phrases	**0.944**	0.166
6	VHA and noun phrases	**0.88**	−0.161
7	Adjective and noun phrases	**0.862**	−0.138
8	Non-repeated multi-character words	0.074	**0.836**
9	Non-repeated two-character words	0.337	**−0.819**
10	Non-repeated four-character words	0.402	**0.669**

Chinese health translations. As may be seen in Table 8.2, this new analytical model has streamlined the corpus analysis by reducing the large number of original textual features from thirty-nine lexical indexes to ten textual and linguistic features which explain the largest amount of variance in the original data set. The first latent factor contains seven textual and linguistic features: total words; total characters; punctuations; types of words; consecutive noun phrases; VHA (abbreviation for Chinese predicate adjectives) and noun phrases; adjective and noun phrases. These seven textual variables have large loadings on the first dimension or latent factor which indicate their contribution to the first dimension.

Examples of consecutive noun phrases are 鐮狀 細胞 疾病 (lián zhuàng xì bāo jí bìng) (sickle-cell disease); 前 胚胎 遺傳 診斷 (qián pēi tāi yí chuán zhěn duàn) (pre-embryo genetic diagnosis); β珠蛋白 基因 (B zhū dàn bái jī yīn) (β globin gene); 結核 分枝 桿菌 (jié hé fēn zhī gǎn jùn) (Mycobacterium tuberculosis); 男性 荷爾 濛睾丸素 (nán xìng hè ěr méng gāo wán sù) (male hormone testosterone); 腹膜 透析 (fù mó tòu xī) (peritoneal dialysis); 腎小球 濾過率 (shèn xiǎo qiú lǜ guò lǜ) (glomerular filtration rate); and 皮質 類固醇 鼻噴劑 (Pízhí lèigùchún bí pēn jì) (corticosteroid nasal spray). Examples of patterned VHA and noun phrases are 精 囊 膀胱 輸精 (jīng náng pang guāng shū jīng) (seminal vesicle bladder insemination); 增長 繁殖 (zēng zhǎng fánzhí) (growth and reproduction); 超重 範圍 (chāo zhòng fàn wéi) (overweight range); 特異 抗原 (tè yì kàng yuán) (specific antigen); 異常 宮頸 塗片 結果 (yì cháng gōng jǐng tú piàn jié guǒ) (abnormal cervical smear results); and 免疫 化學 FOBT 檢驗 (miǎn yì huà xué FOBT jiǎn yàn) (immunochemical faecal occult blood test). Examples of Chinese patterned adjective and noun phrases are 慢性 腸道 炎性 疾病 (màn xìng cháng dào yán xìng jí bìng) (chronic intestinal inflammatory diseases); 綜合 治療 小組 (zòng hé zhì liáo xiǎo zǔ) (comprehensive treatment group); 惡性 腫瘤 論斷 (È xìng zhǒng liú lùn duàn) (cancer diagnosis); 慢性 乙型 肝炎 (Mànxìng yǐ xíng gānyán) (chronic hepatitis B); 慢性 心力衰竭 (Mànxìng xīnlì shuāijié) (chronic heart failure); 循環式 透析 (xún huán shì tòu xī) (circulating dialysis); and 急性 排斥 反應 (jí xìng pái chì fǎn yìng) (acute rejection).

The three textual and linguistic features of total words, total characters and types of words are related to the amount of information in health translations. The four textual features of noun and noun phrases, VHA and noun phrases, adjective and noun phrases and the number of punctuation marks are related to the semantic and textual coherence of Chinese health translations. Chinese is different from languages using the Latin alphabet, as there is no space between Chinese words made of characters. The comprehension of Chinese texts often starts with the segmentation and isolation of character words within long character strings. In written Chinese, punctuation marks are mainly used for separating long sentences into smaller textual segments. The understanding of smaller textual segments largely depends on the collocation patterns of Chinese character words which are written with no space in between. High-frequency phrasal patterns include phrases made of consecutive nouns, phrases combining VHA and nouns, and phrases containing an adjective followed by a noun. These conventionalised lexical and phrasal patterns provide culturally loaded, effective communication methods to facilitate the comprehension of Chinese written texts including translations. The enhanced use of patterned phrases can significantly increase the amount of information to be delivered in written materials, adding to the information load and reading difficulty among certain population groups.

The second latent factor contains three textual and linguistic features which are non-repeated multi-character words, non-repeated two-character words and non-repeated four-character words. Patterned character words represent another effective communication method in written Chinese. Historical Chinese was overwhelmingly monosyllabic, with the majority of historical Chinese words made of one character only. As the language evolved, an increasing number of disyllabic, trisyllabic, quadrisyllabic and multi-character expressions were created and gradually assimilated into the original Chinese lexical system. In contemporary Chinese, disyllabic words represent the largest number of words in modern Chinese lexis. The majority of Chinese idioms are made of four characters, and to a lesser extent, three- or five-character words. Patterned character words represent more explicit, idiomatic and highly accessible lexical resources for Chinese-speaking populations.

In written Chinese, the enhanced use of patterned character expressions can effectively increase the textual and semantic coherence of the written materials. It is useful to notice that in our study, whereas four-character and multi-character words have large positive loadings on the second latent factor, 0.669 and 0.836, respectively, two-character words have large negative loading on the same dimension. This corpus finding suggests that the use of two-character expressions may well have the opposite effect from the use of four- and five-character expressions in the Chinese health translations under study. To understand and interpret this corpus finding, a large number of relevant expressions were extracted from the health translation corpus. It was found that while in general Chinese writing, four-character and multi-character expressions tend to be idiomatic expressions, patterned character words retrieved from the health translation corpus were mostly medical expressions and technical terms including the transliteration of medications and names of diseases. As a result, the large positive loadings of four-character and multi-character expressions on this dimension imply that the second dimension of the factor analysis provides a measurement of the lexical technicality of health translations. The large negative loading of two-character expressions on the second dimension indicates that an increased use of this linguistic feature will lead to enhanced readability or lexical familiarity of the health translation materials.

The two latent factors extracted from the exploratory factory analysis point to two important scales of Chinese health translation readability evaluation: information load (Factor 1) and lexical technicality (Factor 2). In Section 8.5, we will evaluate the effectiveness of the model by using confirmatory discriminant analysis. This will be achieved by comparing the readability assessment scales developed by statistics and the human-based readability assessment provided by health communication experts with extensive experience of working with the targeted populations. At this stage, two human annotators were contracted to develop the human judgement variable. The two independent annotators were accredited bilingual health communication experts in Australia. They were native Chinese speakers with near native English proficiency.

Each annotator was given access to the entire corpus of Chinese health translations and enough time to read through and compare the translations. Based on their experience of working with Chinese Australians over the years, they provided their own binary marks of the reading difficulty of the translation materials. The coding of the dependent variable followed a binary scheme: one for translations of low reading difficulty, and two for translations of high reading difficulty. The increased value of the dependent variable signifies the increased reading difficulty of the health translation materials. The reading difficulty scores provided by the two human annotators were verified in a statistical reliability test. The Cronbach's alpha score of inter-annotator reliability was 0.861, which confirmed the internal consistency of the human assessment of the difficulty of the Chinese health translations selected for readability testing.

Table 8.3 *Model fit: Discriminant analysis*[a]

Eigenvalues				
Function	Eigenvalue	Per cent of variance	Cumulative per cent	Canonical correlation
1	0.860[a]	100.0	100.0	0.680

[a] First 1 canonical discriminant function was used in the analysis

The next task was to evaluate the effectiveness of the data-driven readability scales derived from the original textual features in a confirmatory factor analysis or discriminant analysis. This was achieved by matching and comparing the human-assessed difficulty of the health translations with the predicted difficulty of translations based on the statistically built assessment model. As explained above, the human annotation of the reading difficulty of health translations created a binary dependent variable (1 = low-difficulty text; and 2 = high-difficulty text). This binary dependent variable was used to assess the predictive power of the function extracted in the discriminant analysis. Table 8.3 shows the fitness of the discriminant model. The function derived has an eigenvalue of 0.860 and a canonical correlation of 0.680. Both statistics point to a reasonably efficient model.

Table 8.4 shows the component variables in the statistical function built. In Table 8.4, the key statistical indicator is Wilks' lambda. The Wilks' lambda provides a measurement of how well the function identified by the discriminant analysis separates the dependent variable into groups, which in this case are the two reading difficulty levels of Chinese health translations. Wilks' lambda is equal to the proportion of the total variance in the discriminant scores not explained by differences among the groups of the dependent variable. Smaller values of Wilks' lambda indicate greater discriminatory ability of the function. The small significance value of the associated chi-square indicates that the discriminant function does better than chance at separating the groups.

Table 8.4 displays the five textual and linguistic features entered successively into the function to reduce the Wilks' lambda. Items entered earlier into the function contribute to the predictive power of the function more than those entered at a later stage. For example, total words and non-repeated two-character words were first entered into the function. This indicates that these two textual features have greater discriminatory ability when assessing the readability level of Chinese health translations. As we can see in Table 8.4, the original ten-item model developed in the exploratory factor analysis has been refined to a five-item function. Compared with the factor analysis model constructed, the function derived has removed five textual features due to their limited contribution to the discriminant function. The resulting

Table 8.4 *Discriminant analysis (stepwise)*

Variables entered[a,b]									
		Wilks' lambda							
						Exact F			
Step	Entered	Statistic	df1	df2	df3	Statistic	df1	df2	Sig.
1	Total words	0.751	1	1	96.000	31.773	1	96.000	0.000
2	Non-repeated two-character words	0.644	2	1	96.000	26.313	2	95.000	0.000
3	Types of words	0.601	3	1	96.000	20.780	3	94.000	0.000
4	Consecutive noun phrases	0.564	4	1	96.000	17.954	4	93.000	0.000
5	Non-repeated four-character words	**0.538**	5	1	96.000	15.828	5	92.000	0.000

[a] At each step, the variable that minimises the overall Wilks' lambda is entered.
[b] Minimum partial F to enter is 3.84; Maximum partial F to remove is 2.71.

discriminant function thus provides an effective instrument for the prediction of the readability level of Chinese health translations.

Tables 8.5 and 8.6 provide a structural analysis of the function derived from discriminant analysis. Textual factors which have larger standardised canonical discriminant function coefficients and larger correlation scores in the structural matrix are more useful to the function which predicts and labels the readability level of Chinese health translations included in the Australian Chinese Health Translation Corpus. The structural matrix is based on within-groups correlations between discriminating variables and standardised canonical discriminant functions. The independent variables are ordered by the absolute size of correlation within the function derived from the discriminant analysis. The statistics presented in Tables 8.5 and 8.6 point to similar findings. The textual variable of total character words is most strongly correlated with the discriminant function. Similarly, types of words and double noun phrases are also strongly correlated with the function. By contrast, non-repeated two-character and four-character words exhibit a modest correlation with the discriminatory function derived.

Table 8.7 shows the result of the predictive classification using the statistical function derived from the discriminant analysis. Table 8.7 contains two sets of classification results. The first one is based on the original health translation data set; 84.7 per cent of the original grouped cases were correctly classified. Specifically, the function of discriminant analysis has correctly predicted forty-four of the fifty-two health translations of low reading difficulty. This accounts for 86.3 per cent of the total low-difficulty-translation sub-data set. Similarly, in

Table 8.5 *Standardised canonical discriminant function coefficients*

Textual features	Function
Total words	4.024
Types of words	−2.126
Non-repeated two-character words	0.357
Consecutive noun phrases	−1.12
Non-repeated four-character words	−0.483

Table 8.6 *Structure matrix of the five-item model*

Textual features	Function
Total words	0.62
Types of words	0.543
Non-repeated two-character words	0.523
Consecutive noun phrases	0.499
Non-repeated four-character words	−0.065

Table 8.7 *Classification result*

			Predicted group membership		
Human judgement			Low difficulty	High difficulty	Total
Original	Count	Low difficulty	44	7	51
		High difficulty	8	39	47
	per cent	Low difficulty	**86.3**	13.7	100
		High difficulty	17	**83**	100
Cross-validated	Count	Low difficulty	43	8	51
		High difficulty	9	38	47
	per cent	Low difficulty	**84.3**	15.7	100
		High difficulty	19.1	**80.9**	100

predicting and identifying health translations of high reading difficulty, the function has accurately labelled thirty-nine of the total forty-six health translations in that group. This represents a high prediction score of 83 per cent. To further verify the result, cross-validation was performed for all the cases in the analysis. In the cross-validation process, each health translation was classified by the function derived from all other translations in the database. An equally high overall function accuracy score was reported: 82.7 per cent of the total cross-validated grouped health translations were correctly classified. In the cross-validation, forty-three of the fifty-two low-difficulty translations were labelled correctly by the function (84.3 per cent), whereas thirty-eight of the forty-six high-difficulty translations retrieved by the function matched the human-based assessment (80.9 per cent).

The success of the factor model thus built raises another question, i.e. whether this health text readability model can be extended from Chinese health translations to original health education texts in the Chinese language. If this model can be effectively extended to encompass both non-translated and translated Chinese health education materials, this will enable the design, development and objective assessment of Chinese health translations, as the computerised analytical model can effectively identify and suggest specific areas for improvement in health translation based on the statistical analysis of textual, linguistic and stylistic features of popular, non-translated Chinese health promotion and education resources. To address this question, Section 8.5 of the chapter will continue to test the validity and efficiency of the Chinese health translation readability assessment instrument with non-translated, popular Chinese digital health education resources.

8.5 Testing the Chinese Health Readability Instrument with Non-Translated Chinese Health Materials

This section verifies the ten-item analytical instrument developed in the exploratory analysis of Chinese health translations. This is achieved through the inclusion of ten original Chinese health education articles written by health experts for people with limited education and health literacy in China. The ten original health education articles were carefully chosen from two creditable sources of popular health communication and education materials: the Chinese Centre for Disease Control and Prevention, and the China Science Communication Digital Portal, which are developed and regularly updated by the Chinese health authorities: the Ministry of Health of China and the China Association for Science and Technology. Health education materials circulated on these two digital health portals have important features which contribute to the wide circulation and endorsement of these health education materials: the credibility of the scientific and health knowledge conveyed in the health materials distributed, and the high level of readability or the perceived persuasiveness or actionability of these materials among the target audiences. Health education materials published on the China Science Communication Digital Portal are often developed collaboratively between medical professionals and health communication specialists.

The ten original Chinese health education articles were chosen particularly for the fact that they represent important joint efforts between experienced health communication experts and domain specialists, as indicated by their joint signatures provided at the end of the articles. The topics of the ten original Chinese health materials cover osteoporosis, adult dietary guidelines, high blood pressure control, children's dietary guidelines, pain management, salt intake reduction methods, drinking water safety surveillance, pregnancy health and disease management such as for irritable bowel syndrome. The diverse topics selected for non-translated texts mirrored the topical complexity of the Australian Chinese Health Translation Corpus used in the previous sections.

To verify the applicability of the factor analysis model in the study of both Chinese health translation and original Chinese health education resources, a discriminant analysis was run with the mixed data set which contained both the translated and non-translated Chinese education materials. This was to compare the human-assessed readability level with the predicted readability level of the Chinese health education materials included in the enlarged data set. Since the ten non-translated Chinese health education articles were popular readings among the target audiences, they were labelled as low-difficulty texts following the same binary classification scheme described in Section 8.4 (1= low difficulty; 2 = high difficulty). Tables 8.8 and 8.9 show the statistics which indicate the fitness and efficiency of the function derived from the augmented data set. Similar to the discriminant analysis in the Section 8.4, one function was extracted with the mixed corpus containing both health translations and original Chinese health education materials. The function has an eigenvalue of 0.703 and the canonical correlation is 0.642.

Table 8.10 shows the classification results of the function derived from the enlarged data set. The result contains two parts: 83.3 per cent of original grouped cases were correctly classified, and 75.9 per cent of the cross-validated grouped cases were correctly classified. The rates of correct

Table 8.8 *Model fit*[a]

Function	Eigenvalue	per cent of variance	Cumulative per cent	Canonical correlation
1	0.703	100	100	0.642

[a] First 1 canonical discriminant function was used in the analysis.

Table 8.9 *Wilks' lambda*

Test of function(s)	Wilks' lambda	Chi-square	Df	Sig.
1	0.587	53.487	11	0

Table 8.10 *Classification results*

Human judgement			Predicted group membership: Low difficulty	Predicted group membership: High difficulty	Total
Original	Count	Low difficulty	53	9	62
		High difficulty	9	37	46
	per cent	Low difficulty	**85.5**	14.5	100
		High difficulty	19.6	**80.4**	100
Cross-validated	Count	Low difficulty	51	11	62
		High difficulty	15	31	46
	per cent	Low difficulty	**82.3**	17.7	100
		High difficulty	32.6	**67.4**	100

classification were slightly lower than those with the health translation corpus. It dropped from 86.3 to 85.5 per cent in the prediction of low-difficulty texts, and from 83 to 80.4 per cent in the prediction of high-difficulty texts of the original cases. In a similar pattern, the rate of correct classification decreased from 84.3 to 82.3 per cent in the prediction of low-difficulty texts, and from 80.9 to 67.4 per cent in the prediction of high-difficulty texts of the cross-validated group cases.

The relatively large decrease in the predictor power of the function with high-difficulty texts may be explained by the imbalanced distribution of health resources of low versus high readability levels. With the addition of highly readable, non-translated Chinese health education texts in the enlarged data set, the total number of translations and non-translated health education materials of high readability outweighed articles of low readability. Two possible methods may improve the model. One is to add more low-readability health education materials to enlarge the data set with more abstract and technical Chinese health materials, such as research papers and medical professional readings. The other way to improve the model is to develop and include more textual and linguistic features in the online Chinese Readability Analyser, which will be the topic for future research. Overall, the classification results confirmed that the health readability assessment instrument can be used as a reliable model to diagnose and label the readability level of both Chinese health translations and non-translated Chinese health education resources as a cost-effective alternative to human-judged readability assessment and evaluation.

8.6 Conclusion and Future Research

Despite the growing needs for quality health communication and translation resources in multicultural societies, the study of the readability of health translations represents a largely under-explored research area. This chapter presented a useful effort to advance current health translation readability research, with a focus on computerised Chinese health translation readability assessment. This was achieved through leveraging and integrating empirical research methodologies from corpus translation studies, Chinese linguistics, Chinese educational literacy and computer science. The evaluation of Chinese health educational resources was facilitated by two new empirical analytical tools which form the core of the computerised readability assessment system: the first part is an online Chinese lexical profile analyser that incorporates a wide range of Chinese lexical indexes from individual lexical and textual features such as total word count, total character count, punctuations, non-repeated words, to Chinese lexical and phrasal collocation patterns and lexical features derived from the relative frequency ranking. The second part is a data-driven statistical instrument which extracts two measurement scales from the extensive list of original lexical features included in the online Chinese lexical profiler. The two measurement scales constructed in the factor analysis model identify ten lexical features which point to the information load and the lexical technicality as two indicators of the readability and accessibility of Chinese health translations and non-translated education resources among populations with limited education and health literacy levels.

It was found that seven textual and linguistic features were highly related to the information load of Chinese health materials. These were total words, total characters, total number of punctuations, types of words, consecutive noun phrases, patterned VHA (abbreviation for Chinese predicate adjectives) and noun phrases, and combined adjective and noun phrases. By contrast, three lexical features were detected as the largest contributors to the lexical technicality of Chinese health communication materials: non-repeated multi-character, two-character and four-character words. In general-purpose Chinese writing, the use of multi-character and four-character words tends to be associated with the enhanced idiomaticity of the language, as the majority of Chinese idioms are made of four characters. However, it was found in the Australian Chinese Health Translation Corpus that with the translation of medical and health education materials, the occurrence of multi-character and four-character expressions was likely to be triggered by specific source textual features such as the names of diseases, medications, complex physiological mechanisms and proper nouns related to locations and organisations. On the scale which measures the lexical technicality, the textual feature of two-character words has a large negative loading which suggests that in Chinese health educational resources, the use of two-character words which represent the majority of modern Chinese lexis can reduce the reading difficulty caused by a tense, abstract and highly technical writing and communication style.

The assessment of the readability of Chinese health translations was followed by the testing of the statistical model with non-translated, popular Chinese health education materials published and circulated online by authoritative Chinese health organisations and scientific research bodies. It was found that the two measurement scales of information load and lexical technicality can also successfully detect and discriminate the readability level of a mixed selection of translated and non-translated Chinese health education materials. The rates of correct prediction showed a minor decrease with the classification of low-difficulty texts, whereas a relatively large decrease in the correct prediction rate was found with the discrimination of texts of high reading difficulty. The results suggest new areas for future research to further develop the Chinese text readability testing system. These include the inclusion of more textual, grammatical, syntactical and discourse features in the online Chinese textual feature analyser which currently focuses on Chinese lexical features. It is hypothesised that grammatical and syntactical features also contribute to the readability of the written materials in terms of the textual coherence and the linguistic idiomaticity of the language. The performance of the data-driven statistical instrument can be enhanced by incorporating more varieties of Chinese health education materials, especially those written for medical professionals and thus of high reading difficulty, as the corpus analysis result shows that the predictive power of the model can be affected by the changed relative proportion of Chinese texts of high and low readability when non-translated, popular Chinese health communication and education resources were added to the Australian Chinese Health Translation Corpus.

Appendix 8A.1 *Brief description of the textual features analysed in this study*

1	Total number of Chinese words
2	Total number of Chinese characters
3	Total number of punctuations
4	Ratio between punctuations and Chinese characters
5	Ratio between punctuations and Chinese words
6	Non-repeated words
7	Ratio between word types and word tokens
8	Percentage of non-repeated one-character words
9	Percentage of non-repeated two-character words
10	Percentage of non-repeated three-character words
11	Percentage of non-repeated four-character words
12	Percentage of non-repeated multi-character words

Appendix 8A.1 (*cont.*)

13	Percentage of band one words
14	Percentage of band two words
15	Percentage of band three words
16	Percentage of band four words
17	Percentage of band five words (*)
18	Average band ranking
19	Noun and noun phrases
20	VH and noun phrases
21	A and noun phrases
22	Percentage of three phrase types
23	Average length of phrases in Chinese characters

* In total, twenty-one bands of Chinese words were included.

References

Caperchione, Cristina M., Gregory S. Kolt, Rebeka Tennent and W. Kerry Mummery (2011). Physical activity behaviours of culturally and linguistically diverse (CALD) women living in Australia: A qualitative study of socio-cultural influences, BMC Public Health 11(26). Available at: https://doi.org/10.1186/1471–2458-11–26; www.biomedcentral.com/1471-2458/11/26.

Crossley, Scott A., Jerry Greenfield and Danielle S. McNamara (2008). Assessing text readability using cognitively based indices, TESOL Quarterly, 42(3), 475–493.

Crossley, Scott A., David B. Allen and Danielle S. McNamara (2011). Text readability and intuitive simplification: A comparison of readability formulas, Reading in a Foreign Language 23(1), 84–101.

Dale, Edgar and Ralph W. Tyler (1934). A study of the factors influencing the difficulty of reading materials for adults of limited reading ability, The Library Quarterly 4(3), 384–412.

Doak, Cecilia Conrath, Leonard G. Doak and Jane H. Root (1985). Teaching Patients with Low Literacy Skills. Philadelphia: J. B. Lippincott.

Friedman, Daniela B. and Laurie Hoffman-Goetz (2006). A systematic review of readability and comprehension instruments used for print and web-based cancer information, Health Education and Behaviour 33(3), 352–373.

Graesser, Arthur C., Danielle S. McNamara, Max M. Louwerse and Zhiqiang Cai (2004). Coh-Metrix: Analysis of text on cohesion and language, Behaviour Research Methods 36(2), 193–202.

Jowsey, Tanisha, James Gillespie and Clive Aspin (2011). Effective communication is crucial to self-management: The experiences of immigrants to Australia living with diabetes, Chronic Illness 7(1), 6–19.

Kreps, Gary L. and Lisa Sparks (2008). Meeting the health literacy needs of immigrant populations, Patient Education and Counselling 71(3), 328–332.

Lively, Bertha A. and Sidney Leavitt Pressey (1923). A method for measuring the 'vocabulary burden' of textbooks, Educational Administration and Supervision, 9, 389–398.

Sung, Yao-Ting, Ju-Ling Chen, Yi-Shian Lee, Jih-Ho Cha, Hou-Chiang Tseng, Wei-Chun Lin, TaoHsing Chang and Kuo-En Chang (2013). Investigating Chinese text readability: Linguistic features, modelling, and validation, Chinese Journal of Psychology 55(1), 75–106.

Thorndike, Edward L. (1921). The Teacher's Word Book. New York City, NY: Columbia Teacher's College, Columbia University.

Thow, Anne Marie and Anne-Marie Waters (2005). Diabetes in Culturally and Linguistically Diverse Australians: Identification of Communities at High Risk. Canberra: Australian Institute of Health and Welfare.

9 Reordering Techniques in Japanese and English Machine Translation

Masaaki Nagata

9.1 Introduction

'Machine translation' is a technology which translates one language to the other language using a computer. There are many web pages written in foreign languages such as Chinese, Korean and Arabic, and some of them could include the information we need. Multinational companies have to translate their manuals and product information, quickly and accurately, into local languages. Communication beyond the language barrier is one of the common dreams of human beings.

Research on machine translation began in the 1950s, almost as far back as the birth of the computer. For a full history of machine translation, readers are advised to see Hutchins (2010). In this chapter, we will focus on the transition from rule-based approaches to corpus-based approaches for language pairs with very different word orders such as Japanese and English, by the research and development of reordering techniques for statistical machine translation.

'Rule-based machine translation' is the first generation of machine-translation technology, in which large-scale translation rules and bilingual dictionaries are developed manually for each language pair. It is a labour-intensive task requiring dozens of specialists working over several years. Around the 2000s, a corpus-based approach called 'statistical machine translation' had become the major focus of many research groups (Hutchins, 2010).

'Statistical machine translation' was proposed in the 1990s by researchers at IBM as an alternative to rule-based machine translation (Brown et al., 1993). It automatically learns statistical models which correspond to translation rules and bilingual dictionaries from bilingual sentences in the order of millions. Its goal is to develop a machine-translation system for a new language pair or a new domain at low cost in a short period of time. Figure 9.1 shows the outline of statistical machine translation.

In the mid-2000s, the accuracy of statistical machine translation had achieved a level of practical usefulness in language pairs with similar word order, such as French and English, by using a type of statistical machine

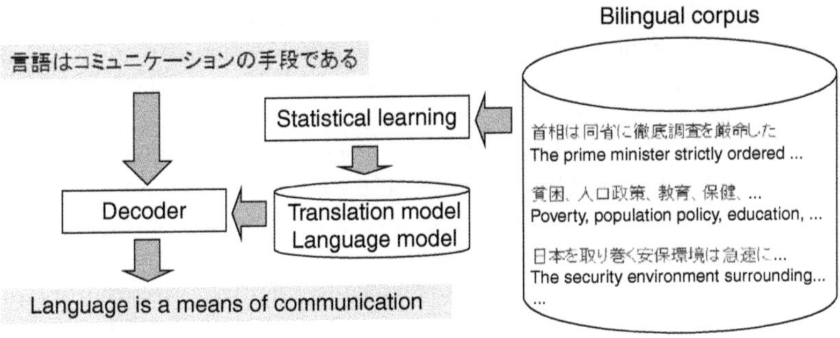

Figure 9.1 Outline of statistical machine translation

translation called 'phrase-based translation' in which the translation unit is changed from words to phrases (Koehn, Och and Marcu, 2003). But statistical machine translation could not outperform rule-based translation for those language pairs with highly different word order such as Japanese and English.

'Pre-ordering', which is the topic of this chapter, was first proposed in the early 2000s (Xia and McCord, 2004) and actively researched in the first half of the 2010s. It was the state-of-the-art machine-translation method for language pairs with highly different word order, until the advent of a radically new technology called 'neural machine translation' (Bahdanau, Cho and Bengio, 2014; Cho et al., 2014; Luong, Pham and Manning, 2015) in the autumn of 2016. We believe, however, that pre-ordering is still effective in the areas where neural machine translation is not good, where there are a large number of bilingual sentences and extensive vocabulary must be accounted for, such as in patent translation.

9.2 Pre-ordering Method Based on Head-Final Word Order in Japanese

'Pre-ordering' is a preprocessing task in statistical machine translation, in which the word order of the source-language sentence is reordered into that of the target-language sentence before translation. It was first proposed in the early 2000s (Xia and McCord, 2004), and started to attract attention as a promising technology to overcome word-order difference in around 2010 from major research institutes including Google, Microsoft, IBM and Nippon Telegraph and Telephone (NTT). In pre-ordering, in order to obtain the target sentence word order, 'reordering rules' are applied to the syntactic structure obtained from the syntactic parsing of the source-language sentence. Reordering rules are made either manually or automatically from bilingual sentences with word alignments.

We proposed a pre-ordering method for English-to-Japanese translation which is focused on the head-final nature of Japanese syntactic structure, called 'head finalization', in which only one rule, 'move the syntactic head to the end of the constituent', is used (Isozaki et al., 2012). Figure 9.2 shows an example of head finalization applied to an English binary constituent tree. Here, =H stands for the head of each binary branch. If the head is the first child, the two children are swapped and the head becomes the last child, which results in the same word order as its Japanese translation.

We found that head finalization dramatically improves the accuracy of English-to-Japanese translation. In 2011, the joint team of NTT and the University of Tokyo achieved the top score in the evaluation of the NTCIR-9 patent translation task (Goto et al., 2013) by combining the University of Tokyo's accurate English parser, Enju, with NTT's pre-ordering by head finalization (Sudoh et al., 2011). As far as we know, this is the first time in history that, based on human evaluation, the accuracy of statistical machine translation outperformed that of rule-based translation in English-to-Japanese translation.

Figures 9.2 and 9.3 show examples of head finalization applied to English and Chinese dependency structures. The core idea of head finalization can be understood easily by using the dependency structure. 'Head' is a word in a phrase which determines its grammatical role in a sentence. For example, a proposition is the head of a propositional phrase. In other words, in the syntactic dependency relation, the word modified is the head. In the dependency structure of a Japanese sentence, a dependency link 'always goes

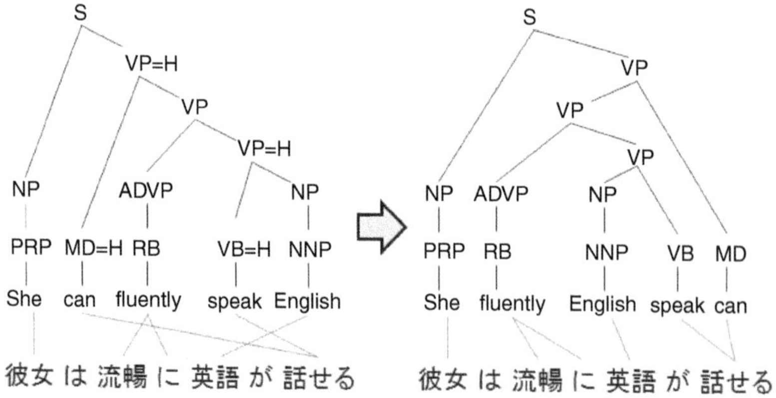

Figure 9.2 Pre-ordering method based on head finalization applied to an English binary constituent tree. '=H' stands for the head of each binary branch. If the head is the first child, it should be reordered

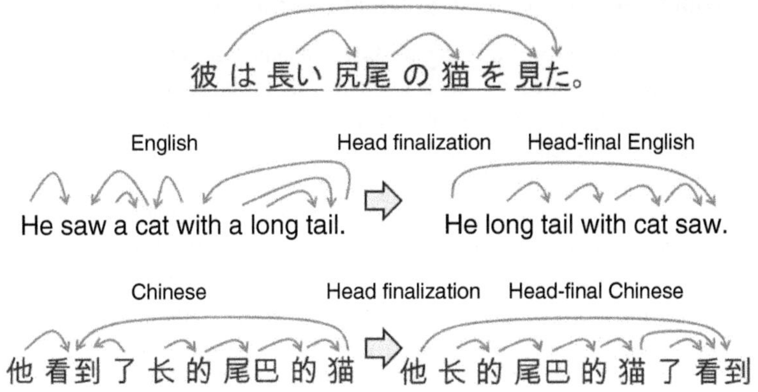

Figure 9.3 Pre-ordering method based on head finalization applied to English and Chinese dependency structures

from left to right' if we draw an arrow representing the dependency link from a modifier to its head, that is, headwords are always placed at the sentence-end side of the modifying words. This is the 'head-final' property of Japanese.

In fact, Japanese is a strictly head-final language, which is very rare in the languages of the world. In general, as shown in the English and Chinese examples in Figures 9.2 and 9.3, dependency goes both 'from left to right' and 'from right to left'. For example, for verbs in English, subjects are placed to the left of their head verb and objects are placed to the right. With respect to nouns, adjectives are placed to the left of their head noun and prepositional phrases are placed to the right. In Chinese, with respect to verbs, the subject precedes its head verb and the object follows its head verb, but as for nouns, a modifier always precedes its head noun.

Because of this head-final property of Japanese, if we reorder the words in the source-language sentence so that its dependency always goes from left to right based on its original syntactic structure, the resulting word order is the same as its Japanese translation. This is the core idea of pre-ordering based on head finalization. If the word order of the source-language sentence is the same as that of the target sentence, the remaining task is word-to-word translation, which can be solved accurately by phrase-based statistical machine translation. We find that head finalization is also effective for Chinese-to-Japanese translation (Dan et al., 2012). Since head finalization only uses the linguistic property of the target language, it can be applied to translations from any language to Japanese as long as we can obtain the syntactic structure of the source language automatically.

9.3 Multilingual Translation of Patent Documents

In order to investigate the feasibility of statistical machine translation from foreign languages to Japanese based on head finalization, we have built a statistical machine-translation system for patent documents from English, Chinese and Korean to Japanese (Sudoh et al., 2014). In patents, there are so-called 'patent families', which are sets of patents applied to different countries sharing priority claims to a patent. Patent documents in a patent family are not a perfect translation of each other, but they include a lot of sentences which are translations of each other. So, by mining patent families, we can extract a large-scale bilingual corpus. We have built bilingual corpora, English–Japanese (about 3 million sentences), Chinese–Japanese (about 9 million sentences) and Korean–Japanese (about 2 million) from Japanese, US, Chinese and Korean patents documents after 2004.

In order to apply the proposed pre-ordering method based on head finalization, we need an accurate syntactic parser of the source-language sentence. We prepared a set of training data with manually annotated syntactic structure, for English (40,000 sentences from news articles and 10,000 sentences from patent documents), and for Chinese (50,000 sentences from news articles and 20,000 sentences from patent documents). We then built a dependency parser for English and Chinese using a semi-supervised learning technique developed by our group (Suzuki et al., 2009), which achieved the best published accuracy on the standard benchmark data for English and Czech dependency parsing. As for word segmentation and part-of-speech tagging of English, Chinese, Korean and Japanese, we used a joint analysis method based on dual decomposition (extended Lagrangian relaxation) described in Suzuki et al. (2012). It should be noted that we did not apply pre-ordering in Korean-to-Japanese translation because the word order in Korean is almost the same as that in Japanese.

Table 9.1 shows the accuracy of word segmentation, part-of-speech tagging, and dependency parsing of English, Chinese and Korean for patent documents. Table 9.2 shows the translation accuracy of the proposed pre-ordering based on head finalization in BLEU (BiLingual Evaluation Understudy) for English, Chinese and Korean to Japanese, compared with the baseline of phrase-based statistical machine translation. We can see that there is significant improvement in the English-to-Japanese and Chinese-to-Japanese translation accuracies due to the head-finalization reordering.

9.4 Pre-ordering Method Based on Maximization of the Rank Correlation Coefficient

Compared to translation into Japanese, translation from Japanese into other languages is difficult, because, for each dependency relation in the syntactic structure of the source Japanese sentence, we have to decide whether or not we

Table 9.1 *Word segmentation, part-of-speech tagging and dependency parsing accuracies for patent sentences*

	Word	Part of speech	Dependency
English	99.3	94.7	86.7
Chinese	92.7	85.2	81.2
Korean	93.2	-	-

Table 9.2 *Translation accuracy in BLEU for baseline (phrase-based SMT)*[a] *and head finalization (phrase-based SMT with pre-ordering)*

	Baseline	Head finalization
English to Japanese	34.8	**37.4**
Chinese to Japanese	47.9	**49.8**
Korean to Japanese	70.4	

[a] SMT = statistical machine translation.

should keep its direction, depending on the grammar of the target language. In the first half of the 2010s, in the Japanese-to-English direction, rule-based translation still outperformed statistical machine translation although the difference in accuracy was becoming smaller.

We first proposed a simple discriminative pre-ordering method, which traverses binary constituent trees, and classifies whether children of each node should be reordered (Hoshino et al., 2015). For a given bilingual sentence with a binary constituent tree for the source sentence and with word alignment between the source sentence and the target sentence, the method first determines oracle labels for pre-ordering (monotone or swap) for each tree node, so as to maximize the Kendall rank correlation coefficient τ between the reordered source words and the associated target words based on the automatic word alignment. We call them oracle labels because they are assigned based on the target sentence (the ideal translation result of the source sentence), which is not available at the time of translation. From these labelled source trees, a discriminative classifier is trained to assign a label for pre-ordering for each node in the given source tree, using the word forms, parts of speech and non-terminal labels of subtrees as features. Support vector machines (SVM) are used for the classifier.

For two given rankings, the Kendall rank correlation coefficient is defined as the difference between the number of concordant pairs and the

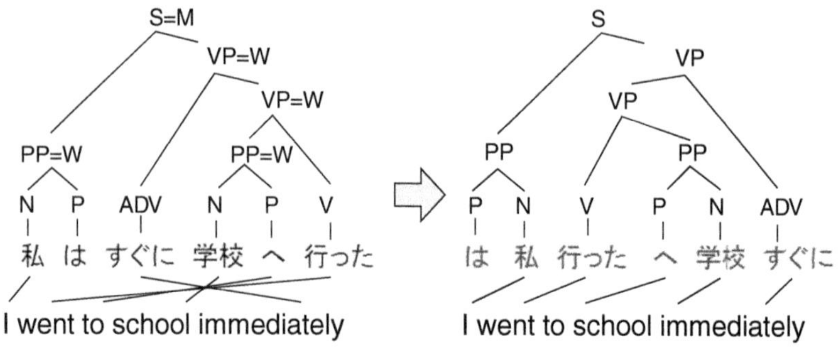

Figure 9.4 Pre-ordering method-based maximization of rank correlation coefficient applied to Japanese binary constituent tree. '=M' indicates that the children should not be reordered (monotone), while '=W' indicates that the children should be reordered (sWap)

number of discordant pairs divided by the total number of pair combinations. If the two rankings are in the same order, the coefficient has a value of 1, and if one ranking is the reverse of the other, the coefficient has a value of –1. For source and target sentences which are translations of each other, the number of discordant pairs is equal to the number of crossings in the word alignment. Thus, maximizing the Kendall rank correlation coefficient is equivalent to minimizing the number of crossings in the word alignment. Figure 9.4 shows an example of a Japanese binary constituent tree whose leaf nodes are aligned to its English translation. A node labelled with '=M' indicates that its two child nodes should not be reordered (monotone), while a node labelled with '=W' indicates that its two child nodes should be reordered (sWap). By swapping the nodes with '=W', the leaf nodes in the Japanese tree and the words in its English translations are aligned monotonically.

We extended the discriminative pre-ordering method from a constituent tree to a dependency structure (Sudoh and Nagata, 2016). We used a learning-to-rank model based on pairwise classification to obtain the reordering of multiple children of a parent node, as the dependency structure is a multiple tree. Figure 9.5 is an example of pre-ordering based on the maximization of the rank correlation coefficient. Here, the input is a word-based typed dependency for Japanese, which is described in Section 9.5.

9.5 Word-Based Typed Dependency Parser for Japanese

In Japanese, syntactic structures are usually represented as dependencies between chunks called 'bunsetsu'. A bunsetsu is a Japanese grammatical and

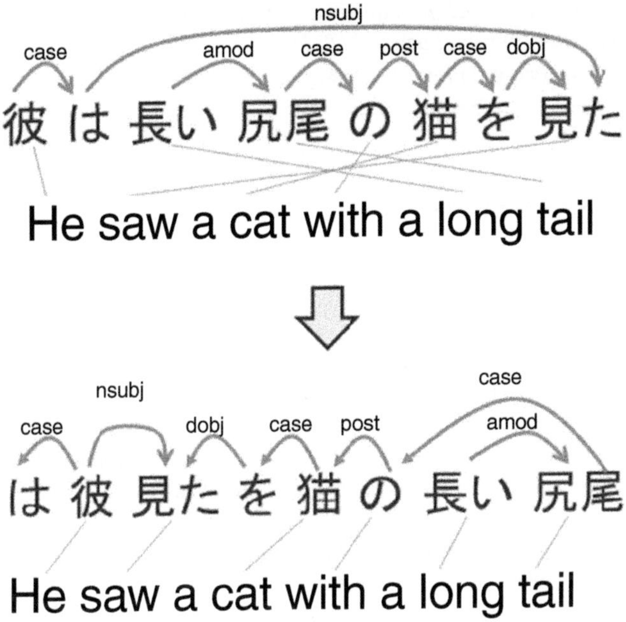

Figure 9.5 Pre-ordering method-based maximization of rank correlation coefficient applied to word-based typed dependency for Japanese

phonological unit that consists of one or more content words such as a noun and verb, followed by a sequence of zero or more function words such as postpositional particles, auxiliary verbs and sentence-final particles. Popular publicly available Japanese parsers, such as CaboCha and KNP, return bunsetsu-based dependency as syntactic structure.

However, the bunsetsu-based Japanese representation is not suitable for reordering in statistical machine translation for two reasons. The first is that there is a discrepancy between syntactic and semantic units. This is apparent when it includes co-ordinating conjunctions because bunsetsu-based dependencies do not convey information about the left boundary of each noun phrase. For example, from a Japanese bunsetsu structure of a noun phrase '技術-の (technology-GEN)/ 向上-と (improvement-CONJ)/ 経済-の (economy-GEN) / 発展 (growth)', where the bunsetsu boundary is indicated by '/', it is difficult to make an English constituent structure with the resulting word order ((technology improvement) and (economic growth)). The other reason is that it does not have a label for each dependency arc such as subject (nsubj) and object (dobj). This makes manual writing and/or automatic learning of reordering rules complicated.

Table 9.3 *Translation accuracy in BLEU for baseline (phrase-based SMT) and bunsetsu-based pre-ordering and word-based pre-ordering*

	BLEU
Baseline	27.0
Bunsetsu-based pre-ordering	28.2
Word-based pre-ordering	28.9

We developed a word-based typed dependency parser for Japanese (Tanaka and Nagata, 2015). To be more specific, we built a word-based Japanese constituent treebank (Tanaka and Nagata, 2013) whose size is about 40,000 sentences, and converted it to a word-based typed dependency Japanese treebank. We then used it as training data for our dependency parser (Suzuki et al., 2009), which is also used for English and Chinese as described in the previous sections.

Table 9.3 shows the comparison of Japanese-to-English translation accuracy for the patent corpus between bunsetsu-based pre-ordering and word-based pre-ordering. The baseline is phrase-based statistical machine translation (SMT) without pre-ordering. It shows that both bunsetsu-based pre-ordering and word-based pre-ordering improve the translation accuracy, but word-based pre-ordering is better than the bunsetsu-based one.

As a side note, it may also be pointed out that our efforts to build a word-based typed dependency treebank for Japanese was one of the origins of the universal dependencies for Japanese (Tanaka et al., 2016).

9.6 Automatic Evaluation of Translation Accuracy

Finally, we will briefly explain the automatic evaluation of translation accuracy. Objective evaluation of machine-translation accuracy is a very difficult problem. There are many correct translations for a sentence, and it is a subjective decision whether you focus on word-translation errors or word-order errors. An automatic evaluation measure for translation, BLEU (BiLingual Evaluation Understudy) (Papineni et al., 2002), brought about a revolutionary change and accelerated the research on machine translation when it was presented in the early 2000s. There is a problem with BLEU, however, in that it does not agree with human evaluation for translations between English and Japanese. Figure 9.6 shows the correlation between human evaluation and automatic evaluation by BLEU for the Japanese-to-English translation of a patent translation task in NTCIR-7, an evaluation workshop held in 2008. Among statistical machine-translation systems,

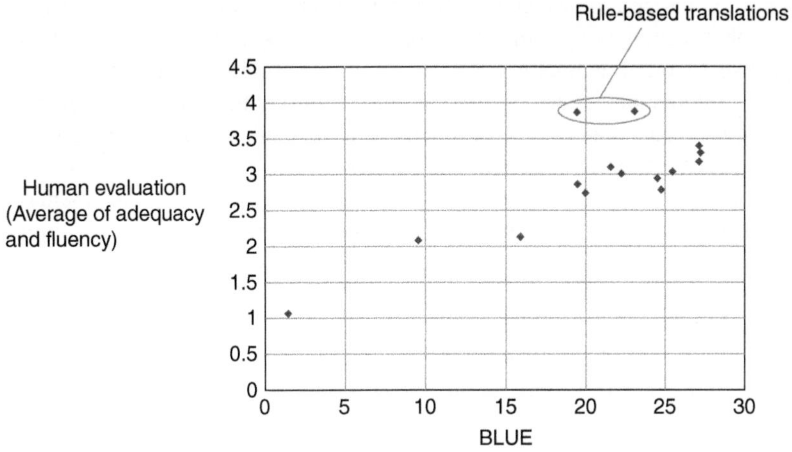

Figure 9.6 Correlation between human evaluation and BLEU

BLEU correlates with human evaluation relatively well, but rule-based systems are underestimated by BLEU.

In order to solve the problem, we proposed a novel automatic evaluation measure, RIBES (Rank-Based Intuitive Bilingual Evaluation Score) (Isozaki et al., 2010) and released it to the public as open source software (RIBES, n.d.). RIBES is a weighted product of unigram word precision and the rank correlation coefficient between system output sentence and reference sentence. Compared to BLEU, it focuses more on the degree of word-order agreement between the translation result and the reference translation. RIBES was adopted as one of the official evaluation measures in the previously mentioned NTCIR-9, and it was also shown, in the evaluation by the contest organizers, that it agrees better than BLEU with the human evaluation in English-to-Japanese, Japanese-to-English and Chinese-to-English translation tasks (Goto et al., 2013).

9.7 Conclusion and Future Projects

This chapter described a series of tasks conducted at our laboratories on statistical machine translation between Japanese and other languages (English, Chinese and Korean). The problem to be tackled was a large difference of word order. To solve the problem, we had to refine the pre-ordering method from a rule-based one to a discriminative one. We also had to refine the Japanese parser from a bunsetsu-based one to a word-based one. Moreover, we developed a new evaluation metric for translation accuracy for a fair comparison between rule-based translation systems and statistical machine translation systems. One of the important topics in translating Japanese to other languages, which is not mentioned in this chapter, is empty category detection. Empty categories are phonetically null elements and are used for representing dropped (zero) pronouns, controlled elements and traces of movement, such as WH-questions and relative clauses. They are important for machine translation from pro-drop languages such as Japanese, to non-pro-drop languages such as English. We first developed an empty category detection as a post-processor of a constituent parser (Takeno, Nagata and Yamamoto, 2015), and we then integrated it into the constituent parser (Hayashi and Nagata, 2016). We also have a preliminary result of integrating empty category detection into pre-ordering SMT (Takeno, Nagata and Yamamoto, 2016). As the reordering problem has been largely solved by neural machine translation, it turns out that translation of empty categories is one of the major remaining problems in Japanese-to-English neural machine translation. Based on our experience on empty category detection and pre-ordering translation, we proposed a method which jointly predicts empty elements and their translations from a source sentence in a neural machine-translation framework (Takeno, Nagata and Yamamoto, 2017). Although fluency and average translation accuracy have been improved by neural machine translation, translation of context-dependent information such as zero pronouns and articles is still an open problem. As we did in statistical machine translation, we would like to keep working on linguistically motivated approaches in this new area.

References

Bahdanau, Dzmitry, Kyunghyun Cho and Yoshua Bengio (2014). Neural machine translation by jointly learning to align and translate. In Proceedings of the 3rd International Conference on Learning Representations. CoRR, abs/1409.0473.

Brown, Peter F., Stephen A. Della Pietra, Vincent J. Della Pietra and Robert L. Mercer (1993). The mathematics of machine translation: Parameter estimation, Computational Linguistics 19(2), 263–311.

Cho, Kyunghyun, Bart van Merrienboer, Caglar Gulcehre, Dzmitry Bahdanau, Fethi Bougares, Holger Schwenk and Yoshua Bengio (2014). Learning phrase representations using RNN encoder-decoder for statistical machine translation. In Proceedings of the 2014 Conference on Empirical Methods in Natural Language Processing (EMNLP), pp. 1724–1734.

Dan, Han, Katsuhito Sudoh, Xianchao Wu, K. Doh, Hajime Tsukada and Masaaki Nagata (2012). Head finalization reordering for Chinese-to-Japanese machine translation. In Proceedings of Sixth Workshop on Syntax, Semantics and Structure in Statistical Translation, Jeju, Republic of Korea, 12 July, pp. 57–66.

Goto, Isao, Bin Lu, Ka Po Chow, Eiichiro Sumita and Benjamin K. Tsou (2013). Overview of the Patent Machine Translation Task at the NTCIR-10 Workshop.

Proceedings of NTCIR-10 Workshop Meeting, NII, Tokyo, Japan, 18–21 June, pp. 559–578.
Hayashi, Katsuhiko, and Masaaki Nagata (2016). Empty element recovery by spinal parser operations. In Proceedings of the 54th Annual Meeting of the Association for Computational Linguistics, pp. 95–100.
Hoshino, Sho, Yusuke Miyao,Katsuhito Sudoh, Katsuhiko Hayashi and Masaaki Nagata (2015). Discriminative preordering meets Kendall's maximization. In Proceedings of the 53rd Annual Meeting of the Association for Computational Linguistics and the 7th International Joint Conference on Natural Language Processing, pp. 139–144.
Hutchins, W. John (2010). Machine translation: A concise history, Journal of Translation Studies 13(12), 29–70.
Isozaki, Hideki, Tsutomu Hirao, Kevin Duh, Katsuhito Sudoh and Hajime Tsukada (2010). Automatic evaluation of translation quality for distant language pairs. In Proceedings of the 2010 Conference on Empirical Methods in Natural Language Processing EMNLP 2010, MIT, Massachusetts, 9–11 October, pp. 944–952.
Isozaki, Hideki, Katsuhito Sudoh, Hajime Tsukada and Kevin Duh (2012). HPSG-based preprocessing for English-to-Japanese translation, ACM Transactions on Asian Language Information Processing 11(3) (September), Article 8, 8:11–8:16.
Koehn, Philipp, Franz Josef Och and Daniel Marcu (2003). Statistical phrase-based translation. Proceedings of the Joint Conference on Human Language Technologies and the Annual Meeting of the North American Chapter of the Association of Computational Linguistics. Edmonton, May–June, pp. 48–54.
Luong, Thang, Hieu Pham and Christopher D. Manning (2015). Effective approaches to attention-based neural machine translation. In Proceedings of the 2015 Empirical Methods in Natural Language Processing. Lisbon: The Association for Computational Linguistics, pp. 1412–1421.
Papineni, Kishore, Salim Roukos, Todd Ward and Wei-Jing Zhu (2002). BLEU: A method for automatic evaluation of machine translation. Proceedings of the 40th Annual Meeting of the Association for Computational Linguistics, Philadelphia, PA, pp. 311–318.
RIBES (n.d.) Rank-Based Intuitive Bilingual Evaluation Score software. Available at: www.kecl.ntt.co.jp/icl/lirg/ribes/index.html.
Sudoh, Katsuhito and Masaaki Nagata (2016). Chinese-to-Japanese patent machine translation based on syntactic pre-ordering for WAT 2016. In Proceedings of the 3rd Workshop on Asian Translation, Osaka, Japan, pp. 211–215.
Sudoh, Katsuhito, Kevin Duh, Hajime Tsukada, Masaaki Nagata, Xianchao Wu, Takuya Matsuzaki and Jun'ichi Tsujii (2011). NTT-UT statistical machine translation in NTCIR-9 PatentMT. In Proceedings of NTCIR-9 Workshop Meeting. Tokyo: National Institute of Informatics, pp. 585–592.
Sudoh, Katsuhito, Jun Suzuki, Yasuhiro Akiba, Hajime Tsukada and Masaaki Nagata (2014). Statistical machine translation system for patent sentences from English, Chinese, Korean to Japanese. In Proceedings of the 20th Annual Meeting of the Association for Natural Language Processing. Tokyo: The Association for Natural Language Processing, pp. 606–609 (Japanese).
Suzuki, Jun, Hideki Isozaki, Xavier Carreras and Michael Collins (2009). An empirical study of semi-supervised structured conditional models for dependency parsing. In Proceedings of the 2009 Conference on Empirical Methods in Natural Language

Processing (EMNLP). Singapore: Association for Computational Linguistics, pp. 551–560.
Suzuki, Jun, Kevin Duh and Masaaki Nagata (2012). A joint natural language analysis method using extended Lagrangian relaxation. In Proceedings of the 18th Annual Meeting of the Association for Natural Language Processing. Hiroshima: The Association for Natural Language Processing of Japan, pp. 1284–1287 (in Japanese).
Takeno, Shunsuke, Masaaki Nagata and Kazuhide Yamamoto (2015). Empty category detection using path features and distributed case frames. In Proceedings of the 2015 Conference on Empirical Methods in Natural Language Processing, pp. 1335–1340.
Takeno, Shunsuke, Masaaki Nagata and Kazuhide Yamamoto (2016). Integrating empty category detection into preordering machine translation. In Proceedings of the 3rd Workshop on Asian Translation, pp. 157–165.
Takeno, Shunsuke, Masaaki Nagata and Kazuhide Yamamoto (2017). Controlling target features in neural machine translation via prefix constraints. In Proceedings of the 4th Workshop on Asian Translation. Osaka: Association of Computational Linguistics, pp. 55–63.
Tanaka, Takaaki and Masaaki Nagata (2013). Constructing a practical constituent parser from a Japanese treebank with function labels. In Proceedings of the Fourth Workshop on Statistical Parsing of Morphologically Rich Languages. Seattle, WA: Association for Computational Linguistics, pp. 108–118.
Tanaka, Takaaki and Masaaki Nagata (2015). Word-based Japanese typed dependency parsing with grammatical function analysis. In Proceedings of the 53rd Annual Meeting of the Association for Computational Linguistics and the 7th International Joint Conference on Natural Language Processing. Beijing: The Association for Computational Linguistics, pp. 237–242.
Tanaka, Takaaki, Yusuke Miyao, Masayuki Asahara, Sumire Uematsu, Hiroshi Kanayama, Shinsuke Mori and Yuji Matsumoto (2016). Universal dependencies for Japanese. In Proceedings of the Tenth International Conference on Language Resources and Evaluation. Portorož, Slovenia: Association of Computational Linguistics.
Xia, Fei and Michael McCord (2004). Improving a statistical MT system with automatically learned rewrite patterns. Proceedings of COLING 2004. Geneva: Association of Computational Linguistics, pp. 508–514.

10 Audiovisual Translation in Mercurial Mediascapes

Jorge Díaz-Cintas

10.1 Introduction

In recent decades, audiovisual translation (AVT) has been, without a doubt, one of the most prolific areas of research in the field of translation and interpreting studies, if not the most prolific. For many years ignored in academic circles, AVT has existed as a professional practice since the invention of cinema, though it was not until the mid-1990s, with the advent of digitisation, that it began to gain in scholarly prominence and in number of acolytes. The flurry of activity observed in the media and the technology industries has had a positive knock-on effect on the raising of the visibility and status of AVT at academic level too, as attested by the exponential growth in the number of publications, conferences, research projects as well as undergraduate and postgraduate courses that have been developed around the world in a relatively short period of time.

In a technologically driven multimedia society like the present one, the value of moving images, accompanied with sound and text, is crucial when it comes to engaging in communication. We live our working and personal lives surrounded by screens of all shapes and sizes: television sets, cinema screens, desktop computers, laptops, video game consoles and mobile phones are a common and recurrent feature of our socio-cultural environment, heavily based on the omnipresence of the image. Entanglements with technology punctuate our daily routine as we experience a great deal of exposure to screens and consume vast amounts of audiovisual programmes to enjoy ourselves, to obtain information, to carry out our work, to learn and study, and to develop and enhance our professional and academic careers. Moving images are ubiquitous in our time and age and their power and influence are here to stay and live on via the screens.

This tallies well with the constant linear increase that has been observed in the use of computers and digital devices, particularly amongst the younger generations (Ferri, 2012). In his discussion on the new divide between 'digital natives' and 'digital immigrants', the latter aka 'Gutenberg natives', Prensky argues that today's students, making special reference to graduates in the USA:

> have spent their entire lives surrounded by and using computers, videogames, digital music players, video cams, cell phones, and all the other toys and tools of the digital age. Today's average college grads have spent fewer than 5,000 hours of their lives reading, but over 10,000 hours playing video games (not to mention 20,000 hours watching TV). Computer games, e-mail, the Internet, cell phones and instant messaging are integral parts of their lives. (Prensky, 2001, 1)

Along the same lines, but in the case of the UK, Elks (2012, online) highlights that 'children will spend an entire year sat in front of screens by the time they reach seven', with an average of 6.1 hours a day spent on a computer or watching TV and with 'some ten and 11-year-olds having access to five screens at home'. In the battle between paper and the digital page, it is the latter that seems to be winning, which, coupled with the affordances of technology and the pervasiveness of the Internet, means that audiovisual communication is now a daily occurrence for millions of netizens around the globe.

All forms of communication are based on the production, transmission and reception of a message amongst various participants. Though, on the surface, this seems to be a rather straightforward process, human interaction of this nature can be complex even when the participants share the same language, and more so when they belong to different linguacultural communities. That is why practices like translation have existed for centuries, to facilitate communication and understanding amongst cultures, as well as to promote networks of power and servitude. To a large extent, translation can be said to be running parallel to the history of communication and has experienced a similar transition in recent decades from the printed page to the more dynamic, digital screen. From this perspective, and given the exponential growth experienced by audiovisual communication, the boom witnessed in the industry's increased volume of audiovisual translation comes as no surprise. Technological advancements have had a great impact on the way we deal with the translation and distribution of audiovisual productions, and the switchover from analogue to digital technology at the turn of the last millennium proved to be particularly pivotal and a harbinger of things to come. Known as the fourth industrial revolution (Schwab, 2016), we are in the midst of a technical transformation that is fundamentally changing the way in which we live, work and relate to one another. In an age defined by technification, digitisation and internetisation, the world seems to have shrunk, contact across languages and cultures has accelerated and exchanges have become fast and immediate. Symbolically, VHS tapes have long gone, the DVD and VCD came and went in what felt like a blink of an eye, Blu-rays never quite made it as a household phenomenon, 3D seems to have stalled and, in the age of the cloud, we have become consumers of streaming, where the possession of actual physical items is a thing of the past.

The societal influence of AVT has expanded its remit in terms of the number of people that it reaches, the way in which we consume audiovisual productions and the nature of the programmes that get to be translated. If audiovisual translation came first to be as a commercial practice to enhance the international reach of feature films, the situation has changed quite drastically and the gamut of audiovisual genres that get translated nowadays is virtually limitless, whether for commercial, ludic or instructional purposes: films, TV series, cartoons, sports programmes, reality shows, documentaries, cookery programmes, current affairs, edutainment material, commercials, educational lectures and corporate videos to name but a few. The digital revolution has also had an impact on the very essence of newspapers, which have migrated to the web and now host videos on their digital versions that are usually translated with subtitles when language transfer is required. Consumption of audiovisual productions has also been altered significantly, from the large public spaces represented by cinema, to the segregated family experience of watching television in the privacy of the living room, to the more individualistic approach of binge watching in front of our personal computer, tablet or mobile telephone. The old, neat distinction between the roles of producers and consumers has now morphed into the figure of the prosumer, a direct result of the new potentiality offered by social media and the digital world. In addition to watching, consuming and sharing others' programmes, netizens are also encouraged to become producers and create their own user-generated content that can be easily assembled with freely available software programs and apps on their computers, smartphones or tablets, uploaded to any of the numerous sharing platforms that populate the ether and distributed throughout the world in an instantaneous manner.

As foregrounded by Shetty (2016, online), digital video has been in hyper growth mode over the last few years, 'with a projected 80% of all internet traffic expected to be video by 2018. This is because of improvements in video technology, wider viewing device options, and an increase in content made available online both from television broadcasters and from other video services.' Simultaneously, giants like YouTube estimate that more than 60 per cent of a YouTube channel's views come from outside its country of origin (Reuters, 2015), clearly pointing to the pivotal role of translation in cross-cultural communication. The parallel commercial upsurge of translation activity in the audiovisual industry has been corroborated by research conducted on behalf of the Media & Entertainment Services Alliance Europe, underlining that audiovisual media content localisation across Europe, the Middle East and Africa is expected to increase from $2 billion in 2017 to over $2.5 billion before 2020 (MESA News, 2017). The mushrooming of channels and video on-demand platforms, driven partly by so-called over-the-top (OTT) players like Netflix, Amazon Prime, Viki, Hulu, iQiyi or Iflix to name but a few, who specialise in the delivery of content over the Internet, has opened up more opportunities for programme makers to sell their titles into new markets. To be successful in this venture, most audiovisual productions come accompanied by subtitled and dubbed versions in various languages, with many also including subtitles for the deaf and the hard of hearing (SDH) and audio description (AD) for the blind and the partially sighted. Never before has translation been so prominent on screen.

A collateral result from this fast-growing global demand for content that needs to be translated – from high-profile new releases to back-catalogue TV series and films for new audiences in regions where they have not been commercialised previously, without forgetting the myriad of new genres that a few years back would not have been translated – is the perceived critical 'talent crunch' (Estopace, 2017) in the industry, when it comes to dubbing and subtitling. Given the lack of formal AVT training in many countries, the situation is likely to get worse in the short term, especially in the case of certain language combinations.

Yet, what is certain is that the demand for audiovisual translation is here to stay, as companies and organisations around the world continue to recognise the immense value of adapting their content into multiple languages to extend their global reach. Its playbook, however, is still an evolving paradigm.

10.2 The Multimodality of Audiovisual Translation

In her attempt to dispel inherited assumptions that have had the pernicious effect of academically marginalising certain translational practices, O'Sullivan (2013, 2) remarks that '[t]ranslation is usually thought of as being about the printed word, but in today's multimodal environment translators must take account of other signifying elements too'; a warning also echoed by Pérez-González (2014, 185), who bemoans the excessive emphasis placed by AVT researchers on the linguistic analysis of often decontextualised dialogue lines, and for whom the need 'to gain a better understanding of the interdependence of semiotic resources in audiovisual texts has become increasingly necessary against a background of accelerating changes in audiovisual textualities'. In this respect, greater scholarly attention to the interplay between dialogue and the rest of semiotic layers that configure the audiovisual production can only be a positive, if challenging, development for the discipline.

One of the early scholars to discuss the significance for translation of the multimodal nature of the source text is Reiss (2000/1971), who in her text typology for translators distinguishes three initial groups, namely (1) content-focused texts, (2) form-focused texts and (3) appeal-focused texts. To these, she adds a fourth, overarching category that she refers to as audio-medial texts and, in her own words, 'are distinctive in their dependence on non-linguistic (technical) media and on graphic, acoustic, and visual kinds of expression. It is only in combination with them that the whole complex literary form realizes its full potential' (ibid., 43). Primary examples of this category are texts that require 'the use of and a degree of accommodation to a non-linguistic medium in order to communicate with the hearer' (ibid.), as in radio and television scripts, songs, musicals, operas and stage plays. Audio-medial texts seem then to be aimed at hearers, since they 'are *written* to be *spoken (or sung)* and hence are not *read* by their audience but *heard*' (ibid., 27). From the perspective of AVT, the term is clearly problematic and Reiss's taxonomy is also rather wanting as any reference to the main film translation modes, whether dubbing or subtitling, is conspicuously absent in her work and the emphasis is placed, symptomatically, on the 'hearer' rather than the 'viewer/reader'. In fact, the only mention of dubbing is hidden away in a footnote, where she quotes directly from Jumpelt (1961, 24) – 'in the setting of filming dialog the critical factor may well be the necessity for finding expressions that effectively carry the meaning and match most closely the actors' lip movements' – and refers the reader to the pioneering 1960 special issue of the journal *Babel*, entitled *Cinéma et Traduction* and guest-edited by Pierre-François Caillé (Reiss, 2000/1971, 46).

A decade later, she revisited the term and changed it to 'multi-medial', after acknowledging the fact that:

> the translating material does not only consist of 'autonomous' written texts, but also, to a large extent, firstly of verbal texts, which, though put down in writing, are presented orally, and, secondly, of verbal texts, which are only part of a larger whole and are phrased with a view to, and in consideration of, the 'additional information' supplied by a sign system other than that of language (picture + text, music and text, gestures, facial expressions, built-up scenery on the stage, slides and text, etc.). (Reiss, 1981, 125)

In effect, this hypertext continues to function as a superstructure for the three basic types and allows her to include texts like comics and advertising material, which resort to visual but not acoustic elements. In an attempt to overcome the limitations of Reiss's terminological framework of reference and to dispel any potential confusion, Snell-Hornby (2006, 85) defines four different terms for four different classes of text that all depend on elements other than the verbal:

1. *Multi-medial* texts (in English usually *audiovisual*) are conveyed by technical and/or electronic media involving both sight and sound (e.g. material for film or television, sub-/surtitling),
2. *Multimodal* texts involve different modes of verbal and non-verbal expression, comprising both sight and sound, as in drama and opera,
3. *Multisemiotic* texts use different graphic sign systems, verbal and non-verbal (e.g. comics or print advertisements),
4. *Audio-medial* texts are those written to be spoken, hence reach their ultimate recipient by means of the human voice and not from the printed page (e.g. political speeches, academic papers).

In all cases, we are dealing with texts that go beyond language and that in translation studies 'until well into the 1980s were hardly investigated as a specific challenge for translation' (ibid.). Delabastita (1989) was one of the first scholars to elaborate further this multimodal dimension that so characterises what he calls 'film and TV translation' and that rests on the intricate combination of the acoustic and the visual channels, which together with the verbal and the non-verbal dimensions of communication, results in the four basic elements that define the audiovisual text and validate its semiotic texture:

1 The acoustic–verbal: dialogue exchanges, monologue, lyrics, voice-off.
2 The acoustic–non-verbal: instrumental music, sound effects, laughter, crying, background noises.
3 The visual–verbal: street signs, banners, opening/closing credits, text on screen, letters, messages on computer screens, newspaper headlines.
4 The visual–non-verbal: images, lighting, gestures, facial expressions.

The interdependence that exists amongst these various meaning-making resources has been theorised by Baldry and Thibault (2006) and their resource integration principle, which refers to the way in which multiple semiotic layers co-exist in the same multimodal text and affect each other in various ways. They argue that multimodal texts do not function as a mere juxtaposition of resources and assert that meaning is ultimately created through the interrelations of modes within a given text. The ensuing meaning is thus the result of the highly complex relationships that get established amongst the various semiotic elements and that cannot be expressed as a sum of meanings individually conveyed by each of the resources. When confronted with this vast array of communicative layers and signs, and as foregrounded by Pérez-González (2014, 188), viewers 'are normally able to make inter-modal connections and process the information realized through different modes in a routinized, often subconscious, manner'.

Although, a priori, all dimensions can be thought to play an equally important role within the communicative encounter, their degree of interdependence will vary depending on the genre and nature of the audiovisual production as well as the intended audience. Thus, the visual–non-verbal dimension, i.e. the image, might carry more weight than the word in the case of some of the big blockbuster films touring the world, whereas the acoustic–verbal, i.e. the spoken word, will be more prevalent in certain *films d'auteur* and documentaries. Naturally, this imbalance can also be found at different points within the same audiovisual programme, where some scenes may be of a verbose nature, whilst others will rely on special effects to the detriment of dialogue. From a translational perspective, such interplay amongst the various semiotic resources can on occasions be decisive when deciding on the preferred approach to activate for the language transfer. From a scholarly angle, it is this enmeshment and communicative richness inherent to multimodality that makes audiovisual productions so arresting to produce and to consume as well as to interpret and to investigate.

10.3 The Many Instantiations of Audiovisual Translation

Used as an umbrella term, AVT subsumes a raft of translation practices that differ from each other in the nature of their linguistic output and the translation strategies on which they rely. In addition to having to deal with the communicative complexities derived from the concurrent delivery of aural and visual input, audiovisual translators have to be conversant with the spatial and temporal constraints that characterise this translation activity as well as with the specialised software that is used in this profession. The various ways in which audiovisual productions can be translated into other languages have been discussed by many authors over the years, of which the typology presented by Chaume (2013) is perhaps one of the most recent and complete. What follows is a panoptic overview of each of the main modes.

Two fundamental approaches can be distinguished: either the source text oral output is transferred aurally in the target language (i.e. revoicing) or is converted into written text that appears on screen (titling, text localisation). Within these two all-encompassing approaches, further sub-categorisations can be established. Thus, revoicing subsumes interpreting, voiceover, narration, dubbing, fandubbing and audio description.

In simultaneous interpreting, the source speech is transferred by an interpreter, who listens to the original and verbally translates the content. Voiceover consists in orally presenting the translation of the source text speech over the still audible original voice, usually allowing the speaker to be heard for a few seconds in the foreign language, after which the volume of the soundtrack is reduced and the translation is then overlaid. In the case of narration, the original speech is obliterated and replaced by a new soundtrack containing only the voice of the target language narrator. Dubbing, also known as lip-sync, consists in the substitution of the dialogue track of an audiovisual production with another track containing the new lines in the target language. To make viewers believe that the characters on screen share the same language, three types of synchronisation need to be respected: (1) lip synchrony, to ensure that the translated sounds fit into the mouth of the onscreen characters, (2) isochrony, to guarantee that the duration of the source and the target utterances coincide in length, especially when the characters' movements of the mouth can be seen, and (3) kinetic synchrony, to assure that the translated dialogue does not contradict the thespian performance of the actors. Fandubbing refers to the dubbing or redubbing, done by fans, of audiovisual productions that have not been officially dubbed or whose available dubbed versions are deemed to be of poor quality. Mostly interlingual, some of them are also intralingual, in which case the intent is primarily humorous and they are known as 'fundubs'. Finally, audio description converts images and sounds into text by describing any visual or audio information that will help visual impaired audiences to follow the plot of the story, such as body language and facial expressions, scenery, costumes and the like.

The second main approach to AVT, titling, comprises subtitling, fansubbing, surtitling, subtitling for the deaf and the hard of hearing and respeaking. Subtitling is the rendition in writing of the translation of the original dialogue exchanged amongst the various speakers, as well as of all other verbal information that is transmitted visually (letters, banners, inserts) or aurally (lyrics, voices-off). Subtitles are usually confined to a maximum of two lines, each containing some 39 to 42 characters and displayed at the bottom of the screen. They appear in synchrony with the dialogue and the image and remain visible for between one and six seconds (Díaz-Cintas and Remael, 2007). Technically similar to subtitling, though still exhibiting some remarkable differences in terms of layout and activated translation strategies, fansubbing designates the subtitling carried out on the Internet by fans and amateurs. Surtitling, or supertitling, refers to the translation or transcription of dialogue and lyrics in live opera, musical shows and theatre performances, which is then displayed on a screen located above the stage or placed in the seat in front of the patron. As an assistive service, subtitling for the deaf and the hard of hearing, aka captioning, presents on screen a written text that accounts for the dialogue and its paralinguistic dimension as well as for music, sounds and noises contained in the soundtrack so that audiences with hearing impairments can access audiovisual material. Respeaking is the production of subtitles for live programmes or events, whereby a professional listens to the original utterances and repeats them, including punctuation marks, to a speech-recognition software that then displays the text on screen.

For some, AVT fell short of being a case of translation proper because of the various spatial and temporal limitations that constrain the end result, a conceptualisation that for many years stymied the academic development of this discipline. Today, translation has evolved from a corseted, outdated notion of a term coined many centuries ago – when the cinema, the television, the computer and Internet had not yet been invented – into a more flexible and inclusive concept that accommodates new professional practices and realities. In this evolution, AVT has come to question and reframe long-established tenets such as text, authorship, original work, translation unit or fidelity to the original.

Yet, when it comes to investigating the different professional practices, the general approach has been to study them together under the umbrella term of audiovisual translation, even though their study would gain in depth and substance if approached individually. Although some commonalities can be certainly discerned, the differences that separate them warrant more targeted analyses. For instance, the challenges raised by the shift from speech to written text are typically encountered in subtitling but not in dubbing; the transfer of discourse markers, exclamations and interjections plays a crucial role in the perceived naturalness of the dubbed exchanges but not so much in subtitling; the nature and recurrence of the translation strategies activated in dubbing and subtitling vary greatly and whilst condensation and deletion can be considered pivotal to subtitling, they are not so pervasive in dubbing; the ineffability of linguistic variation in written subtitles can be easily overcome by dubbing actors' voice inflection; and the cohabitation of source and target languages in the subtitled version straightjackets potential translation solutions in a way that does not happen in dubbing.

10.4 Research Hotspots in Audiovisual Translation

The sprouting media interest in AVT can also be tracked in academia, where a vast number of publications and doctoral projects have seen the light in the last two decades. However, as foregrounded by Gambier and Ramos Pinto (2016, 185), this exponential growth 'does not negate the fact that it is still a very young domain of research currently exploring an incredible number of different lines of inquiry without a specific methodological and theoretical framework', which means that any attempt to provide a comprehensive overview of the main developments taking place in such a vibrant area is bound to be partial.

If empiricism is to be broadly understood as an approach to knowledge that is based on observation and experience rather than on conjecture and abstract theorisation, then research in AVT can be said to have been firmly rooted in empirical endeavours since its humble beginnings in the second half of the twentieth century. Many of the early studies conducted in this field are of a descriptive nature and concentrate on the translation product – i.e. the actual translation – rather than on the process. As can be expected, the object of research in these pioneering scholarly publications, by antonomasia, was the film, which in more recent times has diversified to encompass other genres, notably TV series and animation, and, to a lesser extent, documentaries.

As already mentioned, a common drawback observed in some publications on the topic is reflected in the fact that they do not seem to take proper account of the semiotic dimension and, when discussing the translation solutions, tend to focus on the linguistic aspects and the translational strategies activated by the translators, at the expense of the images and the sound. Mirroring other types of translation, the scholarly exploration of AVT has been typically partisan to examinations centred on linguistics and discourse analysis; arguably a direct consequence of a research tradition that, in the case of translation, has been clearly literary, printed-text oriented and has drawn its inspiration largely from comparative linguistics. Notwithstanding the potential limitations, it is also true that their results have decisively contributed to the painting of a more rounded picture of the discipline by addressing its practical needs. With the passing of the years, the scope of the research has widened considerably to encompass many other aspects that directly impinge on the interlingual transfer that takes place. This has enabled the profusion of works in which particular emphasis has been placed on the challenges presented by the transfer of humour (Zabalbeascoa, 1996; Martínez-Sierra, 2008), cultural references (Ramière, 2007; Pedersen, 2011; Ranzato, 2016) and, more recently, taboo language (Ávila Cabrera, 2014; Yuan, 2016) and multilingualism (de Higes Andino, 2014; Beseghi, 2017).

The trope of translation as a bridge that enables understanding between cultures and communities requires urgent revision as it has been proven once and again that it can also stress differences and perpetuate negative stereotypes, hence dynamiting those very bridges it is supposed to build. The act of translating is never neutral and AVT scholars are awakening to the reality that mass media is an extraordinarily powerful tool, not only in the original but also in their translation. This heightened awareness of the power of translation has led to the realisation that commercial and political dominance, rather than linguistic asymmetries between languages, are often catalysts in the way cultural values are transferred in interlingual exchanges. Translation has come a long way to be understood as a form of rewriting (Lefevere, 1992), i.e. a discursive activity embedded within a system of conventions and a network of institutions and social agents that, acting as gatekeepers of a given ideology, condition textual production and activate manipulation, to varying degrees, of the original text in the service of the powers that be. Since no translation can ever be the same as the original, unavoidable departures from the original will happen to a greater or lesser extent. In academic exchanges, the term 'manipulation' is closely linked to censorship, though a distinction can be established, in the specific field of AVT, between technical manipulation, prompted by space and time limitations imposed by the medium, and ideological manipulation or censorship, which, irrespective of the technical constraints, unscrupulously misconstrues what is being said (or shown) in the original and is usually instigated by agents in a position of power, who act according to a certain political agenda (Díaz-Cintas, 2012). Given the vastness of the topic, any scholarly approach will benefit from charting it on the basis of different national, historical and sociopolitical environments. Historical accounts of how censorial forces have expurgated political, ethnic, religious, moral and sexual references in audiovisual materials, particularly from the perspective of dubbing, have been conducted by authors like Pruys (1997) in Germany, Mereu Keating (2016) in Italy, and Díaz-Cintas (2019), Gutiérrez Lanza (2002) and Vandaele (2002) in Spain.

Case studies are a convenient, easy-to-articulate research method that can help collect data and shed light on different contexts and domains by closing in on a given subject matter. As a regular feature in AVT scholarship, they tend to focus on small bodies of work, raising issues about their limited scope of action and the difficulty of generalising and extrapolating any of their findings. To counteract some of these shortcomings, scholars have approached AVT from other angles, taking inspiration from paradigms that allow the analysis of larger data, such as corpus linguistics. In this respect, corpora and corpus-analysis tools have been successfully used to systematically identify the idiosyncratic, recurrent features and patterns of larger sets of translated audiovisual productions across time, genres and languages (Freddi and Pavesi, 2009; Baños, Bruti and Zanotti, 2013). As already discussed, the multimodality of audiovisual texts demands that any study considers not only the dialogue but also the visual and the acoustic–non-verbal components. So, whilst this methodology has proven successful in the exploration of language, the design and construction of corpora that also include video material is not without its challenges as tagging the clips is a rather onerous task and securing permission to use and share them can prove most elusory. These are some of the reasons why corpus-based AVT studies tend to draw on relatively small corpora, as having a controllable amount of data allows for a quantitative and qualitative analysis that takes into consideration not only information transmitted through codes other than the linguistic one, but also permits the researcher to reflect on the many other factors that might have influenced certain solutions: synchrony between subtitles and soundtrack, respect of shot changes, semiotic cohesion, and adherence to spatial and temporal constraints, to name but a few.

Social inclusion in the form of accessibility to audiovisual media for people with sensory impairments has become an important issue in many countries around the globe, featuring prominently in legislation, academic exchanges and broadcasters' output. As government regulators impose new rules and regulations on broadcasters and other distributors regarding access services to audiovisual media, the various stakeholders in the field are joining efforts to conduct empirical research that can inform the professional world. Its novelty and alluring nature have triggered a great deal of interest in a relatively short period of time, emphasising its role as a tool for social integration and proving its versatility when it comes to the application of different inquiring methodologies, like Action Research in the case of subtitling for the deaf and the hard of hearing (Neves, 2005) and Actor Network Theory in the study of audio description (Weaver, 2014). The lobbying of interest groups has been instrumental in bringing about changes in this field, which has evolved fast in some countries but is still in its infancy in many other parts of the world. Pioneering research in this field has also proven instrumental in the professional development of access services that have taken off in some countries thanks to the championing of scholars, as in the case of SDH in the UK (Baker, Lambourne and Rowston, 1984) and in Portugal (Neves, 2005), and that of AD in Hong Kong (Leung, 2015).

In addition to the works that explore the specific nature of the various access services like SDH (de Linde and Kay, 1999; Neves, 2005) and AD (Fryer, 2016; Vercauteren, 2016) many other studies focus on end-reception with the aim of identifying the likes and dislikes of the audience and improving access to audiovisual productions, such as the projects by Zárate (2014) and Tamayo-Masero (2015) on children's reception of SDH, and the work by Romero-Fresco (2011) on subtitling through speech recognition. As for AD, interest has also been placed on reception issues (Maszerowska, Matamala and Orero, 2014) as well as on the drafting of pan-European protocols and the training of professional AD specialists (ADLAB-Pro project).[1] The EU-funded project Digital Television for All[2] and its follow-up, Hybrid Broadcast Broadband for ALL[3] have both taken a technological slant and focused on fostering and facilitating the provision of access services on digital television. Romero-Fresco's (2013) notion of accessible filmmaking, as a potential way to integrate AVT and accessibility during the filmmaking process through collaboration between filmmakers and translators, is a brave attempt to exploit synergies, cement links and narrow the breach between translation studies and film and television studies.

To a very large extent, AVT has been at the mercy of the twists and turns of technology, which has had a considerable impact in our field, visible in the way professional practice has changed, the profile of translators and other professionals has evolved, and existing forms of AVT have adapted and developed into new hybrid ones. It is thanks to the instrumental role played by technology that subtitles can today be perfectly synchronised and produced live with minimal latency; that subtitlers' productivity has been boosted with the manufacturing of user-friendly software; and that new workflows, like crowdsubtitling, have emerged under the shelter of the cloud.

The role played by technology has been crucial not only with regard to the way AVT professional practices have evolved but also to the manner in which research has responded to these changes. The difficulty of getting hold of the actual physical material, together with the tedium of having to transcribe the dialogue and translations, and having to wind and rewind the video tape containing them, may help partly justify the reluctance to conduct research on AVT before the 1990s. Against this backdrop, the advent of digital technology can be hailed as an inflection point for the industry and the academe. A new distribution format, the DVD, acted as a research accelerator as it facilitated access to multiple language versions of the same production on the same copy

[1] ADLAB-Pro project, https://adlabpro.wordpress.com. [2] DTV4All, www.psp-dtv4all.org.
[3] HBB4ALL, http://pagines.uab.cat/hbb4all.

(Kayahara, 2005) and allowed the easy extraction (ripping) of the subtitles and the timecodes. Conducting comparative analyses across languages, or getting hold of a seemingly infinite number of audiovisual programmes with their translations, had now become a walk in the park. It is not surprising, therefore, that the number of scholarly publications started to grow exponentially around this time, which coincided with the then upcoming descriptive translation studies paradigm postulated by Toury (1995), thus explaining why a large number of projects carried out in the field subscribed to this theoretical framework. The industry had come up with a novel way of distributing audiovisual material that not only had captivated the audience, but it had also revolutionised the way in which translations were produced, distributed, consumed and studied. The more recent introduction of streaming continues to put the consumer firmly in the driver's seat, with the offering of productions that have been translated into several languages and are available in dubbed and subtitled versions, though obtaining the material for research purposes may not be as straightforward as before.

An area of great interest to the industry has been the application of computer-assisted translation (CAT) tools and machine translation to increase productivity and cope with high volumes of work and pressing deadlines (Bywood, Georgakopoulou and Etchegoyhen, 2017). Whilst in regular use in the more traditional localisation industry, these have not seen a significant uptake in the AVT arena. Yet, the relative ease with which quality subtitle parallel data can be procured has been the catalyst for the recent uptake in experimentation in subtitling with statistical machine translation (SMT). Under the aegis of the European Commission, projects like SUMAT (SUbtitling by MAchine Translation, 2011–2014) have focused on building large corpora of aligned subtitles in order to train SMT engines in various language pairs. Its ultimate objective is to automatically produce subtitles, followed by human post-editing, in order to increase the productivity of subtitle translation procedures, and reduce costs and turnaround times whilst keeping a watchful eye on the quality of the translation results. A similar project, conducted also around the same time, 2012–2014, was EU-BRIDGE,[4] whose main goal was to test the potential of speech recognition for the automatic subtitling of videos.

As highlighted by Jenkins (2006, 17–18), 'new media technologies have lowered production and distribution costs, expanded the range of available delivery channels, and enabled consumers to archive, annotate, appropriate, and recirculate media content in powerful new ways'. This transformative shift brought about by the affordances of digital technology and the activity of the crowds in the cloud is best illustrated by the rise of collaborative practices like fansubbing and fandubbing, fuelled by the availability of cheap and free

[4] EU-BRIDGE, www.eu-bridge.eu.

applications for working with multimedia and subtitling software. Usually less dogmatic and more creative than their commercial counterparts, the underlying philosophy of these practices is the sharing amongst their unofficial networks of audiovisual programmes which have been dubbed and subtitled by fans for fans (Díaz-Cintas and Muñoz-Sánchez, 2006). Although the early fansubbers started operating in the niche genre of Japanese anime, their reach has broadened substantially and, nowadays, these close-knit Internet communities with shared affinities engage in the subtitling of most audiovisual genres and languages. For scholars like Dwyer (2017), these new sites of cultural production hold much potential for democratising access to screen media and providing audiences with a voice as well as means of intervention and participation. Already, fansubbing and crowdsubtitling are being deployed as tools for literacy, education and language preservation. These newfangled collaborative practices raise numerous questions, not least from an ethical perspective, that have already attracted the attention of scholars like Pérez-González (2014) and Massidda (2015) and will no doubt continue to dominate the audiovisual landscape in the years to come.

A more contemporary, novel way of appropriating AVT for political causes has been initiated by networks of activists who make use of interventionist forms of mediation like subtitling, and to a lesser extent dubbing, to enact their own political sensitivities and structure their resistance movements. In a paradoxical way, translation is a tool used by the audiovisual media industry, which relies on professional translators, to reach and influence global audiences, whilst at the same time also exploited, in the form of subtitling and dubbing, by groups of activists that challenge and resist the established world order and try to undermine existing structures of power. These activist communities of translators and interpreters have become the recurrent object of scholarly inquiry in the wider field of translation and interpreting. Yet, their activity in AVT is less well documented although is clearly gaining momentum and attracting the attention of scholars in film studies (Nornes, 2007; Dwyer, 2017). By focusing on the subtitling of online video, Notley, Salazar and Crosby (2013) examine the way in which these instances of what they call 'citizen translation' empower activists to address social and environmental justice issues in the South East Asia region. Pérez-González's (2014) article explores how communities of politically committed individuals without formal training in subtitling come together on the Internet to raise their voice and oppose the socio-economic structures that sustain global capitalism. Entrenched in film studies, Dwyer (2017) also discusses resistant modes of screen translation that she knows as 'guerrilla screen translation' and, in her opinion, are helping shift language patterns and hierarchies in the distribution of AVT on the net, resisting the traditional flows from the West to the rest of the globe; an assertion that seems to be sanctioned by one of the largest streaming distributors in the world: 'Netflix says English won't be its primary viewing language for much longer' (Rodríguez, 2017, online). Despite the appealing nature of these practices, and after recognising that they raise 'a host of issues relating to the broader social and political context of subtitling and dubbing in the global era' (Dwyer, 2017, 123), the scholar goes on to bemoan that their social relevance has been little discussed and remains largely beyond the purview of academia.

The communicative possibilities of AVT have expanded beyond its prima facie role of acting as a service for viewers to facilitate the understanding of a production originally shot in another language, to embrace its potential as a tool for foreign language learning (Talaván, 2010; Gambier, Caimi and Mariotti, 2015). The exploration conducted on the benefits that using subtitles or other AVT modes can have on second language education is eminently empirical in nature and has attracted the interest of bodies like the European Union, which, from 2011 to 2014, funded ClipFlair (Foreign Language Learning through Interactive Captioning and Revoicing of Clips),[5] a research project focused on the design and development of a cloud-based platform as well as educational material for the teaching and learning of foreign languages. In a similar vein, the more recent PluriTAV[6] exploits the conception of AVT as a tool for the development of multilingual competences in the foreign language classroom.

Without a shred of doubt, one of the areas prospering these days is that of reception studies. Traditionally, approaches contingent on human behaviour have been avoided in AVT as they were considered to be too complex in their implementation, costly and lengthy. In addition, technology to conduct experimental research was not easily available and researchers' expertise was lacking. Yet, there is a growing consensus these days that reception studies are crucial for the sustainability of the discipline and the buttressing of links between industry and academe. In this drive to expand our knowledge of AVT, some researchers have shifted their focus from contrastive comparisons between source and target texts to zoom in on the effects that the ensuing translations have on their viewers. In this regard, AVT is a perfect example of a research area markedly interdisciplinary and increasingly eager to resort to technology, statistical analysis and social sciences methodologies to interrogate users and scrutinise data. Reception and process have taken pole position in recent scholarly exchanges and viewers, end users, as well as translation professionals and trainees are becoming the focal point of empirical and intercultural inquiry. Researchers working in AVT are no longer content with describing a product or blindly accepting inherited principles that have survived unchallenged in the printed literature. Rather, by adhering to psychometric methodologies and making use of statistical data analysis tools, they are

[5] ClipFlair, http://clipflair.net. [6] PluriTAV, http://citrans.uv.es/pluritav.

keen to explore the impact of AVT practices on the audience, and to investigate the cognitive effort required by professionals and translators-to-be when processing translation tasks. The research project conducted by Beuchert (2017) on the exploration of the subtitling processes, by observing *in situ* the working routine of a sample of professional subtitlers, is a case in point.

Of particular note in this attempt to measure and understand human behaviour is the application of physiological instruments, such as eye trackers, to the experimental investigation (Perego, 2012). These devices, which offer metrics about visual information by measuring eye positions and eye movement, are helping scholars in AVT to move away from speculation to the analysis of data based on the observation of subjects. In this new research ecosystem, eye tracking is used to monitor viewers' attention to the various parts of the screen, in an attempt to gain a better understanding of their cognitive processes when presented with diverse concurrent stimuli such as images, sound and written subtitles in audiovisual productions. It is also a fruitful tool to gauge the audiences' enjoyment of a given size and type of font, to find out about their preferred maximum number of lines and number of characters per line of subtitle, to observe their reaction to the use of different colours and explicative glosses in the subtitles, to test their ability to read fast subtitles, to confirm their favourite positioning of the subtitles on screen or to check whether they are aware of text crossing over shot changes and how this may affect their reading pattern.

In addition to instruments like eye trackers, and more traditional cognitive and evaluative tools such as questionnaires, interviews, think-aloud protocols and keystroke logging, a wide array of other biometric tools are also being used to conduct multisensorial experiments, such as galvanic skin-response devices, that measure participants' levels of arousal, and webcams, which allow investigators to record participants and conduct facial expression analysis that, in turn, can provide cues about respondents' basic emotions (anger, surprise, joy) and levels of engagement. The potential of electroencephalography (EEG) and electrocardiograms (ECG) is also being tested with the ultimate aim of gaining an insight into cognitive–affective processes. EEG is a neuroimaging technique that helps to assess brain activity associated with perception, cognitive behaviour and emotional processes by foregrounding the parts of the brain that are active whilst participants perform a task or are exposed to certain stimulus material. By tracking heart activity, ECG monitors respondents' physical state and stress levels.

From the perspective of AVT process analysis, potential areas for research could be the study of the similarities and discrepancies that can be observed in the performance of translators with differing levels of expertise (students, professionals, amateurs), the assessment of the impact that technological resources have in the activity of the professionals (use of various subtitling programs), or the evaluation of translators' productivity and enjoyment when confronted with certain tasks (spotting vs working with templates, translating vs post-editing vs quality revising). Results yielded from this experimentation could contribute to the maturation of a largely underdeveloped area, such as the training of audiovisual translators, by informing trainers of future audiovisual translators about the cognitive load involved in the translation process and suggesting ways of improving their curricula. The outcomes could also help language service providers specialising in AVT to adapt their practices to new workflows, to update their in-house style guides when necessary or to reconsider some of the traditionally accepted spatial and temporal considerations that influence the translation and reception of their audiovisual programmes.

10.5 Conclusion

Today, the leading modes of AVT, subtitling and dubbing, are amongst the most ubiquitous translation types encountered in everyday life. This contribution has charted some of the key developments that have punctuated the evolution of AVT and has framed some of the most topical and current trends, whilst promoting new perspectives and pointing to the potential opened up by new research initiatives. As evidenced, the multimodal dimension of the object of study and the interdisciplinary nature of the research being conducted in AVT speak of a rich and complex academic subject in the making and reflect the many crossroads and junctions it presently faces. Part of the broader discipline of translation, which straddles humanities and social sciences, and confidently situated in what is increasingly being known as 'applied humanities', AVT has traditionally shown a good synergetic balance amongst all stakeholders (lecturers, scholars, practitioners, software developers, media producers and distributors) and is now forcibly pursuing an audience-centred approach in an attempt to understand the likes and dislikes of the various audiences that consume AVT in its many forms and shapes.

Although much has been done in AVT scholarship in a relatively short time span, there is still ample scope for further advancement. No doubt, there remain some conceptual and methodological gaps in the research that has been produced, and no doubt academics need to continue conducting investigations and generating new knowledge to try and fill those gaps and gain a better understanding of the field of study. Paradoxically, its inter- and multidisciplinary spirit is not only one of its most alluring attributes, it is also one of the main hoops to be jumped through as it is becoming increasingly evident that the research questions now being put forward require investigators to be competent and well versed in different fields and, ideally, members of cross-disciplinary teams. Promoting and responding to new links between different types of knowledge and technologies can be judged a challenging prospect, albeit one worth taking and full of promise in a field as rewarding as AVT.

Acknowledgements

This research is part of the project PluriTAV, ref. FFI2016-74853-P (2017–2019), financed by the Spanish Ministry of Economy and Competitiveness (Programa Proyectos I+D Excelencia).

References

Ávila Cabrera, José Javier (2014). The subtitling of offensive and taboo language: A descriptive study. PhD thesis. Madrid: Universidad Nacional de Educación a Distancia.

Baker, Robert G., Andrew D. Lambourne and Guy Rowston (1984). *Handbook for Television Subtitlers*. Winchester, UK: Independent Broadcasting Authority.

Baldry, Anthony and Paul J. Thibault (2006). *Multimodal Transcription and Text Analysis*. London: Equinox.

Baños, Rocío, Silvia Bruti and Serenella Zanotti (2013). Corpus linguistics and audiovisual translation: In search of an integrated approach, *Perspectives* 21(4), 483–490.

Beseghi, Micòl (2017). *Multilingual Films in Translation: A Sociolinguistic and Intercultural Approach*. Oxford: Peter Lang.

Beuchert, Kathrine (2017). The web of subtitling: A subtitling process model based on a mixed methods study of the Danish subtitling industry and the subtitling processes of five Danish subtitlers. PhD thesis. Aarhus: Aarhus University.

Bywood, Lindsay, Panayota Georgakopoulou and Thierry Etchegoyhen (2017). Embracing the threat: Machine translation as a solution for subtitling, *Perspectives* 25(3), 492–508.

Chaume, Frederic (2013). The turn of audiovisual translation: New audiences and new technologies, *Translation Spaces* 2, 105–123.

de Higes Andino, Irene (2014). Estudio descriptivo y comparativo de la traducción de filmes plurilingües: el caso del cine británico de migración y diáspora. PhD thesis. Castellón: University Jaume I.

Delabastita, Dirk (1989). Translation and mass-communication: Film and TV translation as evidence of cultural dynamics, *Babel* 35(4), 193–218.

de Linde, Zoe and Neil Kay (1999). *The Semiotics of Subtitling*. Manchester: St. Jerome.

Díaz-Cintas, Jorge (2012). Clearing the smoke to see the screen: Ideological manipulation in audiovisual translation, *Meta* 57(2), 279–293.

Díaz-Cintas, Jorge (2019). Film censorship in Franco's Spain: The transforming power of dubbing, *Perspectives* 27(2), 182–200.

Díaz-Cintas, Jorge and Aline Remael (2007). *Audiovisual Translation: Subtitling*. London: Routledge.

Díaz-Cintas, Jorge and Pablo Muñoz Sánchez (2006). Fansubs: Audiovisual translation in an amateur environment, *The Journal of Specialised Translation* 6, 37–52.

Dwyer, Tessa (2017). *Speaking in Subtitles: Revaluing Screen Translation*. Edinburgh: Edinburgh University Press.

Elks, Sonia (2012). Children 'spend one year in front of screens by the age of seven', *Metro*, 21 May. http://metro.co.uk/2012/05/21/children-spend-one-year-in-front-of-screens-by-the-age-of-seven-433743.

Estopace, Eden (2017). Audiovisual translation hits a sweet spot as subscription video on-demand skyrockets, Slator, Language Industry Intelligence, 23 November. https://slator.com/features/audiovisual-translation-hits-sweet-spot-subscription-video-on-demand-skyrockets.

Ferri, Paolo (2012). Digital and inter-generational divide. In Antonio Cartelli (ed.), *Current Trends and Future Practices for Digital Literacy and Competence*. Hershey PA: IGI Global, pp. 1–18.

Freddi, Maria and Maria Pavesi (eds.) (2009). *Analysing Audiovisual Dialogue: Linguistic and Translational Insights*. Bologna: Clueb.

Fryer, Louise (2016). *Introduction to Audio Description: A Practical Guide*. London: Routledge.

Gambier, Yves, Annamaria Caimi and Cristina Mariotti (eds.) (2015). *Subtitles and Language Learning: Principles, Strategies and Practical Experiences*. Bern: Peter Lang.

Gambier, Yves and Sara Ramos Pinto (2016). Introduction, *Target* 28(2), 185–191.

Gutiérrez Lanza, Camino (2002). Spanish film translation and cultural patronage: The filtering and manipulation of imported material during Franco's dictatorship. In Maria Tymoczko and Edwin Genzler (eds.), *Translation and Power*. Massachusetts: University of Massachusetts, pp. 141–159.

Jenkins, Henry (2006). *Convergence Culture: Where Old and New Media Collide*. New York, NY: New York University Press.

Jumpelt, Rudolf Walter (1961). *Die Übersetzen naturwissenschaftlicher und technischer Literatur: sprachliche Maßstäbe und Methoden zur Bestimmung ihrer Wesenszüge und Probleme*. Berlin: Langenscheidt.

Kayahara, Matthew (2005). The digital revolution: DVD technology and the possibilities for audiovisual translation studies, *The Journal of Specialised Translation* 3, 64–74.

Lefevere, André (1992). *Translation, Rewriting and the Manipulation of Literary Fame*. London: Routledge.

Leung, Dawning (2015). Audio description in Hong Kong. In Rocío Baños Piñero and Jorge Díaz-Cintas (eds.), *Audiovisual Translation in a Global Context. Mapping and Ever-Changing Landscape*. Basingstoke: Palgrave Macmillan, pp. 266–281.

Martínez-Sierra, Juan José (2008). *Humor y traducción: Los Simpson cruzan la frontera*. Castellón: Universitat Jaume I.

Massidda, Serenella (2015). *Audiovisual Translation in the Digital Age: The Italian Fansubbing Phenomenon*. Basingstoke: Palgrave Macmillan.

Maszerowska, Anna, Anna Matamala and Pilar Orero (eds.) (2014). *Audio Description – New Perspectives Illustrated*. Amsterdam: John Benjamins.

Mereu Keating, Carla (2016). *The Politics of Dubbing. Film Censorship and State Intervention in the Translation of Foreign Cinema in Fascist Italy*. Oxford: Peter Lang.

MESA News (2017). Study: EMEA content localization service spending hits $2 billion, Media & Entertainment Services Alliance, 27 June. www.mesalliance.org/2017/06/27/study-emea-content-localization-service-spending-hits-2-billion.

Neves, Josélia (2005). Subtitling for the deaf and hard of hearing. PhD thesis. London: Roehampton University.

Nornes, Abé Mark (2007). *Cinema Babel: Translating Global Cinema*. Minneapolis: University of Minnesota Press.

Notley, Tanya, Juan Francisco Salazar and Alexandra Crosby (2013). Online video translation and subtitling: Examining emerging practices and their implications for media activism in South East Asia, *Global Media Journal – Australian Edition* 7(1), 1–15. http://researchdirect.westernsydney.edu.au/islandora/object/uws%3A17810/datastream/PDF/view.

O'Sullivan, Carol (2013). Introduction: Multimodality as challenge and resource for translation, *The Journal of Specialised Translation* 20, 2–14.

Pedersen, Jan (2011). *Subtitling Norms for Television: An Exploration Focussing on Extralinguistic Cultural References*. Amsterdam: John Benjamins.

Perego, Elisa (ed.) (2012). *Eye Tracking in Audiovisual Translation*. Rome: Aracne.

Pérez-González, Luis (2014). *Audiovisual Translation: Theories, Methods and Issues*. London: Routledge.

Prensky, Marc (2001). Digital natives, digital immigrants part 1, *On the Horizon* 9(5), 1–6.

Pruys, Guido Marc (1997). *Die Rhetorik der Filmsynchronisation. Wie ausländische Spielfilme in Deustschland zensiert, verändert und gesehen werden*. Tübingen: Gunter Narr.

Ramière, Nathalie (2007). Strategies of cultural transfer in subtitling and dubbing. PhD thesis. Brisbane: University of Queensland.

Ranzato, Irene (2016). *Translating Culture Specific References on Television: The Case of Dubbing*. London: Routledge.

Reiss, Katharina (1981). Type, kind and individuality of text: Decision making in translation, *Poetics Today* 2(4), 121–131.

Reiss, Katharina (2000/1971). *Translation Criticism – The Potentials and Limitations: Categories and Criteria for Translation Quality Assessment*. Translated by Erroll F. Rhodes. Manchester and New York: St Jerome and American Bible Society.

Reuters (2015). YouTube introduces new translation tools to globalise content, ET Brand Equity, 21 November. https://brandequity.economictimes.indiatimes.com/news/digital/youtube-introduces-new-translation-tools-to-globalize-content/49860574.

Rodríguez, Ashley (2017). Netflix says English won't be its primary viewing language for much longer, *Quartz*, 30 March.https://qz.com/946017/netflix-nflx-says-english-wont-be-its-primary-viewing-language-for-much-longer-unveiling-a-new-hermes-translator-test.

Romero-Fresco, Pablo (2011). *Subtitling through Speech Recognition: Respeaking*. London: Routledge.

Romero-Fresco, Pablo (2013). Accessible filmmaking: Joining the dots between audio-visual translation, accessibility and filmmaking, *The Journal of Specialised Translation* 20, 201–223.

Schwab, Klaus (2016). *The Fourth Industrial Revolution*. Geneva: World Economic Forum.

Shetty, Amit (2016). VAST 4.0 arrives, championing the technology behind the growth of digital video advertising, *iab*, 21 January. www.iab.com/news/vast-4–0-arrives-championing-thetechnology-behind-the-growth-of-digital-video-advertising.

Snell-Hornby, Mary (2006). *The Turns of Translation Studies: New Paradigms or Shifting Viewpoints?* Amsterdam: John Benjamins.

Talaván, Noa (2010). Subtitling as a task and subtitles as support: Pedagogical applications. In Jorge Díaz-Cintas, Anna Matamala and Josélia Neves (eds.), *New Insights into Audiovisual Translation and Media Accessibility.* Amsterdam: Rodopi, pp. 285–299.

Tamayo-Masero, Ana (2015). Estudio descriptivo y experimental de la subtitulación en TV para niños sordos: una propuesta alternativa. PhD thesis. Castellón: Universitat Jaume I.

Toury, Gideon (1995). D*escriptive Translation Studies – and Beyond.* Amsterdam: John Benjamins.

Vandaele, Jerome (2002). Funny fictions: Francoist translation censorship of two Billy Wilder films, *The Translator* 8(2), 267–302.

Vercauteren, Gert (2016). A narratological approach to content selection in audio description. PhD thesis. Antwerp: University of Antwerp.

Weaver, Sarah (2014). Lifting the curtain on opera translation and accessibility: Translating opera for audiences with varying sensory ability. PhD thesis. Durham: Durham University.

Yuan, Long (2016). The subtitling of sexual taboo from English into Chinese. PhD thesis. London: Imperial College.

Zabalbeascoa, Patrick (1996). Translating jokes for dubbed television situation comedies, *The Translator* 2(2), 235–57.

Zárate, Soledad (2014). Subtitling for deaf children: Granting accessibility to audiovisual programmes in an educational way. PhD thesis. London: University College London.

11 Exploiting Data-Driven Hybrid Approaches to Translation in the EXPERT Project

Constantin Orăsan, Carla Parra Escartín, Lianet Sepúlveda Torres and Eduard Barbu

11.1 Introduction

Technologies have transformed the way we work, and this is also applicable to the translation industry. In the past thirty to thirty-five years, professional translators have experienced an increased technification of their work. Barely thirty years ago, a professional translator would not have received a translation assignment attached to an e-mail or via an FTP and yet, for the younger generation of professional translators, receiving an assignment by electronic means is the only reality they know. In addition, as pointed out in several works such as Folaron (2010) and Kenny (2011), professional translators now have a myriad of tools available to use in the translation process.

All parties in the translation industry agree that Computer-Assisted Translation (CAT) tools are now their main working instruments. Back in the early 1990s, when such tools started to be developed and used, they were little more than a set of Microsoft Word macros that integrated a translation memory (TM) engine and some sort of terminology management. Currently, these are comprised of a wide variety of features that range from TM and terminology management systems, to machine translation (MT) plug-ins and quality assurance tools, with new features added on a regular basis. In addition to supporting translators during the translation process, CAT tools allow translators and project managers to carry out a complete translation cycle if needed.

Most of the components of a CAT tool rely on some kind of data in order to be useful to translators: translation memories rely on a database of previous translations, terminology management tools require access to term databases, whilst concordancers need corpora to extract examples of usages. For this reason, a significant amount of research in the field of translation technology has focused on the development of methods which can create such resources.

The EXPERT (EXPloiting Empirical appRoaches to Translation) project was an EC-funded FP7 project whose main aim was to promote the research, development and use of data-driven hybrid language translation technology.[1] The project appointed twelve Early Stage Researchers (ESRs) and three Experienced Researchers (ERs) who worked on independent, but related, projects on various topics related to translation technology. The core objective of these projects was to create hybrid technologies which incorporate the best features of the existing corpus-based approaches and to improve the state of the art for data-driven empirical methods used in translation.

The translation industry is now facing more challenges than ever. Translators are required to deliver high-quality professional translations, whilst having lower rates and increased time pressure imposed, as clients expect to get the translations they demand as quickly as possible and for the lowest possible rate. One of the aims of the EXPERT project was to help translators with this issue by developing data-driven translation technologies which speed the translation process up, whilst maintaining the quality of translation. In addition, the EXPERT project aimed to bridge the gap between academia and industry by applying some of the methods developed in the project to real-life situations.

Prior to the EXPERT project, hybrid corpus-based solutions considered each approach individually as a tool, not fully exploiting the integration possibilities. The proposed EXPERT solution was to fully integrate corpus-based approaches to improve translation quality and minimise translation effort and cost. This chapter offers an overview of several technologies developed as part of the project which implemented the EXPERT solution. Given the limited space available and the fact that the EXPERT project focused on a variety of topics, in most cases the research is presented only briefly, with references to articles which provide further information.

The remainder of the chapter is structured as follows: Section 11.2 provides an overview of the EXPERT project, highlighting its most important outputs with emphasis on the hybrid data-driven research. Given the importance of translation memories in the work of professional translators, Section 11.3 presents the work on this topic carried out as part of the EXPERT project. The chapter closes by presenting our conclusions.

11.2 The EXPERT Project

The EXPERT) project was an EC-funded FP7 project initiated under the 'People' programme. The main aim of the project was to train young

[1] See the EXPERT project website: http://expert-itn.eu.

researchers, namely ESRs and ERs, to promote the research, development and use of data-driven hybrid language translation technologies, and create future world leaders in the field. From the research perspective, the main objectives of the EXPERT project were to improve the corpus-based TM and MT technologies by addressing their shortcomings, and to create hybrid technologies which incorporate the best features of corpus-based approaches. The research also focused on how to incorporate user requirements and translators' feedback in the translation process, as well as how to integrate linguistic knowledge that is usually ignored by the existing technologies.

The scientific work was organised into fifteen individual projects, each linked to one of the main themes of the project: the user perspective, data collection and preparation, incorporation of language technology in translation memories, the human translator in the loop, and hybrid approaches to translation. This section presents a brief overview of the main research themes pursued in the project. A more detailed description can be found in Orăsan et al. (2015).

The researchers had access to a vibrant training programme, which consisted of four large training events that ran across the whole consortium and engaged all the fellows: (1) a scientific and technological training session, (2) a complementary skills training session, (3) a scientific and technological workshop and (4) a business showcase. In addition, they were involved in intersectoral and transnational mobilities via secondments and short visits to industrial and academic partners. Each researcher received training from their hosting institutions and all ESRs were registered on doctoral programmes.

The project was co-ordinated by the University of Wolverhampton, UK and consisted of six academic partners: University of Wolverhampton (UK), University of Malaga (Spain), University of Sheffield (UK), University of Saarland (Germany), University of Amsterdam (Netherlands) and Dublin City University (Ireland); three companies, Translated (Italy), Hermes (Spain) and Pangeanic (Spain); and four associated partners, eTrad (Argentina), Wordfast (France), Unbabel (Portugal) and DFKI (Germany).

The rest of this section presents the work carried out across the main themes of the project.

11.2.1 The User Perspective

The research on the user perspective sought to better understand the needs of professional translators by carrying out a large survey on their views and requirements regarding various technologies and their current work practices (Zaretskaya, Pastor and Seghiri, 2015, 2018). The survey showed that from the various technologies available, professional translators only use TM on a regular basis, and that the adoption of different tools depends very much on the translator's background. Because current TM software performs many tasks in addition to the simple retrieval of previously translated segments, the survey revealed that translators use these tools to perform a variety of other operations, such as terminology management and quality assurance.

On the same theme of user perspective, Hokamp and Liu (2015) proposed HandyCAT, an open-source CAT tool[2] that allows the user to easily add or remove graphical elements and data services to or from the interface. Moreover, new components can be directly plugged into the relevant part of the translation data model. These features make HandyCAT an ideal platform for developing prototypes and conducting user studies with new components.

11.2.2 Data Collection and Preparation

The focus of the project was on data-driven technologies. For this reason, extensive research on data collection and preparation was also carried out. Costa et al. (2015) developed iCorpora, a tool which can semi-automatically compile monolingual and multilingual parallel and comparable corpora from the web. In addition to compiling corpora, the tool also enables users to manage corpora and exploit them. Barbu (2015) worked on the cleaning of TMs. This became the focus of a shared task organised by the consortium and which is presented in more detail in Section 11.3.3.

11.2.3 Language Technology in Translation Memory

As demonstrated by the survey mentioned above, TMs are among the most successfully used tools by professional translators. However, most of these tools hardly use any language processing when they match and retrieve segments. Section 11.3 presents the research carried out in the EXPERT project that incorporates information from a paraphrase database into matching and retrieval from TMs, and shows how this can improve the productivity of professional translators, and how to deal with large TMs. In the same vein of research, Tan and Pal (2014) proposed several methods for terminology extraction and ontology induction with the aim of integrating them in TMs and statistical MT.

11.2.4 The Human Translator in the Loop

The work dedicated to the 'human translator in the loop' investigated approaches that could inform end users about the quality of translations,

[2] HandyCAT at GitHub: http://handycat.github.io/.

as well as learn from their feedback on the quality of translations in order to improve translation systems and workflows. The work focused on ways of collecting and extracting useful information from post-edited sentences to feedback into statistical machine translation (SMT) systems (Logacheva and Specia, 2015), as well as discourse-level-quality estimation, a topic that has been largely neglected by the research community (Scarton and Specia, 2014). Carla Parra Escartín, Hanna Béchara and Constantin Orăsan (2017) analysed the work of professional translators when they were asked to post-edit segments of various qualities, in an attempt to better understand how the quality of automatically translated segments influences the post-editing process.

To better understand the post-editing process, researchers working on the EXPERT project developed CATaLog (Nayek et al., 2015, 2016) and CATaLog Online (Pal et al., 2016), the online version of CATaLog. Both tools are language-independent CAT tools which provide a user-friendly CAT environment to post-edit TM segments and MT output. They were implemented in order to minimise the translators' and post-editors' efforts during the post-editing task. One of the main innovations of CATaLog online consists of integrating a colour-coded scheme, both for the source and target segments, to highlight the chunks in a particular segment that should be changed. Whilst most CAT tools highlight fuzzy match differences, this is only done on the source side and it is left to the translator to locate the part of the target segment that needs to be changed. Additionally, the tool includes automatic logging of user activity. It automatically records keystrokes, cursor positions, text selection and mouse clicks together with the time spent post-editing each segment. In this way it collects a wide range of logs with post-editors' feedback, which could be very useful for research on post-editing and could also be used as training materials for automatic post-editing tasks. These features make the tool ideal for MT developers and researchers in translation studies.

11.2.5 Hybrid Approaches to Translation

A significant amount of research was carried out on hybrid approaches to translation and delivered a general framework for the combination of SMT and TM which outperforms the state-of-the-art work in SMT (Li, Parra Escartín and Liu, 2016), better ways of incorporating a dependency tree into an SMT model (Li, Way and Liu, 2015), methods for performing source-side pre-ordering for improving the quality of SMT (Daiber and Sima'an, 2015) and a method that produces better translations by considering the domain of the text to be translated (Cuong, Sima'an and Titov, 2016).

This section has briefly presented the context in which the research described in this chapter took place. Given that the EXPERT project was a four-year project, it produced much more than the research described here. For example, given its importance for many of the topics researched in the project, there were a number of systems submitted for the task of Semantic Text Similarity organised at SemEval conferences.[3,4,5] The same happened with various evaluation metrics submitted at several editions of the Workshop on Statistical Machine Translation (WMT workshops).[6,7,8] The project's webpage provides the complete list of publications which resulted from the project and links to the resources released.

11.3 Translation Memories

As shown in Zaretskaya et al. (2018), TM systems are very important for professional translators and constitute a key component of CAT tools. Translation memories store past translations which can be retrieved when either an identical or a very similar new sentence has to be translated. This process is called TM leveraging. In order to leverage past translations, TM systems rely on an algorithm to measure the similarity between a sentence to be translated and those stored in the TM. For each new sentence, the TM system computes this similarity and assigns all identical or similar translations a score called the fuzzy match score (FMS). Given that the TMs store the sentence in both the source language and its translation, TM systems will offer the translation of the sentence from the TM with the highest FMS as a translation for the new sentence. This is done even in cases where the two sentences are not identical, the assumption being that if they are similar enough the effort needed to post-edit the suggested translation is lower than the effort necessary to translate from scratch.

Translators are used to post-edit the so-called fuzzy matches and the TM leverage is also used to compute rates and allocate resources at the planning stage of a translation project. As the FMS decreases, sentences are more difficult to post-edit and at some point they are not worth post-editing. That is why in the translation industry a threshold of 75 per cent FMS is used. Segments with a 75 per cent FMS or higher undergo TM post-editing (TMPE), and segments below that threshold are translated from scratch.

The EXPERT project proposed two main ways of improving TM systems. The first focused on improving the way in which TM systems carry out the TM-leveraging process, by proposing new ways of identifying similar sentences in the translation memories. Section 11.3.1 proposes a new method for calculating the similarity between sentences which goes beyond surface matching and

[3] http://alt.qcri.org/semeval2014/. [4] http://alt.qcri.org/semeval2015/.
[5] http://alt.qcri.org/semeval2016/. [6] www.statmt.org/wmt14/. [7] www.statmt.org/wmt15/.
[8] www.statmt.org/wmt16/.

incorporates a database of paraphrases in the process. The usefulness of TM systems improves when translators have access to larger TMs. Section 11.3.2 describes a fast and scalable tool for translation memory management (TMM). Another direction of research investigated in the EXPERT project focused on the task of curating TMs to ensure their high quality, and automatically cleaning them. This is presented in Section 11.3.3.

11.3.1 Incorporating Semantic Information in the Matching and Retrieval Process

Translation memory leveraging is key for professional translators, as it determines the amount of segments that can be re-used in a new translation task. When they are given a segment to be translated, CAT tools look for an identical or similar segment in the available TMs. As previously explained, TMs will not only retrieve the exact matches found, but also fuzzy matches (i.e. similar segments to the one that needs to be newly translated). Fuzzy matches are retrieved using some sort of edit-distance metric such as Levenshtein distance.

Gupta and Orăsan (2014) explore the integration of paraphrases in matching and retrieval from TMs using edit distance in an approach based on greedy approximation and dynamic programming. The proposed method modifies Levenshtein distance to take into consideration paraphrases extracted from the paraphrase database (PPDB) (Ganitkevitch, Van Durme and Callison-Burch, 2013) when it is calculated. In addition, it is possible to paraphrase existing TMs to allow for offline processing of data and alleviate the need for translators to install additional software. Their system is based on the following five-step pipeline:

1 Read the TMs.
2 Collect all paraphrases from the paraphrase database and classify them in classes:
   a Paraphrases involving one word on both the source and target side.
   b Paraphrases involving multiple words on both sides but differing in one word only.
   c Paraphrases involving multiple words but the same number of words on both sides.
   d Paraphrases with differing number of words on the source and target sides.
3 Store all the paraphrases for each segment in the TM.
4 Read the file to be translated.
5 Get all paraphrases for all segments in the file to be translated, classify them and retrieve the most similar segment above a pre-defined threshold.

They report a significant improvement in both retrieval and translation of the retrieved segments. This research was further expanded with a human-centred evaluation in which the quality of semantically informed TM fuzzy matches was assessed based on post-editing time or keystrokes (Gupta et al., 2015). This evaluation revealed that both the editing time and the number of keystrokes are reduced when the enhanced edit-distance metric is used, without a decrease in the quality of the translation. The tool has been publicly released under an Apache License 2.0 and is available on GitHub.[9]

11.3.2 ActivaTM: A Translation Memory Management (TMM) System

The previous section demonstrated how it is possible to improve matching and retrieval from TM by incorporating semantic information from a database of paraphrases in the matching algorithm. This can be very useful for professional translators, but is not enough. The survey carried out by Zaretskaya et al. (2018) showed that a fast response is an essential feature for TMs. When working on large translation projects, translators usually have access to massive background translation memories, which are sometimes augmented with input from fully automatic translation engines. In these cases speed of access can become a problem and specialist solutions have to be sought.

ActivaTM is a fast and scalable translation memory management (TMM) system developed in the EXPERT project to ensure fast access to large TMs. It is based on a full-text search engine which has the ultimate goal of providing TM capabilities for a hybrid MT workflow. It can be used in a CAT environment to provide almost perfect translations to the human user, with mark-ups highlighting the translated segments that need to be checked manually for correctness.

This TMM system was designed in such a way that it can be successfully integrated into an online CAT tools environment, where several translators work simultaneously in the same project, adding and updating TM entries. ActivaTM can also outperform pure SMT when a good TM match is found, and in the task of automatic website translation. Preliminary experiments showed that the ActivaTM system overcomes the limitations of current TM systems in terms of storage and concordance searches. The remainder of this section presents the main features of ActivaTM.

11.3.2.1 ActivaTM Design and Capabilities Figure 11.1 presents an overview of the ActivaTM system. It consists of two principal components, tmSearchMap and tmRestAPI, and aims to ensure the following requirements:

- **Great storage capacity:** The system has the capacity to store large numbers of segments (over 10 M), along with their corresponding metadata (source

[9] TMAdvanced on GitHub: https://github.com/rohitguptacs/TMAdvanced.

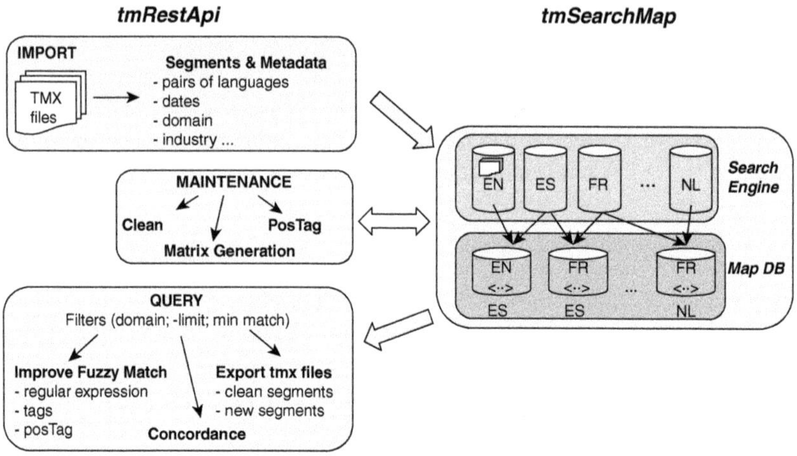

Figure 11.1 Main components of ActivaTM

and target language, segment creation and modification date, part-of-speech tags for all tokens in a given segment and for both languages, domains, etc.).

- **Fast and efficient retrieval algorithm**: The system is able to retrieve fuzzy matches quickly regardless of their FMS score.
- **Reasonable import time of new segments**: It is foreseen that occasionally the existing TMs will need to be updated by importing a massive number of new segments in TMX[10] or a similar format. ActivaTM is able to achieve this task within a reasonable amount of time.
- **Effective segment filtering, retrieval and export**: The system is able to retrieve sets of segments fulfilling certain criteria (e.g. domain, date, time span, file name, and terms appearing in the source or target language). Such subsets can be exported as one or several TMs in the TMX format that can subsequently be used to train MT systems, like those available in the PangeaMT platform.[11]

11.3.2.2 The tmSearchMap Component As the name suggests, tmSearchMap is the component in charge of retrieving segments from the TM. It is based on Elasticsearch[12] and takes advantage of its Information Retrieval (IR)-based indexing technique to speed up the time-consuming TM retrieval procedure. Elasticsearch was selected because is a mature project that dominates the

[10] TMX stands for Translation Memory eXchange and is an XML-based format for exchanging TMs between computers. The details of the standard can be accessed at www.gala-global.org/tmx-14b.

[11] PangeaMT: http://pangeamt.com/description/. [12] Elasticsearch: www.elastic.co/.

open-source search engine market, and supports fast mapping of source segments considering exact match, fuzzy match and regular expression. The tmSearchMap component consists of two principal applications: Search Engine and MapDB.

The purpose of Search Engine is to store monolingual indices of segments and provide a flexible search interface, whilst MapDB aims to complement Search Engine by storing pairs of bidirectional mappings. MapDB stores both the source and target texts together with their metadata, extracted from TMX files, such as domain, industry, type, organisation, several dates etc. MapDB also supports quick bulk import and update operations. The purpose of the update operation is to enable future updates of a segment including updating the modification date to indicate when translators edited it. This design enables the corresponding ID and text of the target language segment to be quickly retrieved, after identifying a match in a monolingual index. Additionally, the design conserves a significant amount of memory by only storing each unique segment once, which is necessary when dealing with large TMs.

Using the above design, a query to ActivaTM is conducted as follows, taking an EN–ES language pair as an example:

- A client queries ActivaTM by providing a source (EN) language segment.
- ActivaTM uses its search engine to identify the most suitable segment in the EN index and retrieves its ID.
- MapDB index EN–ES is queried using the retrieved ID and then the bilingual properties are retrieved, returning the stored translation to the client.

11.3.2.3 The tmRestAPI Component The tmRestAPI component implements a series of operations which allow importing, maintenance and query of TMs.

Importing From time to time, it is foreseen that the existing TMs will need to be updated by importing new segments in TMX formats. The tmRestAPI component is capable of importing large numbers of segments (over 10 M), along with their corresponding metadata (source and target language, segment creation and modification date, domains, industry, etc.). The ActivaTM system implements a TMX parser to extract the above properties from the input files and is able to store the new pairs of segments in a database within a reasonable amount of time.

Maintenance Maintenance tasks aim to improve the quality of the existing data, generate new data and aggregate new properties to the existing data. To increase efficiency and minimise interference with the work done by translators, all of these processes occur in the background and are performed on specific segments which are selected on the basis of a pre-defined set of characteristics.

The following tasks are performed during the maintenance: part-of-speech (POS) tagging, cleaning and matrix generation.

1. **POS tagging:** In order to improve the retrieval operation, all the tokens in source and target segments are tagged with POS information. ActivaTM is able to use different taggers, depending on the language to be analysed, and the precision and performance of those taggers. For example, it uses TreeTagger[13] (Schmid, 1994) for segments in English, Spanish, French, for Japanese it employs KyTea[14] (Neubig, Nakata and Mori, 2011) whereas for other languages it relies on RDRPOSTagger[15] (Nguyen et al., 2014), which includes the pre-trained Universal POS tagging models for forty languages. To allow for comparisons across languages, the Universal POS tag set (Petrov, Das and McDonald, 2012) is also used.
2. **Cleaning**: As discussed in Section 11.3.3, it is not unusual to have noise in TMX files. The cleaning task aims to identify and penalise pairs of noisy segments on a database. This will ensure that during the query, Elasticsearch does not rank spurious segments among the best. Currently, ActivaTM distinguishes most punctuation and numerical inconsistencies in the source language and in the target language.
3. **Matrix generation**: This task implements a triangulation algorithm which takes advantage of the tmSearchEngine design to create new pairs of segments from existing ones. The algorithm considers the stored data as an undirected graph where each monolingual segment is a node and each bilingual entry is an arc connecting nodes of different languages which are known to be correct. In this way, if for one of the segments we have translations into more than one target language, we can generate translations between these target languages even if they are not explicitly specified.

The tmRestAPI: Query Task Function ActivaTM takes advantage of the powerful Elasticsearch query language to implement a fast and efficient retrieval algorithm. The sets of segments retrieved using this language can be restricted to fulfil certain criteria such as coming from a specific domain, containing certain terms in the source or target language and/or having specific time stamps. These sets can be exported as one or several TMs in a TMX format and used to train customised translation engines (both TM and SMT engines).

An innovation of ActivaTM is its FMS, which was created specifically for the tool and leads to better ranking of the segments retrieved by Elasticsearch. The FMS is based on the well-known Levenshtein distance; however, the score between the query and the TM source is calculated taking into account the

[13] TreeTagger: www.cis.uni-muenchen.de/~schmid/tools/TreeTagger/.
[14] KyTea: www.phontron.com/kytea/.
[15] RDRPOSTagger: http://rdrpostagger.sourceforge.net/.

similarities of both strings considering the following features: characters, words, punctuation and stop words.

In addition, ActivaTM exploits existing linguistic knowledge to improve the fuzzy matching algorithm, and as a consequence the TM leveraging. The fuzzy match algorithm consists of a pipeline that integrates several language-dependent and language-independent features, such as: regular expressions, tag processing and POS sequence matching. Regular expressions are used to improve the recognition of place-able and localisable elements (e.g. numbers and URLs). Part-of-speech matches are used to detect grammatical similarities between source and target segments. Currently, only segments having a very similar grammatical structure benefit from POS matches. This procedure is also used to identify mismatches between source and target segments, and relies on a glossary or the output of an SMT system to obtain translations of the mismatched words in the target segment.

11.3.3 Translation Memory Cleaning

As reiterated throughout this chapter, TMs are very important tools for translators. However, in order to be beneficial to translators, the contents already stored in a TM must be of high quality and correct. This is not always the case when TMs are built by communities[16] or they are automatically harvested from the web. Manual cleaning is expensive and is sometimes not possible due to the lack of domain experts. For this reason, the researchers involved in the EXPERT project proposed a method for the automatic cleaning of translation memories and organised a shared task which focused on this.

11.3.3.1 TM Cleaner Barbu (2015) has developed a machine-learning-based tool which is able to identify false translations in pairs of segments stored in TMs. The system is trained and tested on a dataset extracted from MyMemory. Analysis of the data revealed four main sources of errors:

- random text where a contributor copies random text for the source and/or target segment. These cases usually indicate a malevolent contributor.
- chat-like contributions in which the TM users exchange messages instead of providing translations. For example the English text 'How are you?' translates in Italian as 'Come stai?' Instead of providing this translation, the contributor answers 'Bene' ('Fine').

[16] For example, MyMemory (https://mymemory.translated.net/) (Trombetti, 2009) allows anyone to register and translate using their online portal. During this process, users also build translation memories which can be used in other translation processes. Because anyone can participate, by default there is no quality control on the translation memories and some of the entries contain mistakes.

- language errors, when languages of the source or target segments are mistaken or swapped. This type of error usually occurs in TMs which have several target languages.
- partial translations, where only part of the source segment is translated.

The method proposed uses seventeen features to train a machine-learning classifier to identify false translation pairs. These features cover a range of phenomena which can indicate correct or incorrect translations such as presence of URLs, tags or e-mail addresses, and the cosine similarities between the use of punctuation, tags, e-mail addresses, and URLs between the source and the target. The full list of features and their descriptions can be found in Barbu (2015).

Evaluation of six different machine-learning algorithms revealed that with the exception of Naive Bayes, all of them perform much better than two baselines (both random, and one of which respects the training set class distribution). However, a detailed error analysis of the results shows that the classifiers produce a large number of false negatives, which means that around 10 per cent of good examples would need to be discarded. A solution to this problem is to develop methods which have higher precision, even if this means a lower recall.

An enhanced version of TM Cleaner is freely available on GitHub.[17] The main differences between the algorithm presented in Barbu (2015) and the implementation on GitHub are features designed to make it easily usable by the translation industry. The main differences are:

1. Integration of the HunAlign aligner (Varga et al., 2005): This component is meant to replace the automatic translation component, as not every company can translate huge amounts of data. The score given by the aligner is smoothly integrated with the training model.
2. Integration of the Fastalign word aligner as a web service: As above, this component is meant to replace the automatic translation. Based on the alignments returned by the word aligner, new features are computed (e.g. number of aligned words in source and target segments). For more details please see (Barbu, 2017).
3. Addition of two operating modes, the train modality and the classify modality: In the train modality, the features are computed and the corresponding model is stored. In the classify modality, a new TM is classified based on the stored model.
4. Passing arguments through the command line: It is now possible to indicate the machine-learning algorithm that will be used for classification.
5. Implementation of handwritten rules for keeping/deleting certain bilingual segments: These handwritten rules are necessary to decide, in certain cases

[17] TM Cleaner on GitHub: https://github.com/SoimulPatriei/TMCleaner.

with almost 100 per cent precision, if a bilingual segment should be kept or not. This component can be activated/deactivated through an argument passed through the command line.

6 Integration of an evaluation module: When a new test set is classified and a portion of it is manually annotated, the evaluation module computes the precision/recall and F-measure for each class.

The tool has been evaluated using three new data sets coming from aligned websites and TMs. Moreover, the final version of the tool has been implemented in an iterative process based on annotating the data and evaluating it using the evaluation module. This iterative process has been followed to boost the performance of the cleaner.

11.3.3.2 Automatic Translation Memory Cleaning Shared Task This shared task was inspired by the work carried out by Barbu (2015) in the EXPERT project as presented above, and was one of the outcomes of the First Workshop on Natural Language Processing for Translation Memories (NLP4TM).[18] The purpose of the first Automatic Translation Memory Cleaning Shared Task was to invite teams from both academia and industry to tackle the problem of cleaning TMs and submit their automatic systems for evaluation.

As this was the first shared task on this topic, the focus was on learning to better define that task and on identifying the most promising approaches with which to tackle the problem. The proposed task consisted of identifying translation units that had to be discarded because they were inaccurate translations of each other, or corrected as they contained ortho-typographical errors such as missing punctuation marks or misspellings.

For this first task, bi-segments for three frequently used language pairs were prepared: English–Spanish, English–Italian and English–German. The data was annotated with information on whether the target content of each TM segment represented a valid translation of its corresponding source. In particular, the following three-point scale was applied:

1 The translation is correct (tag '1').
2 The translation is correct, but there are a few ortho-typographical mistakes and therefore some minor post-editing is required (tag '2').
3 The translation is not correct and should be discarded (content missing/added, wrong meaning, etc.) (tag '3').

Besides choosing the pair of languages with which they wanted to work, participants could participate in one or all of the following three tasks:

1 Binary classification (I): In this task, it was only necessary to determine whether a bi-segment was correct or incorrect. For this binary classification option, only tag ('1') was considered correct because the translators did not

[18] See webpage on the workshop: http://rgcl.wlv.ac.uk/nlp4tm/.

need to make any modification, whilst tags ('2') and ('3') were considered incorrect translations.

2 Binary classification (II): As in the first task, it was only required to determine whether the bi-segment was correct or incorrect. However, in contrast to the first task, a bi-segment was considered correct if it was labelled by annotators as ('1') or ('2'). Bi-segments labelled ('3') were considered incorrect because they require major post-editing.

3 Fine-grained classification: In this task, the participating teams had to classify the segments according to the annotation provided in the training data: correct translations ('1'), correct translations with a few ortho-typographical errors ('2') and incorrect translations ('3').

The data was, for the most part, sampled from the public part of MyMemory. In the initial phase, we extracted approximately 30,000 translation units (TUs) for each language pair. The TUs were heterogeneous and belonged to different domains, ranging from medicine and physics to colloquial conversations. A set of filters was applied in order to reduce this number to 10,000 units per language, from which approximately 3,000 TUs per language pair were manually selected. Since the proportion of units containing incorrect translations is low, to facilitate their manual selection we computed the cosine similarity score between the MT of the English segment and the target segment of the TU. The hypothesis to test was that low cosine similarity scores (less than 0.3) can signal bad translations. Finally, we ensured that the manually selected TUs did not contain inappropriate language or other errors that could not be identified automatically. The data was manually annotated by two native speakers.

In total, six teams participated in the shared task, by submitting a total of forty-five runs. Barbu et al. (2016) contains a detailed description of the participating teams and a comparative evaluation of their results. In addition, the reports from each of the participating teams can be found on the shared task's webpage.[19]

11.4 Conclusion

This chapter has presented the main research topics addressed in the EXPERT project and summarised some of the project's innovations related to data-driven hybrid approaches to translation. Some of the researchers employed in EXPERT have focused on improving already existing algorithms with linguistic information, whilst others have researched how to create new tools that can be used in the translation industry. As a result, the TMAdvanced tool developed

[19] See webpage on the shared task: http://rgcl.wlv.ac.uk/nlp4tm2016/shared-task/.

by Gupta and Orăsan (2014) can already be used by any translator or translation company, as can the ActivaTM and the TM Cleaner.

The CAT tools CATaLog (Nayek et al., 2015; Pal et al., 2016) and HandyCAT (Hokamp and Liu, 2015), and the terminology management system proposed by Hokamp (2015), are also examples of how academic research can produce open-source tools that aim to fulfil all the features of existing CAT tools whilst adding new functionalities, with the sole purpose of helping translators translate better and focus on the task at hand: delivering high-quality translations in a timely manner.

Several EXPERT researchers have explored ways of integrating new advances in computational linguistics and MT into the translation workflow. The research carried out as part of the EXPERT project proved there is room for a successful hybridisation of the translation workflow, and such hybridisation may be implemented in different components with a unique goal: enabling the end users (i.e. the translators) to work more efficiently and effectively as a benefit of the research undertaken.

Acknowledgements

We would like to acknowledge the contributions of all the partners and all the researchers in this project. This chapter would not have been possible without their hard work. The research described here was partially funded by the People Programme (Marie Curie Actions) of the European Union's Seventh Framework Programme FP7/2007–2013/under REA grant agreement no. 317471.

References

Barbu, Eduard (2015). Spotting false translation segments in translation memories. In Proceedings of the Workshop Natural Language Processing for Translation Memories. Association for Computational Linguistics. Hissar, Bulgaria, September 2015, pp. 9–16. www.aclweb.org/anthology/W15-5202.

Barbu, Eduard (2017). Ensembles of classifiers for cleaning web parallel corpora and translation memories. In Proceedings of the International Conference Recent Advances in Natural Language Processing, RANLP 2017, Varna, Bulgaria, September 2017, pp. 71–77. https://doi.org/10.26615/978–954-452–049-6_011.

Barbu, Eduard, Carla Parra Escartín, Luisa Bentivogli, Matteo Negri, Marco Turchi, Constantin Orăsan and Marcello Federico (2016). The first Automatic Translation Memory Cleaning Shared Task. Machine Translation, 30 (3–4) (December 2016), 145–166. ISSN 0922–6567. DOI:10.1007/s10590-016-9183-http://link.springer.com/10.1007/s10590-016–9183-x.

Costa, Hernani, Gloria Corpas Pastor, Miriam Seghiri and Ruslan Mitkov (2015). Towards a Web-based tool to semi-automatically compile, manage and explore comparable and parallel corpora. In New Horizons in Translation and Interpreting Studies (Full papers), December 2015, 133–141.

Cuong, Hoang, Khalil Sima'an and Ivan Titov (2016). Adapting to all domains at once: Rewarding domain invariance in SMT. Transactions of the Association for Computational Linguistics 4, 99–112. https://transacl.org/ojs/index.php/tacl/article/view/768.

Daiber, Joachim and Khalil Sima'an (2015). Machine translation with source-predicted target morphology. In Proceedings of MT Summit XV. Miami, Florida, 2015, pp. 283–296.

Folaron, Deborah (2010). Translation tools. In Yves Gambier and Luc van Doorslaer (eds.), Handbook of Translation Studies, vol. 1, Amsterdam; Philadelphia: John Benjamins Publishing Co., pp. 429–436.

Ganitkevitch, Juri, Benjamin Van Durme and Chris Callison-Burch (2013). PPDB: The paraphrase database. In Proceedings of NAACL-HLT 2013 Atlanta, Georgia, June 2013, pp. 758–764. www.aclweb.org/anthology/N13-1092.pdf.

Gupta, Rohit and Constantin Orăsan (2014). Incorporating paraphrasing in translation memory matching and retrieval. In Proceedings of the European Association of Machine Translation (EAMT–2014), pp. 3–10.

Gupta, Rohit, Constantin Orăsan, Marcos Zampieri, Mihaela Vela and Josef van Genabith (2015). Can translation memories afford not to use paraphrasing? In Proceedings of the 2015 Conference on European Association of Machine Translation (EAMT-2015). Antalya, Turkey, 2015, pp. 35–42.

Hokamp, Chris (2015). Leveraging NLP technologies and linked open data to create better CAT tools. Localisation Focus – The International Journal of Localisation, 14(1), 14–18. www.localisation.ie/resources/publications/2015/258.

Hokamp, Chris and Qun Liu (2015). HandyCAT: The flexible CAT tool for translation research. In Proceedings of the 18th Annual Conference of the European Association for Machine Translation, Istanbul, Turkey, May, p. 216.

Kenny, Dorothy (2011). Electronic tools and resources for translators. In Kirsten Malmkjær and Kevin Windle (eds.), The Oxford Handbook of Translation Studies, pp. 455–472. Oxford, UK: Oxford University Press. www.oxfordhandbooks.com/view/10.1093/oxfordhb/9780199239306.001.0001/oxfordhb-9780199239306-e-031.

Li, Liangyou, Andy Way and Qun Liu (2015). Dependency graph-to-string translation. In Proceedings of the 2015 Conference on Empirical Methods in Natural Language Processing, Lisbon, Portugal, 2015, pp. 33–43. http://aclweb.org/anthology/D15-1004.

Li, Liangyou, Carla Parra Escartín and Qun Liu (2016). Combining translation memories and syntax-based SMT: Experiments with real industrial data, Baltic Journal of Modern Computing 4(2) (June), 165–177.

Logacheva, Varvara and Lucia Specia (2015). The role of artificially generated negative data for quality estimation of machine translation. In Proceedings of the 18th Annual Conference of the European Association for Machine Translation, Antalya, Turkey, 2015, pp. 51–58. www.aclweb.org/anthology/W/W15/W15-4907.pdf.

Nayek, Tapas, Sudip Kumar Naskar, Santanu Pal, Marcos Zampieri, Mihaela Vela and Josef van Genabith (2015). CATaLog: New approaches to TM and post editing interfaces. In Proceedings of the 1st Workshop on Natural Language Processing for Translation Memories. Workshop on Natural Language Processing for Translation Memories (NLP4TM), located at RANLP 2015, September 11, Hissar, Bulgaria, pp. 36–43. www.aclweb.org/anthology/W15-5206.

Nayek, Tapas, Santanu Pal, Sudip Kumar Naskar, Sivaji Bandyopadhyay and Josef van Genabith (2016). Beyond translation memories: Generating translation suggestions based on parsing and POS tagging. In Proceedings of the 2nd Workshop on Natural Language Processing for Translation Memories (NLP4TM 2016), Portorož, Slovenia, May 2016.

Neubig,Graham, Yosuke Nakata and Shinsuke Mori (2011). Pointwise prediction for robust, adaptable Japanese morphological analysis. In The Proceedings of the 49th Annual Meeting of the Association for Computational Linguistics: Human Language Technologies (ACL-HLT), Portland, Oregon, USA, June 2011, pp. 529–533. www .phontron.com/paper/neubig11aclshort.pdf.

Nguyen,Dat Quoc, Dai Quoc Nguyen, Dang Duc Pham and Son Bao Pham (2014). RDRPOSTagger: A ripple down rules-based part-of-speech tagger. Proceedings of the Demonstrations at the 14th Conference of the European Chapter of the Association for Computational Linguistics, Gothenburg, Sweden, 26–30 April. Association for Computational Linguistics, pp. 17–20.

Orăsan, Constantin, Alessandro Cattelan, Gloria Corpas Pastor, Josef van Genabith, Manuel Herranz, Juan José Arevalillo, Qun Liu, Khalil Sima'an and Lucia Specia (2015). The EXPERT project: Advancing the state of the art in hybrid translation technologies. In Proceedings of Translating and the Computer 37, London, UK, 2015. Geneva: Editions Tradulex.

Pal, Santanu, Marcos Zampieri, Sudip Kumar Naskar, Tapas Nayak, Mihaela Vela and Josef van Genabith (2016). CATaLog online: Porting a post-editing tool to the web. In Nicoletta Calzolari (Conference Chair), Khalid Choukri, Thierry Declerck, Sara Goggi, Marko Grobelnik, Bente Maegaard, Joseph Mariani, Helene Mazo, Asuncion Moreno, Jan Odijk and Stelios Piperidis (eds.), Proceedings of the Tenth International Conference on Language Resources and Evaluation (LREC 2016), Paris, France, May 2016. European Language Resources Association (ELRA).

Parra Escartín, Carla, Hanna Béchara and Constantin Orăsan (2017). Questing for quality estimation: A user study, The Prague Bulletin of Mathematical Linguistics 108, 343–354. DOI:10.1515/pralin-2017-0032.https://ufal.mff.cuni.cz/pbml/108/art-bechara-escartin-orasan.pdf.

Petrov,Slav, Dipanjan Das and Ryan McDonald (2012). A universal part-of-speech tagset. In Nicoletta Calzolari (Conference Chair), Khalid Choukri, Thierry Declerck, Mehmet Uğur Doğan, Bente Maegaard, Joseph Mariani, Asuncion Moreno, Jan Odijk and Stelios Piperidis (eds.), Proceedings of the Eighth International Conference on Language Resources and Evaluation (LREC'12). European Language Resources Association (ELRA). Istanbul, Turkey, May 2012.

Scarton,Carolina and Lucia Specia (2014). Document-level translation quality estimation: Exploring discourse and pseudo-references. In Proceedings of the Seventeenth Annual Conference of the European Association for Machine Translation (EAMT 2014), Dubrovnik, Croatia, 2014. Zagreb: Hrvatsko društvo za jezične tehnologije, pp. 101–108.

Schmid,Helmut (1994). Probabilistic part-of-speech tagging using decision trees. In Proceedings of the International Conference on New Methods in Language Processing, Manchester, UK.

Tan,Liling and Santanu Pal (2014). Manawi: Using multi-word expressions and named entities to improve machine translation. In Proceedings of the Ninth Workshop on Statistical Machine Translation, Baltimore, Maryland, USA, 2014, pp. 201–206.

Trombetti,Marco (2009). Creating the world's largest translation memory. In MT Summit XII: Proceedings of the Twelfth Machine Translation Summit, Ottawa, ON, Canada, 2009, pp. 9–16.

Varga, Dániel, Péter Halácsy, András Kornai, Viktor Nagy, László Ńemeth and Viktor Trón (2005). Parallel corpora for medium density languages. In Recent Advances in Natural Language Processing (RANLP 2005). Bulgaria: INCOMA Ltd., pp. 590–596.

Zaretskaya,Anna, Gloria Corpas Pastor and Miriam Seghiri (2015). Translators' requirements for translation technologies: Results of a user survey. In Proceedings of the AIETI7 Conference: New Horizons in Translation and Interpreting Studies (AIETI), Malaga, Spain, 2015. Geneva: Editions Tradulex, pp. 103–108.

Zaretskaya, Anna, Gloria Corpas Pastor and Miriam Seghiri (2018). User perspective on translation tools: Findings of a user survey. In Gloria Corpas Pastor and Isabel Duran (eds.), Trends in E-tools and Resources for Translators and Interpreters. The Netherlands: Brill, pp. 37–56.

12 Advances in Speech-to-Speech Translation Technologies

Mark Seligman and Alex Waibel

Introduction

The dream of automatic speech-to-speech translation (S2ST), like that of automated translation in general, goes back to the origins of computing in the 1950s. Portable speech-translation devices have been variously imagined as *Star Trek*'s "universal translator" for negotiating extraterrestrial tongues, Douglas Adams' Babel Fish in the *Hitchhiker's Guide to the Galaxy*, and more. Over the past few decades, the concept has become an influential meme and a widely desired solution, not far behind the videophone (already here!) and the flying car (any minute now).

Back on planet Earth, real-world S2ST applications have been tested locally over the past decade to help medical staff talk with other-language patients; to support military personnel in various theaters of war; to support humanitarian missions; and in general-purpose consumer products. A prominent current project aims to build S2ST devices to enable cross-language communications at the 2020 Olympics in Tokyo, with many more use cases in the offing. Systems are now on offer for simultaneous translation of video conferences or in-person presentations.

Automated speech translation has arrived: The technology's entry into widespread use has begun, and enterprises, application developers, and government agencies are aware of its potential. In view of this general interest, we provide here a survey of the field's technologies, approaches, companies, projects, and target use cases. Sections follow on the past, present, and future of speech-to-speech translation. The section on the present surveys representative participants in the developing scene.

12.1 Past

This section of our review of S2ST recaps the history of the technology. Later sections will survey the present and look toward the future.

The field of *speech* – as opposed to *text* – translation has an extensive history which deserves to be better known and understood. Text translation is already quite difficult, in view of the ambiguities of language; but attempts to automatically translate *spoken* rather than *written* language add the considerable difficulties of converting the spoken word into text. Beyond the need to distinguish different meanings, systems also risk additional errors and ambiguity concerning what was actually said – due to noise, domain context, disfluency (errors, repetitions, false starts, etc.), dialog effects, and many more sources of uncertainty. They must not only determine the appropriate meaning of "bank" – whether "financial institution," "river bank," or other; they also run the risk of misrecognizing the word itself, in the face of sloppy speech, absence of word boundaries, noise, and intrinsic acoustic confusability. "Did you go to the bank?" becomes /dɪd͡ʒəgoʷdəðəbæŋk/, and each segment may be misheard in various ways: /bæŋk/ → "bang"; /goʷdəðə/ → "goat at a"; and so on. This extra layer of uncertainty can lead to utter confusion: When a misrecognized segment (e.g. "Far East" → "forest") is translated into another language (becoming e.g. Spanish: "selva"), only consternation can result, since the confused translation bears neither semantic nor acoustic resemblance to the correct one. A speaker may even mix input languages, further compounding the problems.

12.1.1 Orientation: Speech-Translation Issues

As orientation and preparation for our brief history of speech translation, it will be helpful to review the issues confronting any system. We start by considering several dimensions of design choice, and then give separate attention to matters of human interface and multimodality.

12.1.1.1 Dimensions of Design Choice Because of its dual difficulties – those of speech recognition *and* machine translation (MT) – the field has progressed in stages. At each stage, attempts have been made to reduce the complexity of the task along several dimensions: range (supported linguistic flexibility, supported topic or domain); speaking style (read vs. conversational); pacing (consecutive vs. simultaneous); speed and latency (real-time vs. delayed systems); microphone handling; architecture (embedded vs. server-based systems); sourcing (choice among providers of components); and more. Each system has necessarily accepted certain restrictions and limitations in order to improve performance and achieve practical deployment.

- **Range (supported linguistic flexibility, supported topic or domain)**
  - ***Restricted syntax, voice phrase books***: The most straightforward restriction is to severely limit the range of sentences that can be accepted, thereby restricting the allowable syntax (grammar). A voice-based phrase book, for example, can accept only specific sentences (and perhaps near variants). Speech recognition need only pick one of the legal words or sentences, and

translation requires no more than a table lookup or best-match operation. However, deviations from the allowable sentences will quickly lead to failure, so free conversations, dialogs, speeches, etc. are out of range.

- ***Restricted-domain dialogs:*** Systems can limit the domain of a dialog rather than the range of specific sentences, such as those related to registration desk and hotel reservation systems, facilities for scheduling or medical registration, and so on. Users can in theory say anything they like . . . *if* they remain within the supported topic or domain. Users need not remember allowable phrases or vocabularies. Domain restrictions simplify the work of developers, too: for both recognition and translation, we know the typical transactional patterns; can apply domain-dependent concepts and semantics; and can train appropriate models given large data and corpora from dialogs in that domain. Even so, limited-domain dialog systems are typically more difficult to engineer than those limited to phrase books, as they include varied expressions; greater disfluency and more hesitations; and, in general, less careful speech. Procurement of sufficient data for training limited-domain systems is also a constant challenge, even when users can contribute.
- ***Open-domain speech:*** In open-domain systems we remove the domain restriction by permitting any topic of discussion. This freedom is important in applications like translation of broadcast news, lectures, speeches, seminars, and wide-ranging telephone calls. However, developers of these applications confront unrestricted vocabularies and concept sets, and must often handle continuous streams of speech, with uncertain beginnings and endings of sentences.
- **Speaking style (read vs. conversational speech):** Among open-domain systems, another dimension of difficulty is the clarity of the speech – the degree to which pronunciation is well articulated on one hand, or careless and conversational on the other. The speech of a TV anchor, for example, is mostly read speech without hesitations or disfluencies, and thus can be recognized with high accuracy. Lectures are harder: they are not pre-formulated, and some lecturers' delivery is halting and piecemeal. At the limit, spontaneous and conversational dialogs like meetings and dinner-table exchanges tend toward even more fragmentary and poorly articulated speech.
- **Pacing (consecutive vs. simultaneous):** In *consecutive* speech translation, a speaker pauses after speaking to give the system (or human interpreter) a chance to produce the translation. In *simultaneous* interpretation, by contrast, recognition and translation are performed in parallel while the speaker keeps speaking. Consecutive translation is generally easier, since the system knows where the end of an utterance is. Articulation is generally clearer, and speakers can try to cooperate with the system. In simultaneous interpretation, speakers are less aware of the system and less prone to cooperate.

- **Speed and latency (real-time vs. delayed systems):** In a given task, excessive latency (waiting time) may be intolerable. For simultaneous speech interpretation, the system must not fall too far behind the speakers, and it may be desirable to produce a segment's translation before the end of the full utterance. In that case, accurate rendering of the early segments is vital to supply complete context. Fortunately, use cases differ in their demands: when an audience is following along *during* a lecture, parliamentary speech, or live news program, low latency is essential; but if the same discourses are audited *after the fact* for viewing or browsing, the entire discourse can be used as context for accuracy.
- **Microphone handling:** Speakers can sometimes use microphones close to them, yielding clear speech signals, e.g. in telephony, in lectures with headset or lapel microphones, and in mobile speech translators. Similarly, broadcast news utilizes studio-quality recording. However, performance degrades when speakers are far from their mics, or when there is overlap among several speakers, as when table mics are used in meetings (though array mics are progressing), or in recordings of free dialog captured "in the wild."
- **Architecture (mobile vs. server-based systems):** Must speech-translation technology run embedded on a mobile device, or is a network-based solution practical? Good performance and quality is generally easier to engineer in networked implementations, because more extensive computing resources can be brought to bear. Network-based solutions may also enable collection of data from the field (privacy regulations permitting). On the other hand, in many speech-translation applications, such solutions may be unacceptable – for example, when network-based processing is unavailable, or too expensive, or insufficiently secure. For interpretation of lectures or for broadcast news, network-based solutions work well; by contrast, in applications for travel or for medical, humanitarian, military, or law-enforcement apps, embedded mobile technology is often preferable.
- **Sourcing (choice among providers of components):** We have been discussing mobile vs. server-based system architectures. Architecture choices also have organizational and business implications: where will the technology – the speech, translation, and other components – come from? Given the global character of the field, speech-translation vendors can now build applications without owning those components. A vendor may for example build an interface that captures the voice utterance; sends it to an Internet language service (e.g. Nuance, Google, and Microsoft) to perform speech recognition; sends the result to another service to perform MT; and finally sends it to a third service for speech synthesis. An embedded system might similarly be built up using licensed components. With either architecture,

value might (or might not) be added via interface refinements, customization, combination of languages or platforms, etc. This systems-integration approach lowers the barrier of entry for smaller developers but creates a dependency upon the component providers. The advantages of tight integration among system components may also be forfeit.

In the face of all these dimensions of difficulty and choice, speech-translation solutions differ greatly. Direct comparison between systems becomes difficult, and there can be no simple answer to the question, "How well does speech translation work today?" In each use case, the answer can range from "Great! Easy problem, already solved!" to "Not so good. Intractable problem, research ongoing." In response to the technical challenges posed by each dimension, speech translation as a field has progressed in stages, from simple voice-activated command-and-control systems to voice-activated phrase books; from domain-limited dialog translators to domain-unlimited speech translators; from demo systems to fully deployed networked services or mobile, embedded, and general-purpose dialog translators; and from consecutive to simultaneous interpreters.

12.1.1.2 Human Factors and Interfaces Interfaces for speech translation must balance competing goals: we want maximum speed and transparency (minimum interference) on one hand, while maintaining maximum accuracy and naturalness on the other. No perfect solutions are to be expected, since even human interpreters normally spend considerable time in clarification dialogs.

As long as perfect accuracy remains elusive, efficient error-recovery mechanisms can be considered. (We will discuss their usefulness later in this section.) The first step is to enable users to recognize errors, both in speech recognition and in translation. To correct errors once found, mechanisms for correction, and then for adaptation and improvement, are needed.

Speech-recognition errors can be recognized by literate users if speech-recognition results are displayed on a device screen. For illiterate users, or to enable eyes-free use, text-to-speech playback of automatic speech recognition (ASR) results could be used (but has been used only rarely to date). To correct ASR mistakes, some systems may enable users to type or handwrite the erroneous words. Facilities might instead be provided for voice-driven correction (though these, too, have been used only rarely to date). The entire input might instead be repeated; but then errors might recur, or new ones might erupt. Finally, multimodal resolutions can be supported, for instance involving manual selection of an error in a graphic interface followed by voiced correction. (More on multimodal systems in Section 12.1.1.3.)

Once any ASR errors in an input segment have been corrected, the segment can be passed to machine translation (in systems whose ASR and MT components are separable). Then recognition and correction of translation results may be facilitated.

Several spoken-language translation (SLT) systems aid recognition of MT errors by providing indications of the system's confidence: low confidence flags potential problems. Other systems supply back-translations, so that users can determine whether the input is still understandable after its round trip through the output language. (However, back-translation can yield misleading results. Some systems have minimized extraneous mistakes by generating back-translations directly from language-neutral semantic representations; and one system has enhanced accuracy by forcing the MT engine to reuse during back-translation the semantic elements used in the forward translation.)

User-friendly facilities for real-time *correction* of translation errors are challenging to design. They may include tools for choosing among available meanings for ambiguous expressions (as discussed in the short portrait of coauthor Seligman in Section 12.2.3.4).

Some systems have experimented with robot avatars designed to play the role of mediating interpreters. In one such system, intervention was ultimately judged too distracting, and a design has been substituted in which users recognize errors by reference to a running transcript of the conversation. When misunderstandings are noticed, rephrasing is encouraged.

Whether in ASR or MT, repeated errors are annoying: Systems should learn from their mistakes, so that errors diminish over time and use. If machine learning is available, it should take advantage of any corrections that users supply. (Dynamic updating of statistical models is an active development area.) Alternatively, interactive update mechanisms can be furnished.

One more interface issue involves frequent recurrence of a given utterance, e.g. "What is your age?" Translation memory (TM) can be supplied in various forms: Most simply, a system can record translations for later reuse.

12.1.1.3 Multimodal Translators Flexible and natural cross-language communication may involve a wide range of modalities beyond text and speech. On the input side, systems can translate not only speech but text messages, posts,[1] images of road signs and documents (Yang et al., 2001a, 2001b; Waibel, 2002; Zhang et al., 2002a, 2002b; Gao et al., 2004)[2] . . . even silent speech by way of muscle movement of the articulators, as measured through electromyographic sensors (Maier-Hein et al., 2005)![3] Going forward, multimodal input will be needed to better capture and convey human elements of

1 E.g. in Facebook: Facebook Help Centre, "How do I translate a post or comment written in another language?": www.facebook.com/help/509936952489634?helpref=faq_content.

2 E.g. in Google. Google Translate Help, "Translate images": https://support.google.com/translate/answer/6142483?hl=en.

3 See YouTube, "Silent speech translation by InterACT." Posted by CHILukaEU on January 3, 2008: www.youtube.com/watch?v=aMPNjMVlr8A.

communication: emotions, gestures, and facial expressions will help to transmit speakers' intent in the context of culture, relationships, setting, and social status.

Multimodal *output* choices will likewise vary per situation. In lectures, for example, audible speech output from multiple sources would be disruptive, so delivery modes may involve headphones, targeted audio speakers,[4] etc. Text may be preferred to spoken output, or may be added to it – on-screen in presentations, on personal devices, in glasses, etc.

12.1.2 Chronology and Milestones

Having gained perspective on the issues facing speech-translation systems – the design choices and considerations of human interface and multimodality – we can now begin our historical survey.

The earliest demonstration seems to have been in 1983, when the Japanese company NEC presented a system at that year's ITU Telecom World.[5] It was limited to domain-restricted phrasebooks, but did illustrate the vision and feasibility of automatically interpreting speech.

Further progress would await the maturation of the main components of any speech-translation system: speech recognition, MT, speech synthesis, and a viable infrastructure. Continuous speech recognition for large vocabularies emerged only at the end of the 1980s. Text-based MT was then still an unsolved problem: it was seriously attempted again only in the late 1980s and early 1990s after a multi-decade hiatus. Meanwhile, unrestricted speech synthesis was just appearing (Allen et al., 1979). Also emerging was a medium for transmission: several companies – Uni-verse, Amikai, CompuServe, GlobalLink, and others – attempted the first chat-based text-translation systems, designed for real-time use but lacking speech elements.[6]

12.1.2.1 Japan: ATR and Partners By the early 1990s, speech translation as a vision had generated sufficient excitement that research in the space was

4 E.g. in the work of Jörg Müller and others: Paul Marks, "Beams of sound immerse you in music others can't hear," *New Scientist* (Web), January 29, 2014, www.newscientist.com/article/mg22129544-100-beams-of-sound-immerse-you-in-music-others-cant-hear/.

5 See for example: Karmesh Arora, Sunita Arora, and Mukund Kumar Roy, "Speech to speech translation: A communication boon," *CSI Transactions on ICT* 1(3) (September 2013), 207–213: http://link.springer.com/article/10.1007/s40012-013–0014-4; or "TELECOM 83: Telecommunications for all," *ITU 3* (Web), https://itunews.itu.int/En/2867-TELECOM-83BRTelecommunications-for-all.note.aspx.

6 Translating chat systems have survived to the present, spurred by the recent explosion of texting. San Diego firm Ortsbo, for example, was primarily a chat aggregator, supplying a bridge among many different texting platforms; but it also enabled multilingual translation of the various streams and, with speech translation in mind, purchased an interest in Lexifone, a speech-translation company. Ortsbo was acquired by Yappn Corporation in 2015.

funded at the national level. In Japan, the Advanced Telecommunications Research (ATR) Institute International opened officially in April 1989, with one of its four labs dedicated to interpreting telephony. A consortium underwritten by the Japanese government brought together investment and participation from a range of Japanese communication firms: NTT, KDD, NEC, and others.[7] Researchers from all over the world joined the effort, and collaborative research with leading international labs was initiated. The Consortium for Speech Translation Advanced Research (C-STAR) was established in 1992 by ATR (initially under the direction of Akira Kurematsu), Carnegie Mellon University in Pittsburgh (CMU), and the Karlsruhe Institute of Technology (KIT) in Germany (coordinated by Alexander Waibel), and Siemens Corporation. In January 1993, the same group mounted a major demo linking these efforts as the culmination of an International Joint Experiment on Interpreting Telephony. It was widely reported – by CNN, the *New York Times, Business Week*, and many other news sources – as the first international demonstration of SLT, showing voice-to-voice rendering via dedicated long-distance video hook-ups for English↔Japanese, English↔German, and Japanese↔German.

At the Japanese end, the speech-translation system was named ASURA, for a many-faced Buddhist deity (Morimoto et al., 1993). The system was potentially powerful, but extremely brittle in that its hand-built lexicons were narrowly restricted to the selected domain, conference registration. The system was also slow, due to the hardware limitations of the time and the computational demands of its unification-based MT.

In the demo, the speech-translation system for German and English was the first in the United States and Europe, coincidentally named for another two-faced god, JANUS (Waibel et al., 1991; Waibel, Lavie, and Levin, 1997).[8] The system was also one of the first to use neural networks for its speech processing. Analysis for translation was performed in terms of Semantic Dialog Units, roughly corresponding to speech acts. Output was transformed into a common semantic exchange format. This representation yielded two advantages: Domain semantics could be enforced, so that all sentences, even if stuttered or otherwise disfluent, would be mapped onto well-defined semantic concepts to support generation of output utterances; and additional languages could be added relatively easily.

At the participating sites, a wide variety of studies tackled example-based translation, topic tracking, discourse analysis, prosody, spontaneous speech

[7] This consortium followed upon another ambitious government-sponsored R&D effort in the 1980s: the Fifth Generation project, which aimed to build computers optimized to run the Prolog computer language as a path toward artificial intelligence.

[8] Its name, beyond the classical reference, also served as a tongue-in-cheek acronym for Just Another Neural Understanding System.

features, neural-network-based and statistical system architectures, and other aspects of an idealized translation system. In cooperation with CMU and KIT, ATR also amassed a substantial corpus of close transcriptions of simulated conversations for reference and training.

12.1.2.2 C-STAR Consortium As the 1993 demo was taking shape, the parties also expanded the international C-STAR cooperation into its second phase. To the original US, German, and Japanese research groups (CMU, KIT, and ATR International) were added organizations from France (GETA-CLIPS, University Joseph Fourier); Korea (Electronics Telecommunications Research Institute); China (National Laboratory of Pattern Recognition, Institute of Automation, Chinese Academy of Sciences); and Italy (ITC-IRST, Centro per la Ricerca Scientifica e Tecnologica). Over the following decade, plenary meetings were held annually to compare and evaluate developing speech-translation systems. Locations included Pittsburgh, Grenoble, Taejon (Korea), Guilin (China), Trento (Italy), Munich, and Geneva.[9]

To facilitate comparison among C-STAR systems, all employed the same underlying representation for the meanings of utterances – the language-neutral Interchange Format, or IF (Levin et al., 1998). This use of a common interlingua, however, also had two drawbacks. First, it was necessary to develop and maintain this representation and the parsers mapping into it – at the time, manually. Second, the representation was domain-limited, so that the resulting systems could operate only in the chosen domains (hotel reservation, travel planning, etc.). Hand-coded parsers were gradually replaced by parsers trainable via machine learning, but the limitation to specific domains remained, yielding systems appropriate only for tightly goal-driven transactional dialogs. The need for extension to domain-independent tasks became apparent.

Accordingly, as an alternate approach, the consortium also became the context for the first practical demonstration, in Grenoble in 1998, of unrestricted or open-ended speech translation. Under the auspices of the French team, the demo was built by adding in-device speech input and output elements to a server-based chat translation system for several European languages created by CompuServe under the management of Mary Flanagan (Seligman, 2000). The resulting SLT system enabled interactive correction of ASR errors.

The C-STAR consortium also became the venue for the first speech translation via a cellular phone connection – in Guilin, China, in 2002, by the Korean group. The first two SLT products for telephony entered the Japanese market

[9] And quite enjoyable they were. Someone suggested renaming the association as Consortium for Sightseeing, Travel, and Restaurants.

four and five years later: NEC's mobile device for Japanese–English (2006) and the Shabete Honyaku service from ATR-Trek (2007).[10]

12.1.2.3 Germany: Linguatec and Verbmobil An early boxed product for speech translation on PCs used similar component technologies. This was *talk & translate* for German↔English, produced by Linguatec (later Lingenio) in 1998. To the company's own bidirectional translation software were added ViaVoice from IBM and its associated text-to-speech. The product required a twenty-minute training session for the speaker-dependent software of the time and failed to find a market in German business.[11]

Also in Germany, the government supported a major speech-translation endeavor during the 1990s – the Verbmobil project, headed by Wolfgang Wahlster and Alex Waibel and sponsored by the German Federal Ministry of Research and Technology from 1993.[12] As in the C-STAR consortium, studies were undertaken of discourse, topic tracking, prosody, incremental text generation, and numerous other aspects of a voice-to-voice translation system. The combination of many knowledge sources, however, became unwieldy and hard to maintain. One research element did prove seminal, though: the use of statistical machine translation (SMT) for speech translation. Originally proposed for text translation at IBM (Brown et al., 1993), the approach was championed by Verbmobil researchers at KIT, Carnegie Mellon University (CMU) (Waibel, 1996), and the Rheinisch-Westfälische Technische Hochschule (RWTH) (Och and Ney, 2002), who then further developed SMT to create the first statistical *speech* translators. Statistical techniques enabled the training of the associated MT systems from parallel data, without careful labeling or tree-banking of language resources. Although the significance of the approach was not immediately recognized (see e.g. Wahlster, 2000, 16), SMT often yielded better translation quality than rule-based methods, due partly to the consistency of its learning. The approach went on to become dominant within C-STAR and other programs.

12.1.2.4 Other Early Projects Other noteworthy projects of the time:

- A prototype speech-translation system developed by SRI International and Swedish Telecom for English↔Swedish in the air-travel domain (Alshawi et al., 1992);
- The VEST system (Voice English/Spanish Translator) built by AT&T Bell Laboratories and Telefonica Investigacion y Desarrollo for restricted

[10] See the next section (Section 12.2, "Present") concerning current phone-based systems by SpeechTrans and Lexifone.
[11] Subsequent products have fared better, however.
[12] See Verbmobil at: http://verbmobil.dfki.de/overview-us.html.

domains (Roe et al., 1992) (using finite state transducers to restrict language processing in domain and syntax);

- KT-STS, a prototype Japanese-to-Korean SLT system created in 1995 by KDD in cooperation with Korea Telecom (KT) and the Electronics and Telecommunications Research Institute (ETRI) in Korea, also for limited domains.[13]

12.1.2.5 Big Data and Apps Approaching the present, we come to twin watersheds which together shape the current era of speech translation: the advent of big data and of the app market.

As big data grew ever bigger, Google Translate took off in 2006–2007 as a translator for text (initially in Web pages), switching from earlier rule-based translation systems to statistical MT under the leadership of Franz Och (who had developed early SMT under Verbmobil and at ISI, the Information Science Institute). In this effort, general-purpose, open-domain MT became available to every Internet user – a dramatic milestone in worldwide public use. Equally significant was SMT's broad adoption as the method of choice for MT, as Google took full advantage of its massive databanks.

Och oversaw a massive expansion of words translated and language pairs served. (The service now bridges more than 100 languages and counting, and translates 100 billion words per day.) Machines were soon to generate 99 percent of the world's translations. True, the results were often inferior to human translations; but they were often sufficiently understandable, readily available, and free of charge for everyone's use via the Internet. Translation of speech, however, was not yet being attempted at Google. (At IWSLT 2008, Och argued at a panel discussion against its feasibility and its readiness and usefulness to Google as a Web company.)

Then came the transition to mobile. As mobile phones became smartphones and the mobile app market took shape, sufficient processing punch was packed into portable or wearable devices to enable creation of fully mobile and embedded speech translators. With the advent of the iPhone 3G, advanced speech and MT technology could fit on a phone. A newly enabled system could exploit advanced machine learning and include sufficiently large vocabularies to cover arbitrary traveler needs.

In 2009, Mobile Technologies, LLC, a start-up founded by Alex Waibel and his team in 2001, launched Jibbigo (Eck et al., 2010), the first speech translator to run without network assistance on iPhone and Android smartphones. The product featured a 40,000-word vocabulary and produced voice output from voice input faster than a chat message could be typed. While it was designed with travelers or healthcare workers in mind, it was domain-independent and thus served as

[13] See www.researchgate.net/publication/2333339_Kt-Sts_A_Speech_Translation_System_For_Hotel_Reservation_And_A_Continuous_Speech_Recognition_System_For_Speech_Translation.

a general dialog translator. The first Jibbigo app provided open-domain English↔Spanish speech translation and offered several user interface features for quick error recovery and rapid expansion of vocabularies in the field: for instance, back-translations – secondary translations from the output (target) language back into the input (source) language – helped users to judge translation accuracy. The app incorporated customization features as well: Users could enter proper names missing from a system's ASR vocabulary (like "München" in English and "Hugh" in German), thereby automatically converting and loading associated elements (dictionaries, models of word sequence, etc. in ASR, MT, and text-to-speech) without requiring linguistic expertise (Waibel and Lane, 2012a, 2012b, 2015); and system extensions for humanitarian missions featured user-definable phrasebooks that could be translated by machine and then played back at will (Waibel and Lane, 2015). Via machine-learning technology, Jibbigo added fifteen languages in the following two years. Network-free, it could be used by off-grid travelers and healthcare workers in humanitarian missions (2007–2013) (Waibel et al., 2016). A free network-based version with chat capabilities was also provided. The company was acquired by Facebook in 2013.

Google entered the SLT field with a network-based approach to mobile speech translation, demonstrating Conversation Mode in 2010, releasing an alpha version for English↔Spanish in 2011, and expanding to fourteen languages later that year. Microsoft launched Skype Translator in 2014, judging that exploitation of neural networks for ASR and MT had finally brought S2ST past the usability threshold.

12.1.2.6 Vertical Markets In the 2010s also, movement could be seen from research systems, constrained by the limitations of the technology, toward those designed for commercial use in vertical markets, purposely focused for practicality within a use case.

In healthcare, an early challenger was the S-MINDS system by Sehda, Inc. (later Fluential) (Ehsani et al., 2008). It relied upon an extensive set of fixed and pre-translated phrases; and the task of speech recognition was to match the appropriate one to enable pronunciation of its translation via text-to-speech, using the best fuzzy match when necessary. In this respect, the system was akin to the earlier Phraselator,[14] a ruggedized handheld device for translation of fixed phrases, provided to the US military for use in the first Gulf War and various other operations. Later versions added licensed Jibbigo technology to enable more flexible speech input.

Other phrase-based systems designed for specific use cases included Sony's TalkMan[15] – a system sporting an animated bird as a mascot – and several

[14] See Wikipedia entry for Phraselator: https://en.wikipedia.org/wiki/Phraselator.
[15] See Wikipedia entry on Talkman: https://en.wikipedia.org/wiki/Talkman.

voice-based phrase-book translators on dedicated portable devices from Ectaco, Inc.[16]

Converser for Healthcare 3.0, a prototype by Spoken Translation, Inc., was pilot-tested at Kaiser Permanente's Medical Center in San Francisco in 2011 (Seligman and Dillinger, 2011; 2015). Converser provided full speech translation for English↔Spanish. To overcome a perceived reliability gap in demanding areas like healthcare, business, emergency response, military and intelligence, facilities for verification and correction were integrated: As in Jibbigo and MASTOR (Gao et al., 2006), users received feedback concerning translation accuracy in the form of back-translation, but Converser also applied semantic controls to avoid back-translation errors. If errors due to lexical ambiguity were found, users could interactively correct them using synonyms as cues. To customize SLT for particular use cases, the system also included pre-translated frequent phrases. These could be browsed by category (e.g. **Pickup** or **Consultation** within the larger **Pharmacy** category) or discovered via keyword search, and were integrated with full MT.

12.1.2.7 US Government Projects In 2004, the Defense Advanced Research Projects Agency (DARPA) launched several research programs in the United States to develop speech translators for use by government officers. On the subject of Project DIPLOMAT, see Frederking et al. (2000); for Project BABYLON, see Waibel et al. (2003); and for Project TRANSTAC, see Frandsen, Riehemann, and Precoda (2008). The substantial Project GALE also developed technology for translation and summarization of broadcast news: see Cohen (2007) and Olive, Christianson, and McCary (2011). Both research directions were advanced in tandem in Project BOLT.[17]

Initial efforts in DARPA programs (e.g. in DIPLOMAT) had led only to the development of voice-based phrase books for checkpoints, but ongoing DARPA research programs BABYLON and TRANSTAC advanced to development of flexible-dialog (in DARPA parlance, "two-way") speech translators. Several players – BBN, IBM, SRI, and CMU – participated. IBM's MASTOR system (Gao et al., 2006) incorporated full MT and attempted to train the associated parsers from tree-banks rather than build them by hand. MASTOR's back-translation provided feedback to users on translation quality, making good use of an interlingua-based semantic representation (also found helpful in compensating for sparseness of training data). BBN, SRI, and CMU

[16] See Wikipedia entry for Ectaco: https://en.wikipedia.org/wiki/Ectaco.

[17] On Project BOLT, see Dr. Boyan Onyshkevych, "Broad Operational Language Translation (BOLT)," DARPA (Web), n.d.: www.darpa.mil/program/broad-operational-language-translation and "Broad Operational Language Technology (BOLT) Program," SRI International (Web), 2018: www.sri.com/work/projects/broad-operational-language-technology-bolt-program.

developed similar systems on laptops, while CMU also implemented systems on (pre-smartphone) mobile devices of the day. Interestingly, the systems developed and evaluated under Program BOLT demonstrated the feasibility of error correction via spoken disambiguation dialogs (Kumar et al., 2015). However, voice fixes were found less efficient than typed or cross-modal error repair when these were available, thereby confirming conclusions drawn earlier for speech-based interfaces in general (Suhm, Myers, and Waibel, 1996a; 1996b).

Program GALE, perhaps the largest speech-translation effort ever in the US, focused upon translation of broadcast news from Chinese and Arabic into English using statistical core technologies (ASR, MT, and summarization). The effort produced dramatic improvement in this tech, yielding tools usable for browsing and monitoring of foreign media sources (Cohen, 2007; Olive, Christianson, and McCary, 2011).

Serious R&D for speech translation has continued worldwide, both with and without government sponsorship. Some notable efforts have included the following (with apologies to those not listed):

- Raytheon BBN Technologies (Stallard et al., 2011)
- IBM (Zhou et al., 2013)
- Nara Institute of Science and Technology (NAIST) (Shimizu et al., 2013)
- Toshiba[18]
- VOXTEC[19]
- Japan Global Communication Project, especially the National Institute of Information and Communications Technology (NICT)[20]

. . . which brings us to the present.

12.2 Present

Having traversed the history of automatic speech-to-speech translation, we arrive at the somewhat paradoxical present. On one hand, the technology has finally emerged from science fiction, research, and forecasts. It has finally become real, and is really in use by many. On the other hand, some knowledgeable industrial parties remain skeptical. The IT advisory firm Gartner, for example, recently showed speech translation as at the Peak of Inflated

[18] See Toshiba's website for details: "Beginning an in-house pilot project in preparation for practical use," *Toshiba* (Web), October 29, 15: www.toshiba.co.jp/about/press/2015_10/pr2901.htm.

[19] See www.voxtec.com.

[20] See e.g. NICT News, www.nict.go.jp/en/index.html and Una Softic, "Japan's translation industry is feeling very Olympian today," *TAUS: The Language Data Network* (Web), February 2, 2016: www.taus.net/think-tank/articles/japan-s-translation-industry-is-feeling-very-olympic-today.

Expectations,[21] in spite of dramatic recent progress and despite its current deployment in actual products and services.

Two factors seem to be at play in this caution. First, large profits have remained difficult to identify. Second, current usage remains largely in the consumer sphere: Penetration remains for the future in vertical markets like healthcare, business, police, emergency response, military, and language learning.

Both shortfalls seem to have the same origin: that the current era of speech translation is the age of the giants. The most dramatic developments and the greatest expenditure are now taking place at the huge computation/communication corporations. These have until now viewed SLT not as a profit center but as a feature for attracting users into their orbits. Speech-to-speech translation has been included as added value for existing company services rather than as stand-alone technology.

The result has been, on the one hand, stunning progress in technology and services; and, on the other, rampant commoditization. Consumers already expect S2ST to be free, at least at the present level of accuracy, convenience, and specialization. This expectation has created a challenging climate for companies depending on profit, despite continuing universal expectation that worldwide demand for truly usable speech translation will soon yield a hugely profitable world market.

Accordingly, this section on the present state of S2ST will provide not a report on an established market or mature technology, but rather a representative survey of the present activities and strivings of the large and small. We proceed in three subsections: (1) a snapshot of state-of-the-art systems by Google, Microsoft, and InterACT; (2) a short list of other participating systems, plus a long list of features which each system may combine; and (3) short portraits of four participants in speech-translation R&D.

12.2.1 Some State-of-the-Art Systems

Here is a snapshot – a selfie, if you will – of a few leading technical accomplishments at the current state of the art.

- **Google Translate mobile app:**
  - ***Speed:*** Barring network delays, speech recognition and translation proceed and visibly update while you speak: no need to wait till you finish. When you do indicate completion by pausing long enough – about a half-second – the pronunciation of the translation begins instantly.
  - ***Automatic language recognition:*** Manually switching languages is unnecessary: The application recognizes the language spoken – even by a single

[21] See "Newsroom," *Gartner* (Web), 2018: www.gartner.com/newsroom/id/3114217.

speaker – and automatically begins the appropriate speech recognition and translation cycle. End-of-speech recognition, too, is automatic. As a result, once the mic is manually switched on in automatic-switching mode, the conversation can proceed back and forth hands-free until manual switch-off. (Problems will arise if speakers overlap, however.)

- ***Noise cancellation**:* Speech recognition on an iPhone works well in quite noisy environments – inside a busy store, for instance.
- ***Offline capability (text only)**:* Since travelers will often need translation when disconnected from the Internet, Google has added to its app the option to download a given language pair onto a smartphone for offline *text* translation. However, *speech* translation still requires an Internet connection at time of writing.[22]
- ***Dynamic optical character recognition**:* While this capability plays no part in *speech* translation per se, it now complements speech and text translation as an integral element of Google's translation suite. It enables the app to recognize and translate signs and other written material from images (photos or videos), rendering the translation text within the image and replacing the source text as viewed through the smartphone's camera viewer. The technology extends considerable previous research in optical character recognition (OCR),[23] and builds on work by WordLens, a start-up acquired by Google in 2014 that had performed the replacement trick for individual words. The current version handles entire segments and dynamically maintains the positioning of the translation when the camera and source text move.
- ***Earbuds synced to smartphone**:* Google's Pixel 2 smartphone features a synchronized set of earbuds which can be used for conversational speech translation. The phone's owner can hold it or hand it to a conversation partner, press a button on the right earbud, and then say, for instance, "Help me speak Japanese." To activate the phone's mic, she can again press the right earbud (as an alternative to tapping on the phone's screen). Her words will then be recognized, translated, and pronounced aloud, just as if the buds were absent; but when the partner responds, translation will be pronounced only via the buds, for her ears only. The ergonomic advantages over phone-only use, then, are: (1) it is unnecessary to hand the device back and forth; (2) the owner can adjust her private volume by swiping the bud; and (3) since translation in only one direction is pronounced out loud, auditory confusion is less likely. (Compare the translating earbuds promised by Waverly Labs.)

[22] Jibbigo had previously introduced a comparable option as an "in-app purchase": Users could buy untethered offline speech-translation systems as an alternative to an otherwise free networked app.

[23] See for example mention of Yang et al. (1999) in Alex Waibel's portrait in Section 12.2.3.3.

- **Microsoft's Skype Translator:**
  - ***Telepresence:*** Microsoft's Skype isn't the first to offer speech translation in the context of video chat: as one example, by the time Skype Translator launched, Hewlett-Packard had for more than two years already been offering a solution in its bundled MyRoom application, powered by systems integrator SpeechTrans, Inc. And speech translation over phone networks, but lacking video or chat elements, had been inaugurated experimentally through the C-STAR consortium and commercially through two Japanese efforts (as mentioned in Section 12.1.2.2). But the launch of Skype Translator had great significance because of its larger user base and consequent visibility – it exploits the world's largest telephone network – and in view of several interface refinements.
  - ***Spontaneous speech***: The Microsoft translation API contains a dedicated component to "clean up" elements of spontaneous speech – hesitation syllables, errors, repetitions – long recognized as problematic when delivered to an SLT system's translation engine. The component's goal, following a long but heretofore unfulfilled research tradition, is to translate not what you said, stutters and all, but what you meant to say.
  - ***Overlapping voice:*** Borrowing from news broadcasts, the system begins pronunciation of its translation while the original speech is still in progress. The volume of the original is lowered so as to background it. The aim of this "ducking" is to encourage more fluid turn-taking. The aim is to make the technology disappear, so that the conversation feels maximally normal to the participants.
- **Microsoft's Presentation Translator:**
  - ***Simultaneous subtitling of presentations:*** Microsoft has recently released a Presentation Translator add-in to its PowerPoint application which displays in real time a running transcription of the speaker's words while broadcasting text translations in multiple languages. The speaker wears a cordless headset and speaks normally, taking advantage of the above-mentioned TrueText facility for handling disfluencies. (The vocabulary of the slides can also be pretrained for greater speech recognition accuracy via the Custom Speech Service from Azure's Cognitive Services. Up to 30 percent improvement is claimed.) Transcriptions are continually updated as the speaker talks, and can appear below the slides in the manner of subtitles or superimposed above them. Listeners navigate to a one-time-only webpage (via a shared QR or five-letter code) to indicate the preferred reception language. They can respond to the speaker (if they are unmuted) by speaking or typing in that language. (Currently, ten-plus languages are enabled for spoken responses, and more than sixty for written interactions.) As a final communication aid, the slides themselves can be translated at presentation time, with formatting preserved. The new facility follows

upon, and now offers an alternative to, the InterACT interpreting service described next.

- **Interpreting Services InterACT (Waibel, KIT/CMU):**
  - ***First simultaneous interpreting services:*** Following its release of consecutive speech translators – including Jibbigo, the first network-free mobile SLT application – the team at InterACT[24] pioneered real-time and simultaneous automatic interpreting of lectures. The technology was first demonstrated at a press conference in October 2005 (Fügen, Waibel, and Kolss, 2007; Waibel and Fügen, 2013). It was later deployed in 2012 as a lecture interpretation *service* for German (compare Microsoft's add-in for a specific application, as just described) and now operates in several lecture halls of KIT. Target users are foreign students and the hearing-impaired.
  - ***Subscription-based online interpretation:*** Lecturers can subscribe to the KIT Service for online streaming to the institution's servers. Speech recognition and translation are then performed in real time, and output is displayed via standard Web pages accessible to students.
  - ***Offline browsing:*** Transcripts are offered offline for students' use after class. Students can search, browse, or play segments of interest along with the transcript, its translation, and associated slides.
  - ***Speed:*** Translations appear incrementally as subtitles with a delay of only a few words. The system may anticipate utterance endings, revising as more input becomes available.
  - ***Readability:*** The system removes disfluencies and automatically inserts punctuation, capitalization, and paragraphs. Spoken formulas are transformed into text where appropriate ("Ef of Ex" → f(x)).
  - ***Trainability:*** Special terms are added to ASR and MT dictionaries from background material and slides.
  - ***Multimodality:*** Beta versions include translation of slides, insertion of Web links giving access to study materials, emoticons, and crowd-editing. These versions also support alternative output options: speech synthesis, targeted audio speakers instead of headphones, or goggles with heads-up displays.
  - ***European Parliament pilots:*** Variants and subcomponents are being tested at the European Parliament to support human interpreters. (A Web-based app automatically generates terminology lists and translations on demand.) The system tracks numbers and names – difficult for humans to remember while interpreting. An "interpreter's cruise control" has been successfully tested for handling repetitive (and boring) session segments like voting.

[24] The International Center for Advanced Communication Technologies (InterACT) is a network of Research Universities and Institutes. See www.interact.kit.edu.

12.2.2 Additional Contributors

At the time of writing, the speech-translation field is evolving rapidly: A hundred flowers are blooming in research and in commerce. Among the current systems are these, in alphabetical order (and more are appearing monthly):

- BabelOn
- Baidu
- Converser for Healthcare
- Easy Language Translator
- Google Translate
- iFlyTek
- ili (Logbar)
- iTranslate Pro/Voice
- Jibbigo
- Microsoft Translator
- Pilot (Waverly Labs)
- Samsung
- SayHi Translate
- Skype Translator
- Speak & Translate
- SpeechTrans
- Talkmondo
- Triplingo
- Vocre Translate
- Voice Translate Pro
- Waygo
- Yandex.Translate

The systems offer widely varying combinations of the features tabulated in Table 12.1 (many discussed in Section 12.1.1.1, "Dimensions of Design Choice").

12.2.3 Selected Portraits

Aiming for an interesting cross-section of the current speech-translation field, we now profile four contributors, touching on their respective backgrounds, viewpoints, and current directions. Included are one research and development leader from the United States, one from Japan, and the coauthors. See (Seligman, Waibel, and Joscelyne, 2017) for interviews with additional representative participants.[25]

[25] Thirteen interviews appear in the cited report. Four have been recast in discursive form for this chapter: those of Chris Wendt (Microsoft); Eiichiro Sumita (NICT); and coauthors Mark Seligman (Spoken Translation, Inc.) and Alex Waibel (CMU/Karlsruhe Institute of Technology). Remaining interviewees are: Eric Liu (Alibaba); Chengqing Zong (Chinese Academy of Sciences); Siegfried "Jimmy" Kunzmann (EML); Yuqing Gao (IBM); Ike Sagie (Lexifone); Takuro Yoshida (Logbar); Ronen Rabinovici (SpeechLogger); John Frei and Yan Auerbach (SpeechTrans); and Sue Reager (Translate Your World).

Table 12.1 *Features combined in current speech-translation systems*

- Business model
  - Pay-per-use
  - Subscription
  - Free/Freemium
- Operating system
  - iOS
  - Android
  - Desktop (Mac/PC)
- Available language paths
  - European
  - Asian
  - Others (including long-tail)
- Audio and text translation combinations
  - Speech-to-speech (STS)
  - Speech-to-text (STT)
  - Text-to-speech (TTS)
  - Text-to-text (TTT)
- Text-to-speech features
  - Choice of voices
  - Quality, expressiveness
- Video and text translation
  - Still scenes only
  - Dynamic scenes
  - For both of the above
    - With/without replacement of text
- Conversational arrangement
  - Face-to-face
    - Two devices
    - One shared device
      - Automatic language switching
  - Remote
    - Text/Chat
    - Audio
      - VOIP
      - Telephony
      - For both of the above
        - With/without voice messaging
    - Video
    - For all the above
      - One-to-one
      - Group
        - Audience can/cannot respond
- Verification, correction capability
  - Of speech recognition
  - Of translation
    - Back-translation
    - Lexical disambiguation
- Customization tools per use case
  - Vocabulary
  - Phrases
    - Personalized
    - Sharable
- Specialized devices
  - Wrist-borne
  - Eyeglass-borne
  - Necklace-borne
  - Directional microphone(s)
- Text-translation capability
  - Website
  - Document
  - Email
  - Other apps
- Social-network features
  - Friends
  - Interest groups
  - Upload translation to social media
- Connectivity
  - Online
    - Via URL
    - Via dedicated app
  - Offline
  - Hybrid (e.g. speech online, translation offline)
- Instructional features
  - Dictionaries
  - Grammar notes
  - Speech-related
- User Interface (UI) features
  - Comments
  - Note-taking aids
  - Personal information
  - Still images
    - Personal
    - Background
  - Cultural communication tools
    - Pictures
    - Videos

12.2.3.1 Microsoft's Skype (Chris Wendt) In his capacity as Principal Group Program Manager of the Microsoft translation team, Wendt decided that the time was right for speech translation, as several factors had converged in a perfect storm over the previous few years: ASR underwent dramatic improvements through application of deep neural networks; MT on conversational content had become reasonably usable; and Skype provided an audience already engaged in global communication.

However, ASR, MT, and text-to-speech (TTS) by themselves were not found sufficient to make a translated conversation work. Clean input to translation was thought necessary; so elements of spontaneous language – hesitations, repetitions, corrections, etc. – had to be cleaned between ASR and MT. For this purpose, Microsoft built a facility called TrueText[26] to turn raw input into clean text more closely approaching expression of the speaker's intent. Training on real-world data covers the most common disfluencies.

Another necessity is a smooth user experience. The problem was to effectively guide speakers and protect them from errors and misuse of the system. The initial approach was to model the interpreter as a *persona* who could interact with each party and negotiate the conversation as a "manager," but this approach was abandoned for several reasons.

First, a simulated manager does not always simplify. On the contrary, it can add ambiguity by drawing attention to possible problems and adding additional interaction, so that the experience becomes overly complex. Instead, the aim was formed to let people communicate directly, keeping the technology behind the scenes. The translation should appear as a translated version of the speaker, with no intermediary.

Further, it was noticed that people who use human interpreters professionally tend to ignore the presence of the interpreter, focusing instead on the speaker. By contrast, novices tend to talk to the interpreter as a third person. The presence of an additional party can be distracting and requires the system to distinguish between asides to the interpreter and material intended for translation.

In the revised Skype interface, users see a transcript of their own speech and the translation of the partner's speech. They can also *hear* what the partner said via speech synthesis. But in fact, in usability tests, only 50 percent of the users wanted to hear translated audio – the others preferred to hear only the original audio and follow the translation by reading.

[26] Hany Hassan Awadalla, Lee Schwartz, Dilek Hakkani-Tür, and Gokhan Tur, "Segmentation and disfluency removal for conversational speech translation," in *Proceedings of Interspeech, ISCA – International Speech Communication Association*, September 2014 (ISCA): www.microsoft.com/en-us/research/publication/segmentation-and-disfluency-removal-for-conversational-speech-translation/.

The relation between the original voice and the spoken translation poses an additional issue. The most straightforward procedure is to wait until the speaker finishes, and then produce the spoken translation; but to save time and provide a smoother experience, a technique called *ducking* has been incorporated. The term is borrowed from broadcasting: One hears the speaker begin in the foreign language, but the spoken translation starts before he or she finishes, and as it proceeds the original voice continues at a lower volume in the background. The technique is intended to encourage speakers to talk continuously, but many still wait until the translation has been completed.

Unlike a text translation, spoken translation cannot be undone: Once the translation has been finalized, the listener will hear it. This factor poses difficulties for simultaneous translation, since segments later in the utterance might otherwise affect the translation of earlier segments.

Microsoft offers the speech-translation service via a Web service API, free for up to two hours a month, and at an hourly base price for higher volumes, heavily discounted for larger contingents. Thirteen languages are presently handled for SLT, in all directions, any to any. Multidirectional text translation can be handled for more than sixty languages, along with various combinations of speech-to-text and text-to-speech.

The system is deemed especially useful for general consumer conversation, e.g. for family communication. Names, however, remain problematic, given the difficulty of listing in advance all names in all the relevant languages, either for speech recognition or for translation.

Still, the range of use cases is expected to grow. As a case in point, the Presentation Translator described above is now in release, with automatic customization available for the words and phrases used in the PowerPoint deck. Increasing interest is expected from enterprises, e.g. those active in consumer services. On the other hand, Wendt observes that speech as a medium of communication may be losing out to text for some use cases – young people tend to IM or to use Snapchat more than to phone each other, for instance. The demand for speech translation may grow more slowly than the need for translation of text.

12.2.3.2 NICT (Eiichiro Sumita) Eiichiro Sumita serves as Director of the Multilingual Translation Laboratory in the Universal Communication Research Institute of the National Institute of Communication and Technology (NICT) in Kyoto. The Institute was established for research, but now sells speech and translation technologies to private companies in Japan. Its history goes back to that of ATR International, which itself has a somewhat complicated history (partly mentioned above).

In 1986, the Japanese government began basic research into MT. Because the Japanese language is unique, it was felt that Japanese people needed MT systems, but little practical technology was then available. Consequently, this R&D area attracted government sponsorship, and this research became the source of the ATR project, adding speech translation to the goal set. There was no commercial goal at that time.

In 1992, ATR 1 was followed by ATR. Then, in 2008, a group of ATR researchers moved to NICT. A more accurate system presented in 2010 drew the attention of many companies, some of which then created their own speech-translation systems. The DoCoMo system was particularly prominent.

However, NICT is still completely sponsored by the Japanese government. The center still carries out research, organized in five-year plans. Currently the main goals are systems to be used in the 2020 Olympics. The Institute provides basic technology for development at private companies – not only APIs for ASR, MT, and TTS, but OCR, noise reduction, and more. Ten languages are presently emphasized, including English, Japanese, Chinese, Korean, Indonesian, Thai, French, Spanish, and Burmese (the language of Myanmar).

The goal is to handle basic conversations for everyday life: hospitals, accident response, shopping, and many other community functions.

Associated business models depend upon the companies and products – advertising or licensing, for instance. Current examples: DoCoMo's Hanashita Honyaku product; the Narita airport translator; or Logbar's development of wearable hardware.

Sumita encourages development of special-purpose devices for SLT, such as Fujitsu's hands-free devices for hospitals. (Two form factors have been shown: a twin mic setup for desktop, and a wearable pendant. For both, the source language is identified by analyzing the direction of speech input.)

Free downloads are available on app stores for a product named VoiceTra which handles all covered language pairs. Notably, no pivot languages are used in this pairing; instead, some 900 direct paths have been developed. The strongest current use case is in communication for tourism. Quality is claimed to be higher than that of the Microsoft or Google program within this domain, especially in the hotel service area. Overall, a market of 40 billion yen is anticipated by 2020. An associated weakness: No provision has yet been made for general-purpose systems. Thus development of SLT systems for translation of broadcasts remains for the future. There are some technological lags, too: there has been no effort yet to combine statistical and neural network approaches, for instance.

The only real threat, in Sumita's view, is lack of money! The R&D budget for SLT in Japan is modest.

12.2.3.3 CMU/KIT (Alex Waibel, Coauthor) Research at InterACT aims to address cross-cultural understanding quite broadly, with studies of speech, gesture, text, images, facial expression, cultural and social understanding, emotion, emphasis, and many other cues and sources of information. Speech translation involves many of these elements. While studying technical problems, the organization has attempted to transfer the results to society through start-up companies, services deployed for universities and governments, and humanitarian deployments.

Initial speech translators (which were the first in the United States or Europe) began with a mix of rule-based, statistical, and neural processing. To capture the ambiguities, complexities, and contextual interactions of human language, machine learning and adaptation have continually been stressed, within the limits of currently available resources: Rule-based translation could be replaced by statistical and neural methods as computing and data resources grew. Actually, deep neural networks were already being used for speech recognition in the late 1980s. In 1987, the group applied to speech recognition the Time-Delay Neural Network (TDNN), the first convolutional neural network. The TDNN delivered excellent performance in comparison to Hidden Markov Models (HMMs) (Waibel, 1987; Waibel et al., 1987; Waibel et al., 1989); but, due to lack of data and computing power, the superiority of neural network approaches over statistical methods could not yet be demonstrated conclusively. Now, however, with several orders of magnitude more computing and data, comparable models generate up to 30 percent better results than the best statistical systems.

Better algorithms and more powerful computing also affected the practical range of systems and deployments. Limited vocabulary and complexity have given way to interpreting systems with unlimited vocabularies, operating in real time on lectures (as described above), and reduced versions can now run on smartphones.

The work also extended to human interface factors. For example, a first implementation was presented of translated "subtitles" on wearable devices or heads-up displays during mobile conversations (Yang et al., 1999). A variant became an application in Google Glass.[27]

With respect to use cases, tourism and medical exchanges have been in focus. Initially, in the early 1990s, pocket translators were envisioned for these domains and for humanitarian missions in the field. Accordingly, a central goal was to enable embedded systems to be used off the grid – that is, not necessarily networked. The associated start-up company Jibbigo built and deployed the first offline speech-translation app that ran in real time over a 40,000-word vocabulary. Used in various humanitarian missions, it was also sold to travelers via the iPhone and Android app stores. Jibbigo was acquired by Facebook in 2013; and projects researching speech and translation are ongoing, but to date without announcements of any activity in speech translation per se.

[27] See e.g. Michelle Starr, "Real-time, real-world captioning comes to Google Glass," *CNET* (Web), October 2, 2014: www.cnet.com/news/real-time-real-world-captioning-comes-to-google-glass/.

Broadcast news has been another use case of special interest: The goal is to make content available rapidly in multiple languages, for instance for YouTube and TV programs. In 2012, Waibel led the Integrated Project EU-Bridge, funded by the European Commission. Nine research teams developed cross-lingual communication services, aiming to produce automatic transcription and interpretation services (via subtitles) for the BBC, Euronews, and Sky News. Deployment activities have been continuing since the completion of the project in 2015.

Since 2005, research has been performed on the interpretation of lectures and seminars and of political speeches and debates, yielding the system described earlier in this section, which delivers translated text output via a Web browser on mobile phones, tablets, or PCs. The service is now deployed in multiple lecture halls in Karlsruhe and other German cities, interpreting German lectures for foreign students. (The automatic subtitling also aids the hearing-impaired.) Field tests are also underway at the European Parliament with the aim of facilitating workflow between human interpreters and technology to decrease stress and increase productivity.

Under-resourced languages have been a continuing concern. Jibbigo covered fifteen to twenty European and Asian languages and pairings between them, but the cost of developing new languages remains too high to address all 7,000 languages of the world: Khmer, Arabic dialects, provincial languages in Africa or Southeast Asia, and so on remain neglected.

Yet another concern relates to cross-language pairings. When interlingua-based approaches gave way to statistical translation – which learns translation directions between specific language pairs – arbitrary languages could no longer be connected through an unambiguous intermediate concept representation. Neural networks, however, are reviving the interlingua approach, and this revival is a current research theme at KIT.

Waibel expresses a few final concerns:

- Semantics is still poorly understood: Too often, programs continue to operate on surface words rather than on the intended meaning. Better models of conceptual representation are required, along with better models of the conversational context to help deduce the underlying meaning – models including the speaker's gender, emotions, dramatic performance, social setting (chatting or lecturing), social relationships (status, gender, rank), etc. Broader context could also help ASR to resolve names, help MT to automatically resolve ambiguity, and so on.
- The status of SLT research and development is poorly understood. On one hand, the problem is thought to have been solved, with the result that funding for advanced research becomes scarce. On the other, the problem is thought to be unsolvable. Waibel argues for a more balanced view: that while practical, cost-effective solutions do exist today, considerable work is still needed.

- Machine translation should be integrated with multimodal graphics and sensing technology.
- Large companies are helping people to connect across languages, but create obstacles for small, agile innovators. They also restrict research by not sharing results and data.

12.2.3.4 Spoken Translation, Inc. (Mark Seligman, Coauthor) On completing his Ph.D. in computational linguistics, Seligman took a research position at ATR (see Section 12.1.2.1) from 1992 to 1995. He participated in the first international demonstration of speech-to-speech translation early in 1993, which involved teams in Pittsburgh, Karlsruhe, and Takanohara, near Nara, Japan, and has researched various related topics (Seligman, 2000).

Once back in the United States, he proposed to CompuServe a "quick and dirty" (pipeline architecture) speech-translation demonstration, based upon their experimental translating chat. The result was the first successful demonstration, in 1997 and 1998, of unrestricted – broad coverage or "say anything" – speech-to-speech translation. Crucial to the success of the demo were facilities for interactive correction of speech-recognition errors.

Spoken Translation, Inc. (STI) was founded in 2002, adding verification and correction of translation to the mix. The healthcare market was targeted because the demand was clearest there; and, after a long gestation, a successful pilot project was mounted at Kaiser Permanente in San Francisco in 2011. Since then, the prototype product, Converser for Healthcare, has been refined based upon lessons learned.

Since the goal has been to demonstrate and test the company's proprietary verification, correction, and customization technology, Converser has adopted, rather than invented, third-party core components for MT, speech recognition, and TTS. The present implementation for English and Spanish uses a rule-based MT engine. Nuance currently supplies software for speech elements.

With respect to verification and correction: Having said in English, "This is a cool program," the user might learn, via a translation from Spanish back into English, that the tentative translation would actually express, "This is a chilly program." (Patented semantic controls are applied during the reverse translation to avoid extraneous errors and faithfully render the tentative translation's meaning.) The mistranslation can be verified using proprietary cues indicating the tentative meaning of each input expression, for example showing via synonyms that "cool" has been misunderstood as "chilly, nippy ... "; and that the preferred meaning can be specified as "awesome, great ..." Another round of translation can then be executed, this time giving the back-translation, "This is an awesome program." Reassured that the intended meaning has been expressed in Spanish, the user can give the go-ahead for transmission, pronunciation, and entry into a bilingual transcript. Such reassurance is considered crucial for demanding use cases; but the verification and correction tools also enable even monolingual users to provide effective feedback for machine learning, thus expanding the potential crowdsourcing base.

Spoken's patents describe in detail the implementation of its verification and correction technology in rule-based and statistical MT systems; techniques for systems based on neural networks are also suggested, but more tentatively, as monitoring and control of neural networks remains a forefront research area.

With respect to customization: Prepackaged translations are provided for frequent or important phrases in the current use case. Users can browse for desired phrases by category and subcategory, or can search for them by keywords or initial characters. If an input phrase matches against translation memory, the stored translation is used, and verification is bypassed; otherwise, full translation is applied.

At the time of the 2011 pilot project, the major components (ASR, MT, and TTS) and the infrastructure (cloud computing, mobile platforms, the application market, etc.) were still immature, and the difficulties of penetrating very large and conservative organizations were underestimated. The company judges that speech translation is now ready for this and other demanding vertical markets (customer service, B2B communications, emergency response, intelligence, and many more), provided products can deliver the necessary degree of reliability and customizability.

The challenge facing STI is to integrate with third-party APIs to add proprietary verification, correction, and customization tools to many languages and platforms. The APIs recently offered by Microsoft, Google, and other large companies are now possibilities; but these programs present themselves as black boxes, which complicates integration.

One obstacle facing this integration is the push toward a maximally simple user interface. The hope is now widespread that machine learning will yield SLT systems accurate enough to operate *without* feedback and correction even in critical use cases, but STI views this hope as illusory: even human interpreters typically spend some 20 percent of their time in clarification dialogs. The company argues that while the push toward simplicity is certainly right in principle, reliability must be enhanced, and that this need must be met by facilities for feedback and control which demand some attention, at least sometimes. To achieve a balance between seamless use and reliability, interface facilities have been developed to enable users to easily turn verification and correction on when reliability is most needed, but off when speed is more important. (Alternatively, the adjustment could be made automatically in response to programs' confidence scores.) Testing has convinced some companies (Microsoft, for example; see 12.2.3.1) that users will reject feedback or correction tools; but STI believes that acceptance will depend on the need for reliability and the specific interface design.

Spoken Translation, Inc. views the issue of feedback and control in SLT as a special case of the black-box issue in AI: At the present early stage of the neural net era, users must often accept AI results with no idea how they were reached. The company sees its work as part of a long-term effort to pry open the black box – to learn to fully exploit automaticity while keeping humans in the loop.

12.3 Future

As Yogi Berra said, it's hard to make predictions, especially about the future. Nevertheless, in this section, we try. Following are our best guesses about future directions for automatic speech-to-speech translation.

Advances in speech translation will often be driven by advances in text translation (but see Section 12.3.2 concerning possible S2ST training regimes which entirely bypass text). Lacking space here to examine these general MT directions, we refer readers to Seligman (Chapter 4 in this volume) for consideration of trends in semantic processing, with due attention to the explosive development of neural machine translation (NMT). Here we limit discussion to progress expected to involve speech and related technology specifically: platforms and form factors; big speech-translation data and associated correction data; integration of knowledge sources; and integration of human interpreting.

12.3.1 Platforms and Form Factors

One obvious trend in speech translation's future is the technology's migration into increasingly mobile and convenient platforms and form factors. Most immediately, these will be wearable and other highly mobile devices.

Wrist-borne platforms integrating SLT are already available. SpeechTrans, Inc., for example, has offered S2ST, including output voice, via both a wristband and a smart watch. Translation apps from iTranslate and Microsoft are already available on iPhone and Android devices, though neither app appears to offer text-to-speech yet. (In compensation, Microsoft's watch offering can exchange translations with a nearby smartphone.)

Eyeglass-based delivery of real-time translation is likewise available now in early implementations. Google Glass did include the functions of Google Translate, but the device has now been withdrawn. In 2013–2014, SpeechTrans, Inc. was offering computational glasses incorporating translation functions, but availability is now unclear. Still, second- and third-generation smart glasses will soon appear; and, given the current state of optical character recognition – for example, the dynamic OCR in the Google Translate app – it is inevitable that near-future smart glasses will support instant translation of written material in addition to speech translation.

And wristbands and glasses hardly exhaust the wearable possibilities. Start-up Logbar is developing a translating necklace; Google has released linked earbuds which can channel the translation capabilities of its Pixel 2 device (as described in Section 12.2.1); Waverly Labs will offer phone-free earbuds with translation software built in; and dedicated handheld devices are already on sale, e.g. in China. Further afield, the anticipated Internet of Things will embed myriad apps, certainly including speech translation, into everyday objects.

Not all such devices will succeed. The survivors of the shakedown will need to address several issues already discernible. First, some balance must be found between supplying all software on the local machine and exploiting the many advantages of cloud-based delivery. (Recently, Google has begun enabling users to download modules for individual languages to their local devices, though these do not yet enable speech input at time of writing. As the computational and storage capacities of these devices grow, this option will increasingly be offered.) Second, since special-purpose devices (necklaces, earbuds, rings) risk being left at home when needed, they will have to compete with multi-purpose devices carried every day and everywhere (watches, smartphones, prescription glasses), so they may find niches by offering compelling advantages or by customizing for specific use cases, as in healthcare or police work. And finally, the new devices must be both nonintrusive and . . . cool. Google Glass, while presaging the future, failed on both fronts; but Google and others, one can bet, are even now planning to do better.

12.3.2 Big Data

Big data has undeniably played a crucial – if not decisive – role in improvement and scaling of MT to date. More data is better data, and plenty more is on the way (though the rise of neural network technology is increasing the importance of data quality as well as quantity). The crucial new element for improving speech translation, however, will be increasingly massive and high-quality *speech translation* data. To augment already massive and good-enough text-translation data – both parallel and monolingual – for MT training, along with copious and acceptable audio data for ASR training, organizations will be able to collect the audio (and video) components of natural conversations, broadcasts, etc. along with the resulting translations. Training based upon these sources can enable speech recognition and translation to assist each other: Speech data can provide context for training text translation and vice versa. A virtuous circle can result: As systems built upon speech-translation sources improve, they will be used more, thus producing still more speech-translation data, and so on.

While S2ST data will accumulate rapidly, it may sometimes be necessary to process and curate it in preparation for training, for example by correcting (human or automatic) transcriptions of the input and output spoken languages. Cleanup and/or postediting of the original translation into the target language will sometimes be desirable as well. Since such processing will hinder scaling, much interest currently accrues to the possibility of machine learning based upon speech-only corpora, gathered for example by recording both source and target languages in human interpreting situations. Such training approaches currently remain in the stage of early research (or just discussion): They will confront noisy data, and will forgo any chance to attack specific problems within the speech-to-speech chain by isolating them. Attempts to integrate semantic information would also be forfeit in corpora strictly limited to speech, though not necessarily in future corpora including video or other multimedia input (concerning which, again see Seligman [Chapter 4 in this volume]).

In any case, to massive speech and translation data can be added massive correction data. Users can correct the preliminary speech-recognition and translation results, and these corrections can be exploited by machine learning to further improve the systems. Google Translate has made a strong beginning in this direction by enabling users to suggest improvement of preliminary machine-made translations via the company's Translate Community. And just as more data is desirable, so are more corrections. At present, however, there is a barrier which limits the crowdsourcing community: To correct translations most effectively, users must have at least some knowledge of both the source and target language – a handicap especially for lesser-known languages. However, verification and correction techniques designed for monolinguals might greatly enlarge the feedback base. This exploitation of feedback to incrementally improve speech translation jibes with a general trend in machine learning toward continual learning, as opposed to batch learning based on static corpora.

12.3.3 Knowledge Source Integration

Projects ASURA and Verbmobil, mentioned in our short history in Section 12.1.2, were ahead of their time in attempting to integrate into speech-translation systems such multiple knowledge sources as discourse analysis, prosody, topic tracking, and so on. The computational, networking, architectural, and theoretical resources necessary for such complex integration did not yet exist. These resources do exist now, though, as witness the progress of IBM's Watson system.[28] Watson calls upon dozens of specialized programs to perform question-answering tasks like those required to beat the reigning human champions in Jeopardy, relying upon machine-learning techniques for selecting the right expert for the job at hand. In view of these advances, the time

[28] See IBM website: www.ibm.com/watson/.

seems right for renewed attempts at massive knowledge-source integration in the service of MT. Just two examples:

- In many languages, questions are sometimes marked by prosodic cues only, yet these are ignored by most current speech-translation systems. A specialized prosodic "expert" could handle such cases. Of course, prosody can signal many other aspects of language as well – pragmatic elements like sarcasm, emotional elements like anger or sadness, etc.
- As discussed above, the Microsoft translation system which powers Skype Translator features an auxiliary program that addresses issues of spontaneous speech by cleaning and simplifying raw speech input, for example by eliminating repetitive or corrected segments.

While current techniques for knowledge source integration are already available for exploitation, the nascent neural paradigm in natural language processing promises interesting advantages: As suggested in Seligman (Chapter 4 in this volume), neural networks appear especially attractive for such integration.

12.3.4 Integrating Human and Automatic S2ST

Combinations of human and automatic interpreting are already in operation, and more can be expected. SpeechTrans, Inc., for example, has offered an API which includes the option to quickly call in a human interpreter if automatic S2ST is struggling. More flexible facilities would enable seamless interleaving of automatic and human interpreters, perhaps including feedback tools to help users judge when (inevitably more expensive) human interventions are really necessary. Whenever human interpreters are in fact brought in, whether in formal situations (e.g., at the UN) or in relatively informal ones (e.g., in everyday business meetings), a range of aids can be provided for them. Alex Waibel's group, as already mentioned, has experimented with an "interpreters' cruise control," able to handle routine meeting segments like roll calls which would tire and bore humans. For more challenging episodes, well-designed dictionaries and note-taking tools can be useful, while more advanced aids could exploit automatic interpreting operating alongside the human, in the manner of an assistant or coach. Such interaction would extend into speech translation the current trend toward interactive text translation, as promoted for instance by the start-up Lilt:[29] rather than wait to postedit the finished but rough results of MT, translators can intervene during the translation process. (Or is it the MT which can intervene while the human is translating?)

The movement toward human–machine interaction within automatic speech and text translation can be seen as part of a larger trend within artificial intelligence: The increasing effort to maintain traceability, comprehensibility,

[29] See Lilt website: https://lilt.com/.

and a degree of control – keeping humans in the loop to exert that control and avoid errors. In Google's experiments with driverless cars, for instance, designers have struggled to maintain a balance between full autonomy on the car's part, on one hand, and enablement of driver intervention on the other.

The larger issue, briefly mentioned above: Should we treat MT, S2ST, and other AI systems as black boxes – as oracles whose only requirement is to give the right answers, however incomprehensibly they may do it? Or should we instead aim to build windows into artificial cognitive systems, so that we can follow and interrogate – and to some degree control – internal processes? The black-box path is tempting: It is the path of least resistance, and in any case organic cognitive systems have until now always been opaque – so much so that behaviorism ruled psychology for several decades on the strength of the argument that the innards were bound to remain inaccessible, so that analysis of input and output was the only respectable scientific method of analysis.

However, because artificial cognitive systems will be human creations, there is an unprecedented opportunity to peer within them and steer them. As we build fantastic machines to deconstruct the Tower of Babel, it would seem healthy to remember the Sorcerer's Apprentice: best to have our minions report back from time to time, and to provide them with a HALT button.

References

Allen, Jonathan, Sharon Hunnicutt, Rolf Carlson, and Bjorn Granstrom (1979). MITalk: The 1979 MIT Text-to-Speech system. *The Journal of the Acoustical Society of America* 65 (S1).

Alshawi, Hayan, David Carter, Steve Pulman, Manny Rayner, and Björn Gambäck (1992). English-Swedish translation dialogue software. In *Translating and the Computer*, 14. Aslib, London, November, pp. 10–11.

Brown, Peter F., Stephen A. Della Pietra, Vincent J. Della Pietra, and Robert L. Mercer (1993). The mathematics of Statistical Machine Translation: Parameter estimation. *Computational Linguistics* 19(2) (June), 263–311.

Cohen, Jordan (2007). The GALE project: A description and an update. In *Institute of Electrical and Electronics Engineers (IEEE) Workshop on Automatic Speech Recognition and Understanding (ASRU)*. Kyoto, Japan, December 9–13, pp. 237–237.

Eck, Matthias, Ian Lane, Y. Zhang, and Alex Waibel (2010). Jibbigo: Speech-to-Speech translation on mobile devices. In *Spoken Technology Workshop (SLT), Institute of Electrical and Electronics Engineers (IEEE) 2010*. Berkeley, CA, December 12–15, pp. 165–166.

Ehsani, Farzad, Jim Kimzey, Elaine Zuber, Demitrios Master, and Karen Sudre (2008). Speech to speech translation for nurse patient interaction. In *COLING 2008: Proceedings of the Workshop on Speech Processing for Safety Critical Translation and Pervasive Applications. International Committee on Computational Linguistics (COLING) and the Association for Computational Linguistics (ACL)*. Manchester, England, August, pp. 54–59.

Frandsen, Michael W., Susanne Z. Riehemann, and Kristin Precoda (2008). IraqComm and FlexTrans: A speech translation system and flexible framework. In *Innovations and Advances in Computer Sciences and Engineering*. Dordrecht, Heidelberg, London, New York: Springer, pp. 527–532.

Frederking, Robert, Alexander Rudnicky, Christopher Hogan, and Kevin Lenzo (2000). Interactive speech translation in the DIPLOMAT project. *Machine Translation* 15(1–2), 27–42.

Fügen, Christian, Alex Waibel, and Muntsin Kolss (2007). Simultaneous translation of lectures and speeches. *Machine Translation* 21(4), 209–252.

Gao, Jiang, Jie Yang, Ying Zhang, and Alex Waibel (2004). Automatic detection and translation of text from natural scenes. Institute of Electrical and Electronics Engineers (IEEE) Transactions on Image Processing 13(1) (January), 87–91.

Gao, Yuqing, Liang Gu, Bowen Zhou, Ruhi Sarikaya, Mohamed Afify, Hong-kwang Kuo, Wei-zhong Zhu, Yonggang Deng, Charles Prosser, Wei Zhang, and Laurent Besacier (2006). IBM MASTOR SYSTEM: Multilingual Automatic Speech-to-speech Translator. In *Proceedings of the First International Workshop on Medical Speech Translation, in conjunction with the North American Chapter of the Association for Computational Linguistics, Human Language Technology (NAACL/HLT)*. New York City, NY, June 9, pp. 57–60.

Kumar, Rohit, Sanjika Hewavitharana, Nina Zinovieva, Matthew E. Roy, and Edward Pattison-Gordon (2015). Error-tolerant speech-to-speech translation. In *Proceedings of Machine Translation (MT) Summit XV, Volume 1: MT Researchers' Track, MT Summit XV.* Miami, FL, October 30–November 3, pp. 229–239.

Levin, Lori, Donna Gates, Alon Lavie, and Alex Waibel (1998). An interlingua based on domain actions for machine translation of task-oriented dialogues. In *Proceedings of the Fifth International Conference on Spoken Language Processing, ICSLP-98*. Sydney, Australia, November 30–December 4, pp. 1155–1158.

Maier-Hein, Lena, Florian Metze, Tanja Schultz, and Alex Waibel (2005). Session independent non-audible speech recognition using surface electromyography. In *Proceedings of the 2005 Institute of Electrical and Electronics Engineers (IEEE) Workshop on Automatic Speech Recognition and Understanding, ASRU 2005*. Cancun, Mexico, November 27–December 1, pp. 331–336.

Morimoto, Tsuyoshi, Toshiyuki Takezawa, Fumihiro Yato, Shigeki Sagayama, Toshihisa Tashiro, Masaaki Nagata, and Akira Kurematsu (1993). ATR's speech translation system: ASURA. In *EUROSPEECH-1993, the Third European Conference on Speech Communication and Technology*. Berlin, September 21–23, pp. 1291–1294.

Och, Franz Josef, and Hermann Ney (2002). Discriminative training and maximum entropy models for statistical machine translation. In *Proceedings of the 40th Annual Meeting of the Association for Computational Linguistics (ACL)*. Philadelphia, PA, July, pp. 295–302.

Olive, Joseph, Caitlin Christianson, and John McCary (eds.) (2011). *Handbook of Natural Language Processing and Machine Translation: DARPA Global Autonomous Language Exploitation*. New York City, NY: Springer Science and Business Media.

Roe, David B., Pedro J. Moreno, Richard Sproat, Fernando C. N. Pereira, Michael D. Riley, and Alejandro Macaron (1992). A spoken language translator for restricted-domain context-free languages, *Speech Communication 11*(2–3) (June), 311–319.

Seligman, Mark (2000). Nine issues in speech translation, *Machine Translation* 15(1–2) Special Issue on Spoken Language Translation (June), 149–186.

Seligman, Mark, and Mike Dillinger (2011). Real-time multi-media translation for healthcare: A usability study. In *Proceedings of the 13th Machine Translation (MT) Summit*. Xiamen, China, September 19–23, pp. 595–602.

Seligman, Mark, and Mike Dillinger (2015). Evaluation and revision of a speech translation system for healthcare. In *Proceedings of International Workshop for Spoken Language Translation (IWSLT) 2015*. Da Nang, Vietnam, December 3–4, pp. 209–216.

Seligman, Mark, Alex Waibel, and Andrew Joscelyne (2017). *TAUS Speech-to-Speech Translation Technology Report*. Available via www.taus.net/think-tank/reports/translate-reports/taus-speech-to-speech-translation-technology-report#download-purchase.

Shimizu, Hiroaki, Graham Neubig, Sakriani Sakti, Tomoki Toda, and Satoshi Nakamura (2013). Constructing a speech translation system using simultaneous interpretation data. In *Proceedings of the International Workshop on Spoken Language Translation (IWSLT) 2013*. Heidelberg, Germany, December 5–6, pp. 212–218.

Stallard, David, Rohit Prasad, Prem Natarajan, Fred Choi, Shirin Saleem, Ralf Meermeier, Kriste Krstovski, Shankar Ananthakrishnan, and Jacob Devlin (2011). The BBN TransTalk speech-to-speech translation system. In Ivo Ipsic (ed.), *Speech and Language Technologies*. InTech, DOI:10.5772/19405. Available from: www.intechopen.com/books/speech-and-language-technologies/the-bbn-transtalk-speech-to-speech-translation-system.

Suhm, Bernhard, Brad Myers, and Alex Waibel (1996a). Interactive recovery from speech recognition errors in speech user interfaces. In *Proceedings of the Fourth International Conference on Spoken Language Processing (ICSLP) 1996*. Philadelphia, PA, October 3–6, pp. 865–868.

Suhm, Bernhard, Brad Myers, and Alex Waibel (1996b). Designing interactive error recovery methods for speech interfaces. In *Proceedings of the ACM Conference on Human Factors in Computing Systems (CHI) 1996, Workshop on Designing the User Interface for Speech Recognition Applications*. Vancouver, Canada, April 13–18.

Wahlster, Wolfgang (ed.) (2000). *Verbmobil: Foundations of Speech-to-Speech Translation*. Springer: Berlin.

Waibel, Alex (1987). Phoneme recognition using time-delay neural networks. In *Meeting of the Institute of Electrical, Information, and Communication Engineers (IEICE), SP87-100*. Tokyo, Japan, December.

Waibel, Alex (1996). Interactive translation of conversational speech. *Computer* 29(7), July, 41–48.

Waibel, Alex (2002). *Portable Object Identification and Translation System*. US Patent 20030164819.

Waibel, Alex, Naomi Aoki, Christian Fügen, and Kay Rottman (2016). *Hybrid, Offline/Online Speech Translation System*. US Patent 9,430,465.

Waibel, Alex, Ahmed Badran, Alan W. Black, Robert Frederking, Donna Gates, Alon Lavie, Lori Levin, Kevin Lenzo, Laura Mayfield Tomokiyo, Jurgen Reichert, Tanja Schultz, Dorcas Wallace, Monika Woszczyna, and Jing Zhang (2003).

Speechalator: Two-way speech-to-speech translation on a consumer PDA. In *EUROSPEECH-2003, the Eighth European Conference on Speech Communication and Technology*. Geneva, Switzerland, September 1–4, pp. 369–372.

Waibel, Alex, and Christian Fügen (2013). *Simultaneous Translation of Open Domain Lectures and Speeches*. US Patent 8,504,351.

Waibel, Alex, Toshiyuki Hanazawa, Geoffrey Hinton, and Kiyohiro Shikano (1987). Phoneme recognition using time-delay neural networks. Advanced Telecommunications Research (ATR) Interpreting Telephony Research Laboratories Technical Report. October 30.

Waibel, Alex, Toshiyuki Hanazawa, Geoffrey Hinton, Kiyohiro Shikano, and Kevin Lang (1989). Phoneme recognition using time-delay neural networks. *Institute of Electrical and Electronics Engineers (IEEE) Transactions on Acoustics, Speech and Signal Processing* 37(3) (March), 328–339.

Waibel, Alex, Ajay N. Jain, Arthur E. McNair, Hiroaki Saito, Alexander G. Hauptmann, and Joe Tebelskis (1991). JANUS: A speech-to-speech translation system using connectionist and symbolic processing strategies. In *Proceedings of the International Conference on Acoustics, Speech and Signal Processing (ICASSP) 1991*. Toronto, Canada, May 14–17, pp. 793–796.

Waibel, Alex and Ian R. Lane (2012a). *System and Methods for Maintaining Speech-to-Speech Translation in the Field*. US Patent 8,204,739.

Waibel, Alex and Ian R. Lane (2012b). *Enhanced Speech-to-Speech Translation System and Method for Adding a New Word*. US Patent 8,972,268.

Waibel, Alex and Ian R. Lane (2015). *Speech Translation with Back-Channeling Cues*. US Patent 9,070,363 B2.

Waibel, Alex, Alon Lavie, and Lori S. Levin (1997). JANUS: A system for translation of conversational speech. *Künstliche Intelligenz* 11, 51–55.

Yang, Jie, Weiyi Yang, Matthias Denecke, and Alex Waibel (1999). Smart Sight: A tourist assistant system. In *The Third International Symposium on Wearable Computers (ISWC) 1999, Digest of Papers*. San Francisco, CA, October 18–19, pp. 73–78.

Yang, Jie, Jiang Gao, Ying Zhang, and Alex Waibel (2001a). Towards automatic sign translation. In *Proceedings of the First Human Language Technology Conference (HLT) 2001*. San Diego, CA, March 18–21.

Yang, Jie, Jiang Gao, Ying Zhang, and Alex Waibel (2001b). An automatic sign recognition and translation system. In *Proceedings of the Workshop on Perceptual User Interfaces (PUI) 2001*. Orlando, FL, November 15–16.

Zhang, Jing, Xilin Chen, Jie Yang, and Alex Waibel (2002a). A PDA-based sign translator. In *Proceedings of the Fourth IEEE International Conference on Multimodal Interfaces (ICMI) 2002*. Pittsburgh, PA, October 14–16, pp. 217–222.

Zhang, Ying, Bing Zhao, Jie Yang, and Alex Waibel (2002b). Automatic sign translation. In *Proceedings of the Seventh International Conference on Spoken Language Processing (ICSLP) 2002,* Second INTERSPEECH Event. Denver, CO, September 16–20.

Zhou, Bowen, Xiaodong Cui, Songfang Huang, Martin Cmejrek, Wei Zhang, Jian Xue, Jia Cui, Bing Xiang, Gregg Daggett, Upendra Chaudhari, Sameer Maskey, and Etienne Marcheret (2013). The IBM speech-to-speech translation system for smartphone: Improvements for resource-constrained tasks. *Computer Speech and Language* 27(2) (February), 592–618.

13 Challenges and Opportunities of Empirical Translation Studies

Meng Ji and Michael Oakes

13.1 From Descriptive Translation Studies to Empirical Translation Studies: The Empirical Turn

In Holmes' first map of translation studies, descriptive translation studies was identified as a 'pure' as opposed to 'applied' research branch which was dedicated to the study of the product, process and function of translation (Holmes, 1988). The inclusion of the descriptive research branch within 'pure' academic research alongside theoretical translation studies has brought both benefits and limitation to this nascent research field in the following decades. The conceptualised adjacency as illustrated in Holmes' map between theoretical and descriptive translation studies has led many translation scholars over the years to leverage the latter in their search and verification of theoretical assumptions regarding universally existent patterns, norms and laws which govern and can help us to understand the production, consumption, assimilation and recreation of written materials between languages, cultures, communities and societies. That is, since its early days, descriptive translation studies has been conceptualised and served as the testing ground for the proposition and contestation of theoretical hypotheses and tenets which have underscored the growth of the discipline.

Over the decades that followed, the growth of the descriptive branch has been intrinsically linked with and, indeed benefited from the increasing research interests, needs and demands from theoretical translation studies, as more scientifically rigorous research approaches, methodologies and analytical schemes have been called upon from descriptive translation studies to testify the validity, verifiability and wide applicability of the original set of theoretical hypotheses on ever larger translation data sets and with more diverse, less-known language combinations. The growth of the descriptive research branch has thus become increasingly focused on the methodological sophistication and advancement of the field (Baker, 1993, 1996, 2004). Significant, notable efforts have been made by early, pioneering translation scholars to explore and introduce emerging digital resources such as language corpora to the field, enabling the development of more systematic, empirically replicable analytical procedures at a later stage for the purpose of translation studies (Laviosa, 1995, 1998, 2004; Olohan, 2004). It should also be noted that descriptive translation studies was amongst the first humanities research fields to proactively and effectively engage with the digital resources and methodologies which gave rise to the 'computational turn' in the arts and humanities around the mid-2000s, a phenomenon that is also widely known today as digital humanities (Schreibman, Siemens and Unsworth, 2004).

Following the introduction of language corpora, important efforts have been made to borrow and adapt established research methods from cognate fields, especially corpus linguistics and quantitative linguistics, to systematically document, describe and analyse linguistic and textual events and phenomena in different types of language corpora developed for translation research purposes. A range of specialised, noticeably methodologically oriented research terms were created, experimented with, adopted or contested by the global translation studies community; these have contributed to the rapid growth of the descriptive research branch, as well as to the wide acceptance and endorsement of particular research methodologies that have proved valid, effective and efficient with the study of larger and more diverse language corpora. A number of corpus search tools and software were also developed to facilitate the exploration and empirical analysis of large-scale language corpora, as the descriptive research field witnessed an important, gradual but decisive methodological transition from individual, circumscribed case study of translation features to systematic, frequency-based, pattern-oriented analysis of textual and linguistic events that recur in language corpora. There has been important interaction between the design of corpus-exploration tools and the development and establishment of specific corpus analytical procedures and methodologies for corpus-assisted translation research. For example, the translation of multi-word units such as fixed expressions, idioms, collocations, lexical bundles, clusters, and formulaic sequences can be effectively identified, analysed and compared using the concordancing function of most corpus software. Statistical lexical profiling functions such as lexical collocation patterns can give important clues to the best translation candidate amongst various possible options based on the immediate textual environment in which the keyword occurs.

Much of descriptive translation research in the last few decades has been geared towards the development of a set of robust, widely replicable analytical procedures that can be used to systematically interrogate language corpora. The availability of corpus software has enabled the retrieval of recurrent linguistic and textual analogies and variations. However, this identification of the differences and variations within and amongst language corpora has yet to be leveraged or exploited to allow insights into the production, process and function of translation as the central aim and purpose of the descriptive research branch. Efforts were made in the late 2000s to introduce, experiment with and establish more advanced statistical, quantitative research methodologies in the bourgeoning corpus translation research paradigm (Oakes and Ji, 2012). This has opened up new possibilities of studying language corpora and developed novel approaches to analysing the differences and similarities amongst language corpora. The search for 'meaning patterns' in corpora is no longer an end of corpus-assisted descriptive translation research, but rather the beginning, and essential groundwork for the analysis of the latent relations between textual and contextual entities, as well as of their interaction which has given rise to the observed and detected differences or similarities in language corpora. The descriptive research branch has thus been equipped with a new set of advanced, powerful research tools and instruments that are particularly effective and useful when exploring large-scale digital language resources.

After four decades of strenuous academic efforts amongst a growing global research community, it may be said that descriptive translation research has been leading up to what Gideon Toury envisaged as the rise of the field as a distinctively empirical or scientific research field: 'no empirical science may make a claim for completeness, hence be regarded a (relatively) autonomous discipline, unless it has developed a descriptive branch' (Toury, 1982). In this regard, the descriptive translation research which has underscored the rapid development of translation studies since the early 1980s, has fulfilled its mission to 'study, describe (to which certain philosophers of science add: predict), in a systematic and controlled way, that segment of "the real world" which it takes as its object' (Toury, 1982). In this concluding chapter, we argue that the proposed 'empirical turn' in translation studies, particularly in the descriptive research branch, reflects the practical needs of the growth of the whole discipline. The term of empirical translation studies – in the context of this book – is intrinsically linked with and purposefully reminiscent of descriptive translation studies, as it is intended to serve as a useful landmark in the search for, development and establishment of scientifically rigorous research methodologies and analytical procedures to advance translation studies as a developing academic discipline.

13.2 From 'Pure' Research to Socially Oriented Research: The Social Turn

As discussed earlier, the conceptualisation of descriptive translation as part of the pure branch of translation studies has brought both benefits and limitations to the nascent descriptive research branch. The benefits consist in the importance attached to the branch for the development of the whole discipline, as it has largely been seen as the platform and testing ground on which translation scholars could experiment with and develop useful, reliable research methodologies and analytical procedures to advance theoretical translation studies, still seen as the core of the discipline (Toury, 1995, 2000). Descriptive translation research has served as the engine which has driven much of the methodological growth and innovation of the field over the last four decades. It is argued in the concluding chapter that the early definition and limitation of descriptive translation research as part of 'pure' translation studies needs to be revisited, as the research branch has, over the last four decades, developed important research capacities to directly address and tackle the new research issues and problems that have arisen from changing social environments in many parts of the world. Translation studies, especially the descriptive, empirical research branch, no longer needs to be limited to the documentation or description of the production, process and function of translation, when it can offer translation-based innovative, effective solutions to help address practical, pressing social issues. Such issues include: strategies related to the effective translation, cross-cultural communication and adaptation of global environmental policy in national contexts; the assessment of the social diffusion and uptake of environmental translation materials to build much-needed multi-sectoral interaction and cooperation amongst societal stakeholders, in order to increase national environmental performance; and the objective, computerised assessment and evaluation of the linguistic readability and accessibility of specialised health and medical translation resources amongst immigrant groups with limited English proficiency and health-literacy levels, so as to significantly reduce health risks amongst target populations.

The chapters in this book illustrated the purposed 'social turn' in the descriptive or empirical research branch of translation studies. These chapters explored and demonstrated how advanced statistical methods can be deployed to construct empirical analytical instruments in order to enable socially oriented empirical translation research. Using different exploratory statistics, three new types of translation-derived, empirical analytical instruments were developed and tested with a variety of translation genres and language pairs appearing in different translation directions. Chapter 2 illustrates the development of a new ranking scheme to offer insights into important, latent social mechanisms that may impact a country's overall environmental performance as measured by global environmental performance indexes. Specifically, this chapter first developed a multilingual terminology which contained Chinese, Spanish and Portuguese translations of original English multilateral environmental agreements. Five large lexical categories were developed to label different dimensions of the interaction amongst social agencies in the communication and diffusion of environmental knowledge and management strategies specified in, and endorsed by, multilateral environmental agreements. This multilingual and multi-dimensional terminology framework provided the basis for comparison amongst fifteen countries with regard to the multi-sectoral interaction between social agencies in the communication and materialisation of environmental protection. Frequency information regarding the distribution of translated terminologies in published sectoral materials was extracted on a yearly basis from different societal sectors within each country. This has led to the computation of the cross-sectoral correlation score matrix, and the composite score which represents the overall multi-sectoral interaction level for each of the fifteen countries. This newly developed country ranking of the internal multi-sectoral interaction around environmental knowledge communication and management was then compared against the widely endorsed global Environmental Performance Index (EPI). The EPI ranks world countries based on their national performance in achieving two objectives: the protection of human health and maintenance of the country's ecosystems. Spearman's correlation test detected important similarities between the two ranking schemes. This confirmed the original hypothesis of the study, i.e. that stronger multi-sectoral interaction amongst societal sectors within a country can effectively contribute to better, more competitive overall environmental performance by that country at the international level.

The aim of Chapter 2 was to illustrate the viability and productivity of constructing empirical analytical instruments to enable socially oriented empirical translation research. The development and validation of the country-based cross-sectoral interaction ranking scheme – an innovative, empirically derived analytical instrument – was facilitated by the compilation of specialised multilingual terminology which constitutes an important practice in applied translation research. In this way, Chapter 2 demonstrates the usefulness of integrating and combining research approaches from 'pure' and 'applied' translation studies to develop innovative, problem-oriented intra-disciplinary research approaches and methodologies that further enhance the research capacities of the discipline of translation studies as a whole.

Chapter 5 illustrates the development of another type of empirical analytical instrument which is based on a different translation genre that supports cross-national institutional collaboration: i.e. the translation and adaptation of international health policy material in national contexts, in this case, the translation and social dissemination of drinking-water guidelines stipulated by the World Health Organization (WHO) in Japan. This chapter experimented with a different type of exploratory statistics, i.e. structural equation modelling, also known as path analysis for the purpose of empirical translation studies. Structural equation modelling is a powerful statistical technique widely used in the social sciences. It provides a formalised approach to testing theoretical hypotheses regarding the combined effects of two sets of external variables – i.e. independent variables and mediating variables – on the observed dependent variable(s). Specifically, Chapter 5 leverages structural equation modelling as an analytical instrument to further the study of the translation and cross-cultural adaptation of the WHO drinking-water guidelines, which informed the development and establishment of local discourses regarding the management and consumption of drinking water in Japan in the last two decades. This study combined corpus translation research with political discourse analysis to explore the social process through which institutional translation plays an instrumental role in disseminating authoritative international health materials to influence and enhance public-health surveillance in national contexts. Chapter 5 provides a formalised analysis of the dissemination of the key terminology and associated concepts in institutional health translations which have underscored the development of social awareness and accountability mechanisms towards the management and regulation of drinking water amongst different societal sectors and agencies in Japan since the early 2000s. The chapter argued that an important aspect of the cross-cultural adaptation and diffusion of sustainable practices conducive to a new drinking-water management system was the social accountability attribution process, i.e. the responsibility attached or ascribed to industrial sectors by creditable and authoritative social agencies such as governmental, legislative or industrial regulatory bodies.

To configure the international policy translation and the subsequent cross-cultural knowledge-diffusion process, three key elements were required to initiate and establish the attribution of social accountability: a source of information, a mediating agent and an industrial actor engaged in relevant social and industrial activities. In Chapter 5, it is hypothesised that the social accountability attributed to industrial sectors was susceptible to direct effects of the main sources of information and indirect effects of the media as a mediating agent. The term 'effect' was used to describe and gauge the visibility given by sources of information and the media to industrial sectors in discussions of specific aspects and issues related to the management and consumption of drinking water in Japan. More specifically, the level of sectoral visibility was gauged through the frequency analysis of industrial sectors in materials published by different sources of information such as governmental agencies, industrial sources, business sources and by mediating agencies such as newspapers and journals. The corpus analysis demonstrated that in the social diffusion of the translated drinking-water-quality discourse, as part of the 'translation' process, different sources of information in Japan played distinct roles in engaging with different industrial sectors regarding the management and surveillance of the consumption of drinking water by the public. The mediating variables included in the corpus study, i.e. newspapers and journals, can significantly improve the predictive power of the structural equation model. The mass media played a dynamic role in moderating the transmission of the translated drinking-water discourse from different sources of information, e.g. government, business, top industrial bodies from industrial sectors. This study provided empirical evidence on the role of the mass media as a social intervention that can influenced and influenced by the level of public visibility of specific industrial sectors in the complex process of the translation, diffusion and local adaptation of international policy and regulatory materials in national contexts.

Chapter 5 illustrates an alternative approach to that explored in Chapter 2 to the development of empirical social and political analytical instruments which are directly derived from an important type of translation resources, i.e. international institutional translation. Cross-cultural institutional translation sets in motion the social dissemination of the key principles and recommendations provided by organisations of global governance, such as the WHO, in terms of achieving international health standards in national contexts. The corpus analysis demonstrated that the social dissemination process requires not only effective interaction amongst social sectors, but also relies on the existence of an effective social transmission network able to link the main sources of information, such as government agencies and industrial and business sources, with the end users of the information distributed; i.e. a wide range of industrial sectors. It integrated quantitative corpus linguistic methods with political discourse analysis to identify and construct a formalised empirical model of the social dissemination and culturally adapted development of drinking-water-management discourse in Japan. In doing so, the corpus analysis used structural equation modelling to illustrate the three important components of the social diffusion of translated knowledge and policy recommendations which are: first, the pathways of social accountability attribution; second, the role of the media as a social intervention that can be moderated in such a way as to alter the social accountability attribution pathways; and third, the importance of the interaction between main sources of information, i.e. governmental, business, industrial, official and legal and the mass media, as both constitute integral parts of the social accountability attribution process.

In contrast to Chapters 2 and 5, which focus on the role of institutional translations in enabling and facilitating important social and cultural changes, Chapter 8 illustrates the development of empirical analytical instruments to advance current multicultural and multilingual health-literacy and public-health promotion, which represents another important emerging research area for the application of empirical translation studies. Health research was amongst the earliest applications of readability evaluation. A strong correlation between readability and health literacy was identified in the early days of readability formulas, when these were first developed. Whilst English readability formulas have been used by health professionals for a long time, readability in other languages remains under-explored, especially in the context of health promotion. With a changing global demographic, and especially with the influx of multicultural migrants, refugees and displaced populations to more developed countries, there is a pressing need to explore the readability of health resources that are translated to the first languages of migrants in order to reduce the large and increasing health and economic burdens caused by these populations with limited English-language and health-literacy levels. For example, effective health communication with culturally and linguistically diverse populations holds the key to the success of the prevention and self-management of lifestyle-related diseases such as Type 2 diabetes mellitus, cancers and cardiovascular diseases, which represent leading health burdens in many developed countries.

Health translation provides a useful and powerful intervention tool to facilitate the engagement of service providers with migrants with diverse language, cultural and health-literacy backgrounds. The effectiveness and usability of health translation is contingent upon the readability and accessibility of those translated materials amongst multicultural populations. As a public-health intervention instrument, health translations of high readability can, amongst populations with limited English and health literacy, effectively motivate and support the much-needed behaviour changes that prevent and reduce the development of health risks. Objective, consistent and cost-effective evaluation of health translation readability thus represents an integral and critical part in the development of multicultural health-promotion resources. In health translation, three key factors contribute to the usability and effectiveness of the translated material: scientific precision, linguistic accuracy and textual readability. Whilst the first two factors have been studied extensively in translation quality assessment, the readability of health translation remains largely under-explored in translation studies, representing a critical knowledge gap.

Existing publications in this area have chiefly been written by health and medical professionals who are keenly aware of the importance of the readability of health translations to the effectiveness and success of any multicultural health-promotion and intervention programmes. Health translation readability represents an important and innovative application of readability research, a field which originated in education studies. Text readability is linked with a range of orthographic, linguistic and textual features such as the number of complex, high-stroke character words, in Asian languages, total number of words or character words, average sentence length, average word length, syntax and grammar which have direct impact on the accessibility and comprehensibility of the text. Readability score is derived quantitatively from the frequency data of relevant linguistic features of the text.

The development of English readability formulas such as the widely used Simple Measure of Gobbledygook (SMOG) system rests on the hypothesis that polysyllabic lexis is the sole key factor that contributes to textual complexity.

The assessment of the readability of multilingual translations is more complex than the original English readability testing formula. It is well known that translated materials tend to exhibit translation-induced textual features such as lexical variation, syntactic reposition and grammatical conversion, as well as new health terminology and/or medical jargon. These variations can significantly reduce the linguistic readability and cultural accessibility of health translations amongst their target multicultural populations. Research shows that the perceived usability and practicality of translated health materials is directly linked with adherence to medical and self-care instructions, and the motivation to sustain behavioural change, amongst the target users of the health materials.

Chapter 8 illustrates the development of a computerised readability testing system which is capable of processing and analysing linguistic and textual features of health translations in traditional and simplified Chinese. The corpus study analysed a wide range of Chinese translated health-promotion resources currently used by national health-promotion organisations in Australia. Using exploratory and confirmatory statistics, the corpus study identified two important dimensions of health translation textual features which represent major barriers to the effective understanding of Chinese health translations: i.e., the information load and lexical technicality of the translated materials. In order to assess the level of accessibility of health translations, this chapter analysed and compared Chinese health translations with original Chinese health-promotion resources using comparable corpus materials. The triangulation of contrastive and comparable corpus resources represents a well-established methodology in corpus translation studies. The comparison between Chinese translations and original Chinese health-promotion materials covered morphological, lexical and textual coherence features related to the readability and accessibility of the text material amongst the target populations. Chapter 8 illustrates the deployment of statistical methods to investigate linguistic and textual features contributing to the readability, accessibility and motivational effectiveness of health translation and promotion materials.

13.3 Enabling Technological Advances for Empirical Translation Research

Even though empirical translation studies (ETS) grew out of descriptive translation studies, which was originally proposed as a pure branch of translation studies in the 1980s, as opposed to applied translation studies (the latter including research into translation aids, which would later on include machine translation and speech translation technology) – it has both benefited from and contributed to the growth of applied translation studies as well. Chapter 11 by Orăsan et al., on hybrid approaches to machine-translation research, is a very good example of this. Therefore, the initial proposal to separate ETS and applied translation studies by restricting the former to pure translation studies now perhaps needs to be revisited and reformulated given the rapid growth of the field as a whole and the increasing interaction between these two sub-branches.

In Chapter 3, Oakes compares corpus-based and corpus-driven approaches to empirical translation studies. The corpus-based approaches (t-test, linear regression, ANOVA, multi-level/mixed modelling) were to compare the use of high-frequency words in English texts in translations from various languages in the Europarl Corpus of Native, Non-Native and Translated Texts (ENNTT) (Rabinovich et al., 2016), whilst corpus-driven studies used principal component analysis (PCA) with the same corpus to show that texts translated into English could be distinguished from each other according to their language of origin. This ability to discriminate between translated texts based on their original language has a number of practical applications: it sheds light on the possible existence and nature of translation universals; it has a role in translation plagiarism detection; it helps with the task of author profiling for either literary or forensic purposes; and is a first step to enabling native-language-specific grammar correction for learners of another language (Rabinovich et al., 2016).

Two chapters cover state-of-the-art corpus-processing tools and their applications in translation. Löfberg and Rayson (Chapter 6) write about their experience of developing multilingual automatic semantic annotation systems, which are valuable corpus-processing tools with the ability to annotate each word in the corpus with a semantic tag in the form of a code number to represent its meaning class. They describe the building of single-word and multi-word expression lexicons for a semantic tagging system and also the updating and transporting of a semantic tagging system to other languages using both manual and automatic approaches. There is discussion of how the system can be made domain-specific, and of its practical applications, which include both web-content filtering and psychological profiling.

Moze and Krek (Chapter 7) describe the Sketch Engine suite of corpus-processing tools. Whilst these have many monolingual applications, such as in lexicography, the emphasis of this chapter is on their usefulness in aiding human translators. Sketch Engine is particularly useful in helping the translator choose between translation equivalents. For example, distributional semantics are used to automatically suggest synonyms, antonyms and other related words for almost any word in a language. The 'Sketch Difference' feature allows the user to compare the collocates of a pair of semantically related words. Parallel corpora may be used like translation memories, where each different translation of a word or phrase may be examined, so that the translator can choose the most suitable one. The translation equivalents are found using a statistical machine dictionary. In fact, these parallel corpora may be generated from the translator's personal translation memory.

Four chapters discuss the latest developments in machine translation. Seligman and Waibel (Chapter 4) write about the evolving treatment of semantics in machine translation. Their chapter takes Searle's Chinese Room as a starting point from which to discuss whether machine-translation systems could ever understand semantics. Three main areas of machine translation are discussed – rule-based, statistical and neural – and how and to what extent they can capture semantics. Neural approaches have very recently become very successful, and zero-shot neural machine-translation systems can even learn without bilingual training data.

Nagata (Chapter 9) writes about machine translation for languages with very different word orders. This is a personal account from someone who has been personally involved at the highest level over at least three phases in the development of machine translation. Whilst there is a lot of enthusiasm in the world about neural machine translation, this paper points out that the latter presents problems when translating with a large vocabulary. Nagata discusses in detail the alternative approach of pre-ordering in order to make the word order match in language pairs which have very different word orders such as English and Japanese, and Chinese and Japanese.

Orăsan, Parra Escartín, Sepúlveda Torres and Barbu (Chapter 11) write about their experience of exploiting data-driven hybrid approaches to translation on the EU-funded Expert Project. The chapter gives various examples of how translation memories can be enhanced for use by professional translators, including a data-driven approach to cleaning them. Existing translation memories are most successful at retrieving previous sentences when these are similar to the one being translated. The chapter describes an algorithm that retrieves more distantly related sentences by using paraphrases, and a new model for reordering input words, which helps with the difficult task of translating into morphologically rich languages. The most radical example given by the authors is of a hybrid machine-translation method which integrates statistical machine translation with translation memory.

Seligman and Waibel (Chapter 12) write on advances in speech-to-speech translation technologies. This chapter considers many aspects of different speech-to-speech translation approaches, which makes direct comparison between them difficult. There is a discussion of recovery mechanisms, whereby if an erroneous translation is made, it can be corrected by user feedback. The opening sections of the chapter are a fascinating exploration of the desiderata – what one would like to see in a speech-to-speech translation system. The chapter also contains very recent information on apps for interpreting and subtitling. It demonstrates Alex Waibel's contribution to this field, including his leadership of the EU-Bridge project, and also contains a short study/account of Seligman's own research.

13.4 Conclusion

This book raises and addresses the key question of the relation between empirical translation studies and the descriptive branch of pure translation research that was initially proposed in the late 1980s. It analyses, explains and illustrates the rationale and viability of the proposed 'empirical turn' in translation studies, whose goal is to better align the central aims and purposes of the discipline with the new, practical research needs arising from the changes to our social environments in many parts of the world. It is argued that, as demonstrated by the diverse chapters in the book, translation studies, especially the descriptive, empirical research branch, has benefited and will continue to benefit from the integration of advanced quantitative research methodologies and advances in corpus analytical software development and natural language processing technologies such as machine translation. This bourgeoning field of translation research is thus well equipped to play a larger, more significant role by addressing practical, pressing social and research issues such as environmental communication, sustainable development and health literacy; this focus has been described as the 'social turn' in empirical translation studies. This book illustrates and demonstrates the social and research values of the proposed socially oriented and data-driven approach to empirical translation studies in particular, and translation studies in general. Its set of highly interdisciplinary and problem-oriented research approaches will significantly expand the horizons of contemporary translation studies by stimulating scholarly debates around the engagement with real-life issues in theoretical translation research. We are of the view that the development of quantitative research methods and the integration of applied translation technologies in empirical translation research have significantly increased, and will continue to increase, the capacity of translation studies to tackle the new social and research problems which have emerged in more recent times, such as environmental protection and multicultural health promotion. Using innovative and representative case studies, T=this book illustrates the interaction, dynamics and growing dependency that have developed between theoretical and applied translation studies in more recent times, in an attempt to mitigate the long-existing divide between the two research fields. This effort to bring together theoretical (descriptive) and applied translation studies, especially corpus translation studies and applied translation technology, will significantly expand the horizon of the research field as a whole.

References

Baker, M. (1993). Corpus linguistics and translation studies: Implications and applications. In M. Baker, G. Francis and E. Tognini-Bonelli (eds.), *Text and Technology: In Honour of John Sinclair*. Amsterdam: John Benjamins, pp. 233–250.

Baker, M. (1996). Corpus-based translation studies: The challenges that lie ahead. In H. Somers (ed.), *Terminology, LSP and Translation: Studies in Language*

Engineering in Honour of Juan C. Sager. Amsterdam and Philadelphia: John Benjamins, pp. 175–186.

Baker, M. (2004). A corpus-based view of similarity and difference in translation, *International Journal of Corpus Linguistics* 9(2), 167–193.

Holmes, J. S. (1988). The name and nature of translation studies. In *Translated! Papers on Literary Translation and Translation Studies*. Amsterdam: Rodopi, pp. 66–80.

Laviosa, S. (1995). Comparable corpora: Towards a corpus linguistic methodology for the empirical study of translation. In M. Thelen and B. Lewandowska-Tomaszczyk (eds.), *Translation and Meaning (Part 3)*. Maastricht: Universitaire pers Maastricht, pp. 71–85.

Laviosa, S. (1998). Universals of translation. In M. Baker (ed.), *Routledge Encyclopedia of Translation Studies*. Oxford and New York: Routledge.

Laviosa, S. (2004). Corpus-based translation studies: Where does it come from? Where is it going? *Language Matters* 35(1), 6–27.

Oakes, M. and M. Ji (2012). *Quantitative Research Methods in Corpus-Based Translation Studies*. Amsterdam: John Benjamins.

Olohan, M. (2004). *Introducing Corpora in Translation Studies*. London: Routledge.

Rabinovich, E., S. Nisioi, N. Ordan and S. Wintner (2016). On the similarities between native, non-native and translated texts. In Proceedings of the 5th Annual Meeting of the Association for Computational Linguistics, Berlin, Germany, August 7–12. Association of Computational Linguistics, pp. 1870–1881.

Schreibman, S., R. Siemens and J. Unsworth (eds.) (2004). *A Companion to Digital Humanities*. Oxford: Blackwell.

Toury, G. (1982). A rationale for descriptive translation studies, *Dispositio* 7 (19–21), 23–40.

Toury, G. (1995). *Descriptive Translation Studies and Beyond*. Amsterdam: John Benjamins.

Toury, G. (2000). The nature and role of norms in translation. In Lawrence Venuti (ed.) *The Translation Studies Reader*, vol. 2. London: Routledge.

Index

For EU product safety concerns, contact us at Calle de José Abascal, 56–1°,
28003 Madrid, Spain or eugpsr@cambridge.org.

www.ingramcontent.com/pod-product-compliance
Ingram Content Group UK Ltd.
Pitfield, Milton Keynes, MK11 3LW, UK
UKHW021616111026
15749UKWH00004BA/37
9781108423274